KEEP THIS MAJOR WORK
UP TO DATE

It is the intention of LLP Limited to keep all major works up to date and ensure that our customers have the very latest information.

A supplement to this work is planned and we would like to ensure that you receive this as soon as it is published. To reserve your copy, simply return this card. You may also use it to order additional copies of *The Law of Tug and Tow.*

Please reserve for me .... copies of the forthcoming supplement to *The Law of Tug and Tow.* I understand that you will send me a pre-payment invoice prior to publication.

Please send me .... additional copies of *The Law of Tug and Tow* (ISBN 1 85044 967 8) at £85 each.

Other available titles
Please send me details of: (tick box)
Lloyd's Shipping Law Library ☐
Lloyd's Commercial Law Library ☐

Please send me a copy of your complete catalogue ☐

L|L|P

Method of Payment
☐ Payment enclosed (payable to LLP Limited) in £ Sterling.
☐ Please send me a pre-payment invoice. (Goods will be despatched on payment of invoice.)
☐ Please debit my credit/charge card:

☐ Amex ☐ Diners ☐ Visa ☐ Access/Mastercard

Card No.: ☐☐☐☐☐☐☐☐☐☐☐☐☐☐☐☐

Signature: .... Expiry Date: .... / ....

Note: When paying by credit card please quote registered card address.

If you are in an EC Country please provide the VAT registration number of your company: ....

Postage and packing charges
UK: Please add £5 per book
Overseas: Please add £10 for one book, £15 for two or more books.

Please give your preferred delivery address:

Name (Mr/Mrs/Miss): ....

Job Title: ....

Company Name: ....

Address: ....

....

Town/City: .... Postcode: ....

Country: ....

Tel: ....

Orders from North America and the Far East will be processed by our relevant overseas offices in local currency.

KEEP THIS MAJOR WORK
UP TO DATE

It is the intention of LLP Limited to keep all major works up to date and ensure that our customers have the very latest information.

A supplement to this work is planned and we would like to ensure that you receive this as soon as it is published. To reserve your copy, simply return this card. You may also use it to order additional copies of *The Law of Tug and Tow.*

Please reserve for me .... copies of the forthcoming supplement to *The Law of Tug and Tow.* I understand that you will send me a pre-payment invoice prior to publication.

Please send me .... additional copies of *The Law of Tug and Tow* (ISBN 1 85044 967 8) at £85 each.

Other available titles
Please send me details of: (tick box)
Lloyd's Shipping Law Library ☐
Lloyd's Commercial Law Library ☐

Please send me a copy of your complete catalogue ☐

L|L|P

Method of Payment
☐ Payment enclosed (payable to LLP Limited) in £ Sterling.
☐ Please send me a pre-payment invoice. (Goods will be despatched on payment of invoice.)
☐ Please debit my credit/charge card:

☐ Amex ☐ Diners ☐ Visa ☐ Access/Mastercard

Card No.: ☐☐☐☐☐☐☐☐☐☐☐☐☐☐☐☐

Signature: .... Expiry Date: .... / ....

Note: When paying by credit card please quote registered card address.

If you are in an EC Country please provide the VAT registration number of your company: ....

Postage and packing charges
UK: Please add £5 per book
Overseas: Please add £10 for one book, £15 for two or more books.

Please give your preferred delivery address:

Name (Mr/Mrs/Miss): ....

Job Title: ....

Company Name: ....

Address: ....

....

Town/City: .... Postcode: ....

Country: ....

Tel: ....

Orders from North America and the Far East will be processed by our relevant overseas offices in local currency.

CUSTOMER SERVICES
BOOK ORDER DEPARTMENT
LLP LIMITED
FREEPOST
SHEEPEN PLACE
COLCHESTER
ESSEX CO3 4BR
ENGLAND

PLEASE
AFFIX
POSTAGE
STAMP IF
POSTED
OUTSIDE
THE UK

CUSTOMER SERVICES
BOOK ORDER DEPARTMENT
LLP LIMITED
FREEPOST
SHEEPEN PLACE
COLCHESTER
ESSEX CO3 4BR
ENGLAND

THE LAW OF TUG AND TOW

THE LAW OF
TUG AND TOW

BY

SIMON RAINEY

M.A. Cantab.; Lic.Sp.Dr.Eur. (Bruxelles);
of Lincoln's Inn, Barrister

FOREWORD BY
THE HONOURABLE MR JUSTICE CLARKE

LONDON   NEW YORK   HONG KONG
1996

LLP Limited
Legal & Business Publishing Division
27 Swinton Street
London WC1X 9NW
Great Britain

USA AND CANADA
LLP Inc.
Suite 308, 611 Broadway,
New York, NY 10012, USA

SOUTH-EAST ASIA
LLP (Far East) Limited
Room 1101, Hollywood Centre,
233 Hollywood Road
Hong Kong

© Simon Rainey 1996

British Library Cataloguing in Publication Data
*A catalogue record
for this book is available
from the British Library*

ISBN 1-85044-967-8

Typeset in 10/12pt Times
by Interactive Sciences, Gloucester
Printed in England by
Hartnolls Ltd.
Bodmin, Cornwall

To

Sir Barry Cross Sheen

Foreword

BY THE HON. MR JUSTICE CLARKE

I am well qualified to write this foreword for two reasons. The first is that I feel that I owe a good deal to tugs and tows, having spent many years at the Bar attending arbitrations under various editions of Lloyd's Form of Salvage Agreement, most of which seemed to involve the activities of both tugs and tows. The second is that I have just finished grappling with the true construction of Clause 18(3) of the "Towhire" form, which is in the same terms in the "Towcon" form. Fortunately the draft of this book which I have seen came into existence before my decision, which is just as well since the author (who was junior counsel on the losing side) may by now have included a passage demolishing my reasoning!

Despite the above I cannot think of a better person than Simon Rainey to have written a book about a topic which has never been so clearly or comprehensively treated before. On the one hand, with his great knowledge of the principles of maritime law and his considerable experience of the practice of that law in the Commercial and Admiralty Courts he has written a book which I predict will be of inestimable value to the lawyer. On the other hand (subject to any criticism of my decision which may have been included by the time of publication!) by the inclusion of a valuable commentary upon the terms of the standard forms of towage contract, he has written a book which will be of great practical value to those engaged upon the business of negotiating contracts of towage. I have even learned a little about the Admiralty jurisdiction of the High Court. I have often wondered what was meant by a claim "in the nature of towage". Now I know.

Finally, I would like to commend the decision of both author and publishers to produce an entirely new book on tug and tow.

ANTHONY CLARKE

Royal Courts of Justice
25th January 1996

Preface

This book replaces LLP's previous title "The Law of Towage" by Davison and Snelson, published in 1990. When that book was published, one reviewer posed the question, pertinent for any author: is there any need for this book? Putting that question to myself about this book, I think that it has to be answered in two stages.

First, there is certainly a need for *a* book which gives a detailed and comprehensive account of the modern English law specifically relating to the operations of tug and tow and the increasingly important related activities in the field of the offshore service and supply industry. Prior to the advent of Davison and Snelson, the only relevant and widely available English law texts were either out-of-date, or insufficiently detailed on all aspects or both. Alfred Bucknill's treatise *Tug and Tow*, first published in 1913, which attained its second edition in 1927, is exemplary in its terse and didactic style, but, while still a very valuable account of the contractual law of towage before the emergence of the standard form contract, it has been substantially left behind by the widespread use of such contracts and by other developments in the law, for example, in relation to limitation of liability. Kenneth McGuffie's chapter on "Tug and Tow" in his (the Fourth) edition of *Marsden on Collisions at Sea* (1964) gave a very useful account of the collision cases in so far as they touch upon tug and tow. Captain Kovats' account in *The Law of Tugs and Towage* published in 1980 contained some valuable insights but preferred otherwise to present a digest of the towage cases which appear in the indices of the Lloyd's List and Lloyd's Law Reports. Across the Atlantic, Alex Parks' magisterial *The Law of Tug, Tow and Pilotage* (of which the first edition was published in 1971, with the last edition under Parks' sole authorship (the second) being published in 1982; the work is continued in the true Parkseian style by Alex Cattell in the third edition of 1994) marries with an exceptionally well-researched and detailed account of American Law a necessarily abbreviated account of English law which has often served as a good starting point for an English lawyer's researches. The book is designedly encyclopaedic, covering all maritime law as it might impinge upon a tug owner. However, as a primarily American text, it contains no treatment of the standard forms of contract currently in use in an English law context.

As to the second stage of the question and as to whether this book addresses this need, the difficulty for any author of a book on the law of tug and tow and allied services is to steer a course between, on the one hand, simply re-stating the generally applicable maritime law (dealt with in a much better and much more detailed fashion in other books) because tugs and vessels under tow are simply species of "ships" and, on the other hand, giving a detailed account of those principles which apply only to tug and tow or which are particularly pertinent to tug and tow without putting those principles into their broader context. Most practitioners (and reviewers) felt that the course adopted by Davison and Snelson perhaps erred on the former side. For example, very few aspects of the law of employment on board ships, of registration of ships and of marine insurance applicable to hulls (covered *in extenso* in other texts but still dealt with by them) can be said to be peculiar to tug and tow. By contrast, the standard forms of towage contract were only briefly dealt with and no mention at all was made of the common offshore industry form "SUPPLYTIME". Captain Kovats' book adopted a similar approach.

Whether this book will or will not provoke the same question by reviewers remains to be seen. I have adopted a rather different approach from my predecessors and this book attempts to address the gaps and deficiencies in the previously available texts and to provide what is hoped to be a modern and comprehensive account of English towage law. The scheme of this book is therefore as follows:

(i) A detailed account of the English common law of towage which applies in the absence of a contract upon a standard form.

(ii) An account, by reference to English law, of the four principal forms of standard form contract found in towage and allied operations. This aims to be a detailed account but only as far as it goes. For example the BIMCO "TOWHIRE" and "SUPPLYTIME" forms are, in essence, towage or offshore service orientated time charterparties and much of the law is that to be encountered in connection with any time charterparty; that law is admirably dealt with by *Wilford on Time Charters*, another title in the Lloyd's Shipping Law Library. Rather than condense or paraphrase that law, I have attempted to point up the similarities and to make cross-reference to the relevant texts.

(iii) An expanded treatment of the law as to the relationship between towage and salvage (which relationship continues to give rise to relatively frequent disputes between the two and the aspirant salvor) taking account of the enactment of the 1989 Salvage Convention. No attempt has been made to treat otherwise than in outline the subject of salvage in general: this is admirably covered in the current editions of *Brice on Salvage* and *Kennedy on Salvage*.

(iv) An account, purely in the context of towage, of the law of collision and limitation of liability. I have attempted to consider in much greater detail the specifically towage-related questions and have not given any account of the general principles save in very brief outline.

(v) An account of the particular problems which tug and tow present in General Average (not touched on at all by Davison and Snelson), and a more detailed consideration of the jurisdiction of the Admiralty Court in relation to towage disputes.

(vi) I have deliberately not included any sections on employment, registration,

health and safety and marine insurance since I regard them as of marginal
relevance in a book dealing with tug and tow questions.

Where I have thought it necessary to do so, I have tried to set the present law in its
historical and jurisprudential context (for example, in relation to limitation of
liability).

A criticism made of Davison and Snelson which I did not share was its failure to
refer widely to the law in other jurisdictions. The object of that as of this book is to
supply practitioners in *English* law and towage operators facing a problem under an
English law contract with an account of *English* law. This is in common with the other
texts in the Lloyd's Shipping Law Library. While this book may be parochial in the
sense of being confined to English law, it is, therefore, designedly so. However, where
a particular approach has been adopted in the leading Common law jurisdictions upon
a point of interest in the English law of towage, I have tried to refer (albeit sometimes
briefly) to it.

After the book went into page proof and too late for inclusion in the body of the text,
an interesting and important case came before the Admiralty Court upon the
construction and effect of Clause 18(3) of the BIMCO "TOWHIRE" form in which I
was junior counsel, led by Jeremy Russell QC, for the unhappily unsuccessful
Defendant. Judgment was given on 19th January 1996 in open court.

The case concerned a point of construction raised for decision under RSC Order 14A
in the following circumstances. The plaintiff was the salvor, Alexander G. Tsavliris
Limited ("Tsavliris"). It chartered in a tug, the *Herdentor*, from the defendant tugowner, OIL Limited trading as OSA Marine ("OIL"). The tug was chartered in so as
to assist and enable Tsavliris to perform a salvage operation on Lloyd's Open Form in
respect of a VLCC in difficulties off the South African coast. The fixture was at a daily
rate of hire and the contract was concluded on the "TOWHIRE" form. Shortly after the
contract was concluded, Tsavliris entered into a sub-contract with the South African
salvors and tug operators, Pentow. The sub-contract was on the International Salvage
Union sub-contract under which the salvor agrees that the salvage remuneration
eventually payable to him will be shared between himself and the sub-contractor, the
precise share to be determined by an arbitrator. There was a dispute as to what precisely
was agreed between Tsavliris and OIL as to the duration and nature of the services:
Tsavliris contended that it had been agreed that the tug was engaged on an open-ended
basis for as long as the salvage might take while OIL contended that it had been made
clear that the tug was being provided for a limited duration towage in the light of
another towage operation for which the tug was already engaged. Acting on their view
of the contract, OIL withdrew the *Herdentor* after completing the particular towage leg
of the service which had been discussed. Tsavliris performed the salvage but the role
played by Pentow was alleged by it to be greater than it would have been had the
Herdentor stayed. Tsavliris sued OIL for wrongful withdrawal. It claimed damages on
the following basis: first, Tsavliris contended that the base award which was given to
it as contractor in the LOF arbitration was less than it would have been had the tug
stayed until the salvage service was completed and, secondly, it contended that the
share which it had received out of that award under the ISU sub-contract was less than

it would have been. In other words, Tsavliris' overall return on the salvage was said to be less.

While the allegation of wrongful withdrawal was vigorously contested by OIL, OIL raised a preliminary point of law as to whether the recovery of loss of the kind claimed by Tsavliris was barred by the terms of Clause 18(3) of the "TOWHIRE" form as being properly characterised as "loss of profit, loss of use, loss of production or any other indirect or consequential damage". OIL's primary case was that the loss to Tsavliris of its expected return was "loss of profit" within the meaning of the clause and therefore it had an unanswerable defence to the claim, even if the claim were otherwise a good one. OIL's contention was rejected by Clarke J on two principal grounds.

  (i) First, he held that the true nature of Tsavliris' claim was properly characterised as one for reduced remuneration or, as it was put by leading counsel for the contractors (M. N. Howard QC), for a "diminution in the price payable to or receivable by Tsavliris for the salvage service" and was not a loss of profit.
  This ground of decision, it is respectfully submitted, is in part questionable. The judge gave no definition of what loss of profit as used in the clause meant. While the term loss of profit may have different connotations in different contracts, it is submitted that at the very least in the context of the "TOWHIRE" form it is designed to cover a loss of money by tug or tow on an operation which is in excess of the tug or tow's costs of earning that money. On the facts of the case before the court, if Tsavliris had incurred out-of-pocket expenses of x and received an award or share of award of y which was greater than x, Tsavliris' profit on the deal would have been $y - x$. That part of the earnings would have been pure profit and on an ordinary construction of loss of profit would have been caught by the exclusion in Clause 18(3). It is submitted that while the judge was correct in refusing to equate loss of revenue *simpliciter* with loss of profit, he should not have held the exact converse, namely, that a loss of remuneration was not in any sense a claim for a loss of profit. The correct interpretation of Clause 18(3) in the context of a claim for loss of earnings is submitted to be that it excludes that part of the claim which represents a claim for the profit element in those earnings.
  (ii) Secondly and of general significance in the construction of Clause 18(3), the judge held that the words "loss of profit, loss of use and loss of production" were governed and defined by the closing words of the clause "or any other indirect or consequential damage" and that, in particular, the words "any other" were to be read as having the effect that Clause 18(3), in referring to types of loss such as loss of profit etc., was referring only to such types of loss which were indirect but was not excluding recovery of such types of loss which were direct. In other words, Clause 18(3) was simply a variant of the classic exclusion clause which excludes consequential losses and which was considered in cases such as *Croudace Construction* v. *Cawoods Concrete Products* [1978] 2 Lloyd's Rep. 55. Since it was not disputed by

OIL that Tsavliris' loss was a direct loss, that loss fell outside the clause. It is respectfully submitted that this construction of Clause 18(3) is unsound for three reasons. First, it reduces Clause 18(3) which is an integral part of the BIMCO knock-for-knock regime to a provision of very minor effect: the *Croudace* line of cases hold that a "no consequential loss claims" provision leaves unaffected direct loss claims and excludes only indirect loss claims or claims for loss falling within the second but not the first limb of *Hadley* v. *Baxendale*. As submitted in this book, it is questionable of what practical utility such a clause has; it is even more questionable that the draftsmen of the BIMCO forms had in mind this type of distinction when drafting a clause which overall leaves each party bearing its own losses, direct or indirect: see e.g. Clauses 18(1) and (2). Secondly, the construction is not a natural and ordinary reading of the clause. It reads in to the types of loss enumerated the word "indirect"; this jars with the losses listed. What for example is an indirect loss of use as distinct from a direct loss of use? Thirdly, even if "any other" is to be read so as to treat the types of loss listed as types of indirect and consequential damage, it is submitted that what Clause 18(3) is seeking to achieve is to deem certain types of loss, however occurring, as losses which for the purposes of the clause are to be treated as "indirect losses", i.e. financial losses, in distinction to the more direct physical or physically connected losses dealt with in Clauses 18(1) and 18(2) of the form.

Also of general interest in the decision and of wider relevance in construing Clause 18 as a whole was the judge's rejection of Tsavliris' argument that Clause 18(3) was to be construed *contra proferentem* since it was an exemption clause upon which OIL were seeking to rely. He held that as the clause was designed to exclude certain types of loss for both parties to the contract equally and was not a clause inserted by one party solely for its protection, it was not one to which the rule had any application although he held that, as with any clause excluding or limiting rights of recovery at common law, the person relying on the clause had to put himself clearly within it on its ordinary and natural meaning. It is submitted that this approach is clearly right and that the *contra proferentem* rule is inappropriate and inapplicable to mutual exclusion clauses (see e.g. the comments of Lord Upjohn on such clauses in *Suisse Atlantique Société d'Armement* v. *N.V. Rotterdamsche Kolen Centrale* [1967] 1 A.C. 361 at page 420F).

The decision will probably be reported in the Lloyd's Maritime Law Newsletter and the Lloyd's Law Reports. For present purposes, those contracting on the basis of the "TOWHIRE" and "TOWCON" who wish to make it clear beyond doubt that losses of profit etc are excluded whether direct or indirect should amend Clause 18(3) of the form or insert a suitably drawn typed clause.

Acknowledgements are due to Nevil Phillips, barrister, for his assistance in researching the pre-1989 Salvage Convention law relating to the towage and salvage, Mr David Taylor of Clifford Chance and Secretary of the Average Adjusters' Association for his help in relation to the text of the York-Antwerp Rules 1994 and to Miss Sandra Somers, sphinx-like(!) in adversity, who (with the assistance of Miss

Paulette McIntosh) reduced the text into some semblance of order. Warm thanks are also due to Mr Justice Clarke who kindly consented to read the book in page proof and to provide a foreword (which contains the only joke in the book!) notwithstanding the prospect of a critique of his recent decision in *The Herdentor*, to my wife Pia and my children Venetia, Alexander and Nicolas, who more or less cheerfully tolerated the work involved in this book but who now, rather like Davies in Erskine Childers' *The Riddle of the Sands*, object to all mention of towage "on principle", and to the South Devon Hunt, jolly days with which always lighten any task, however onerous.

The law is intended to be that as it was on 1st January 1996, save for the reference to the decision in *The Herdentor* set out above.

SIMON RAINEY

4 Essex Court
Temple
London EC4.

Outline Table of Contents

Table of Contents

CHAPTER 1—THE CONTRACT OF TOWAGE

CHAPTER 2—THE IMPLIED OBLIGATIONS OF TUG AND TOW

CHAPTER 3—STANDARD FORM CONTRACTS: (I) THE U.K. STANDARD CONDITIONS FOR TOWAGE AND OTHER SERVICES

CHAPTER 4—STANDARD FORM CONTRACTS: (II) THE BIMCO FORMS "TOWCON" AND "TOWHIRE"

CHAPTER 5—STANDARD FORM CONTRACTS: (III) THE BIMCO "SUPPLYTIME 89" FORM

CHAPTER 6—TOWAGE AND SALVAGE

CHAPTER 9—TUG AND TOW AND GENERAL AVERAGE

CHAPTER 10—ADMIRALTY JURISDICTION

APPENDICES

Table of Cases

Table of Legislation

*[Page references printed in **bold** indicate where text is quoted]*

Table of Forms

*[Page references printed in **bold** indicate where text is quoted]*

CHAPTER 1

The Contract of Towage

PART A. PRELIMINARY CONSIDERATIONS

1. Defining towage

The towage of one ship by another as a common maritime operation began with the development of the steam paddle tug in the 1820s and 1830s. The first tug upon the River Thames appears to have been the *Lady Dundas* in 1832 (see F. C. Bowing, *A Hundred Years of Towing: A History*). Soon, steam tugs were assisting the sailing ships in the rivers and ports of England. As they grew more powerful, they were engaged to tow sailing ships on longer voyages to hasten the arrival or departure of the ships. So, by the mid-nineteenth century sailing ships would "take steam" to and from the places where the outward pilot was dropped or the inward pilot was taken on board. The definition of towage given by the courts reflected the limited nature of the service which tugs then performed. A towage service was described in *The Princess Alice* (1849) 3 W. Rob. 138 at 139 by Dr Lushington:

"as the employment of one vessel to expedite the voyage of another when nothing more is required than the accelerating [of] her progress".

This definition was adopted and endorsed in successive editions of *Bucknill on Tug and Tow* (1st Edn., 1913; 2nd Edn., 1927).

By the time of the second edition of *Bucknill* (above), Dr Lushington's definition of towage had already become too narrow and did not reflect the varied nature of the services which tugs were performing. Today, his definition aptly describes but one aspect of the varied work upon which tugs are commonly engaged. In addition to the towage of ships and other water-borne objects such as oil and gas rigs, tugs frequently render a wide range of services, both in terms of handling and supply, to the offshore industries.

2. Towage arises *ex contractu*

(1) Towage arises from a contract

However towage is defined and whatever the particular nature of service being performed by the tug, since towage arises from the engagement or employment of the tug by another vessel to perform a particular service or for a particular purpose, towage

1

arises from a contract concluded between the tug and the tow. As was said by *Bucknill* (above) (2nd Edn., p. 1):

"In Admiralty law 'towage' expresses the idea of work done under a towage contract as distinguished from towage work done by a salvor".

The contract of towage is merely a species of contract. With the exception of certain special incidents attaching to the formation and content of the mutual relations under that contract, the ordinary principles of the law of contract will apply (for these, see e.g. *Chitty on Contracts*, 27th Edn.). It is these special incidents which form the subject-matter of this chapter.

(2) The relationship between towage and salvage

The contractual nature of towage is of particular significance in considering the relationship between towage and salvage as the passage cited from *Bucknill supra* demonstrates. Since the service as a service, whether of pure towing work or of any allied operation, being performed by a tug, can be performed by that tug contractually or as a salvage service, the dividing line between contractual towage and towage rendered as salvage will depend upon the presence of a towage contract and upon the extent of the contractual services to be rendered under and as defined in that contract. The old cases when speaking of contractual towage describe it as "ordinary towage" (see *The Strathnaver* (1875) 1 App. Cas. 58 at p. 63) or as "mere towage service" (see *The Reward* (1841) 1 W. Rob. 174 at 177 per Dr Lushington) in distinguishing those services which a tug renders under contract from those which it renders as salvor.

Salvage and the entitlement to remuneration or reward arises irrespective of the existence of a contract between the salvor and the vessel or other property being salved. Although a form of salvage contract is frequently entered into, the most common form being Lloyd's Open Form or "LOF" which has gone through various revisions (the latest form is LOF 1995), salvage does not depend upon the conclusion of a contract. Thus, in *The Hestia* [1895] P. 193, Bruce J. stated at p. 199:

"But salvage claims do not rest upon contract. Where property has been salved from sea perils, and the claimants have effected the salvage, or have contributed to the salvage, the law confers upon them the right to be paid salvage reward out of the proceeds of the property which they have saved or helped to save.

No doubt the parties may by contract determine the amount to be paid; but the right to salvage is in no way dependent upon contract, and may exist, and frequently does exist, in the absence of any express contract, or of any circumstances to raise an implied contract."

Accordingly, where a tug is engaged by a vessel under a towage contract to perform some towage operation, that operation and the work which the tug has to effect to achieve it will not constitute salvage. It is only where the tug has to perform some service outside the contract, and in circumstances of danger to the vessel, that salvage will arise. The touchstone is the scope and nature of the service contemplated by and provided for in the contract. In the celebrated opinion of the Privy Council in *The Minnehaha* (1861) 15 Moo. P.C. 133, per Lord Kingsdown at 152–154, it was put in this way:

"But if in the discharge of this task, by sudden violence of wind or waves, or other accidents, the ship in tow is placed in danger, and the towing vessel incurs risks and performs duties which were not within the scope of her original engagement, she is entitled to additional remuneration for additional services if the ship be saved and may claim as salvor instead of being restricted to be paid for mere towage".

The settled view is that while the tug is acting as salvor and extra-contractually, the towage contract is "superseded" or "suspended" (see per Lord Kingsdown in *The Minnehaha, op. cit.*) or as Sir Samuel Evans P. put it in *The Leon Blum* [1915] P. 90, after an exhaustive review of the authorities, at pp. 101–102:

"The right conclusion to draw from the authorities, I think, is that where salvage services (which must be voluntary) supervene upon towage services (which are under contract), the two kinds of services cannot co-exist during the same space of time. There must be a moment when the towage service ceases and the salvage service begins; and, if the tug remains at her post of duty, there may come a moment when the special and unexpected danger is over, and then the salvage service would end, and the towage service would be resumed. These moments of time may be difficult to fix, but have to be, and are fixed in practice. During the intervening time, the towage contract, insofar as the actual work of towing is concerned, is suspended. I prefer the word 'suspended' to some of the other words which have been used, such as 'superseded', 'vacated', 'abandoned', etc."

As Sir Samuel Evans P. states, the point at which a service being rendered by a tug under a towage contract ceases to be regarded as one rendered under the contract and constitutes salvage is often difficult to discern. The relationship between contractual towage and salvage is considered in greater detail in Chapter 6 below.

(3) Gratuitous towage

While not often encountered in practice, especially in the field of commercial towage or the towage of large water-borne objects, instances occasionally arise where the towing vessel agrees to tow another vessel in difficulties without payment. Thus, a friendly tow may be offered and accepted between small boats such as yachts or between sister ships or ships which, although nominally owned by different companies, are in effect sisters. In such a case there is no contract as such. However, the tug is obliged to exercise reasonable care in the performance of the tow and will be liable to the tow in tort if it executes the tow negligently: see *Skelton* v. *London & North Western Rly.* (1867) L.R. 2 C.P. 631. In that case, a railway company voluntarily followed the practice of shutting a gate by a railway crossing but on one occasion forgot to do so. Willes J., applying the decision in *Coggs* v. *Bernard* (1703) 2 Ld. Raym. 909, stated at 636:

"If a person undertakes to perform a voluntary act, he is liable if he performs it improperly, but not if he neglects to perform it."

Similarly the tow will owe a duty of care to the tug and will also be obliged to exercise reasonable care in respect of its role in the towage. As it is put by *Bucknill* (above) (2nd Edn., p. 1, footnote (b)): where the towage is rendered *gratis* "the general duty to take reasonable care governs the mutual relations of each vessel".

The standard of the reasonable care to be exercised by the "friendly tug" and "friendly tow" will depend on all the circumstances including the type of vessel and nature of the operation proposed; the gratuitous nature of the service will be relevant.

Thus in the Canadian case of *The West Bay III* (*Maurice Federation* v. *Stewart*) [1969] 1 Lloyd's Rep. 158, a "boom-boat" which was used to push floating logs into position suffered an engine failure. A fisheries patrol vessel agreed to give her a tow. She did so gratuitously. During the towage, she increased speed so as to give herself necessary steerage-way but this capsized the boom-boat causing loss of life. The court (Exchequer Court, British Columbia Admiralty District) held that the patrol vessel owed those duties as were usually owed by the tug. Sheppard J., however, held that there was no negligence. At p. 163 he stated:

"In the case of a gratuitous service, such as that of [the patrol vessel's master] in this instance, there is no liability at law where the fault may be excused as an error in judgement."

See also: *Karavias* v. *Callinicos* [1917] W.N. 323 (gratuitous carriage of persons) and *Armand* v. *Carr* [1926] S.C.R. 575, Supreme Court of Canada. See also the American cases of *The Mifflin* 1931 A.M.C. 326 and *The Warrior* 1929 A.M.C. 41 which are to the same effect.

3. The contract of towage is a contract for services

Under a contract of towage, the tug owners agree to provide services for the tow with tug, which they themselves officer, crew and supply, for an agreed or defined service or to attain an agreed defined result or for an agreed or defined period of time in exchange for periodic or lump sum payments.

However, in towage contracts and, in particular, in many of the common standard form towage contracts, terms are often used which imply or connote a lease of the tug to the tow or the hire by the tow of the tug. The tug owner is often described as "letting" the tug to the tow; the tow is usually described as "the hirer" of the tug; the contract will commonly refer to the "delivery" to the tow of the tug and of the "redelivery" by the tow of the tug upon the completion of services. Notwithstanding the use of such terms, a towage contract is not a lease nor a contract for the hire of the tug nor is possession of the tug passed to the tow under the contract. The towage contract is merely a contract for the provision to the tow of services, which services are provided by the tug owners through their tug and tug crew. The position under a towage contract is, therefore, similar to the position under a time charterparty of which Lord Reid said in *The London Explorer* [1971] 1 Lloyd's Rep. 523 at p. 526.

"Under such a charter there is no hiring in the true sense. It is not disputed that, throughout, the chartered vessel remains in the possession of the owners, and the master and crew remain the owners' servants. What the charterer gets is a right to have the use of the vessel."

In *The Madeleine* [1967] 2 Lloyd's Rep. 224 at p. 238, Roskill J. commented as follows in relation to the delivery of a vessel under a time charterparty:

"An owner delivers a ship to a time charterer under this form of charterparty by placing her at the charterers' disposal and by placing the services of her master, officers and crew at the charterers' disposal, so that the charterers may thenceforth give orders (within the terms of the charterparty) as to the employment of the vessel to the master, officers and crew, which orders the owners contract that their servants shall obey."

While under a towage contract the tow does not obtain possession of the tug; on the other hand, the tug will often be put in possession of the tow for the period of the service. So, if the tow is unmanned, such as a dumb barge, or is merely an object which is being conveyed by sea, such as a caisson or a part of a rig, or if the tow is manned by a riding crew put on board by the tug, the tug will have physical possession of the tow. In such cases, the contract may appear to be analogous to a contract of bailment or to a contract for the carriage of goods. The relevance of the distinction lies in the nature of the obligation upon the tug owner. If he is to be regarded as a bailee, then he is liable for loss of or damage to the tow unless he can exculpate himself; if he is merely a provider of services and obliged to exercise care and skill, if the tow sustains loss or damage, the tow must show a breach of the tug's obligations of care and skill in order to recover.

No English authority suggests or supports an analysis of a contract of towage as one of, or akin to one of, bailment although the point has never been specifically addressed. It is submitted that the approach of the Privy Council in *The Julia* (1861) 14 Moo. P.C. 210 and in *The Minnehaha* (1861) 15 Moo. P.C. 133 (considered in detail below at pp. 24–26) in analysing and classifying towage contracts as contracts where the tug is to be engaged to render services and to which specific obligations of due care in and about and performance of those services are attached is plainly inconsistent with the concept of bailment and of the bailee's strict responsibility for the subject-matter of the bailment in the event of loss subject to very limited exceptions such as Act of God. In *Harris* v. *Anderson* (1863) 14 C.B. (N.S.) 499, the Court of Common Pleas rejected an argument that since a tow had grounded during the towage, the tug was to be liable for the same unless it could explain and excuse it. The Court held that the claim was bad since it contained no allegation of fault or neglect on the part of the tug. In *The West Cock* [1911] P. 23, Sir Samuel Evans P. considered the question of the nature of the obligation upon a tug owner to provide a seaworthy tug. He regarded the obligation as an absolute one like that upon a carrier (which is doubtful, see the discussion at pp. 31–33 below), but it is to be noted that he did not seek to support that conclusion by classifying a towage contract as importing the relationship of bailment but kept the two types of contract quite separate (see e.g. [1911] P. 23). The Court of Appeal in the same case, reported at [1911] P. 208, were doubtful as to whether any analogy could be drawn between a towage contract and a contract of affreightment. In *The Kite* [1933] P. 154, a claim for damage to goods on board a lighter being towed on the River Thames was approached by the parties as not being a claim in bailment. Langton J. approved that concession on the basis that the tug did not have custody of the goods but only control over them (see p. 181).

However, there is a considerable body of American authority which has specifically rejected the application of rules of bailment to a contract for towage. In *Brown* v. *Clegg* (1870) 3 Mar L.C. 512 (Supreme Court of Pennsylvania), the owners of barges laden with coal which were damaged during their towage on the River Delaware sought to argue that the owners of the tugs which drew them were liable as bailees and common carriers of the tow. The Court considered the previous American authorities and the English cases (referring principally to the decisions of the Privy Council in *The Julia* and *The Minnehaha*) and held that it was clear both in American and English law that tugs are not common carriers of the vessels which they tow. Similarly, in *The Margaret* 94 U.S. 494 (1876) a tow sued a tug for causing her to ground at the entrance of a harbour during the performance of a towage contract. The court stated (at p. 497):

"The tug was not a common carrier, and the law of that relation has no application here. She was not an insurer. The highest possible degree of skill and care were not required of her. She was bound to bring to the performance of the duty she assumed reasonable skill and care, and to exercise them in everything relating to the work until it was accomplished."

For a more modern consideration of the question see the decision of the U.S. Court of Appeals (5th Circuit) in *Agrico Chemical Co.* v. *M.V. Ben Martin*, 664 F. 2d. 85 (1981). Generally see: *Parks and Cattell on the Law of Tug, Tow and Pilotage* (4th Edn.) at pp. 19–23 where a full list of the American cases is set out and considered.

   Canadian law adopts the same approach as American law as to the rejection of a bailee–bailor relationship. In *The Tug Champlain* [1939] 1 D.L.R. 384, the Exchequer Court, at p. 389, held, after a review of the American decisions and the English decisions in *The Minnehaha* and *Spaight* v. *Tedcastle*, that:

"The obligation to carry out a towage contract requires nothing more than that degree of caution and skill which prudent navigators usually employ in such services. The occurrence of an accident raises no presumption against the tug and the burden is on the complaining party to prove a lack of ordinary care."

See also: *Sewell* v. *B.C. Towing and Transport Co.* (1884) 9 S.C.R. 527. The court in *The Tug Champlain* considered more fully the approach suggested by the decision of the Court of Common Pleas in *Harris* v. *Anderson* (1863) 14 C.B. (N.S.) 499 and made it clear that a claim by the tow against the tug in the event of damage requires the tow to show fault on the part of the tug; the burden of proof is not upon the tug to explain how the damage occurred.

   The position as between tug and tow as separate contractual and contracting entities may be contrasted where the tug and vessel towed are owned or operated by the same person. In such a case, the relationship between the tug and the owner of goods being towed on the vessel will not be one of towage but that of a contract of affreightment. This is the position in American law (e.g. *Agrico Chemical Co., op. cit.*). It is submitted that the position would be the same in English law.

4. The role of the standard form contract

Since the mutual relations of tug and tow are founded upon the existence of a contract of towage between them, the definition of their respective rights and obligations will be defined by the terms of the contract which they have agreed.

   Prior to the development of the use of standard form towage contracts and of contracts on tug owners' terms and conditions, the content of the obligations of the parties was worked out by the courts. By 1860, the principles were sufficiently well-established for the Privy Council to summarise them in its opinions in *The Minnehaha* (1861) 15 Moo. P.C. 133 and in *The Julia* (1861) 14 Moo. P.C. 210. As a result, it is clear that in the absence of express stipulation, the law implies certain specific terms in a contract of towage which limit the rights and define the obligations of tug and tow (see *Bucknill* (above) 2nd Edn., pp. 16–17). The common law principles are considered in detail in Chapter 2.

However, with the development of towage came the increasing use by tug owners of standard form contracts in an attempt to escape from or to dilute their obligations at common law. By the end of the nineteenth century many forms of contract were in use reflecting the wide range of harbour and port authorities, railway and dock companies and tug operators providing towage services. These forms were united by a common purpose: to exclude and restrict to the greatest extent possible the liability of the tug. The Admiralty Court regarded these attempts to "contract out" of the implied obligations of the towage contract, which had been laid down in the line of cases culminating in the opinions of the Privy Council in *The Minnehaha* and *The Julia* in 1860, with considerable hostility and suspicion. Even in 1913 when Butler Aspinall K.C. wrote his introduction to the first edition of *Bucknill on Tug and Tow* (p. xv) it could be said that: "the law relating to towage depends almost entirely, if not entirely, on judicial decisions". However, where the standard forms or conditions were clearly worded to cover a particular situation, they were given their full effect by the court, see for example the approach of the court in *The President Van Buren* (1924) 19 Ll. L. Rep. 185, even if the court did so in many cases with extreme reluctance, see for example *The Newona* (1920) 4 Ll. L. Rep. 156.

Today, the standard form of contract most in use for port and harbour but also some offshore work in the United Kingdom is the "U.K. Standard Conditions for Towage and Other Services". This form has been frequently revised and the current form in use is the 1986 Revision. This form is produced by the British Tugowners' Association and is, even today, a good example of a draconian standard form contract heavily favouring the tug owners. For ocean towage other forms are used. While certain tug operators have their own "house" forms, those forms in most common use both in the United Kingdom and internationally have been produced under the auspices of the Baltic and International Maritime Council or BIMCO: these are the "Towhire" and "Towcon" forms which date from 1985. Reflecting the provision of services by tugs (and other vessels) in connection with the offshore industry, these BIMCO forms are supplemented by the "Supplytime 89" form the predecessor of which first appeared in 1975.

Brief mention should also be made of standard conditions adopted by tug owners in other jurisdictions. Given the volume of towage work in certain places, standard conditions similar to the U.K. Standard Conditions are commonly found in such places. Good European examples of such other conditions are the Netherlands Tug Owners Conditions 1951 and the Scandinavian Tugowners' Standard Conditions 1959 (1974 Revision). Pursuant to Dutch law, towage within Dutch waters by a Dutch tug owner is subject to the Netherlands Tug Owners Conditions unless expressly excluded. They expressly provide for the application of Dutch law (see Article II). The Scandinavian Conditions are published only in Danish, Norwegian and Swedish. For convenience, the text of these conditions is set out in Appendix 6 and 7 respectively, although, since they are rarely encountered in the context of English law contracts, they are not considered in this work.

In large-scale and commercial towage business the mutual relations of tug and tow in present times are habitually defined by standard form contracts. However a place, and an important one, remains for those implied terms in contracts of towage "laid down" (per *Bucknill*, (above) (2nd Edn.), p. 17) by the Privy Council in 1860. This is for two reasons. First, the characteristic of many engagements of a tug or tugs to effect a particular service is a rapid exchange of telexes or faxes between the parties via brokers in circumstances of urgency or where neither party is concerned with the minutiae of offer and acceptance; such operating conditions can and often do prove problematic for the effective incorporation (usually at the tug owner's behest) of the standard form set of conditions. Absent such incorporation, the terms implied at common law will apply. Secondly, although much less importantly, in the engagement of tugs, or of a vessel which can tow, on the more *ad hoc* basis which may be encountered in small ship work, albeit by yachts or other vessels of significant value, the engagement is often rudimentary as to the terms which are to govern it and the parties' rights and obligations will often still be those defined by the decisions of the courts as to the terms to be implied into a contract of towage.

For these reasons, Chapter 2 considers the implied terms and incidents of a towage contract at common law which will pertain where no standard form of contract or standard terms and conditions have been used or have effectively been used by the parties. In Chapters 3, 4 and 5, the standard forms which are commonly used in the realms of towage and allied services and which are encountered in English legal practice are considered separately.

PART B. THE MAKING OF THE CONTRACT

1. Authority of master to contract to be towed

(1) On behalf of his owners

The general position as to the actual and ostensible authority of a ship's master to enter into contracts with third parties on behalf of his owners and so bind his owners has altered considerably with the advent of increased facilities of communication. These mean that in very many cases the master is able to be in constant touch with his owners and that he will be prone to refer to them all but routine navigational and operational decisions. His authority, subject to this limitation, will extend to doing all that is reasonably and ordinarily necessary to effect the usual employment of the vessel (see generally: *Scrutton on Charterparties*, 19th Edn., pp. 38–39 and 254–256).

In relation to contracts for towage, the master of a vessel has authority to engage ordinary towage services which, objectively viewed, are reasonably necessary for the due performance of the vessel's voyage or are reasonably necessary for the safe and proper operation of the vessel and for her preservation from loss or damage. For these purposes, the master has authority to enter into a contract for towage provided that the terms of the contract are reasonable terms. As it was put by Sir Baliol Brett M.R. in *Ocean Steamship Co.* v. *Anderson* (1883) 13 Q.B.D. 651 at 652:

"A captain cannot bind his owners by every towage contract which he may think fit to make; it is binding upon them only when the surrounding circumstances are such as to make it reasonable to be made, and also where its terms are reasonable."

(see also per Baggallay L.J. at p. 663).

The nature of the master's ordinary authority to engage towage services is properly analysed as implied actual authority. The ability and right to engage towage services in circumstances of proper and reasonable necessity is an incident both of the master's authority from and his duty to his owners to prosecute the voyage and to employ the vessel safely and properly and in an ordinary and reasonable fashion. The *Ocean Steamship* test is consistent with the summary of the law given by Brandon J. in *The Unique Mariner* [1978] 1 Lloyd's Rep. 438. He stated at p. 449:

"The principles of law applicable to this issue can, I think, be stated in three propositions as follows. First, the relevant authority of a master, for the purpose of deciding whether his owners are bound, as against a third party, by an act which he has purported to do on their behalf, is his ostensible, rather than his actual, authority. Secondly, the ostensible authority of a master is the same as his implied actual authority, unless the latter has been restricted by express instructions from his owners or their representatives, and the third party concerned is, or should be taken to be, aware of such restriction. Thirdly, the implied actual authority of a master, unless restricted by such instructions lawfully given, extends to doing whatever is incidental to, or necessary for, the successful prosecution of the voyage and the safety and preservation of the ship."

In that case it was held that the authority of the master extended to making a contract for salvage on the basis of Lloyd's Open Form with its system of determining salvage remuneration by arbitration. *Cf. The City of Calcutta* (1898) 8 Asp. M.L.C. 442 in which the Court of Appeal doubted whether a master had authority to bind his owners to a contract involving a Lloyd's salvage arbitration, although it did not decide the point; this expression of doubt must now be considered as ill-founded.

The requirement to establish both the reasonable necessity for the tug and the reasonableness of the terms of the contract under which the tug is employed is illustrated by two cases. In *The Crusader* [1907] P. 15; P. 196 (C.A.), a vessel had run aground and required tug assistance to get her off. The ship's agents were asked by the master to engage a tug and they did so at a rate of £60 per day. The master refused to accept such terms and instead engaged the tug on a lump sum basis of £4,000 if the vessel was refloated "no cure, no pay". The court held that the agreement with its term for the payment of £4,000 was unreasonable and exorbitant and, accordingly, was outside the master's authority. The court refused to uphold the contract against his owners. In *The Luna* [1920] P. 22 the court considered a contract made on a Humber tug operator's standard form contract. The skipper of the Dutch fishing-vessel *Luna* engaged the tug *Kingston* to tow his vessel into dock from the mouth of the River Humber and from the dock to the sea for £15. He spoke very little English but orally negotiated the details of the service and the price. He then signed a form knowing it to be a contract but did not or was unable to read it. The form contained the standard terms which included a typical towage contract indemnity provision under which the tow was to indemnify the tug for all damage even if caused by the tug's negligence. The *Kingston* towed *Luna* into another vessel and was solely to blame. Various arguments were advanced by the owners of the *Luna* to escape from the clause including one that the indemnity clause and standard form were unreasonable and so outside the skipper's authority. This contention was rejected by Hill J. He stated (at p. 27):

"It is said that this clause is unreasonable. It is, and has for many years been, usual for tug owners to protect themselves by such a clause. Nor can I see any ground for saying that it is unreasonable. It is all a question of price . . . . The less the liability of the tug owner . . . the lower the price. There is nothing unreasonable in a bargain which puts the work of towage on the tug and the risks of service on the tow."

The decision in *The Luna* might be criticised on the ground that the incorporation of the standard form at all when signed and agreed to by someone who could not read it is doubtful and might, on this ground, perhaps be decided differently today, at least if it could be shown that the tug owner knew of the skipper's inability to understand the printed conditions (*cf. Geier* v. *Kujawa Weston and Warne Bros* [1970] 1 Lloyd's Rep. 364 per Brabin J. at 368 and 369), although the normal rule is that inability to read the standard terms is no defence by itself to their effective incorporation, see e.g. *Chitty on Contracts* (27th Edn.) Vol. I, para. 122–014 and see also *Watkins* v. *Rymill* (1883) 10 Q.B.D. 178. But, in so far as it establishes that terms in common use in standard forms, albeit onerous, will usually pass the *Ocean Steamship* test of reasonableness for deciding whether or not the entry into a contract on such terms is within the master's authority, it is correctly decided. As *Bucknill* (above) summarised the ratio of the decision: "such a term is usual in forms of contracts of towage, and is reasonable" (2nd Edn., p. 8). Compare the situation where onerous terms are agreed which do not form part of an accepted or usual form of contract, where a master's authority is more easily questioned (see e.g. *The Crusader, op. cit.*).

Outside the master's ordinary implied actual authority to engage ordinary and usual towage services, there will also be authority to engage exceptional towage services for the ship under the master's agency of necessity. The authority of the master in this context derives from the necessity for the engagement of the tug in circumstances where a reasonable person would regard the engagement as likely to be beneficial to the marine adventure on which the vessel is employed and from the master's inability to communicate with his owners: *The Onward* (1874) L.R. 4 A. & E. 38. In *The Alfred* (1884) 50 L.T. 511, 5 Asp., M.L.C. 214, the master of a ship in distress off Cape Finisterre concluded a towage contract with a vessel which had previously towed his vessel, without payment, for two days before letting go. That vessel agreed to stand by and tow for a further two days if the master agreed to pay not only for the future towage but also for the gratuitously rendered past towage. The court held that if it was reasonable as a matter of necessity to contract for the future towage, it was not unreasonable to agree to pay for the towage already done.

"It is clear as a matter of law that the master being the agent *ex necessitate* of his owners was authorised to enter into this agreement . . . . The master acted reasonably. It is clear that he thought he was acting reasonably and that there was some chance of saving the valuable property. This he did for the comparatively small sum of £400."

(per Butt J. at 512).

In reality, however, the relevance to the position as between a master and his owners of the agency of necessity cases will today be very rare given the modern immediacy of ship-to-owners communications. The position may be very different in relation to the agency of necessity conferred on a master or shipowners to act on behalf of cargo interests: see section (2) below.

(2) On behalf of his vessel's cargo

Subject to the exception of agency of necessity (see below), the owners of cargo are not bound by any contract of towage or salvage made by the owner or master of the vessel on which the cargo is laden. Neither the owners of the vessel nor the master have authority to bind the cargo carried or the owners of such cargo by any such contract. In *Anderson Tritton & Co.* v. *Ocean Steamship Co.* (1884) 10 App. Cas. 107, Lord Blackburn stated at p. 117:

"But neither the owners of the ship nor their master have authority to bind the goods or the owners of the goods by any contract."

Similarly, as it was put by Sir Robert Phillimore in *The Onward* (1874) L.R. 4 A. & E. 38 at p. 51:

"According to the law, the master is always the agent for the ship and in special cases of necessity for the cargo also. He is the appointed agent of the former, the involuntary agent of the latter."

The position has been most recently considered in *The Choko Star* [1990] 1 Lloyd's Rep. 516. In that case, the Court of Appeal held in the context of a contract of salvage that the only basis upon which a master might be authorised to contract on behalf of cargo owners was as an agent of necessity. Therefore, however, in the case of a true agency of necessity, i.e. if (1) it is necessary for the ship to take towage or salvage assistance to save the cargo; (2) it is not possible or practical for the ship to communicate with cargo owners; (3) the master or shipowner act *bona fide* in the cargo's interests; and (4) it is reasonable for them to enter into the particular contract in question (see the four-fold formulation of the requirements for such agency summarised by Slade L.J. in *The Choko Star* [1990] 1 Lloyd's Rep. 516 at 525), the cargo may be bound by a contract of towage or salvage entered into by the ship as agent of necessity on its and the ship's behalf. See also the consideration of this case by G. Brice Q.C. [1990] LMCLQ 32.

Commonly, while cargo interests are not bound by a contract of towage entered into by their carrying vessel, such interests will be liable to pay to the owners of the vessel their rateable proportion of the towage costs if the engagement of the tug is properly viewed as a general average measure taken by the vessel to preserve cargo and vessel from loss in time of peril. In such an event, the towage expenses will form part of the general average expenses to which cargo interests will be liable to contribute. As to this: see below in Chapter 9.

2. Authority of a master to take a vessel in tow

(1) The master of a tug

The master of a tug has implied actual authority to make reasonable contracts with regard to the provision by the tug of future towage services. Such authority creates no special difficulties and its extent will depend on the ordinary law of agency. However, in *The Inchmaree* [1899] P. 111, it was held that a tug-master did not have authority to agree retrospectively to deem services to be towage services which services had originally constituted salvage and which had already been completed, although he could do so if the deeming contract was entered into while the service, which had started as a salvage service, was still continuing (see per Phillimore J. at pp. 116–117).

(2) The master of a vessel not a tug

As has been seen above, the master of an ordinary trading vessel has implied actual authority to do such things as are involved in and necessary for the usual employment of the vessel. Since the implied actual authority of the master to contract on behalf of his owners is limited to such contracts as relate to the usual employment of the vessel, it is extremely doubtful whether the master of a vessel other than a tug has any authority to contract to tow another vessel. It is difficult to conceive of circumstances where towing would relate to the usual employment of an ordinary vessel and towing is unlikely to be necessary for such a vessel's safety or for the prosecution of her voyage.

The situation is most likely to arise when a vessel agrees to assist or to tow another vessel in distress. The position is complicated by the fact that a vessel will often by its nature be trading pursuant to some contract of affreightment or charterparty in which third parties are interested as cargo owners or charterers and that undertaking the towage of another vessel may well constitute a deviation putting the vessel outside the contract of carriage and with adverse consequences for her insurance. At common law, the position is that a master of a vessel probably has implied actual authority to deviate and to tow a vessel solely for the purpose of saving life but that he does not have authority to do so for saving property. Any towage other than for saving life will therefore constitute a deviation. The authority of a master to agree to tow a ship in distress was considered in *The Thetis* (1869) L.R. 2 A. & E. 365. In that case, a ship whilst trying to tow another ship collided with her and sank her. In an action by the owners of the sunken vessel against the owners of the towing vessel, the defendants pleaded that they were not liable on the ground that their master had no authority to tow. Sir Robert Phillimore held that the master had an implied authority to tow vessels in distress. He went on to state that he could not assent to the proposition that a deviation for the purpose of rendering salvage services to property would avoid a policy of insurance. However, in *Scaramanga* v. *Stamp* (1880) 5 C.P.D. 295, the Court of Appeal decided that towage for the purpose of saving property was a deviation which avoided the charterparty and rendered the shipowners liable for damage to the cargo caused by the deviation. In that case, Cockburn C.J. pointed out that towage of a disabled vessel was in itself a deviation, "seeing that the effect of taking another vessel in tow is necessarily to retard the progress of the towing vessel and thereby to prolong the risk of the voyage".

Perhaps because of the uncertainty of the position at common law the question of the permissibility of deviation for towing vessels has long been the subject of express clauses in charterparties (see *Scrutton on Charterparties*, 19th Edn., pp. 264–265). In *Stuart* v. *British & African Steam Navigation Co.* (1875) 32 L.T. 275 the clause provided "liberty to tow and assist vessels in all situations". It was argued that the phrase was apt only to extend to towage of vessels in distress which the vessel encountered in her voyage. The court dismissed this construction as too narrow, although it implicitly recognised that some (unspecified) limitation was appropriate. Nevertheless, the court held that the phrase was effective to protect a vessel leaving her berth to tow off a stranded vessel three miles away where no life was in danger and which resulted in the towing vessel being wrecked and her cargo lost. In *John Potter & Co.* v. *Burrell & Son* [1897] 1 Q.B. 97, the charterparty clause read "Steamer to have liberty to tow and be towed and assist vessels in all situations and salvage procured to be for the benefit of owners". In the Court of Appeal, Lindley L.J. stated (at p. 104):

"Therefore, towing is contemplated. What amount of towing is contemplated is another question. Of course, an unreasonable towage service is not contemplated, and, I take it, no towing service which would defeat the object of the parties to the contract is contemplated. But any towage which is consistent with the attainment of the object is contemplated. All towage involves delay. You cannot tow ships and go at the pace you can if you are not towing. Therefore you must read these clauses [i.e., perils of the sea and arrangements for provision of steamers], and, to my mind, it is most important to ascertain exactly what it is the parties are to do."

In that case, the vessel encountered a disabled vessel on her voyage and took her in tow adding a further three weeks to the voyage to the load port.

3. Pre-contractual disclosure: *The Kingalock*

In the last century the Court of Admiralty asserted a general equitable jurisdiction in respect of contracts of towage and salvage. In *Akerblom* v. *Price Potter Walker & Co.* (1881) 7 Q.B.D. 129 Sir Baliol Brett M.R. referred to "the great fundamental rule" (at p. 132) as being:

" ... Whenever the court is called upon to decide between contending parties, upon claims arising with regard to the infinite number of marine casualties, which are generally so urgent in character that the parties cannot be truly said to be on equal terms as to any agreement they make with regard to them, the court will try to discover what in the widest sense of the terms is under the particular circumstances of the particular case fair and just between the parties ... If the parties have made an agreement, the court will enforce it, unless it be manifestly unfair and unjust; but if it be manifestly unfair and unjust, the Court will disregard it and decree what is fair and just. This is the great fundamental rule."

One aspect of that equitable jurisdiction was the insistence of the court that the parties to a towage contract were entitled to full pre-contractual disclosure of all facts likely to affect the performance of the towage contract and which were within the special knowledge of either party. In the absence of such disclosure, the contract could be treated as void *ab initio* and a salvage contract would be substituted by the court, the remuneration under which the court would itself assess. The leading case is *The Kingalock* (1854) 1 Spinks A. & E. 263. In this case, a tug contracted to tow a vessel in very bad weather from the mouth of the River Thames to London for £40. After the towage had commenced the tug discovered that the tow had lost an anchor and had damaged her sails and windlass. The tug declared the contract at an end, but continued to tow the vessel, and after some difficulty brought her to London. The tug then claimed salvage, and the defendants, the owners of the tow, pleaded the towage contract and contended that they were liable only to pay £40. The court upheld the claim to salvage and set aside the contract. The tug received an award of £160. Dr Lushington in his judgment stated (at p. 266):

"I apprehend that the agreement may be said to be somewhat of a mixed nature at that time (when made); it is hardly to be considered an ordinary towage, not on account of the state and condition of the ship, but on account of the state and condition of the weather, which happened to be exceedingly tempestuous. I think whether the omission to state these facts (that the ship had lost an anchor and some sails) would vitiate this agreement or not will depend upon whether they could, with any reasonable probability, affect the service about to be performed. I am of the opinion that they might have an effect on that service, because I apprehend that coming up the River Thames, particularly during weather so tempestuous as this is represented to have been, the services might have been delayed and rendered much more arduous, much more difficult, in consequence of want of ground tackle, which might be of the last importance to the saving of the vessel, and which might, to a certain extent, have governed the manoeuvres of the steamer. I, therefore, come to the conclusion that as it might affect the performance of the service, the agreement was null and void *ab initio*."

Dr Lushington restated the principle 12 years later in *The Canova* (1866) L.R. 1 A. & E. 54. In that case, a tug agreed to tow a vessel into port for a fixed sum. The vessel had not revealed that many of the vessel's crew were ill. The tug performed the contract but claimed salvage on the ground of non-disclosure when the towage contract was made. However, Dr Lushington rejected the claim on the basis that the tow was not in peril when the contract was made. He nevertheless stated as follows:

"If, though unintentionally, there was a concealment of fact so material that it ought to invalidate the agreement, I should not enforce it. We must consider whether the owners of the tug were injured in the performance of their task by the withholding of certain facts, whether, if more time were taken up than should have been, the plaintiffs would be entitled to more than their bargain."

The Kingalock was applied as a case requiring full pre-contractual disclosure in the Canadian case of *Dunsmuir* v. *The Ship Harold* (1894) 3 B.C.R. 128. In that case, when asked by the tug whether any damage on a grounding had occurred, the master, aware that the vessel's hold was 18 inches deep in water, said "I do not know". The Vice-Admiralty Court of British Columbia held that the active concealment by the ship that she was in a leaky and dangerous condition vitiated the contract of towage and entitled the tug to special remuneration (applying *Akerblom's* case).

The Kingalock was considered more recently in *The Unique Mariner* [1978] 1 Lloyd's Rep. 438. A vessel had gone aground. Her owners arranged for a tug to go out to her and notified their master of this. The defendant's salvage tug happened to be in the vicinity and came up to the vessel offering her services. The master wrongly believed her to be the tug arranged for by his owners and accepted it, signing the Lloyd's standard form of salvage agreement (LOF) with the tug-master. When he discovered his mistake he ordered the salvage tug away. The owners sought to have the LOF set aside. One ground on which they did so was that *The Kingalock* established that the contract was a contract *uberrimae fidei* and that the tug should have disclosed all material facts, including, on the facts of that case, that the tug there was there by chance and not pursuant to the owners' own special arrangements. Brandon J. stated at pp. 454–455 as follows:

" . . . *The Kingalock* is not an authority which establishes that all contracts relating to salvage services are contracts *uberrimae fidei*, and therefore voidable by either party on the ground of non-disclosure of material facts by the other. It is rather just one example of the exercise by the Admiralty Court of its equitable power to treat as invalid, on the ground of serious unfairness to one side or the other, one particular kind of salvage agreement, namely an agreement by which the amount to be paid for services, in respect of which those rendering them would otherwise have a claim for salvage at large, is fixed at a definite sum in advance."

It is submitted that Brandon J.'s limited formulation of the type of contract in which the court will intervene as a type of salvage agreement, being towage in salvage conditions or engaged salvage services, correctly reflects the limited cases in which the equitable jurisdiction of the Admiralty Court over towage contracts has in fact been exercised; in all of such cases perilous conditions prevailed at the time of the engagement (see e.g. *The Kingalock*). His formulation is also in accordance with the statement of the "fundamental rule" in *Akerblom* (above) where Brett M.R. emphasised the "urgent character" of the circumstances in which the engagement of the tug took place.

Following *The Unique Mariner* it is therefore submitted that the position is as follows:

(i) In entering into a towage contract, there is no special obligation on tug or tow to make pre-contractual disclosure. The contract of towage is like any other contract and parties are left to the remedy of rescission or damages for misrepresentation as in other contracts. In particular, there is no obligation to disclose material facts.

(ii) However, in the case, in effect, of engaged salvage services where the tug is engaged under a towage contract to render services to a vessel in peril (such as *The Kingalock* was, with no sails or tackle and in very rough weather, but such as *The Canova* was not, merely with her crew being ill) and for a stipulated reward or fixed sum in circumstances where, but for the contract, the tug could have claimed salvage, the court will intervene in the event of a clearly inequitable result and of unfairness caused by a party's non-disclosure at the time the contract was made of matters which had a substantial bearing on the performance of the engaged services under the contract.

PART C. OTHER CONTRACTUAL MATTERS

1. The application of the Unfair Contract Terms Act 1977

(1) The scope of application

In most cases of large-scale commercial towage the towage contract will have been concluded between commercial entities dealing with each other with a fair measure of equality of bargaining power. However, the towage of small boats not operated commercially or in connection with a business, such as yachts and pleasure craft, is not infrequent and in such cases the tow is likely to have to agree to such towage contract as the tug proposes, together with a range of exemption and exclusion clauses in the tug's favour.

The statutory control of such clauses enacted in the Unfair Contract Terms Act 1977 extends to towage contracts in the following way:

(i) By paragraph 2 of Schedule 1 of the Act, "any contract of marine salvage or towage" will be subject to section 2(1) of the Act, which deals with clauses excluding or restricting liability for death or personal injury.

(ii) By the same paragraph, such contracts and their exemption and restriction clauses will not be subject to section 2 (liability for negligence), save for sub-section (1) as to which see (i) above; section 3 (liability in contract); section 4 (unreasonable indemnity clauses); and section 7 (miscellaneous contracts under which goods pass) *except* in the case where the clause is relied upon against any person dealing "as a consumer".

(iii) A person deals "as a consumer" for the purposes of the Act if two conditions, laid down by section 12(1)(a) and (b), are satisfied:

  (a) the person must not enter into the contract in the course of a business nor hold himself out as doing so;

  (b) the other party must make the contract in the course of a business.

  In *R & B Customs Brokers Co. Ltd* v. *United Dominions Trust Ltd* [1988] 1 W.L.R. 321, it was held that, for a contract to be made in the course of a business, the contract in question had to be an integral part of the business carried on, or, if only incidental to the business, nevertheless be of a kind regularly entered into.

In practical terms, parties to most large-scale commercial towage contracts will not be dealing as consumers. However, private boat owners will almost always satisfy the criteria set out in section 12(1) and owners of water-borne objects operated in the course of a business may nevertheless deal with tug owners as consumers if the towage of that object is not an integral part of their business, or is not a regularly incidental transaction of their business. They will not, therefore, deal "as a consumer". Thus, the owner of a floating dry-dock or heavy-lift barge will enter into towage contracts either as part of his business or at least as a transaction frequently incidental to his business. The owner of a floating restaurant or of a diving school run from a houseboat, while running a business, will still deal with the tug owner as a consumer if the towage of his premises is not part of that business and is not something which regularly occurs in and as a part of it.

(2) The provisions of the Act

It is outside the scope of this book to consider the scheme of the provisions of the Act as they affect contracts to which they apply: as to this, see generally e.g. *Chitty on Contracts* (27th Edn.) Vol I, paras. 14–045 to 14–086. In general terms, the Act either strikes down certain exclusion or exemption clauses altogether (e.g. under section 2(1), which applies to all towage contracts, a contractor cannot exclude or restrict his liability for death or personal injury caused by his negligence) or strikes them down if they do not satisfy a requirement of "reasonableness" (e.g. clause purporting to exempt the contractor from liability for breach of contract: section 3). The "reasonableness" of a term is a question of fact in all the circumstances but, in section 11(2), the Act sets out some "guidelines" to which regard is to be had in assessing "reasonableness". These guidelines focus on matters such as the respective bargaining position of the parties and the degree of notice which the other party had of the term in question.

As an example of the effect of the Act, it may be noted that, following the passing of the Act, the U.K. Standard Conditions of Towage and Other Services (see Chapter 3 below) in its 1986 Revision abandoned its exclusion clause in respect of death and personal injury resulting from negligence, i.e. recognising the ineffectiveness of such a clause by virtue of section 2(1) of the Act.

2. The Unfair Terms in Consumer Contracts Regulations 1994

Following the European Communities Council Directive 93/13/EEC on unfair terms in consumer contracts (see Official Journal No. L95, 21.4.1993 at p. 29), the Secretary of State for the Department of Trade and Industry has made regulations implementing the Directive. These are the Unfair Terms in Consumer Contracts Regulations 1994 (S.I. 1994 No. 3159). These Regulations came into force on 1 July 1995.

Pursuant to regulation 3(1) of the Regulations they are to apply to:

"any term in a contract concluded between a seller or supplier and a consumer where the said term has not been individually negotiated."

There is no special exception in respect of towage or salvage contracts (*cf.* the Unfair Contract Terms Act 1977). A "supplier" is defined as a supplier of goods and services acting for purposes relating to his business and a "consumer" is defined as a natural person that is, as distinct from a legal person such as a body corporate or association, who is acting for purposes which are outside his business. It will be seen, therefore, that the potential application of the Regulations to commercial towage is narrower even than that of the Unfair Contract Terms Act 1977. The most likely potential circumstances in which the Regulations might apply is where an individual, such as a yacht owner or a sole trader, enters into a towage contract otherwise than in the course of business with a towage company acting in the course of business and the contract is on a standard form of contract insisted upon by the towage company (i.e., as regulation

3(4) of the Regulations puts it in defining a term which has not been individually negotiated: "a term . . . drafted in advance and [of which] the consumer has not been able to influence the substance".

The detailed provisions of the Regulations are outside the scope of this book. Briefly, the scheme of the Regulations is as follows:

(i) So far as such terms are in plain and intelligible language, terms as to the subject-matter of the contract and price are unaffected by the Regulations: see regulation 3(2).

(ii) An unfair term is one "which contrary to the requirement of good faith causes a significant imbalance in the parties' rights and obligations under the contract to the detriment of the consumer": regulation 4(1).

(iii) Such terms do not bind the consumer: regulation 5(1).

(iv) Ambiguities in any written term of the contract shall be construed in the sense most favourable to the consumer: regulation 6.

(v) Schedule 2 sets out guidelines for how to assess "good faith", these are broadly similar to the guidelines for assessing the reasonableness of a term under section 11(2) of the Unfair Contract Terms Act 1977.

(vi) Schedule 3 sets out "an indicative and non-exhaustive list of terms which *may* be regarded as unfair": see regulation 4(4), emphasis supplied.

3. No special rules of construction for towage contracts

Although the older cases on towage suggest the existence of a canon of strict construction of towage contracts whenever a contract sought to exclude or to limit the terms of the towage contract which are implied at law (see e.g. *The Newona* (1920) 4 Ll. L. Rep. 156 and see *Bucknill on Tug and Tow* (2nd Edn., at p. 13), it is submitted that no special rules of construction apply to towage contracts in respect of exemption or exclusion clauses. The ordinary contract law position accordingly applies (see e.g. *Chitty on Contracts*, 27th Edn., Vol. I, paras. 14–001 to 14–121).

Although a full discussion of general contractual principles is outside the scope of this book, it is useful to consider how the present law leaves previous decisions of the court which have sought to restrict common form towage contract exclusion and exemption clauses.

Since the decision in *Photo Production Ltd* v. *Securicor Transport Ltd* [1980] A.C. 827, the question of whether or not a particular exemption or exclusion clause is effective to relieve the party in breach from liability is one of construction of the clause in question. This is so even if the breach is of a fundamental obligation in the contract. The concept of a "fundamental breach" of a contract, liability for which, as a matter of law could not be excluded or restricted by contractual provisions, was decisively rejected by the House of Lords in that decision.

Whilst in *Suisse Atlantique Soc. d'Armement* v. *N.V. Rotterdamsche Kolen Centrale* [1967] 1 A.C. 361, Lord Upjohn spoke (at p. 427) of a strong though rebuttable presumption that exemption clauses were usually not contemplated by the parties as covering breaches of fundamental or critical terms of the contract, it is doubtful whether this presumption or approach has survived *Photo Production*; it certainly received no express support or recognition by the House of Lords in that case. It is submitted that the question remains simply one of construction whatever the clause and whatever the liability and breach to which it is sought to apply that clause (see the valuable and succinct analysis in *Chitty on Contracts*, 27th Edn., Vol. I at para. 14–022).

In the light of the "construction" approach which the court now adopts, the old decisions on towage contract exclusions and, in particular, upon the very common form of exemption clause found in towage contracts, namely the indemnity by tow of tug for all loss and damage even if caused by the tug itself, have to be treated with great caution. While some would probably still be decided in the same way today, others would not.

(i) In *The West Cock* [1911] P. 23, the towage contract contained a clause that the tug owners were "not to be responsible for any damage to the ship they had contracted to tow arising from any perils or accidents of the seas, rivers or navigation, collision or straining or arising from towing gear (including consequence of defect therein or damage thereto)". It was held that the clause did not cover defects in the towing gear existing before the towage began, inasmuch as the contract evidenced the intention of the parties to refer to defects arising in the course of the towage, but not prior thereto. It is submitted that the language of the exemption clause would today be found to cover a pre-existing defect in the towing gear as well as one arising in the course of the towage and that the case would today be decided differently.

(ii) In *The Cap Palos* [1925] P. 458 an exemption clause provided:

"The acts, neglect or default of the masters, pilots or crew of the steam tugs . . . or any damage or loss that may arise to any vessel or craft being towed, or having been towed . . . whether such damage arise from or be occasioned by any accident or by any omission, breach of duty, mismanagement, negligence or default of the steam tug owner, or any of his servants or employees."

It was held that the clause was insufficiently clearly worded to exempt the tug owner from negligence on the part of the master during a voyage between Immingham and Hartlepool, which resulted in the tugs losing their hawsers and abandoning the tow in Robin Hood Bay, where she foundered. The clause did not expressly cover an unjustifiable handing over of the obligations of the tug owner to someone else for performance or a failure by the tug owner to tow the vessel in the way in which he had contracted to tow her. It is submitted that the clause, concentrating as it does upon damage to a vessel being or having been towed, would probably be construed in the same way by the court today and as not encompassing, as a matter of construction, an abandonment of the towage.

(iii) In *The Refrigerant* [1925] P. 130, the towing hawser broke during the performance of a towage contract, and the tug master left the ship unjustifiably. The tow was subsequently salved by a trawler, which received £2,000 salvage. The owners of the tow recovered this sum from the owners of the tug as damages for breach of contract and duty. Bateson J. held that the tug committed a breach of contract in leaving the tow, and that the very wide clauses of exception, all of which commenced with the words "during the towage service", did not cover such an act. The same construction would probably be adopted by the court today.

(iv) In *The Carlton* [1930] P. 18, the towage contract contained an indemnity in favour of the tug in respect of "loss or damage of any kind whatsoever or howsoever or wheresoever arising in the course of and in connection with the towage". An accident happened due to the tug owner's servant giving the tow the signal to enter a cutting between two docks when it was unsafe to do so. As the accident, although happening "in the course of towage", was not also "connected with towage", the claim for an indemnity failed. The two parts of the clause were not to be read disjunctively. Given the use of the word "and", it is submitted that this decision is plainly correct.

(v) In *The Forfarshire* [1908] P. 339, the tug undertook to tow and, *inter alia*, to find and provide "all items of transportation" such as to include towing gear. Negligently, the tug used the ship's tackle and due to a defective rope and a thimble eye which was too small for the towing hook, the line parted and the ship was damaged. The tug invoked the words, "All transporting to be at owners' risk". The court held that such words did not exempt from liability for negligence and only transferred the risk to the owner where the tug was exercising all reasonable care and skill. This decision is well in line with recent authorities such as *The Raphael* [1982] 2 Lloyd's Rep. 42.

(vi) In *The Riverman* [1928] P. 33, a tug towed six different barges under separate contracts. Due to negligence by the tug, the tug collided with another vessel. The tug admitted liability and then claimed from one of the towed barges under two clauses. The first provided that the tug's crew were to be the employees "of the vessel being towed". The second that any persons interested "in the vessels being so towed" were to indemnify the tug against all claims. The court held that the first clause was inapplicable in a case where there was more than one vessel being towed, but that the second clause applied in the tug's favour. This decision would, it is submitted, be decided in the same way today.

(vii) In *The Clan Colquhoun* [1936] P. 153, a vessel was to be towed by two tugs. The clause provided that the towage, and the exemption regime, was deemed to commence "when the tow rope had been passed to or by the tug". A collision occurred after a rope had been passed to one tug but before one had been passed to the other tug. Bucknill J. held that the clause was to be read as deeming the towage to commence when the rope had been passed to *both* tugs and that, accordingly, the exemptions did not apply at the time of the collision. This decision seems plainly correct; where two or more tugs are used to provide the pulling power they are for the purposes of such a clause collectively being described as "*the* tug".

(viii) *G.W. Rlwy Co.* v. *Royal Norwegian Government* [1945] 1 All E.R. 324 where the clause read:

"The hirer shall not bear or be liable for any loss or damage done by or to the tug otherwise than whilst towing, or for loss of life or injury to the crew of the tug."

The hirers sought to argue that he was not liable for loss of life; the court held that they were so liable "whilst towing" and that these words governed the whole clause. This decision seems plainly correct on the language of the clause.

The approach of the Admiralty Court in cases such as *The West Cock* can be contrasted with its upholding of the exemption or exclusion if, as a matter of construction, the language of the contract was clear and unambiguous. As can be seen from the other cases considered above, such cases are likely to be decided in the same way today. Thus in *The President Van Buren* (1924) 19 Ll. L. Rep 185, the court considered a clause which deemed the tug's crew to be the employees of the tow for all purposes (as to which type of clause, see p. 65 below). The court, foreshadowing the approach adopted in *Photo Production*, rejected an argument that the clause was unfair and too wide and upheld its effect in rendering the tow liable for all damage done to tug or tow, even if caused by the acts of the crew of the tug, simply as a pure matter of construction of the clause.

4. The effect of the general equitable jurisdiction of the Admiralty Court

As seen above (pp. 13 *et seq*.) in the discussion on pre-contractual disclosure, the Admiralty Court has long asserted a general equitable jurisdiction to prevent unfairness in towage contracts. To do what was "fair and just" between the parties was described as "the great fundamental rule" by Sir Baliol Brett M.R. in *Akerblom* v. *Price Potter Walker and Co.* (1881) 7 Q.B.D. 129 at p. 132.

The most recent re-statement of this jurisdiction in *The Unique Mariner* [1978] 1 Lloyd's Rep. 438 makes it clear that this jurisdiction probably exists only in the context of engaged salvage services, that is to say where a tug is engaged under a towage contract to do a fixed price service in circumstances in which it could, absent the contract, have claimed salvage.

The jurisdiction has impinged upon contracts of towage in respects other than pre-contractual disclosure. These may be briefly mentioned.

(i) The court will not uphold a contract of towage if either party has extorted the agreement by taking advantage of the danger to which the property of the other party is exposed (*Bucknill on Tug and Tow*, 2nd Edn., p. 11), or where "there is oppression or virtual compulsion arising from inequality in the bargaining position of the two parties concerned" per Brandon J. in *The Unique Mariner* [1978] 1 Lloyd's Rep. 438 at 454. However, whether this aspect of the jurisdiction amounts to more than the application of ordinary contractual principles as to the effect of duress is extremely doubtful.

(ii) The court will not uphold a contract of towage if the amount agreed upon is utterly inadequate or grossly excessive in comparison to the real value of the services: *The Phantom* (1866) L.R. 1 A. & E. 58. In that case, a towage contract for the towage of a fishing smack worth £700 across Lowestoft harbour in a press of other shipping and in bad weather and with her masts and spars weakened contracted for at 8s. 6d. (42½p) was set aside as inequitable. This aspect of the jurisdiction is sparingly exercised and cannot be invoked merely because subsequent events make the bargain a bad one for one or other party. The fairness or unfairness of the bargain is assessed at the time at which the towage contract was made:

"In forming an opinion of the fairness or unfairness of the agreement, I think that the court must regard the position of the parties at the time the agreement was entered into. The agreement cannot become fair or unfair by reason of circumstances which happened afterwards."

In *The Strathgarry* [1895] P. 264, a vessel engaged a tug for £500 to tow for half an hour believing that it would in that time be able to restart her engines and avoid salvage; the tug towed for half an hour but the hawser broke killing some of the vessel's crew and causing damage to her. In the event, the vessel's engines would not restart so she required to be salved by another tug. Bruce J. held that the £500 was a fair price for the service given the parties' expectations and their circumstances at the time it was agreed.

In *The Unique Mariner* [1978] 1 Lloyd's Rep. 438, Brandon J. referred (at p. 454) to this aspect of the jurisdiction without criticism in his account of the context in which *The Kingalock* had to be viewed. While there are no modern cases on this aspect of the jurisdiction, in the light of Brandon J.'s endorsement of the width of the jurisdiction in *The Unique Mariner* (*op. cit.*), where salvage service is performed under a towage contract the jurisdiction can, potentially, be invoked. However, it is submitted that a very strong case will be required to put the case within the degree of inequity found in *The Phantom* (*op. cit.*). In Brandon J.'s words in *The Unique Mariner* (*op. cit.*), the party seeking to avoid the contract would have to show:

"the gross inadequacy or exorbitancy of the sum agreed, which renders an agreement . . . so inequitable to one side or the other that it should not be allowed to stand."

(or as Dr Lushington put it in *The Phantom* (*op. cit.*) at p. 61, that the level or amount of the contract price was "utterly futile").

(iii) The court will not uphold a contract of towage in the event of "the existence of some collusion of one kind or another": per Brandon J. in *The Unique Mariner* [1978] 1 Lloyd's Rep. at 454. While this is vague, it appears to reflect the old cases on fraud or deceit by the tug, i.e., in bribing or colluding with the tow's master to persuade him to enter into a towage contract on his owner's behalf. See e.g. *The Crus V* (1862) Lush. 583 and *The Generous* (1868) L.R. 2 A. & E. 57. Similarly, if there has been active deceit on the part of the *tow*, as there was in *Dunsmuir* v. *The Ship Harold* (1894) 3 B.C.R. 128 (the facts of which are set out above at p. 14), the contract will be avoided.

CHAPTER 2

The Implied Obligations of Tug and Tow

The law implies certain terms into the contract of towage which define the rights and obligations of tug and tow. These terms will apply to govern the mutual relations of tug and tow under the contract in the absence of express terms having been agreed which are inconsistent with them or which exclude them: see e.g. *The Clan Colquhoun* [1936] P. 153 per Bucknill J. at 164: "Until this has been accomplished, the ordinary provision of the common law applies to the rights and duties of each party." While the implied terms are of little relevance where the towage contract is concluded on one of the commonly used standard forms, where no form or other express terms have been agreed they will define the bounds of the contract between the parties.

PART A. THE OBLIGATIONS OF THE TUG

1. The Supply of Goods and Services Act 1982

The contract for towage is a contract for services. As such it is a contract to which the Supply of Goods and Services Act 1982 applies. This Act provides for certain terms to be implied into all contracts for services unless the service is excluded from the Act by Order made by the Secretary of State (see section 12(4)). No exclusion of towage (or salvage) services has been made.

The relevant sections of the Act are sections 13 and 14. Section 13 provides:

"In a contract for the supply of a service where the supplier is acting in the course of a business, there is an implied term that the supplier will carry out the service with reasonable care and skill."

Section 14 in its turn provides:

"(1) Where, under a contract for the supply of a service by a supplier acting in the course of a business, the time for the service to be carried out is not fixed by the contract, left to be fixed in a manner agreed by the contract or determined by the course of dealing between the parties, there is an implied term that the supplier will carry out the service within a reasonable time.
(2) What is a reasonable time is a question of fact."

These provisions state some fairly basic obligations. Pursuant to section 16(1) of the Act, the duties arising under the Act can be negatived by express agreement or by a course of dealing or a usage binding between the parties.

The extent to which the Act adds anything to the implied obligations long-settled as being applicable to tug (and tow) is minimal as will be seen in the next section.

2. *The Minnehaha* and *The Julia*

(1) The Privy Council decisions

Prior to the Supply of Goods and Services Act 1982, the terms which the law implied into a towage contract were laid down by the courts. Those terms were given their most comprehensive and authoritative statement in two cases before the Privy Council in 1861.

In the first case, *The Julia* (1861) Lush. 224; 14 Moo. P.C. 210, an action was brought by the owners of the tug against the owners of the tow for damage done to the tug by the negligent management of the tow whilst the tug was making fast to the tow under a towage contract made between the masters of the vessels. Lord Kingsdown, who delivered the judgment of the Board, said:

"The case is said to be of the first impression and to involve the decision of nice questions of law . . . . The contract was that the tug should take *The Julia* in tow when required and tow her as far as Gravesend . . . . When the contract was made the law would imply an engagement that each vessel would perform its duty in completing it, that proper skill and diligence would be used on board of each, and that neither vessel, by neglect or misconduct, would create unnecessary risk to the other, or increase any risk which might be incidental to the service undertaken. If, in the course of the performance of this contract, any inevitable accident happened to the one without any default on the part of the other, no cause of action could arise. Such an accident would be one of the necessary risks of the engagement to which each party was subject, and could create no liability on the part of the other. If, on the other hand, the wrongful act of either occasioned any damage to the other, such wrongful act would create a responsibility on the party committing it, if the sufferer had not by any misconduct or unskilfulness on her part contributed to the accident."

In *Spaight* v. *Tedcastle* (1881) 6 App. Cas. 217, Lord Blackburn (at p. 220) described Lord Kingsdown's judgment just cited as one which "clearly and accurately states the law applicable".

In the second case, *The Minnehaha* (1861) Lush. 335; 15 Moo. P.C. 133, the action was for salvage in respect of services rendered by a tug to her tow during the performance of a towage contract. The tow was at anchor and she engaged a passing tug to tow her into the River Mersey and to dock her there for a lump sum. The weather was bad, and shortly after the tug made fast the towing hawser parted, and the tow drifted into danger from which the tug subsequently assisted to salve her. Lord Kingsdown, when delivering judgment, said:

"When a steamboat engages to tow a vessel for a certain remuneration from one point to another, she does not warrant that she will be able to do so and will do so under all circumstances and at all hazards; but she does engage that she will use her best endeavours for that purpose, and will bring to the task competent skill and such a crew, tackle and equipments as are reasonably to be expected in a vessel of her class. She may be prevented from fulfilling her contract by a vis major, by accidents which were not contemplated and which may render the fulfilment of the contract impossible, and in such case by the general rule of law she is relieved from her obligations. But she does not become relieved from her obligations because unforeseen difficulties occur in the completion of the task, or because the performance of the task is interrupted or cannot be completed in the mode in which it was originally intended, as by the breaking of a ship's hawser."

The standard of care and skill imposed upon the tug in the discharge of her duties as stated by Lord Kingsdown in *The Julia* is one of " . . . proper skill and diligence . . . ". In *The Minnehaha*, Lord Kingsdown described the tug's obligation as being one to "use her best endeavours" to achieve the purpose of the contract. At first sight, the obligation of "best endeavours" may appear to connote a significantly higher obligation than one merely to exercise reasonable skill and diligence. However, it is extremely doubtful that when Lord Kingsdown, for the Board, rearticulated in *The Minnehaha* the nature and extent of the duties imposed upon the tug which the Board had considered shortly before in *The Julia*, that it was intended to impose upon the tug a general obligation to exercise best endeavours in and about the towage rather than an obligation to exercise reasonable care and skill. Arguably, *The Minnehaha* and *The Julia* come to the same conclusion and the reference to best endeavours is simply a paraphrase of an obligation to use reasonable care and skill. Indeed in *Bucknill on Tug and Tow* (2nd Edn., p. 19), the obligation on the tug as stated in *The Minnehaha* was summarised as merely being one "to show skill and diligence in the performance of the contract"; interestingly, this is a paraphrase of what was said, not in *The Minnehaha*, but in *The Julia*. The same approach was adopted in *The Ratata* [1898] A.C. 513 where Lord Halsbury L.C. said that tug owners under towage contracts undertake:

"to exercise reasonable care and skill in the performance of the obligations which they have taken upon themselves for hire and reward in conducting the business of towage to its consummation".

So too in *The Marechal Suchet* [1911] P. 1 Sir Samuel Evans P. described the obligations of the tug as follows:

" . . . the owners of the tug must be taken to have contracted . . . that reasonable skill, care, energy and diligence should be exercised in the accomplishment of the work".

In the ordinary contractual context, the obligation to exercise best endeavours to achieve a specified result has usually been construed as one to exercise reasonable efforts to do so. Thus in *Terrell* v. *Mabie Todd & Co. Ltd* [1952] W.N. 434 the court considered a licence agreement under which the licensee of a patent in respect of the "Last-drop Ink Bottle" undertook to make best endeavours to sell the bottle in certain defined sales territories. Sellers J. stated (at p. 435):

"That he did not think that the contract could be construed more favourably for the defendants than that their obligation was to do what they could reasonably do in the circumstances. The standard of reasonableness was that of a reasonable and prudent board of directors acting properly in the interest of their company and applying their minds to their contractual obligations to exploit the invention."

It is accordingly submitted that the tug is only under an obligation to take all reasonable efforts to achieve the towage and to exercise reasonable care and skill to that end. Such a formulation is in line with the American cases (see e.g. *U.S.* v. *Leboeuf*

Bros. Towing Co., 1978 A.M.C. 2195 (E.D.La.), which cases are described in Parks and Cattell, *Law of Tug and Tow*, as applying the same principles as the British cases (4th Edn., p. 127).

However, if the reference to "best endeavours" was intended to signify an enhanced obligation upon the tug, how are the two decisions to be reconciled? The difference in terminology is, it is submitted, to be explained by the fact that the two cases concerned different questions. In *The Julia* the claim was one by the tow for negligent handling of the tow by the tug while the tug was making fast. The issue turned on the nature of the tug's obligation to carry out the towage operation. In *The Minnehaha* the claim was one by the tug for salvage over and above the towage fee of thirty guineas. The issue turned on the nature of the obligation of the tug to stay with the tow and, if she had been parted from her, to rejoin the tow in the event of unforeseen difficulties. The two obligations are qualitatively different. In the former case, the Board was right to characterise the obligation as one to exercise proper care and skill in the execution of the ordinary functions of the tug. In the latter case and given the practical need not to abandon tow or to leave a tow unattended, it was equally justifiable to impose the higher standard of best endeavours upon the tug as to her duty to rejoin and reconnect with the tow and to endeavour to complete the towage. As a *quid pro quo* for the tug, if, in her rejoining or staying with the tow, she exceeds "the scope of her original engagement", she will be entitled to salvage. This higher standard in persevering with the tow may perhaps also be echoed in Lord Kingsdown's words in *The Julia* that there is " . . . an engagement that each vessel would perform its duty in completing it".

(2) The principles summarised

The effect of the decisions in *The Julia* and *The Minnehaha* as to the obligations owed by the tug to the tow can, it is submitted, be summarised as follows:

(a) The tug must be manned by a crew and fitted out with such equipment and tackle as are reasonably to be expected in a vessel of her class.

(b) The tug must exercise reasonable and proper skill and diligence in the execution, performance and accomplishment of the contractual services (see also *The Marechal Suchet* [1911] P. 1).

(c) If, which is unlikely, the reference to "best endeavours" in *The Minnehaha* bears any separate content from the obligation to use reasonable care and skill, it signifies that the tug must exercise best endeavours to complete the towage and, in the event of interruption of the tow, to rejoin and reconnect with the tow; if the reference does not bear any separate content, the obligation is one to use reasonable skill, care and diligence to do so.

(d) The tug is not relieved from performance of the contract by unforeseen difficulties which interrupt the towage or which mean that it cannot be executed or completed as was originally intended.

(e) The tug will be entitled to claim salvage if she incurs risks and performs duties not within the scope of her original engagement (see Chapter 6 on towage and salvage).

(3) *The impact of the Supply of Goods and Services Act 1982 on these principles*

It will be seen that the Supply of Goods and Services Act 1982 has little practical impact upon the content of the terms implied at law in a towage contract. The nature of the obligation upon the tug to carry out the service with proper skill and diligence as stated in *The Julia*, or with "competent skill", as stated in *The Minnehaha*, is of no different quality to that of the obligation to use reasonable care and skill laid down in section 13 of the Act (see e.g. *The Marechal Suchet* [1911] P. 1 in which the President, Sir Samuel Evans, formulated the duty in a way which is no different from the formulation of the duty by section 13). The obligation to use best endeavours to stay with the tow, if it really connotes best endeavours in an enhanced sense (as to which see above), applies only to the perseverance with the tow in the case of interruptions or difficulties and is higher than that of reasonable care and skill. Whether it adds anything to the general contractual obligation on a party to *perform* the service contracted for, in the sense of the obligation actually to carry it out rather than the manner in which it is to be carried out, is doubtful. However, pursuant to section 16(3)(a) of the Act where a stricter duty is imposed upon a supplier by "rule of law", that duty is preserved and is not diluted by the Act. The principles in *The Minnehaha* as followed in the succeeding cases are terms implied by operation of law and amount to a rule of law, and, therefore, the "best endeavours" obligation, to the extent that it has any separate content, is unaffected by the Act.

Section 14 of the Act and the obligation to perform the service within a reasonable time adds little to the obligation already upon the tug to perform the service "with proper skill and diligence" (*The Julia*). That diligence will necessarily oblige the tug to perform the service with reasonable expedition.

3. Preparation for the towage

As part of the obligations upon the tug both to be reasonably crewed, fitted and equipped for the tow and to perform the service with reasonable care and skill, it is implicit that the tug will make all such adequate preparations as are reasonably necessary for the towage. This will usually consist of properly provisioning and equipping the tug. It is not often that the tug will be responsible for the tow although the tug may, as part of its preparations, need to satisfy itself as to the adequacy of the towage connections on the tow and to make necessary modifications and preparations for the reception on board the tow of the towing line(s). The involvement of the tug in preparatory matters on the side of the tow will often be greater in the case of an unmanned tow, where the tug will be directly concerned with the stability and buoyancy of the tow and other matters affecting her tow-worthiness, *a fortiori* if a riding crew is put on board the tow by the tug.

What is the precise scope of the preparations which the tug is to see to is a question of fact in each case. Examples of the areas of preparation for the towage with which the tug must concern itself appear from the cases:

  (i) The tug must make up the tow in a proper and skilful manner. If more than one vessel is to be towed, the tug must satisfy itself as to the sufficiency of its power to tow the vessels. In *The United Service* (1883) 8 P.D. 56; 9 P.D. 3, the tug took another vessel in tow after the towage had commenced but was insufficiently powerful to tow both and as a result the original tow stranded. It was held that, but for the exemption clause, the tug would have been in breach of its obligation of fitness for the service.

(ii) The tug must have the proper tow-lines and equipment on board; so it must ensure that the tow-line used is of the proper length for the tow. In *S.S. Rio Verde (Owners)* v. *S.S Abaris (Owners)* (1920) 2 Ll. L. Rep. 411, a scope of hawser of 120 fathoms in a crowded roadstead behind a defence boom with limited sea-room was held to be unseamanlike.

(iii) The tug must ensure that the navigational requirements of the tow are properly met. This is particularly so where the tow is unmanned where the tug may be responsible for the preparation of the tow's lights. In *The Albion* [1952] 1 Lloyd's Rep. 38, [1953] 2 Lloyd's Rep. 82 (C.A.), an uncompleted and unmanned aircraft carrier was under tow by three tugs and sank a collier at night under tow. The tug was held responsible for the aircraft carrier's failure to show the proper lights.

(iv) The tug must have properly organised the towage and must have a proper and sufficient plan of action to cope with all reasonably foreseeable eventualities: see e.g. *The Albion* (*op. cit.*) in which the defective planning consisted in the sailing of the tug and tow described above in the conditions shown by the falling barometer and in having failed to broadcast warnings to other shipping (see per Somervell L.J., [1953] 2 Lloyd's Rep. at 87).

(v) The tug must properly and securely lash the tow and the tug. In the Canadian case of *Patteson, Chandler & Stephen Ltd* v. *The Senator Jackson* [1969] D.L.R. 166, the failure to lash the tow securely to the tug was held to be negligent on the part of the tug, so that when the barge in tow hit a bridge the tug was liable for the damage.

4. Fitness of the tug for the towage service

(1) The obligation

Absent any special considerations which may apply where the towage contract is for a named tug (as to which, see section 5 below), the tug owner must provide a tug which is:

(i) properly equipped and manned for the service to be carried out, having regard to the weather and circumstances reasonably to be expected and to the class of tug which she is;

(ii) reasonably fit and efficient for the service and capable of performing the service, having regard to the same matters.

See per Lord Kingsdown in *The Minnehaha* (1861) 15 Moo. P.C. 133 at 152–154.

(2) *The nature of the obligation*

As *Bucknill on Tug and Tow* (2nd Edn., at p. 23) stated in 1927 "the precise scope and nature of the warranty by the tug owner as to the efficiency of the tug have not been settled by authority". In particular, the point remains open on the cases as to whether the tug owner's warranty of fitness and efficiency at common law is an absolute one equivalent to the absolute obligation at common law upon a shipowner to provide a seaworthy ship for the carriage of goods (see e.g. *Scrutton on Charterparties*, 19th Edn., Article 48 at pp. 82–90) or whether the tug owner is required only to exercise reasonable care and skill to ensure that the tug shall be fit and efficient.

Until 1911 the trend of the cases was to favour an absolute warranty. In *The Undaunted* (1886) 11 P.D. 46, a tug owner undertook to supply a tug (unnamed), and stipulated that he should be exempted from liability for the negligence of his servants. The tug was inadequately supplied with coal at the commencement of her voyage, and in consequence the voyage was delayed. In an action by the tug owner for the contract price, the owners of the tow counterclaimed for demurrage caused by the tug's insufficient supply of coal. The plaintiffs, as regards the counterclaim, alleged that the shortage of coal was caused by the negligence of their master, for which they were not liable. Butt J. held that there was an implied undertaking on the part of the tug owners to supply an efficient tug, that is to say, one properly equipped and properly supplied with coal, and that the exemption did not exclude liability for breach of this undertaking. As Butt J. put it at 48:

" . . . there being an implied obligation on the tug owners to supply an efficient tug, that is to say, one properly equipped and properly supplied with coal, and as I have found that the tug was deficient in the latter respect, the plaintiffs would be liable, notwithstanding the exception contained on the card. Therefore . . . the plaintiffs had not properly fulfilled their contract."

Although the point was not addressed and did not arise in this decision, Butt J.'s formulation was regarded as laying down an absolute obligation akin to that of seaworthiness (see e.g. Carver in his *Carriage of Goods by Sea*, 3rd Edn., section 112 at p. 140). It may be noted that the case was also interpreted in this sense by Scrutton in his *Law of Charterparties and Bills of Lading*, 1st Edn. (1886), p. 57, footnote (f).

It was similarly so regarded by Sir Samuel Evans P. who explicitly described the obligation of efficiency of the tug as being an absolute one in two decisions in 1910. In *The Marechal Suchet* [1911] P. 1 the President described the obligation as follows:

"The owners of the tug must be taken to have contracted that the tug should be efficient, and that her crew, tackle and equipment should be equal to the work to be accomplished in weather and circumstances reasonably to be expected, and that reasonable skill, care, energy and diligence should be exercised in the accomplishment of the work. On the other hand, they did not warrant that the work should be done under all circumstances and at all hazards, and the failure to accomplish it would be excused if it were due to vis major, or to accidents not contemplated, and which rendered the doing of the work impossible."

In *The West Cock* [1911] P. 23, the tug, whilst towing the plaintiff's vessel on the River Mersey, lost her towing gear. This was due to the shearing-off of her towing plate caused by defective and fatigued rivets which secured the plate to the tug. It was argued by the tug, first, that they were covered by an exemption clause, but, secondly, that the obligation upon them was only to take reasonable care to ensure that the tug, and therefore the towing plate, was fit for the service. The President upheld the claim on the basis that the exemption clause did not cover the tug in respect of a state of things existing before the towage began but only in respect of matters occurring during the towage. He further held that, even if the obligation was one to exercise reasonable care and skill as to fitness, the tug owner failed to do so: "this inefficiency could have been ascertained by reasonable care, skill, and attention": see p. 30. Accordingly, the President's discussion as to the standard of the obligation to provide a tug fit for the service was entirely *obiter*. However, his view was plain:

"In my opinion it is not sufficient for a tug owner in an action like the present one to prove that he is not aware of any unfitness or inefficiency or that it could not be discovered by an ordinary inspection. At the lowest I think his obligation is to prove that the unfitness or inefficiency was not preventable or discoverable by care and skill. But is not the obligation at the outset greater than this? Is it not an obligation which is absolute and which therefore amounts to a warranty? I think it is. It is well-established that the obligation under a charterparty or a bill of lading to provide a vessel which is 'seaworthy', in the commercial and legal sense, is an absolute one and amounts to a warranty of a seaworthiness; and this obligation has been described as 'a representation and an engagement, a contract, by the shipowner that the ship . . . is at the time of its departure reasonably fit for accomplishing the service which the shipowner engages to perform' (per Lord Cairns in *Steel* v. *State Line Steamship Co.*); and as 'a duty on the part of the person who furnishes or supplies the ship . . . unless something be stipulated which should prevent it, that the ship shall be fit for its purpose. That is generally expressed by saying that it shall be seaworthy; and I think also in marine contracts, contracts for sea carriage, that is what is properly called a "warranty", not merely that they should do their best to make the ship fit, but that the ship should really be fit' (per Lord Blackburn)."

The justification for this was said to be as follows:

"It is as important that a tug which undertakes to tow a vessel in some cases for long distances and in varying circumstances, with lives and property at risk, should be efficient for the accomplishment of its work, as it is that a cargo laden ship should be seaworthy, and in this sense fit for the purposes of the services undertaken under a charterparty. The foundation of the obligation is the same in either case, namely, the fitness of the tug or the ship for the purpose of the services to be performed."

The President at pp. 32–33 relied on *The Undaunted* (*op. cit.*) and at p. 33 interpreted *The Minnehaha* (1861) 15 Moo. P.C. 133 as supporting, or at least, as he put it, as being "consistent with", his construction of an absolute warranty. He concluded by stating that, if the matter were one for him to decide then:

"I can see no reason whatever why the same kind of obligation as to efficiency or fitness should not attach to a marine contract of towage as attaches to a marine contract of carriage" (p. 34).

The decision of the President went to appeal in 1911. Although the precise question similarly did not arise for decision on the appeal, the Court of Appeal was specific in distancing itself, with implicit disapproval, from the President's view of the absolute obligation or "warranty". In *The West Cock* on appeal at [1911] P. 208, Vaughan Williams L.J. considered that *The Minnehaha* tended more in favour of an obligation to exercise reasonable care than in favour of an absolute obligation. Further, he stated that he considered contracts of carriage as "entirely different" and that, although he did not need to go into these matters, " . . . I must not be taken to assent to anything . . . " expressed in the first instance decision except the view at first instance as to the ambit of the exemption clause. Farwell L.J. at p. 227 considered it "quite a different matter to extend the category of common law warranties [i.e., in the sense of absolute obligations] by adding another one to them, that is to say, by adding to tugs and tug service to ships the liability for goods carried. As at present advised, I express no opinion on that at all", although he referred to two cases on the hiring of other chattels which pointed in favour of the obligation being merely one to exercise reasonable care and skill. Kennedy L.J., with his unrivalled experience of salvage and towage practice, took a similar approach. He reserved his opinion on the question because it did not arise on the facts (p. 230). However, he commented on the President's alternative formulation of the obligation as being at the very least one of reasonable care as follows: "He describes what I may call the qualified obligation as 'an implied obligation to provide a tug in a fit and efficient condition so far as skill and care can discover its condition'. I accept that statement as correct" (p. 232).

It must be regarded as highly doubtful whether the "absolute obligation" view of the obligation as to the fitness of the tug would today be upheld by the court, notwithstanding Sir Samuel Evans P.'s views. The following matters may be noted.

(i) The contract of towage is only one for services and the cases generally on the hire of a chattel for services do not support and, indeed, are against a special rule where the person providing the service uses an item or object of his own to provide the service.

Thus, in *Hyman* v. *Nye* (1881) 6 Q.B.D. 685 a contract for the provision of the services of a coach, horses, and driver was held to imply an obligation to use reasonable care and skill that they be fit for the service. Farwell L.J. in *The West Cock* on appeal ([1911] P. at 227) expressly adopted and paraphrased the test which was applied by the court in that case in terms of tug and tow rather than of coach and horses:

"I think the liability may be very well stated as Lindley J. put it in respect to the contract of carriage in *Hyman* v. *Nye*. He says (I alter it so as to apply to a tug owner): 'His duty appears to me to be to supply (a tug) as fit for the purpose for which it is hired as care and skill can render it; and if whilst (the tug) is being properly used for such purpose it breaks down, it becomes incumbent on the person who has let it out to shew that the breakdown was in the proper sense of the word an accident not preventible by any care or skill'. Then a little lower down he says: 'As between him and the hirer the risk of defects in (the tug), so far as care and skill can avoid them, ought to be thrown on the owner of (the tug). The hirer trusts him to supply a fit and proper (tug), the lender has it in his power not only to see that it is in a proper state, and to keep it so, and thus protect himself from risk, but also to charge his customers enough to cover his expenses'. That, in my opinion, applies as much to a tug as to a carriage. The same principle was adopted in the case of the refrigerator in *Owners of Cargo of Maori King* v. *Hughes*."

The decision in *Owners of Cargo of Maori King* v. *Hughes* [1895] 2 Q.B. 550 is to like effect as to the fitness for service of a refrigeration plant as is the decision in *Pyman S.S. Co.* v. *Hull & Barnsley Rly. Co.* [1914] 2 K.B. 78;

[1915] 2 K.B. 729 as to the services of a floating dry-dock. (It may perhaps be noted that *Bucknill on Tug and Tow*, 2nd Edn., p. 21, footnote (b) cites *Hyman* v. *Nye* and at p. 23 disapproves of a strict "absolute obligation" approach.)

(ii) The analogy drawn by the President between a contract for towage and the contracts for the carriage of goods is false. As has been seen above, the tug is not in any relation of bailment to the tow whereas the carrier is, hence a strict obligation of seaworthiness. The two cases, contracts for services and contracts for carriage, are as Vaughan Williams L.J. remarked, "entirely different".

(iii) *The West Cock* at first instance and *The Marechal Suchet* are unsupported by any other towage case (save for the assumption of an absolute obligation of efficiency made without discussion in the Canadian case of *McKenzie Barge & Derrick Co.* v. *Rivtow Marine Ltd* [1968] 2 Lloyd's Rep. 505 at 508) and are inconsistent with settled authority. Nothing in *The Minnehaha* (1861) 15 Moo. P.C. 133 suggests an absolute obligation; on the contrary, Lord Kingsdown's formulation in that case suggests much more strongly the exercise of reasonable care and skill as being the tug's obligation; Vaughan Williams L.J.'s view of what Lord Kingsdown had said, which he expressed in *The West Cock* on appeal at [1911] P. at 225, is plainly correct. *The Undaunted* (*op. cit.*) relied on by Sir Samuel Evans P. does not address the question. Further, in *The Ratata* [1898] A.C. 513, Lord Halsbury delivering the judgment of the House of Lords, although not expressly considering the question of the dichotomy of view between an absolute obligation and one only to exercise reasonable care, described the tug's obligation as follows:

" . . . I think it is clear that they undertook to exercise reasonable care and skill in the performance of the obligation which they have taken upon themselves for hire and reward in conducting the business of the towage to its consummation" (p. 516).

"For the time during which this contract business was being performed, it was the tug of the corporation and its inefficiency was an inefficiency for which the corporation, as contractors for towage with reasonable care and skill, were responsible" (p. 517).

This formulation is much more consistent with Lord Kingdown's statement of principle in *The Minnehaha* than that of the "absolute obligation". The President in *The West Cock* had great difficulty in distinguishing *The Ratata* convincingly (see [1911] P. at 33–34). Vaughan Williams L.J. in *The West Cock* correctly thought that Lord Halsbury's formulation in *The Ratata* went against what the President was stating was the law: see [1911] P. at 225. His view appears to be correct.

Compare, however, to the contrary, the implicit assumption of an absolute obligation in successive editions of *Scrutton on Charterparties* citing *The Marechal Suchet* and *The West Cock* (see e.g. the latest (19th) edition, at p. 82, footnote 50).

(iv) An absolute obligation of efficiency and fitness of the tug is anomalous in the relationship between tug and tow which, as the cases rejecting the bailment relationship stress, is one in which the only obligation on the tug is to exercise reasonable care and skill in the performance of the contract: see e.g. *The Tug Champlain* [1939] 1 D.L.R. 384 considered at p. 6 above.

It is therefore submitted that the obligation upon the tug owner to provide a tug which is in a fit and efficient state for the service is one to exercise reasonable care and skill and to ensure that particular fitness and efficiency, and that the views, expressed *obiter* at first instance in *The Marechal Suchet* and *The West Cock*, are wrong in law.

The position may be contrasted with the position in American law which is that the tug owner is under an absolute duty to provide a tug of sufficient power and equipment: see e.g. Parks and Cattell, *Law of Tug and Tow*, 4th Edn. at p. 129:

"The duty of the tower to provide a tug at sufficient power that has a proper and efficient equipment and tackle is relatively absolute, yet it might be qualified by the underlying premise that this duty is to be interpreted in the light of conditions reasonably to be anticipated."

5. Contract for a named tug: special considerations

(1) How the considerations arise

For large-scale operations of ocean towage, the tow may often have in mind the use of the services of a particular tug. Modern tugs for ocean towage work are sophisticated and powerful instruments and most first-class tug operators have several tugs whose names and identities are well-known in the maritime world for their established prowess in complicated ocean tows and, often, in salvage work and whose details are equally well-known.

Particular problems may arise where the tow selects a named tug and the contract is for a named tug. In certain circumstances, the implied term as to the fitness and efficiency of the tug may be excluded.

(2) The cases

In *Robertson* v. *Amazon Tug and Lighterage Co.* (1881) 7 Q.B.D. 598, the contract was less one for towage by a named tug than for the hire by a person of a tug and its crew which person, in effect, took a demise of it for the duration of the tow. The plaintiff, a master mariner, contracted with the defendants for a lump sum to be paid to him by the defendants, to take a certain specified steam tug of the defendants, towing six sailing barges, from Hull to Brazil, the plaintiff paying the crew and providing provisions for all on board for 70 days. The engines of the steam tug were damaged and out of repair at the time of the contract, but neither the plaintiff nor the defendants were then aware of this. The consequence, however, of the engines being so defective was that the time occupied in the voyage was increased, and the plaintiff's gain in performing his contract was much less than it would otherwise have been. At first instance Lord Coleridge C.J. held that the defendants had warranted the reasonable efficiency of the tug. The Court of Appeal reversed this decision (Bramwell L.J. dissenting). Brett L.J. stated at p. 605:

"When there is a specific thing, there is no implied contract that it shall be reasonably fit for the purpose for which it is hired or is to be used. That is the great distinction between a contract to supply a thing which is to be made and which is not specific, and a contract with regard to a specific thing. In the one case you take the thing as it is, in the other the person who undertakes to supply it is bound to supply a thing reasonably fit for the purpose for which it is made."

However, Cotton L.J. held that there was doubt as to the position of a contract for the hire of an ascertained chattel, but described the contract as one by the plaintiff to take the defendants' vessels to a certain place including their named tug. He stated at p. 609:

"The plaintiff here contracts with the defendants for a sum to be paid by them to take a vessel and barge to South America, with liberty to use the vessel as a tug. I say with liberty, for it can hardly be said that it would have been a breach of contract on his part not to use the motive power of the tug, but to tow the *Villa Bella* and the barges to their destination. If the vessel were not at the time of the contract ascertained and known to both parties, probably the contract would imply such a warranty as relied on by the plaintiff. But a contract made with reference to a known vessel in my opinion stands in a very different position. In such a case, in the absence of actual stipulation, the contractor must, in my opinion, be considered as having agreed to take the risk of the greater or a less efficiency of the chattel for which he contracts. He has to determine what price he will ask for the service or work which he contracts to render or to do. He may examine the chattel and satisfy himself of its condition and efficiency. If he does not and suffers from his neglect to take this precaution, he cannot, in my opinion, make the owner liable. He must, in my opinion, be taken to have fixed the price so as to cover the risk arising from the condition of the instrument which might be examined if he had thought fit so to do."

Although the contract was in a rather special form, the approach in that case came to be widely applied as a rule in cases of pure contracts of towage. Thus, in *The West Cock* [1911] P. 208, Kennedy L.J. regarded the rule as applying to towage contracts generally, saying (at p. 231).

"A different set of considerations would have arisen in the present case if the owner of the ship had picked a particular tug and not left it, as he did, to the defendants to supply a tug . . . for the purpose of towing the '*Araby*' ".

In *Point Anne Quarries* v. *The Tug Mary Francis Whalen* (1922) 13 Ll. L. Rep. 40, the Privy Council adopted the rule as a general one, describing the contract as one "for a named tug" falling within *Robertson* v. *Amazon Tug* (at p. 42) and the Board relied upon this rule as one of its grounds for allowing an appeal from a Canadian court which had found for the tow in part because of the tug's incapacity for the towage. In *Fraser & White Ltd* v. *Vernon* [1951] 2 Lloyd's Rep. 175, the issue turned on whether the contract was one "for specific tugs" or one "for towage services" (p. 177). McNair J. held the contract was for the services of two named tugs *FW No. 23* and *Eclair* and that the claim for breaches of implied warranties as to the tugs failed: as the judge put it " . . . the short answer to the whole of this claim is that there is no implied warranty or condition or to the fitness of the tugs to do their work . . . " (p. 178).

But the rule has been distinguished or not applied in other cases. In *The Glenmorven* [1913] P. 141, the contract was for the tug *George V* to tow from Vigo to Jarrow. Sir

Samuel Evans P. held that the principle in *Robertson* v. *Amazon Tug* did not arise because (p. 147):

"I am going to deal with this case upon the basis of the tug itself being chosen by . . . the owners of the ship being towed but not upon the basis that she was so chosen if she went with any defective tackle. It was intended between the parties that the tug should be properly equipped."

This basis of distinction could be applied to almost any case but it is submitted is probably correct on its facts. The tow did not select the tug but asked the tug owner if he had a tug available. It appears that it was the tug owner who put forward the *George V* and who named it in the contract (see p. 142).

A more serious basis of distinction was that set out in *Reed* v. *Dean* [1949] 1 K.B. 188 and *Yeoman Credit Ltd* v. *Apps* [1962] 2 Q.B. 508, neither of which were towage cases. In the former case, the contract was one for the hire of a named motor launch which caught fire. Lewis J. held there was a warranty of fitness notwithstanding the naming of the launch. He distinguished *Robertson* v. *Amazon Tug* as being not a case of hiring but a case of a contract by a master mariner to take specified vessels to a certain port for reward (p. 192) and relied upon Cotton L.J.'s restricted formulation as opposed to Brett L.J.'s more general one (see above). In the subsequent case of *Yeoman Credit* v. *Apps*, the contract was one for the hire purchase of a specified car. Holroyd Pearce L.J. held that *Robertson* did not apply. At pp. 514–515 he commented on that case:

"Therefore Bramwell L.J. was in favour of there being such a warranty in a contract for the hire of a specific article; Brett L.J. was against it and Cotton L.J. doubted it without deciding it . . . The decision does not preclude us from holding that there is a warranty in the ordinary hiring of a specific chattel since for the reasons given by Cotton L.J. the contract in that case was not a contract of hire at all."

(3) *The present position*

It is submitted that the distinguishing of *Robertson* as not being a contract of hire at all, although deriving much support from Cotton L.J.'s views in *Robertson* itself, is artificial. The contract by which the master agreed to take the vessels to South America was in its form plainly one equivalent to a contract of hire (see also per Bramwell L.J. in his dissent at p. 603 and per Brett L.J. at p. 606). Even Cotton L.J. described the contract as excluding warranties because it was "a contract made with reference to a known vessel"; as might a modern contract which was made by reference to a particular contractor's market renowned tug. However, it is to be recognised that in none of the decisions applying *Robertson* does there appear to have been any argument as to precisely what that case decided (e.g. in *Fraser & White* v. *Vernon*, distinguished counsel for both parties, Messrs. Mocatta and Eustace Roskill, were content to proceed upon the assumption of the "named" tug rule). It is also to be recognised that as Thomas Scrutton pointed out in the first edition of his *Law of Charterparties and Bills of Lading* (1886), p. 57, footnote (f) the facts in *Robertson* "were very unusual".

One critical feature may be whether the parties are in fact contracting by reference to a *particular* tug (whether named or not) or by reference to a tug in general (which may be given a name in the contract for ease of identification). This will be a question of fact in each case. In *The M.F. Whalen* and *Fraser & White* v. *Vernon* cases, the parties chose to contract by reference to particular tugs. In *The Glenmorven* it appears they did not. In *Reed* v. *Dean* the contract was one for a launch, which happened to have a name which was used to identify her in the contract. In *Yeoman Credit*, the car was a car but of a particular make and registration number. A further critical feature is whether the contract is one for the *hire* of the tug itself or is for a contract for the *services* to be performed by the tug.

It is submitted that the present status of *Robertson* v. *Amazon Tug* is uncertain. To the extent that it decides a point of general principle, it decides that:

(i) in a contract for the hire of a specific and identified tug where the contract is concluded by reference to that tug, there will be no implied obligation upon the tug owner as to the fitness of that tug (*Robertson* v. *Amazon Tug*);

(ii) however, in a contract for the hire of an unnamed tug or for the performance of a towage service by a named tug or for the performance of a towage service by a tug which the tug owner shall choose, the implied term as to fitness and efficiency applies.

To be sure of the position, where a "named tug" is being contracted for, it should be made clear by the parties in their contract what the agreed position is as to the fitness of the tug.

It should be noted that the American law is to the same effect as *Robertson*: see the decision in *The Dodd*, 1927 A.M.C. 427 (9th Cir.), and that Parks and Cattell in their commentary on the English cases (see *The Law of Tug and Tow*, 4th Edn., at pp. 17–129) accept *Robertson* as laying down a general rule. Similarly Scrutton in the first edition of his work (*op. cit.*) regarded the decision as establishing, albeit on unusual facts, that the naming of the tug "negatived an implied contract of efficiency"; *cf.* the current editors' position in *Scrutton on Charterparties* (19th Edn.), p. 82, footnote 50 who prefer the approach in *Reed* v. *Dean*, considered above. See also the reference to the "naming" of a tug in the Canadian case of *The Tug Champlain* [1939] 1 D.L.R. 384 at p. 389.

The rule in *Robertson* v. *Amazon Tug*, of course, leaves unaffected the position where a specific representation is made as to the named tug or where the parties contract on the basis of a common mistake, i.e., as to the named tug's characteristics: see *The Salvador* (1909) 25 T.L.R. 384, 25 T.L.R. 727 and 26 T.L.R. 149 (lack of power of tug).

6. Performance of the towage service

(1) The general position

The obligation upon the tug in its performance of the towage is to exercise competent skill: see *The Minnehaha* (1861) Lush. 335, or proper skill and diligence: see *The Julia* (1861) Lush. 224. In other words, the tug must exercise reasonable care of and over the tow and in and about the operations which it performs as part of the towage service.

(2) The question of control

Of special relevance in considering the question of the tug's obligations in relation to a particular operation in the towage service is the ascertainment of where the responsibility of tug or tow for a particular operation lies. That responsibility depends upon the allocation of the control of the particular operation. Which is in control of that operation, the tug or the tow?

The question of control is particularly relevant in relation to the navigation of the tug and tow. The question is usually answered as between tug and tow by an express provision in the standard form contracts deeming the tug to be in all respects the tow's servant. In the absence of an express provision, the question as to which of the tug or the tow is in control in a particular operation is a question of fact for the court looking at the contract as a whole. However, a default in the performance of the towage by tug or tow can also result in damage to third parties (i.e., by collision) as well as to the tug and tow. In such a case, the position as to which of tug and tow is in control of the towage operation will be regulated by the court's determination of which is in control, irrespective of what the tug and tow have themselves contractually provided for, either expressly or impliedly, that provision being one incapable of binding anyone other than the parties to the contract (see e.g. *The Panther* and *The Ericbank* [1957] 1 Lloyd's Rep. 57). For this reason, the question of control usually arises in tort in cases of collision with third parties and the legal principles relating to the doctrine of control are dealt with in this context in Chapter 7.

For present purposes however, the law can be stated as follows:

    (i) If the tow is unmanned, generally the tug will be responsible for and will owe contractual obligations, in respect of the navigation of the tow as well as of the tug: see e.g. *The Adriatic* and *The Wellington* (1914) 30 T.L.R. 699 (in which case a dumb barge was held to be under the control of the tug).

    (ii) Where the tow is manned, the question of whether the tug or the tow is in control of a particular towage operation is a question of fact which is to be determined upon the particular facts and circumstances of each case.

This latter rule was laid down by the House of Lords in the *S.S. Devonshire* v. *The Barge Leslie* [1912] A.C. 634. In that case there was a collision between a barge in tow of a tug and a steamship. The tug exercised sole control over the navigation of the tow, and the collision was caused by the joint negligence of the tug and the steamship. It was held in the House of Lords, affirming the Court of Appeal, and the President of the Admiralty Court, that the tow could recover all her damages from the steamship, and that her rights against the steamship were not affected by the negligence of her tug. The case therefore dealt primarily with the right of the tow to recover damages, and not with her liability for damage done by her, but the case decides in general terms that the rights and liabilities of the tow are not affected by the negligence of the tug unless the owners of the tow or their servants have control of the navigation of the tug. In the House of Lords, Lord Ashbourne stated (at p. 648) that there was nothing in the facts of the case to make the tow responsible for the navigation of the tug: "This is not a question of law, but a question of fact to be determined in each case on its own circumstances." Similarly, Lord Atkinson (at p. 656) stated the proposition in these terms: "It must, therefore, I think, now be taken as conclusively established that the question of the identity of the tow with the tug that tows her is one of fact, not law, to be determined upon the particular facts and circumstances of each case." This approach is very similar to the approach adopted by the American cases in applying the "dominant mind" doctrine: see e.g. *Sturgis* v. *Boyer*, 65 U.S. 110 (1861) and *The Margaret*, 94 U.S. 494 (1876).

The rule laid down in the *S.S. Devonshire* dispelled a tendency on the part of the Court of Admiralty under Dr Lushington (see e.g. *The Duke of Sussex* (1841) 1 W. Rob. 270 and *The Christina* (1848) 3 W. Rob.29) to ascribe control to the tow as a matter of presumption so as to avoid an apparent divided "command" of the towage. This presumption was doubted by Sir James Hannen P. in *The Stormcock* (1885) 5 Asp. M.L.C. 470 who stated:

" . . . I myself should have been inclined to think that the decisions of the American courts establish a rule more in conformity with my own ideas of justice; that is, that the particular circumstances should be looked at in each case to see whether the tug or tow or both are liable."

The President returned to the attack in *The Quickstep* (1890) 15 P.D. 196 where, with Butt J., he adopted the American approach of looking to see which of tug and tow exercised the "dominant mind", exemplified in cases such as *Sturgis* v. *Boyer*, 65 U.S. 110 (1861), as applying in cases where no servant or agent relationship existed. He thereby foreshadowed the decision of the House of Lords in *S.S. Devonshire*.

Therefore, in the context of contractual responsibility on the part of tug or tow for some error of navigation during the performance of the towage service, unless there is some express contractual provision regulating the position, the question will be the same as in the context of a claim of a third party for damage sustained by contact with tug or tow. This question is: as a question of fact which of the tug or the tow was in control of the operation in question as a result of or by which the damage has been occasioned?

(3) Examples of identifying which vessel is in control

Although since *S.S. Devonshire* v. *The Barge Leslie* [1912] A.C. 634, the question of control is one of fact to be approached afresh in each case, some tentative guidance as to how the question might be answered can be derived from the pre-*Devonshire* cases. However, these must be read with caution and against the background of the presumptions which the courts were prone to make prior to the decision in the *S.S. Devonshire* case. The approach in the pre-*Devonshire* cases can be summarised as follows:

(i) In open waters where there is plenty of sea-room for tug and tow to manoeuvre, the tow will normally be in control of the towage if it is giving orders as to the course to be followed and the navigation to be adopted. See e.g. in *The Isca* (1886) 12 P.D. 34 per Sir James Hannen P. at 35.

" . . . the general direction is to be given by those on board the vessel in tow . . . "

This is so even if the tow is not directing every aspect of the towage: see *The Sinquasi* (1880) 5 P.D. 241. It is interesting to note that the presumption in the old cases that the tow was in control of the towage, at least in the case of ocean towage, may have arisen because of the poorly-regarded status of many tug operators. Thus, in *The Niobe* (1888) 13 P.D. 55 it was stated (per Sir James Hannen P. at p. 59).

" . . . The authorities clearly establish that the tow has, under the ordinary contract of towage, control over the tug. The tug and tow are engaged in a common undertaking, of which the general management and command belongs to the tow, and, in order that she should efficiently execute this command, it is necessary that she should have a good look-out and should not merely allow herself to be drawn, or the tug to go, in a course which will cause damage to another vessel. As Dr Lushington has pointed out, it is essential to the safety of vessels being towed that there should not be a divided command, and convenience has established that the undivided authority shall belong to the tow. The pilot (if there be one) takes his station on board his tow, and the officers of the tow are usually, as in the present case, of a higher class and better able to direct the navigation than those of the tug. The practice which experience has dictated has received the sanction of many legal decisions, and has been recognised in the House of Lords in *Spaight* v. *Tedcastle* (1881) 6. App. Cas. 217 where Lord Blackburn says that 'it is the duty of the tug to carry out the directions received from the ship' . . . "

Given the very high status of most tug operators today with their extensive experience of complex towages, while the ascertainment of who is in control is a question of fact, if there is any presumption to be made, in many cases it may tend to put the tug in control.

(ii) Where the tow has given only a general order at the start of the towage and gives no further orders or where no orders as such are given at all, the tug will be in control of the towage. In *The Robert Dixon* (1879) 5 P.D. 54 Brett L.J. stated at p. 58:

"I am very much inclined to think that a tug is bound to obey the orders of the captain, and if the captain had insisted on the tug keeping that course, the tug would have been bound to obey; certainly the captain could not have complained of the tug obeying him. But then, on the plaintiff's own showing, the only evidence was that at the beginning of the towage the tug was directed to tow the ship in a particular course. I assume that to have been the right course; but on the way the weather became threatening. Assuming that no further order was given by the captain, it was the duty of the tug to use reasonable care and skill, and unless she was ordered to the contrary, she had the command of the course."

In such a case the tug will have to set the course for the towage: *The Altair* [1897] P. 105.

(iii) In confined waters such as the approaches to a port or in harbour or river towage or in open waters which are congested with other vessels, the control is usually with the tug as the tug is usually the best judge of how to handle the tow and may have local knowledge: see *The Isca* (*op. cit.*) per Sir James Hannen P. (1886) 12 P.D. at 35:

"But it does not follow from this rule that the vessel in tow is to be constantly interfering with the tug, it must depend on the place and on the circumstances as whether there are numerous small vessels about. Those in charge of the tug must exercise their judgement, and not be constantly expecting to receive orders from the vessel in tow, which may be a considerable distance astern of them."

(iv) Where the tow, although manned, is disabled in some respect bearing on her navigation, the tug usually has control of the towage: see *The American* and *The Syria* (1874) L.R. 6 P.C. 127.

(v) Where the tow, although manned, is not herself capable of independent navigation, e.g. such as a barge or where several craft are towed in a convoy or flotilla, the tug will usually be in control: see per Fletcher Moulton L.J. in *S.S. Devonshire* in the Court of Appeal [1912] P. 21 at 49.

(vi) Where the tug executes a sudden and unexpected manoeuvre which the tow is powerless to prevent or to shape up to, cases have gone both ways, i.e., in fixing the tug with control for the purposes of that manoeuvre even if the tow is otherwise in control (see e.g. *The Stormcock* (1885) 5 Asp. M.L.C. 470) and in fixing the tow with control notwithstanding the sudden act of the tug (see e.g. *The Sinquasi* (1880) 5 P.D. 241).

(4) If the tug is in control of the service

On the assumption that the tug is in control of the navigation of the tug and tow for the purposes of the service, the tug, pursuant to the decisions in *The Minnehaha* and *The Julia* is bound to exercise all reasonable care and skill and proper seamanship in the navigation of herself and of the tow.

Thus, for example, amongst its other implied duties involved in its overriding obligation to exercise reasonable care and skill in and about the towage, the tug is under the following particular obligations.

(i) To exercise all reasonable care and skill in anticipating what the tow might do or how she might manoeuvre during the towage.
In *The Cape Colony* (1920) 4 Ll. L. Rep. 116, the tug failed to shift the towing rope from the forward bit to the towing hook sufficiently timeously, held herself too close to the vessel's stern and was collided with when the vessel suddenly used her engine and moved astern. Hill J. stated:

" . . . the tug must anticipate and be on the look out for the engines [i.e. of the tow] being moved to ahead or astern as required."

Similarly, in *The Shanklin* (1932) 43 Ll. L. Rep. 153 there was a collision of a tug towing a barge with a paddle steamer in Portsmouth harbour. The tug was to blame for failing to anticipate the movement of the steamer as she was leaving the landing stage and for failing to take her way off in time. As Langton J. pithily put it at p. 156:

"The moral to be drawn from this case is that if you navigate such unwieldy craft as this tug and barge lashed together you must be unusually on the alert and take no chance. I think Captain Ship took what in ordinary circumstances is an ordinarily fair chance, not perhaps even a sporting chance. He took the chance that the *Shanklin* would not do what she always does, but she did not do it and he lost on the gamble and I am afraid he must also lose on this case."

(ii) To exercise all reasonable care to keep clear of the tow during the service and, especially, while making fast to avoid contact with the tow.

Practically speaking, while tug and tow must each exercise proper care and skill, tugs, being the handier vessels, must take upon themselves the main duty of keeping clear of the tow, e.g. when making fast: see e.g. *Bucknill on Tug and Tow* (2nd Edn.), p. 28. Thus, in *The Lagarto* (1923) 17 Ll. L. Rep. 264 the tug passed under the bow of the tow while taking her tow rope. The tow increased her speed and swung to starboard. She hit the port quarter of the tug and sank her. The tug failed to establish negligence on the part of the tow. At the end of his judgment Hill J. said

" ... In fact, tugs that go out to make fast to steamers which are under way, especially those that go to make fast ahead and have to be close under their bows, do engage in that which is a risky operation. A very slight deflection of the head of the tug, a very slight failure to keep the tug in exactly the right position, may expose it to great danger. That is one of the risks tugs have to run and I suppose it is taken into consideration when their remuneration is fixed; but every now and again it does not come off. This is the second case of the kind heard this term. But that does not justify tug owners seeking to put the blame on the steamers unless it be established that the ship has been guilty of negligence."

The responsibility of the tug in manoeuvring in close quarters has been specifically considered in three cases.

As has been seen in the case of *The Cape Colony* (1920) 4 Ll. L. Rep. 116 the tug failed to shift the towing rope from the forward bit to the towing hook in good time, and thereby held herself too near the stern of the tow, the tug being held to blame for the collision that ensued.

"A tug which is assisting a steamer to manoeuvre ... cannot expect that the steamer will keep her engines stationary",

said Hill J. (at p. 118) and continued:

" ... the tug must anticipate and be on the look out for the engines being moved to ahead or astern as required."

In *The Contest* v. *The Age* (1923) 17 Ll. L. Rep. 172, the tug was putting the ship's hawser on the tow hook. At the end of his judgment, Hill J. said:

" ... however this collision came about it is not suggested, and cannot be suggested, that there was any negligence on the part of the [tow]. Tugs which are making fast to a ship necessarily take upon themselves the main burden of keeping clear; and there are many ways in which careless handling of the tugs in the very close quarters in which they have to work, bring them into contact with the ship."

See also *The Clan Colquhoun* [1936] P. 153 where the tug was criticised for getting too close to the tow's propellers and for failing to inform itself of the exact position of the propellers.

However, the tow owes a duty too to watch the tug in close-quarter operations. In *The Harmony* v. *The Northborough* (1923) 15 Ll. L. Rep. 119, the tug was going around the tow's stern to take the rope on the starboard side in accordance with instructions received from the ship, while she did so the tow used her main engine causing propeller wake. It was contended that the tug bore the sole duty to watch out in close-quarter manoeuvring. The court rejected this:

"There is no unilateral duty of that kind in the relations of tug and tow. Each of them has to exercise proper care. It is quite true that there are acts which are in themselves acts of peril; and a tug which is carrying on business involving risks must incur the proper risks incidental to her occupation; . . . [the tug] being in a position in which her security need not be imperilled . . . is not to be imperilled by unconsidered and hasty action such as was taken by the engines of the [tow]."

(iii) To exercise all reasonable care to keep a good look-out and be ready to take decisions as to the navigation of the tug and tow in an emergency without awaiting orders of approval from the tow.

In *The Isca* (1886) 12 P.D. 34, a tug towed a brigantine in the River Usk downstream against the tide at the brigantine's request. The tug mishandled the tow and the tide drew her into collision with a bridge. The tug argued that it was for the tow to give precise orders as to what to do and that she had not done so. As to this Sir James Hannen P. stated (at p. 35):

"It is true that the general direction is to be given by those on the vessel in tow; and also if a specific order is given by her to the tug, the responsibility must rest with the vessel in tow for the consequences of such order. But it does not follow from this rule that the vessel in tow is to be constantly interfering with the tug; it must depend on the place and on the circumstances and whether there are numerous small vessels about. Those in charge of the tug must exercise their judgement, and must not be constantly expecting to receive orders from the vessel in tow, which may be a considerable distance astern of them."

He was influenced by the narrowness of the river and that the tug was (or should have been) the better judge of how to manoeuvre the convoy in such waters.

Cf. The Niobe (1888) 13 P.D. 55 as to the responsibility of the tow to keep a proper look-out for tug and tow (see Part B below).

(iv) To exercise all reasonable care and skill so to direct the tug and tow as to the course to be taken to avoid other vessels encountered during the towage. See e.g. *The Stormcock* (1885) 5 Asp. M.L.C. 470 (tug towing at night with long scope of hawser; held tug alone to blame as in such circumstances the tow was under no duty to direct the course of movement of the tug). See also *The Duke of Manchester* (1846) 2 W. Rob. 470 at 477.

(v) To exercise all reasonable care for herself and for the tow to proceed at an appropriate speed in thick or foggy weather.

In *The Englishman and The Australia* [1894] P. 239, a tug, whilst towing a vessel, came into collision with, and sank, a third vessel, and was herself damaged. The third vessel and the tug were found to blame for excessive speed in fog. The tow was also found to blame for not controlling the speed of the tug. On these facts it was held by the President (Sir F.H. Jeune) that, although the tow had not been herself in collision, the owners of the tug and the owners of the tow were liable for half the damages of the third vessel after deducting half the damages of the tug for which the owners of the third vessel were liable. See also *Smith* v. *St. Lawrence Tow Boat Co.* (1873) L.R. 5 P.C. 308 (both tug and tow held to blame for proceeding in fog).

(vi) To exercise all reasonable care to proceed at a proper speed for the water and sea conditions.

While this obligation is usually considered in the context of the tug towing the tow at too fast a speed for the conditions (see e.g. *The Altair* [1897] P. 105), the tug must not tow too slowly either. Thus, in *The Ratata* [1898] A.C. 513 the tug was held liable for proceeding so slowly (due to inefficiency at her boilers) that the last vessel in the line of vessels being towed was stranded due to having insufficient way on.

(vii) To exercise all reasonable care where no course has been stipulated by the tow to plan and follow a reasonable, proper and safe course for tug and tow.

In *The Robert Dixon* (1879) 5 P.D. 54, the tug agreed to tow a ship for a fixed sum. The tug towed her too near to the shore. The hawser parted, and the ship was in danger of being driven ashore. The tug re-established a connection and pulled her clear. The tug's claim for salvage was denied. In the Court of Appeal James L.J. said of the relative duties of tug and tow regarding directions:

"Whether the evidence establishes that the tug acted in violation of any positive directions from the ship during the voyage it is not necessary for us to give an opinion, because if it be true that no directions were given to the tug apart from the general directions at the commencement of the towage, it comes to this, that the master of the tug was acting as it was his duty to do on his own discretion to take the ship on a safe course to the Skerries, allowing for possible contingencies and a change of weather."

(viii) Where necessary, to exercise all reasonable care to take soundings as part of the planning and following of a proper course for tug and tow.

In *The Altair* [1897] P. 105, the tug agreed to tow a barque to Hull "without interference from the tow". The tug was held to have been negligent in not taking soundings, as she should have done, when nearing the entrance of the Humber. Gorell Barnes J. stated at p. 115:

"There seems no doubt that the tug is under the control of the master of the ship; but practically the tow cannot be always giving directions as to the course set by the tug, and I am informed by my assessors that the tow usually does leave the course in such towages as the present to the tug, and would not interfere unless there were reasonable grounds for doing so. As a matter of fact, in the present case, the direction of the course was assumed by the tug; and it was perhaps not unreasonable that it should be so, because the master of the tug had been to the Humber several times before, whereas the master of the *Altair* had only once sailed out of that river in the year 1884 . . . as no directions were given by the ship to the tug, the latter was responsible for the direction of the course."

(ix) To exercise all reasonable care to avoid shearing on the part of the tow.

See *R* v. *The Island Challenger* [1959] Ex. C. R. 413 where the tow was on a long hawser and was allowed to shear into a bridge.

7. Completion of the towage service

The overriding obligation upon the tug imposed at common law is to stay with the tow and to persevere in the completion of the towage service. It is as to this obligation which the Board in *The Minnehaha* (1861) Lush. 335; 15 Moo. P.C. 133 stated that the tug "will use her best endeavours for that purpose" and that the tug "does not become relieved from her obligations because unforeseen difficulties occur in the completion of her task, because the performance of the task is interrupted or cannot be completed in the mode in which it was originally intended, as by the weakening of a ship's hawser". Questions often arise in relation to this obligation, in the context of interruptions to the towage service.

8. Interruptions in the course of the towage

Interruptions to a towage service are common: the tow-line parts; the tug is obliged to slip her line in bad weather to avoid colliding with the tow; the tug sustains some mechanical or steering problem; the tug is called away to render some pressing salvage service. In all such cases, the obligation on the tug is the same: to return as soon as possible to the tow, to effect the reconnection of the tow-line and to resume and complete the towage. If this cannot be done, or if the circumstances of the interruption of the towage are such that the service cannot be performed or contemplated, the tug must not leave the tow until she is in a safe place.

(i) In *The Golden Light, The H.M. Hayes, The Annapolis* (1861) Lush. 365, a tug was forced to let go of her tow because of the risk of collision with a third ship. The tow went on to collide with that ship and then with another. The tug came up behind the tow and succeeded in making fast and in preventing a further collision. The tug claimed salvage. It was held by Dr Lushington that the obligations of the tug under the towage contract did not prevent her from letting go but thereafter she had to resume the tow and to take care of the tow in the situation in which she then found herself.

(ii) In *The Aboukir* (1905) 21 T.L.R. 200, the towage consisted of a tow of a vessel from the anchorage into a dock. The vessel was unable to get into the dock. It was held that the obligation under the contract to assist in the docking of the vessel did not come to an end until the tow was left in a safe place, which on the facts of the case meant returning the tow back to anchorage and leaving her there.

(iii) In *The Refrigerant* [1925] P. 130, a tug was held to have breached the contract of towage by abandoning the tow on a towage from Lorient to Liverpool after a hawser parted off the Lizard. The tug went into harbour for a new line and sent out another tug under contract to assist her. Bateson J. held that, while the contract was not one to tow without a break and while it was implicit that there might be interruptions, in the event of such an interruption the tug was under a duty to "do all she reasonably can to take care of and protect" the tow and, in particular, to stand by the tow.

(iv) In *Gamecock Steam Towing Co. Ltd* v. *Trader Navigation Limited* (1937) 59 Ll. L. Rep. 170, the contract was to tow a vessel which had sustained damage from Dartmouth to Southampton; the towage, being short, should have taken two days. However, during the towage, the tow began to take water and had to put into port for temporary repairs. The towage as a result took two weeks. The tugs stood by her during the repairs because the towage contract was a lump sum "no cure–no pay" and they wished to earn the remuneration. Goddard J. considered that as they chose to do so, the service in standing by fell within the contract. He held that the tugs could have left earlier had they wanted to (p. 174) and that they could claim no extra for standing by in this way.

> "I think, the case of *The Refrigerant* ... is authority for saying that the tug must not leave a vessel having once undertaken the service until she is in a safe place. If they could have got her into a safe place they might have left her. They could have said 'It is going to take so long to repair this ship that it will not pay us to go on and as this was not contemplated we threw up the contract'."

As to what is a safe place and as to the content of the obligation to stand by during repairs or similar works, Goddard J. continued (*ibid*):

> " ... if she had been put in dry dock, ... the tug could have gone away and come back. The law would not require a tug to stand by while a ship was in dry-dock."

9. Circumstances in which the towage can be abandoned

Notwithstanding the obligation upon the tug to complete the towage and to rejoin the tow in the event of interruption, there is no absolute warranty on the part of the tug that the service will be performed "under all circumstances and at all hazards": *The Minnehaha* (1861) Lush. 335; 15 Moo. P.C. 133. As was said by the Privy Council in that case, at common law:

> "The tug is relieved from the performance of her contract by the impossibility of performing it."

Where, therefore, for some reason the towage service is rendered impossible of performance, the tug is discharged from the contract and may abandon the towage, having left the tow in a safe place: see e.g. *The Aboukir* (1905) 21 T.L.R. 200. See also *Gamecock Steam Towing Co.* v. *Trader Navigation Co.* (1937) 59 Ll. L. Rep. 170, cited above, where Goddard J., *obiter*, suggested that the same position applied where the performance was still possible but where it was radically different from the contemplated. The test was expressed by Dr Lushington in *The White Star* (1866) L.R. 1 A. & E. 68 as follows at p. 70:

> "The real question is, what are the contracting parties reasonably supposed to have intended by the engagement, and what degree of alteration had they a right to expect, because to suppose that the performance of the service would always be of the same character would be absurd. I apprehend that, when a master of a vessel contracts with the master of a tug, it is upon the supposition that the wind and weather, and the time for performing the service, will be what are ordinary at the time of year, and that the sum contracted for is that which is supposed to be a

sufficient remuneration for the ordinary performance of the voyage. It may be a short voyage if all the circumstances are favourable, and it may be a long one if they are unfavourable. I shall submit to you that when an engagement is made—a contract—for a specific time, that contract must be adhered to, and is not to be broken hastily, unless it be shewn that circumstances have occurred which would not have been within the contemplation of the parties, and that such is the state of circumstances, that to insist upon the contract and hold it binding would be contrary to all principles of justice and equity."

An illustration is given by the case of *The Glenmorven* [1913] P. 141. In that case, the plaintiffs contracted for the sum of £400 to tow the defendant's rudderless steamer from Vigo to the Tyne on the basis of a term which provided "no cure, no pay, no claim to be made for salvage". Whilst the towage was proceeding the master and crew of the steamer left her, and the tug, with other assistance, took the steamer first to Falmouth and then on to the Tyne. It was held by the President (Sir Samuel Evans) that the contract was to tow a partially disabled vessel, with her master and crew on board from Vigo to the Tyne and that that contract came to an end through the fault of those in charge of the steamer, for, though the vessel was not technically a derelict as the tug was in attendance under contract, the master and crew without sufficient justification had abandoned her. From the time of that abandonment the services rendered by the tug were not performed under contract, but were in the nature of salvage for which the award would be £1,400 and, on the basis of a *quantum meruit*, £300 for the previous services. It was held that the contract came to an end when the tow was abandoned, the abandonment not being a temporary one, and when she was left in charge of a tug which was under a legal obligation to go on towing. As the court put it:

"A contract to tow a partially disabled vessel . . . is one thing. A contract to tow a vessel which has been entirely abandoned in the Bay of Biscay is a wholly different contract."

Where, as is common, the tow cannot be left in a safe place immediately upon the performance of the contract becoming impossible, the tug remains under an obligation to render services to the tow. Even where the tug is in no way to blame for the supervening impossibility, she is, apparently, not free to abandon her tow in danger upon the impossibility manifesting itself, but she is obliged to endeavour to save the tow from danger, albeit that in respect of such services she may be entitled to be paid upon a salvage basis: see e.g. *The Galatea* (1858) Swa. 349.

Accordingly, the law implies an obligation on a tug under a towage contract to render assistance to her tow in cases of unusual difficulty or danger, and a corresponding obligation on the tow to pay extra remuneration for these services, and to pay such remuneration on a salvage basis if the tug's services save the tow from the danger in question, or contribute to her ultimate safety.

As it was put by Sir Robert Phillimore in *The I.C. Potter* (1870) L.R. 3 A. & E. 292:

"It is not disputed that circumstances may supervene which engraft upon an original towage agreement the character of a salvage service; and to this proposition of law I must add another, which has an important bearing on my decision, namely, that when the supervening circumstances, from stress of weather or otherwise, are such as to justify the towing vessel in abandoning her contract, it is still her duty to remain by the towed vessel for the purpose of rendering her assistance, but that for such assistance she is entitled to salvage reward."

From the perspective of the tow, it appears that where the tug breaks down and leaves the tow so as to effect repairs at least for a substantial period, the tow may be justified in terminating the towage contract as having been abandoned by the tug thus entitling the tow to engage alternative assistance: see *The Lady Flora Hastings* (1848) 3 W. Rob. 118. This is consistent with the approach suggested (from the perspective of the tug facing a broken-down tow) by Goddard J. in *Gamecock Steam Towing* (1937) 59 Ll. L. Rep. 170 considered above.

PART B. THE OBLIGATIONS OF THE TOW

1. *The Julia*

In its decision in *The Julia* (1861) 14 Moo. P.C. 210, the Privy Council considered the obligations on both tug and tow. In general terms, tug and tow owe each other the same obligations, but it is the nature of the towage and the respective roles played in it by tug and tow which will define the extent and content of each other's obligation. Lord Kingsdown stated (at p. 230):

"The contract was that the tug should take the *Julia* in tow when required and tow her as far as Gravesend . . . When the contract was made the law would imply an engagement that each vessel would perform its duty in completing it, that proper skill and diligence would be used on board of each, and that neither vessel, by neglect or misconduct, would create unnecessary risk to the other, or increase any risk which might be incidental to the service undertaken."

In that case, the steam-tug *Secret* was engaged by a sailing vessel, the *Julia*, to tow her from Folkestone to Gravesend. The *Julia* ran the tug down due to her carrying too much sail in the prevailing wind conditions and to her following dead astern of the tug rather than keeping her helm to starboard. The tug was held to have been blameless since slipping the hawser would have made no difference. The tow was found liable for failing to observe due care and skill in the towage.

The American courts have adopted a virtually identical approach to the mutual duties upon the tug and tow: see *The Raleigh*, 44 F. 781 (1890) and *The Director*, 1927 A.M.C. 1295 (4th Cir.).

2. Fitness of the tow for the towage service

There is an implied term that the tow shall be in a seaworthy condition and fit for the towage service as far as the tow owner can put her into that condition by the exercise of reasonable care and diligence. In *Elliott Steam Tug Co.* v. *The Chester* (1922) 12 Ll. L. Rep. 331 at p. 333, a tug was engaged to tow an obsolete battle-cruiser, the *Chester*. The tow's bottom was then discovered to be heavily fouled making towage by one tug too dangerous. A "without prejudice" agreement was entered into for a second tug to be used by the tug owner. The hirer argued that the contract was for the towage of the *Chester* to destination by however many tugs were needed. This was rejected on various grounds. One ground was that (per Hill J. at p. 333):

"Under a contract for the towage of an obsolete ship, there must be an implied obligation on the part of the tow that she is in a reasonably fit condition to be towed."

Similarly, in *The Smjeli* [1982] 2 Lloyd's Rep. 74 a tug and tow (a dumb barge) were connected by a towing hawser with an insufficiently large breaking strain. The line parted and the barge was cast ashore damaging the plaintiffs' coastal defence groynes. The case concerned questions of limitation of liability (see the consideration of this case below in Chapter 8 at p. 214), but Sheen J. described the position in relation to the condition of the tow to be as follows:

"In this case the duty upon the owners of the tug and barge was the common law duty to use reasonable care to send their vessels to sea in a seaworthy condition and at a proper time."

In *Canada S.S. Lines* v. *S.S. Paisley* [1930] 2 D.L.R. 257 (Can. P.C.), the tow lost its right to limit liability because of its fault, *inter alia*, in allowing the towage to commence without having all proper and sufficient tackle for the service on board the tow and with her anchor left hanging down on the port bow which caused another vessel to be holed during the towage. In *The Bristol City* [1921] P. 444, shipbuilders engaged a tug to tow an unfinished vessel from Bristol to Cardiff. She had no hawse pipes or windlass, no chain cable, only one anchor and a short scope of wire rope. The tow-line parted in bad weather and the tow collided with another ship because she was unable to anchor properly. The Court of Appeal held that the tow's want of ground tackle constituted unseaworthiness and was the cause of the collision and held the tow liable.

The fitness of the tow will depend upon all the circumstances. Thus if the towage contract is to tow a stranded vessel off, there will be an implied obligation upon the tow owners that the tow will be in a position where she can be got off by the tug. In *Elliott Steam Tug Co.* v. *New Medway Steam Packet Co.* (1937) 59 Ll. L. Rep. 35, a tug was hired to tow an eight hundred ton lighter from a mudbank at the end of a shallow and narrow channel. The court held that the contract was subject to an implied term:

"that the owners of the vessel to be towed would have the vessel in such a position that a tug of the size which they knew would have to be sent to perform the voyage would be able to take the lighter in tow, and that the lighter was in such a position that a tug could pick it up and take it out."

Compare the decision in *Gamecock Steam Towing Co. Ltd* v. *Trader Navigation Co. Ltd* (1937) 59 Ll. L. Rep. 170 where the court refused to imply into the contract a term that the vessel should have been lying in midstream in circumstances when she was alongside a berth and lying on mud but could be towed off the mud without difficulty. The court held that the only obligation on the tow was to put herself in a position where she could be taken over by the tug and was lying somewhere whence, at the appropriate state of the tide, she could be floated off and taken in tow.

3. Proper seamanship during the towage service

(1) The general position

Irrespective of whether the tug or the tow is in control of the towage, the tow is obliged to take reasonable care in and about the towage. As Buckley L.J. put it in *The Devonshire* [1912] P. 21 at 61:

"The tow may be a steamship or a sailing vessel, and she may, and sometimes does, use her own means of propulsion to assist the tug in their joint venture. The tow can, by her helm, command, within limits, her direction of motion. She does, in fact, owe the maritime duty towards other vessels of using her helm, and under appropriate circumstances, her steam or other means of propulsion or control, so as to avoid collision. She is not, like cargo, a passive spectator of the manoeuvres. She owes a duty to play a part in them, and is to blame if she plays a wrong part. In this I am not speaking of the responsibility of the tow for the conduct of the tug, but of her responsibility for her own conduct."

(2) The question of control

If, on the factual enquiry made pursuant to the decision in *S.S. Devonshire* v. *The Barge Leslie* [1912] A.C. 634, the tow is found to be in control of the towage, the tow's involvement in and responsibility for navigation during the towage is likely to be increased. But even if the tug is in control of the towage, the tow owes obligations pursuant to the implied terms set out in *The Julia* to use proper skill and diligence and to exercise reasonable care not to increase the risks of the endeavour.

(3) Tow in control

Where the tow has the control of the navigation, the tow is obliged to take reasonable care as to the course chosen and as to the navigation adopted for the tug and tow. Many of the cases and examples cited above in relation to the tug (see Part A, section 6(3) above) will be equally applicable to the duties imposed upon the tow.

(4) Tug in control

Even where the tug is in control, the tow must exercise reasonable care to look out both for herself, for the tug and for the accomplishment of the towage by both (see per Buckley L.J. in *The Devonshire* cited above). Examples of the typical facets of the obligation to take care during and in and about the towage are as follows:

(i) The tow, even if disabled, must anticipate, observe and in so far as she is able, follow the movements of the tug with all proper seamanlike response.

If the tug takes action, the tow should assume that the tug is acting in a seamanlike manner and for a particular purpose and should conduct herself with proper promptitude accordingly. In *The Jane Bacon* (1878) 27 W.R. 35, a tug took action to avoid a fishing vessel. The crew of the tow delayed in shaping their course to follow the tug because they were unaware of why the tug had altered course as she did. The fishing vessel was struck by the towing hawser. It was held by the Court of Appeal that the tow was negligent.

The corollary of this is that if the tow does shape her course in response to the tug's sudden change of course reasonably relying upon the tug's judgement, she will not be negligent even if the tug's movement was itself negligent: see e.g. *Bucknill on Tug and Tow* (2nd Edn.), p. 51, and see also:

Spaight v. *Tedcastle* (1881) 6 App. Cas. 217, where the House of Lords held that the tow was justified in assuming that the master of the tug "knew what he was about and would do what was necessary to avoid getting too close to the bank [at the mouth of Dublin harbour] unless the contrary manifestly appeared".

However, if the navigation of the tug is very bad, a failure to anticipate and act upon a particular manoeuvre may not render the tow liable. In *The Comet (Owners)* v. *The W.H. 1 (and others)* [1911] A.C. 30, the owners of a lightship sued the owners of a hopper barge in tow of a tug for damage by collision between the lightship and the barge. The general control of the navigation was in the tug. The tug executed a sudden and unseamanlike manoeuvre as a result of which the barge collided with the lightship. In the Admiralty Court both the master of the tug and a bargee on the barge were held to have been negligent, and tug and tow were accordingly both held liable. The Court of Appeal and the House of Lords held that the bargee had not been negligent, and that the barge owners were therefore not liable. Lord Loreburn, in the course of his judgment, said:

> "It is the duty of a tow to do her best under all circumstances to avoid collision, but she cannot be held blameworthy because she did not anticipate a thoroughly bad piece of seamanship on the part of the tug which had her in tow."

(ii) The tow must keep a good look-out and must exercise all ordinary navigation precautions.

In *The Minnie Somers* v. *The Francis Batey* (1921) 8 Ll. L. Rep. 247, the Court of Appeal held the tow half to blame for a collision with a wreck-marking vessel. While the tug was to blame for taking the tow in too close a vicinity to the vessel, the tow was held to be blameworthy in not having exercised the necessary navigational precautions; had she parted and slipped the tow-line when she should have, the collision would not have occurred.

(iii) The tow must warn the tug of impending danger and, if it is perceived by the tow to be necessary, must check the tug's speed.

A good example of this principle is the case of *The Niobe* (1888) 13 P.D. 55. In that case, a tug collided with another ship whilst towing; the collision would have been avoided had there been a good look-out on board the tow and had the tow warned the tug of the impending danger of the other ship closing by "girting" the tug (by shearing to the right under a port helm). The tow was held liable. The action of the tug "might have been prevented by those on board the *Niobe*, if they had done their duty": per Sir James Hannen P. at p. 60.

(iv) The tow must not allow the tug to proceed at excessive speed in fog or poor visibility (or to proceed at all if such conditions are severe).

In *The Englishman and The Australia* [1894] P. 239, the tug was found to blame for proceeding too fast in fog and the tow was also found to blame for allowing the tug to proceed at that speed. In *The Challenge and The Duc d'Aumale* [1904] P. 41, the tow was held blameworthy for allowing her tug to continue towing ahead in fog after the fog signal of a vessel forward of the beam had been heard by the tow, but not by the tug.

(v) The tow must exercise all reasonable care in the planning and execution of the towage, e.g. such as the length of the hawser which the tug has out to her. See e.g. *The Abaris* (1920) 2 Ll. L. Rep. 411 (in which it was held that the tow was liable for the use of tow rope of excessive length).

(vi) The tow must exercise reasonable vigilance throughout the towage so as to be able to respond to any sudden events threatening the tug or a third party.

Thus, in busy waters or shipping lanes, she should be ready, if necessary, to slip the tow-line so as to avoid damage or collision: see *The Abaris* (*op. cit.*) and see also *The Jane Bacon* (1878) 27 W.R. 35 where the tow was held to be negligent when proceeding in busy waters in having made the towage connection so fast that it could not be quickly cast off in the event of need.

This need to be alert to slip the lines if necessary is often one of the most important aspects of the tow's duty to exercise reasonable care in and about the towage: see also *The Valsesia* [1927] P. 115 and *The Energy* (1870) 23 L.T. 601.

4. Other aspects of the tow's obligations

The particular facet of the general duty upon the tow to exercise reasonable care about the towage will vary from case to case. Other examples of the duties of the tow to her tug (and to others) are as follows:

(i) The tow must, if it has a crew, and contemplated to be generated as a manned tow be properly manned. This is an incident of the general requirement that the tow shall be seaworthy (as to which see above): see *The Scotia* (1890) Asp. M.L.C. 541.

(ii) Even if the tow is an unmanned object, such as a dumb barge or other water-borne object, the circumstances may be such as to require her to be manned by a riding crew, for example, to tend her lights or to be ready to slip the towing connection. Thus in *The Harlow* [1922] P. 175 a tug towing a tow made up of five barges collided with a steamer in the River Thames. The tow was held to have been negligent on the ground that each barge should have had a lighterman on board to control the lines; had they been so manned they would not have collided (see p. 177).

(iii) The tow must have due regard to the tug's navigational lights and signals. In *The Devonian* [1901] P. 221, the tow was being held up by a tug while waiting to dock in the River Mersey. The tug was burning misleading lights as a result of which a vessel ran into the tow. The Court of Appeal held the tow in part to blame because, although she was in a position to exercise control over the tug, which was alongside her, and of her lights, she had improperly neglected to do so.

CHAPTER 3

Standard Form Contracts:
(I) The U.K. Standard Conditions for Towage and Other Services

PART A. INTRODUCTION

The U.K. Standard Conditions for Towage and Other Services ("the U.K. Standard Conditions") have a long pedigree dating back, through successive revisions, to 1933. In that year negotiation took place between the Chamber of Shipping and the United Kingdom Tug Owners Association on the subject of the large number of towage conditions in operation in various ports. No agreement was reached but a set of "national" conditions came into being and was rapidly adopted by U.K. tug owners. They represent a paradigm standard form contract, being drawn up to protect the interests of the tug owner and relatively draconian in their exclusion and restriction of any possible liability which the tug might be under to the tow. However, while less evident than in the approach of making each party bear its own loss which is found in the "Towcon" and "Towhire" forms, the U.K. Standard Conditions in their latest revision do seek to achieve some measure of balance between tug and tow (see e.g. Clause 4(c)). The U.K. Standard Conditions are in constant use in contracts for domestic towage operations and, as the heading of the Conditions as being conditions for towage "and other services" makes clear, in contracts for allied or connected services, for example to the offshore industry, which are provided by U.K. tug owners and operators. The current form of the Conditions is the 1986 Revision. The terms of this revision are considered below.

PART B. COMMENTARY ON THE CONDITIONS

1. Clause 1: Introductory and definitions

(1) Paragraph (a)

"1.(a) The agreement between the Tugowner and the Hirer is and shall at all times be subject to and include each and all of the conditions hereinafter set out."

The U.K. Standard Conditions, like any standard form of contract, pre-suppose that a valid contract has been effectively concluded between tug and tow and that the Conditions have been effectively incorporated into that contract. As to the requirements for the conclusion of a contract, reference should be made to the leading contract textbooks (see e.g. *Chitty on Contracts*, 27th Edn., Vol. I, Chapters 2 to 7). Useful summaries in the marine context are to be found in *Wilford on Time Charters* (4th Edn.), pp. 49–80 and *Cooke on Voyage Charters*, pp. 3–40.

In practice, the commonest problem is not the question of whether or not a contract has been concluded between tug and tow, but whether the U.K. Standard Conditions (or such other standard forms as are in question) have been effectively incorporated in the concluded contract which the parties have arrived at. The incorporation of terms or conditions can be achieved in one of three ways:

> (i) *Expressly*: This presents the least difficulty. Thus, the fixture recap between tug and tow, or more usually their brokers, will provide that the Conditions are to apply, e.g.: "all other terms as per U.K. Standard Conditions" or "Form/Terms: U.K. Standard Conditions 1986". Towage cases on express incorporation reflect faithfully the general contract cases. In *McKenzie Barge & Derrick Co.* v. *Rivtow Marine Ltd* [1968] 2 Lloyd's Rep. 505, it was held that terms contained in an invoice delivered after the towage contract had been concluded were ineffective. In *Symonds* v. *Pain* (1861) 30 L.J. Ex. 256, however, receipts given to the tow containing standard terms were held to be an effective communication because, *inter alia*, of a previous course of dealing.

> (ii) *By a course of dealing between the parties*: This requires more than just a series of previous transactions: see *McCutcheon* v. *David Macbrayne Ltd* [1964] 1 W.L.R. 125. It requires conduct by both parties showing that they intend their dealings to be on terms to be ascertained by reference to a particular document, for example the sending of invoices over a long series of transactions, which invoices incorporate or refer to a standard form and which have never been questioned by the recipient: see e.g. *J. Spurling Ltd* v. *Bradshaw* [1956] 1 W.L.R. 461. An example of incorporation by a course of dealing in the towage context is given by *The Tasmania* (1888) 13 P.D. 110. The tow engaged the services of the *Tasmania*. The tug owner used to contract with, *inter alia*, the tow owner on terms which excluded liability for damage done by certain named tugs (which did not include the *Tasmania*). The owner of the tow was a director of the tug-owning company and knew well of the terms. The court held that it made no difference that the *Tasmania* was not one of the tugs specifically named in the tug owner's terms. It stated (at p.114):

> "This course of dealing created an agreement with the company that the company should not be liable for damage to his vessels while in tow of the company's tugs and that this would be incorporated into any contract of towage not specifically excluding it, which the plaintiffs their servants or agents might enter into with the company".

> The court continued:

> " . . . if the plaintiff had not been a director of the tug company and had not had previous dealing with it, it would have been necessary for the tug company, in order to free itself from liability for the negligence of its servants in the execution of a contract of towage, to show that the plaintiff had notice of the special terms on which the company did its business. But the plaintiff, both as director and a customer of the

company knew those terms. Suppose that instead of the *Tasmania* one of the tugs named in the printed notice had rendered her services, and the plaintiff, being on board his smack, had thrown the rope to the tug which, from darkness or other cause, he did not recognise as one of the company's fleet, he could not in that case have been heard to say, on discovery that the tug he had employed belonged to the company, that he was not bound by the exemption clause because he did not know at the time that it was one of the company's tugs. This course of dealing created an agreement with the company that the company should not be liable for damage to his vessel while in tow of the company's tugs, and this would be incorporated into any contract of towage not specifically excluding it, which the plaintiff, or his servants, might enter into with the company . . . . The plaintiff impliedly agreed with the tug company that in the event of employing the *Tasmania* it was to be on the same terms as those on which he had previously employed the company's tugs and, therefore, that the clause exempting the company from liability was in the circumstances of the case [i.e., collision caused solely by the negligence of the tug master who was at the wheel of the tug at the time] binding on the plaintiff with reference to the *Tasmania* as well as to the tugs specifically named in the printed notice."

(iii) *By reason of the common understanding in the trade*: In *British Crane Hire v. Ipswich Plant Hire* [1975] Q.B. 303, a standard trade form for crane hiring was held to apply, albeit there was no course of dealing, because as Lord Denning M.R. put it at p. 311:

" . . . both parties knew quite well that conditions were habitually imposed . . . and . . . knew the substance of those conditions . . . the conditions . . . should be regarded as incorporated . . . on the common understanding which is to be derived from the conduct of the parties . . . "

Thus if barge operators at a place know and expect all contracts of towage entered into by the tug operators at that place to be on the U.K. Standard Conditions (for example), this may be sufficient to achieve incorporation even if nothing is said about them in making the particular contract.

(2) Paragraph (b)(i) to (iii)

"(b) For the purposes of these conditions

   (i) 'towing' is any operation in connection with the holding, pushing, pulling, moving, escorting or guiding of or standing by the Hirer's vessel, and the expressions 'to tow', 'being towed' and 'towage' shall be defined likewise.

  (ii) 'vessel' shall include any vessel, craft or object of whatsoever nature (whether or not coming within the usual meaning of the word 'vessel') which the Tugowner agrees to tow or to which the Tugowner agrees at the request, express or implied, of the Hirer, to render any service of whatsoever nature other than towing.

 (iii) 'tender' shall include any vessel, craft or object of whatsoever nature which is not a tug but which is provided by the Tugowner for the performance of any towage or other service."

These definitions show the potential width and breadth of the modern towage service and they extend "towage" and the coverage of the U.K. Standard Conditions to any marine operation being performed by the tug (or tender) to whatever water-borne object is the subject of the service, *cf.* Dr Lushington's definition of towage given in

1849 in *The Princess Alice*, 3 W. Rob. 138 at p. 139. However, while the operations covered by "towing" under Clause 1(b)(i) will embrace the usual towage service such as the towing, holding up and escorting of the tow (whatever it is), they will not extend to cover more general "other services" such as anchor handling, supply and handling work and services ancillary to the offshore industries.

The importance of whether the service performed by the tug falls within "towing", albeit as widely defined as it is in Clause 1(b)(i), or is to be regarded as some "other service" lies in the subsequent provisions in Clause 1(b)(iv) and (v) which define the scope of the service to which the U.K. Standard Conditions, with their exemptions from liability, apply.

(3) Paragraph (b)(iv): "Whilst towing"

"(iv) The expression 'whilst towing' shall cover the period commencing when the tug or tender is in a position to receive orders direct from the Hirer's vessel to commence holding, pushing, pulling, moving, escorting, guiding or standing by the vessel or to pick up ropes, wires or lines, or when the towing line has been passed to or by the tug or tender, whichever is the sooner, and ending when the final orders from the Hirer's vessel to cease holding, pushing, pulling, moving escorting, guiding or standing by the vessel or to cast off ropes, wires or lines has been carried out, or the towing line has been finally slipped, whichever is the later, and the tug or tender is safely clear of the vessel."

"Whilst towing": Significance

The importance of Clause 1(b)(iv) is that it defines the period of the towage service during which the U.K. Standard Conditions and the regime of liability applicable under those conditions applies to the parties and to their operations. Since collisions and mishaps most often occur when the tug is engaged in close-quarter work in effecting the tow or when the line or hawser is being slipped at the conclusion of the service, the precise parameters of "whilst towing" are often of acute importance.

Clause 1(b)(iv) defines the duration of the towage operation in much wider terms than it is defined at common law. At common law, the towage starts or is deemed to start when the towage connection has been passed to or from the tug: see *The Clan Colquhoun* (1936) 54 Ll. L. Rep. 221. Under Clause 1(b)(iv) the start of towage may occur much earlier.

The period "whilst towing" fixed by Clause 1(b)(iv) defines the towage service as continuing between the two fixed points of commencement and termination. Once "towing" commences under the clause, it continues until it ends on the happening of one of the events referred to in the clause irrespective of what the tug is or is not actually doing at any given time. The U.K. Standard Conditions thereby avoid a potential difficulty for the tug which is encountered with other clauses which define the towage on the basis of a continuing operation being performed by the tug. One such clause was that considered in *The Baltyk* [1947] 2 All E.R. 560. The clause provided that the contract terms only applied "whilst the towage . . . or assistant services are being performed". The tug was engaged on a tow from Manchester to Eastham Locks. The towage was interrupted for eight hours en route during which the tug was damaged. The tug sued for an indemnity under the conditions. The tow contended that the towage had been stopped at the time of damage. This argument was rejected by Pilcher J.:

"In the present case there is no question that the towage had commenced and the conditions had unquestionably commenced to be applicable on the passage to Partington. The condition which constituted the master and crew of the tug the servants of the ship only continued 'whilst the towage . . . or assistant services are being performed'. Counsel for the defendants argued that these words meant, 'while some physical force is being exerted by the tug on the ship, either by strain imposed on a tow rope, or by the tug pushing, without a tow rope'. I am satisfied that such an interpretation is too narrow, and that a tug is performing towage, and docking or assistance services when she is fast to the ship, whether at the material time she happens to be exerting any force on the movement of the tow or not. Similarly, it is clear that she may be performing docking or assistance services by pushing with her nose, even though she has no tow rope fast. What precisely is meant by 'piloting' services when used in reference to a tug I do not know and counsel were unable to tell me. It is clear, however, that the conditions in the present contract are intended to apply when such a service is being performed and the word 'piloting' seems at least susceptible of an interpretation which would permit of its being carried out without any physical connection or contact between tug and tow. In the present case the [tug] only moved away from [her tow] and went alongside No. 3 tip because if she had remained moored alongside the vessel she would to some extent have obstructed the passage of vessels up and down the canal. I am satisfied that . . . the [tug] was at all material times 'under the control' of the *Baltyk* in that she was ready to obey orders received from the ship, she was manoeuvring into a position to establish connection so as to continue the physical operation of towage and assistance which her owners had contracted to perform . . .

. . . When, as in this case, the contractual service of towage and assistance in its physical sense has been interrupted for the ship's purposes, it would be wrong to hold that an accident which occurs to the tug while, in response to orders from the ship, she is manoeuvring in close proximity to the tow for the purpose of making fast, did not occur, to use the words of the contract in this case 'whilst the towage or assistance services are being performed'. To hold otherwise would, in my view, put an unduly limited construction on the words 'towage or other services' even when those words appear in a clause of exception, which . . . has to be construed *contra proferentem*."

Similarly in *The Ramsden* [1943] P. 46 the Barrow-in-Furness towage rules applied to any damage " . . . while the tug is in attendance upon or engaged in any manoeuvre for the purpose of making fast . . . ". The tug was in the dock with the tow and from 50 feet away suddenly turned and collided with the tow. Bucknill J. held that the tug could have been doing nothing else other than manoeuvring (albeit very unskilfully) to make fast and that, accordingly, the towage rules applied.

Clause 1(b)(iv) by its different approach to defining the towage avoids the need for the tug to show that the towage services are actually being performed at a time when damage is sustained by the tug or the tow.

Although the tug and tow may be "towing" within the meaning of Clause 1(b)(iv) of the U.K. Standard Conditions, it should be noted that for the purposes of compliance with the Collision Regulations (see Chapter 7 below), the question of whether or not the tug is towing and the tow is being towed will be a question of fact. If the two vessels are either stopped or are making way through the water independently of each other and if no impulsion or traction is being rendered by the tow-line by the tug to the tow, the tow is not under towage for the purpose of the Regulations: see e.g. *The Valiant* [1921] P. 312. This will be so irrespective of whether, as between the tug and tow as parties, the "towage" is deemed contractually to be continuing.

The commencement of "towing"

Rather than deeming towage to commence simply at the moment of the passing of the tow-line between tug and tow as is the position in common law, the U.K. Standard Conditions deem towing to commence at whichever is the sooner of either this moment or "when the tug or tender is in a position to receive orders direct from the Hirer's vessel to commence" the service.

The term "in a position to receive orders" has received consideration in several cases as tug owners have sought to put themselves within the cover of the U.K. Standard Conditions as soon as possible and tow owners and hirers of tugs have sought to push back the moment at which the tug will benefit from the Conditions' exemptions.

In *The Uranienborg* [1936] P. 21, a tug was scheduled to take up her tow at 1100 hours. She came up slightly early. At the time of her arrival the tow was still discharging cargo and she was not in a position to be able to effect the towing connection or to give orders to the tug to that end. The tug approached at too fast a speed, came through a line of buoys and, as the result of excessive speed combined with the failure to give orders to reverse her engine in time, she ran into the *Uranienborg* and did very severe damage. The tug sought to avail herself of the U.K. Standard Conditions on the basis that she was sufficiently close to the tow to be "in a position to receive orders". This was rejected by the Admiralty Court (Sir Boyd Merriman P.). The court stated:

" . . . in effect what [counsel for the tug] has argued is this: If it is shown that the tug was there because of a contract of towage and that she is within reasonable hailing distance of the ship at a reasonable time in reference to the contract of towage, the words are satisfied. Her physical position is within hail, and that is enough. She is there waiting the moment when somebody gives her the orders which she is prepared to receive. She will receive them direct because she is within hailing distance, and there is no more to be said about it.

I do not think that that is a reasonable interpretation of the words. Of course if that be the only possible meaning of the words, then even if they may appear to lead to an absurd conclusion that cannot be helped, and effect must be given to them. But I do not think that that is what this clause means. Whether one looks at the corresponding point of time at which the towage ends, I think one is driven to the conclusion that something narrower than that is meant. I doubt whether the word 'position' is only used in the sense of local situation, I think it involves also the conception of the tug being herself in a condition to receive and act upon the orders. But however that may be, the orders which she is to be in a position to receive are orders to pick up ropes or lines— not orders generally, but those specific orders, and I think that that must have some reference to the intention of those on board the ship to give those orders, and to the readiness of those on board the tug to receive them."

In other words for towing to commence the President held that: (i) at the very least the tug had to be ready to receive and act upon the orders; (ii) additionally, the moment had to be one at which orders might reasonably be expected to be given by the tow. The tug in this case was well within hailing distance, but "in no other sense" was tug or tow, objectively viewed, ready for further orders (see, e.g. at p. 28).

However, in *The Glenaffric* [1948] 1 All E.R. 245 the decision in *The Uranienborg* was distinguished. In that case, the tow lying at anchor off Barry Docks was approached by a tug pursuant to a towage agreement. When the tug was within 20 to

30 feet of the tow, the tug-master was hailed to keep away. He, therefore, dropped astern until he saw the ship's navigation lights put on, when he again approached the ship and was told that he was not wanted yet and that he was to wait until the ship "got in a bit". He waited until the ship had gone further ahead, and then he approached her again, and was ready to take her in tow, but he received an order to tell the dock master that the ship would not dock on that tide. As he dropped back once more, he touched the ship and was damaged.

The Court of Appeal held that the tug was "in a position to receive orders", notwithstanding that the tow had declined her services and had stated her unreadiness to receive the tow-line. The court diluted the requirement stipulated in *The Ura-nienborg* that the tow should have been ready (subjectively?) to give orders for the towage and held that it was enough that the tug reasonably expected to receive orders from the tow. The fact that the tow, subjectively viewed, did not intend to give such orders was immaterial. Scott L.J. stated [1948] 1 All E.R. at p. 247:

"It is clear from the evidence, as the judge held, that the tug was in that position. The mate was standing by ready to heave the line and so pick up a rope from the ship, and I reject the argument of counsel for the shipowner because, to make it good, he has to read into the clause, after the words 'when the tug is in a position to receive orders direct from the hirer's vessel to pick up ropes or lines', the further words 'and the ship is ready to give orders', which are not there. . . . After the tug has arrived at the ship at a proper time, namely, the normal time in accordance with ordinary practice, to take the ship in tow, she is from then in attendance on the ship and necessarily then begins to incur the risk of damage to herself by contact with the ship . . . . I can see no possible ground for implication according to the ordinary rule of construction that nothing can be implied, unless it is necessary to give business efficiency to the bargain that the two parties must have intended when they made the contract . . . "

Somervell L.J. stated (at p. 248):

" . . . the tug did reasonably expect orders to be given from the ship, that is to say, orders in relation to towage and in those circumstances it seems to me that the clause applies . . . "

Bucknill L.J. disregarded the requirement that the tow should be ready to give orders and stated (at p. 247):

"in Clause 1 the period is covered until the tug is safely clear of the vessel. In this case the tug was never safely clear of the vessel, and, if she was 'towing' within the meaning of Clause 1 when she had come alongside and was in a position to comply with orders to proceed to pick up ropes, she was not clear of the vessel at the time the damage was done."

The decision in *The Glenaffric* emphasised the position of *the tug* to receive orders and fell back from Sir Boyd Merriman's interpretation of the clause as having regard also to the position of *the tow* to give such orders. In the Scottish case of *Partafelagid Farmur* v. *Grangemouth & Forth Towing Co. Ltd* [1953] 2 Lloyd's Rep. 699 a similar emphasis on the position of the *tug* rather than the tow was adopted by the court. The Court of Session held that:

" . . . the defenders proved their case that the tug was not only in a position to receive orders direct from the ship to take up ropes or lines, but that an order to this effect was in fact given to the tug by the pilot, and that the collision took place 'whilst towing' in terms of Condition 1 of the United Kingdom Standard Towage Conditions."

However, in *The Impetus* [1953] 2 Lloyd's Rep. 699, the court (Karminski J.) re-emphasised the approach in *The Uranienborg*. In that case, the tug approached the ship at speed in accordance with the usual practice when attending upon her, and when attempting to turn in order to come on a parallel course with the ship the collision occurred by the admitted negligence of the tug. At that moment the tug was ready to receive orders to heave a line on board ship, but was not in the position to throw the heaving line because she was approaching the tow at 90 degrees. Karminski J. rejected the argument that because the tug had, by her turning away from the tow, put herself in a position where she could receive but not comply with the tow's order, she was not "towing" within the clause. As the judge put it:

" . . . Clause 1 means what it says and the conditions attach when the tug is in a position to receive orders to pick up ropes or lines. This presupposes that the ship is ready to give such orders, if such orders are required. I cannot, however, accept counsel's submission that a tug can thereafter put herself outside the conditions by getting into a position which may for a short period make it impossible for her to carry out such orders. To import such a condition when the tug is already in attendance on the ship, and, therefore in danger of incurring damage, would . . . be without justification."

These apparently conflicting decisions were considered by Brandon J. in *The Apollon* [1971] 1 Lloyd's Rep. 476. In that case, the plaintiff's tug was under a towage contract on the terms of the U.K. Standard Conditions to assist the defendant's vessel to a berth in Newport docks. The tug was lying adrift with engines running at standby at the quayside. According to the plaintiff's evidence the master was on the bridge and the crew members were at their stations. When the bridge of the vessel was abreast of the stern of the tug the dock pilot aboard the vessel stated that the tug was to take a line aft and act as stern tug. The tug had to manoeuvre round to starboard in order to fall in astern of the vessel and take a rope from her. Whilst carrying out that manoeuvre the tug's port propeller struck a spare dock gate which was moored to the dock wall. The plaintiff claimed an indemnity against the defendant in respect of the damage done and received by the tug. Brandon J. distilled the principles to be derived from the three decisions referred to above as follows (at p. 480):

"It seems to me that authorities of this kind are only valuable in so far as it is possible to extract from them some general principle. In so far as they are decisions on the facts of the particular cases, which were all different from the facts of this case, while it is helpful to see how other judges approached the matter, it does not seem that the cases assist very greatly. However, I believe that it is possible to extract from these cases taken together certain general principles which I would state in this way. It seems to me that, for a tug to be in a position to receive orders direct from the hirer's vessel to pick up ropes or lines, three conditions must be fulfilled. *The first condition* is that the situation is such that those on board the tug can reasonably expect the ship to give the tug an order to pick up ropes or lines. *The second condition* is that the tug is ready to respond to such orders if given. *The third condition* is that the tug should be close enough to the ship for the orders to be passed direct; in other words, that the tug should be within hailing distance" (emphasis supplied).

He rejected the argument that because the tug, in order to comply with the order received, would have to steam away from the tow and might, as a result thereby put herself out of the position to receive an order, she fell outside the clause. At p. 480 he stated:

" . . . in most cases, when an order is given to a tug to connect to a ship, it will be necessary for the tug to carry out certain manoeuvres in order to execute the order. Those manoeuvres may involve her in turning round a right angle or 180 degrees or even more, or they may involve her in steaming round the ship's bow or stern. There are infinite manoeuvres one can visualise a tug having to execute in such a situation when such an order is given . . . . I cannot see that the fact that a tug has to manoeuvre in some way in order to carry out an order when given shows that she is not in a position to receive that order."

It is submitted that the statement of the law in *The Apollon* correctly summarises the effect of previous authorities. While certain commentators (e.g. Kovats, *Law of Tugs and Towage* (1980) Barry Rose Publishers, p. 43) have in the past criticised the requirement that the tug be within "hailing distance" of the tow by reference to the possibilities of VHF and R/T communication, such criticism seems misplaced. The towage service is to commence under Clause 1(b)(iv) of the U.K. Standard Conditions when the tug, in all practical respects, is alongside and at the disposal of the tow. To extend that state of disposal to the position of the tow several miles out on her approach run in to the tow is both unrealistic and fails to give the meaning of the words "to receive orders *direct* from the Hirer's vessel" (emphasis supplied). The epithet "direct" signifies the close proximity and immediacy of preparation between tug and tow which Brandon J. described as being within hailing distance. Such, realistically and commercially, is when the towage service in fact begins.

Commonwealth authorities have similarly placed emphasis on the readiness of the tug to act on orders received as well as upon the physical proximity of tug to tow. In *Australian Steamship Pty. Ltd* v. *Koninklijke-Java-China-Paketvaart Lynen N.V. Amsterdam* [1955] A.L.R. 462, it has been held in Australia that "whilst towing", commencing from when the tug was in a position to receive orders direct from the hirer's vessel to pick up ropes or lines or when the towrope had been passed to or by the tug whichever was the sooner, meant that:

"the orders that a tug was in a position to receive were orders which could only be carried out when the tug was in a state of readiness, and this means both correctly positioned so far as the vessel was concerned and with everything ready on board the tug itself to pick up the necessary ropes or lines".

If the tug was not in a position to carry into effect any orders which she might be given it was irrelevant that the tug was within hailing distance of the hirer's vessel so that it could receive orders. The tug had to be not only within hailing distance but also in a position to carry the tow's orders into effect at that time and in that place.

The involvement of more than one tug

What if more than one tug or tender is involved in the service? Does the service commence *vis-à-vis* all tugs when the first is in a position to receive orders, or does each tug have to have attained that position before the U.K. Standard Conditions apply to them? The question is one of construction. If two or three tugs are agreed to be "the tug", Clause 1(b)(iv) fits unhappily with treating them all as "the tug" for the purposes of the clause so that if one of them is in the position to receive orders it is sufficient to start the towage service. In *The Clan Colquhoun* [1936] P. 153, the terms (in that case the Port of London Authority's Standard Conditions) deemed towage to commence "when the tow rope has been passed to or by the tug". It was contemplated under the towage contract that there would be two tugs. One made fast forward. The other collided making fast astern. It was held that under the Port of London Authority's clauses (which were very similar to the U.K. Standard Conditions) "the tug" meant "each of the two tugs" so that the second tug's negligence was not covered by the clauses simply because the first tug had achieved the position to receive orders. As Bucknill J. put it (at p. 163):

"Clause 1, to which I have referred, says that the towage must be deemed to have commenced when the tow rope has been passed to the tug. But in this case the contract is for towage by two tugs. In such a case does the expression 'the tug' mean 'each of the two tugs' or does it mean 'either of the tow tugs'? The terms, taken as a whole, appear to contemplate the engagement of two tugs. The view that the words 'the tug' in cl. 1 mean 'each of the two tugs' in this case is borne out by Clause 2. Clause 2 says that during the towage the masters and crews of the tugs shall cease to be under the control of the Port Authority and shall become subject in all things to the orders and control of the master of the ship. But if the towage starts when one of the two tugs makes fast, how can the second tug be under the control of the master of the tow if that tug is at the other end of the dock and is making her way to the ship to be towed?"

It is submitted that the position is the same under the U.K. Standard Conditions.

The cesser of "towing"

Pursuant to Clause 1(b)(iv) the towage service terminates upon the latest of the following two events or occurrences:

(i) *either*: "the final orders from [the tow] to cease holding, pushing, pulling, moving, escorting, guiding or standing by [the tow] or to cast off ropes wires or lines have been carried out".

(ii) *or* "the towing line has been finally slipped".

subject to the proviso that at the time of such event or occurrence "the tug or tender is safely clear of the vessel".

The words "the towing line has been finally slipped" were considered by the Australian High Court in *The Walumba* [1964] 2 Lloyd's Rep. 387. In that case, a tug, the *Walumba*, was requested by the Australian Shipping Commission to refloat and tow a grounded vessel. The tug made fast and began heaving but was carried by the tide towards rocks; in manoeuvring to avoid these rocks, the tow-line parted and fouled the tug's propeller. The tug was immobilised and required salvage assistance. The tug sought to recover the cost of this from the hirer under Clause 3 of the U.K. Standard Conditions. The hirer argued that the tug was no longer towing. In allowing the claim, the High Court of Australia held that the words " . . . ending when . . . the tow rope has been finally slipped" did not refer to the accidental parting of the tow-line during the towing and that accordingly the tug's propeller was fouled "whilst towing" and Clause 3 of the conditions applied.

(4) Paragraph (b)(v) to (vii)

"(v) Any service of whatsoever nature to be performed by the Tugowner other than towing shall be deemed to cover the period commencing when the tug or tender is placed physically at the disposal of the Hirer at the place designated by the Hirer, or, if such be at a vessel, when the tug or tender is in a position to receive and forthwith carry out orders to come alongside and shall continue until the employment for which the tug or tender has been engaged is ended. If the service is to be ended at or off a vessel the period of service shall end when the tug or tender is safely clear of the vessel or, if it is to be ended elsewhere, then when any persons or property of whatsoever description have been landed or discharged from the tug or tender and/or the service for which the tug or tender has been required is ended.

(vi) The word 'tug' shall include 'tugs', the word 'tender' shall include 'tenders', the word 'vessel' shall include 'vessels', the word 'Tugowner' shall include 'Tugowners', and the word 'Hirer' shall include 'Hirers'.

(vii) The expression 'Tugowner' shall include any person or body (other than the Hirer or the owner of the vessel on whose behalf the Hirer contracts as provided in Clause 2 hereof) who is a party to this agreement whether or not he in fact owns any tug or tender, and the expression 'other Tugowner' contained in Clause 5 hereof shall be construed likewise."

Clause 1(b)(v) defines the commencement and termination of services being performed by the tug which do not constitute "towing" within the meaning of Clause 1(b)(i).

For the commencement of the service two geographical locations are contemplated with different states of the tug's readiness to perform the service. Thus the service can either start at one of two places.

(i) At the place designated by the hirer when the tug is placed physically at the disposal of the hirer there. The concept of being "at the physical disposal" of the hirer has been described by past commentators as "a somewhat woolly concept" (Davison & Snelson, *Law of Towage*, 1990) and as a "nebulous phrase" (Kovats, *Law of Tug and Towage*, 1980).

It is respectfully submitted that when read with the requirement that the tug shall be at the place designated by the hirer, the concept presents no difficulties and is clear. The tug is at the physical disposal of the hirer for the terms of the service when she is both tendered to the hirer for hirer's orders and is physically ready to comply with those orders. The concept relates both to the physical readiness of the tug to do what the hirer requires of her as well as to her being put at the hirer's disposal in the sense of "awaiting orders". The state of the tug is akin to that of a vessel which tenders notice of readiness under a charterparty on arrival at the loadport or discharge port. The tug similarly arrives at the "designated place" and will put herself at the disposal of the hirer. If the tug is not in fact physically ready to perform the service required of her, for example, because a particular hawser or item of tackle necessary for the operation is absent, the service will not be deemed to commence irrespective of the tug's arrival at the designated place. Compare in the ordinary charterparty context: *The Tres Flores* [1974] Q.B. 264 (vessel tendered N.O.R. to load but in fact could not do so because infestation made her holds unready to load cargo; held N.O.R. invalid because vessel not ready in all respects for the operation); *The Virginian*

[1989] 1 Lloyd's Rep. 603 (insufficient bunkers for cargo operations). In the United States the courts have adopted the same approach: see e.g. *Fido* v. *Lloyd Brasiliero*, 283 F. 62 (2d. Cir. 1922).

The test of "physical disposal" also signifies that it is the state of the tug which alone determines whether or not the service begins. If the tug arrives at the stated place, is tendered to the hirer and is ready for the service, the service begins, albeit that the hirer is not actually ready to give orders for the service.

(ii) At the vessel (if that is the designated place), when the tug is "in a position to receive and forthwith carry out orders to come alongside". This concept is very similar to that found in Clause 1(b)(iv) which was considered by the court in *The Apollon* [1971] 1 Lloyd's Rep. 476 and it is submitted that the same principles will apply. Instead of being in a position to receive orders "direct" from the tow in Clause 1(b)(iv), the tug is to be "at the vessel", i.e., in her immediate vicinity, and able to come alongside forthwith. The same physical immediacy and proximity between tug and vessel as is required under Clause 1(b)(iv) is achieved by different wording.

Clause 1(b)(v) was briefly considered in *The North Goodwin No. 16* [1980] 1 Lloyd's Rep. 71. This is a rare case of *the tow* seeking to argue that the U.K. Standard Conditions and the contractual towage thereunder had commenced. A tug, the *Northsider*, was engaged to tow a light vessel to Smith's Dock, North Shields. She was held off the River Tyne by another tug awaiting the *Northsider*. Weather conditions were very poor but the *Northsider* left the mouth of the River Tyne and proceeded to the tow where she arrived alongside. The holding tug lost control of the tow which began to drift towards the shore. The *Northsider* took her in tow. She claimed salvage for so doing. The tow argued that the service performed was the contractual towage service which, pursuant to the U.K. Standard Conditions, had commenced and that the *Northsider* was, accordingly, not a volunteer and could not claim salvage. Sheen J. held that the *Northsider* was not a volunteer since the contractual towage or service under Clause 1(b)(v) had already commenced and he dismissed the claim for salvage. It is unclear from the report under which limb of Clause 1(b)(v) the tow argued the case fell. Given that the *Northsider* was to pick up the light vessel from the other tug, it would appear to be the second limb, although Sheen J. at p. 74 stated:

"*Northsider* came out on a towage contract . . . it being conceded that [she] had come out of the protection at the piers pursuant to the terms of her contract",

and based his decision on this; this would appear to put the *Northsider* within the first limb, i.e., physically at the disposal of the light vessel in the waters off the mouth of the River Tyne.

For the termination of the service, the clause provides that the service for which the tug was engaged must have ended. However, if the service ends at or off a vessel, there is the added requirement that the tug must be safely clear of her. This covers the tug while manoeuvring away from the vessel and while slipping any connection which she has out to the tow: see also *The Walumba* [1965] 1 Lloyd's Rep. 121, considered above. If the service is to be ended at some other place other than the vessel, the service ends when any equipment or persons (for example, such as a superintendent or diving team) have been landed or, as the clause rather tritely states, when the service is ended.

Clause 1(b)(iv) makes "tug" include "tugs" but, on the other hand, does not provide that "tugs" shall mean "tug" where the context so requires it. The question which the court had to consider in *The Clan Colquhoun* [1936] P. 153, where two tugs were used and one but not the other had passed the tow rope, that event constituting the commencement of towing under the form being considered, is left unresolved by the U.K. Standard Conditions. Indeed, the U.K. Standard Conditions reinforce Bucknill J.'s conclusion in that case that the "tug" will mean "each tug" if more than one is used when considering the moment at which the line is passed to "the tug": see generally pp. 61–62 above as to the position where more than one tug is used.

Clause 1(b)(vii): see under Clause 5 below.

2. Clause 2: Hirer's warranty of authority

"2. If at the time of making this agreement or of performing the towage or of rendering any service other than towing at the request, express or implied, of the Hirer, the Hirer is not the Owner of the vessel referred to herein as the 'Hirer's vessel', the Hirer expressly represents that he is authorised to make and does make this agreement for and on behalf of the owner of the said vessel subject to each and all of these conditions and agrees that both the Hirer and the Owner are bound jointly and severally by these conditions."

Under this provision, the hirer warrants that he has authority to enter into the contract with the tug on behalf of the owner of the vessel if the hirer is not the owner of the vessel to be towed and purports to agree to bind the owner of the tow to the contract with the tug. This clause is a common one in standard forms but is of very limited efficacy. When the hirer of the tug and owner of the tow are separate entities, the owner of the tow will only be liable upon a contract made by the hirer with the tug owner if the hirer had actual or ostensible authority to contract on the tow owner's behalf. The hirer of the tug cannot by himself, in the absence of actual or ostensible authority, bind the owner of the tow: see e.g. *The Ocean Frost* (*Armagas* v. *Mundogas*) [1986] A.C. 717. However, the hirer of the tug by this clause warrants his authority and in the event that the vessel is not made party to the contract, the hirer will be liable to the tug owner for breach of warranty of authority.

3. Clause 3: Vicarious liability of tow for tug

"3. Whilst towing or whilst at the request, express or implied, of the Hirer, rendering any service other than towing, the master and crew of the tug or tender shall be deemed to be the servants of the Hirer and under the control of the Hirer and/or his servants and/or his agents, and anyone on board the Hirer's vessel who may be employed and/or paid by the Tugowner shall likewise be deemed to be the servant of the Hirer and the Hirer shall accordingly be vicariously liable for any act or omission by any such person so deemed to be the servant of the Hirer."

(1) Generally

This clause in broad terms seeks to transfer all responsibility for the tug's officers and crew and such others of the tug owner's employees who are engaged in the towage service to the hirer by deeming the tug owner's employees to be the hirer's during the service. Since the tug owner's employees are deemed to be the hirer's servants, it is the hirer and not the tug owner who is to be vicariously liable for their negligent acts and omissions during the service. The effect of the clause is different where the tug places reliance on it as between tug and tow and where the tug seeks to rely upon the deeming provision as against a third party who is claiming in respect of negligence on the part of the tug: see (3) and (4) below.

(2) *The period during which the clause operates*

Where the tug is "towing" within Clause 1(b)(i) the deeming provision operates "whilst towing", as to which see the commentary on Clause 1. Where the tug is performing some service other than towing the provision operates "whilst rendering any service other than towing" at the request, express or implied, of the hirer. This period will be defined by Clause 1(b)(v) since it is the "service" which is defined in that clause which the tug will be rendering to the vessel.

(3) *Effect as between tug and tow*

The clause is clearly drafted and is entirely effective as between tug and tow to transfer all responsibility for the acts and omission of the tug owner's servants engaged in the towing or service to the tow. This was established in relation to similar wording in *The President Van Buren* (1924) 16 Asp. M.L.C. 444. As to the provision by which the tug's crew were deemed to be the tow's employees, Hill J. upheld the tug's reliance on the clause.

"The form of the contract aims, in the first place, at making the master and crew of the tug for the time being the servants of the ship which is being towed . . . .If the first section, which begins: 'The masters and crews of the tugs' and ends 'are the servants of the owner or owners' of the vessel towed, is effectual to do that which it sets out to do, it does not much matter what the rest of the conditions provide, because it will be that which the Port of London Authority contemplates; and if it effectually makes the masters and crews of the tugs servants of the ships which are being towed—servants for the time being—then it will follow that the owner of the tow cannot claim for damage brought about by people who for the time being are his own servants; and he must also be liable for damage caused to the Authority's property by persons who for the time being are his servants, the servants of the owners of the tow . . . . [The clause] sets out in terms that for all purposes connected with the towage, the master and crews of tugs are the servants of the owners of the tow."

Accordingly, the effect of the clause as between tug and tow is as follows:

(i) The clause gives the tug a complete defence to claim by the tow based on damage or liability sustained by the tow as a result of negligence by the tug and by the tug owner's servants. If the contract provides that the master and crew of the tug shall become the servants of the tow during the towage, then the owners of the tow cannot claim against the owners of the tug for damage done by the negligence of the crew of the tug, because by the very terms of the contract the tug's crew are for the time being the servants of the owners of the tow.

(ii) The clause will give the tug a cause of action against the tow in the event of negligence by the tug which causes the tug owner loss or damage or as a result of which he incurs a liability. It is to be noted that the mere presence in the towage contract of a deeming provision of this nature will be insufficient to confer upon the tug an indemnity from the tow in respect, for example, of tug crew negligence: see *The Devonshire and The St. Winifred* [1913] P. 23. To achieve an indemnity, an express provision is required to this effect. While the clause, since it is not worded as such, will not be construed as an indemnity by tow in favour of tug (see *Det Forenede D.S. v. Barry Rly. Co.* (1919) 1 Ll. L. Rep. 658; *Cory & Son* v. *France Fenwick* [1911] 1 K.B. 135), nevertheless it establishes that, as a matter of contract between tug and tow, the tug men are the tow's employees and servants.

The use of the word "Hirer" rather than "the vessel being towed" in conjunction with the deeming of the tug's crew to be the servants of the same will not, it is submitted, avoid the problem encountered by the tug owner in *The Riverman* [1928] P. 33 (for the facts of this case, see above at p. 20) in a case where more than one vessel is being towed under separate contracts. In such a case there will be more than one "Hirer", who is described in the singular in this clause just as the towed vessel was in the clause being considered in that case. The potential inapplicability of the deeming clause in such circumstances should, therefore, always be specifically addressed by the tug owner in circumstances where he is towing a flotilla of water-borne objects under separate contracts by a clause in each contract making it clear that each "Hirer" is jointly and severally deemed to be employer of the crew.

(4) Effect as between tug and tow and third parties

Clause 3 has no effect as against third parties, e.g., as against a third party vessel in collision with tug and tow. In such a case, where the third party is injured by or suffers loss and damage as a result of the act of a member of the tug's crew, the question of which of tug and tow is liable for that servant's acts will depend not upon the terms of the contract between tug and tow (being the two possible employers), but will depend upon which of the tug and tow actually had the right to control the servant both as to the task which he was to perform in and about the towage and as to the manner of their performance.

However, the tug will, if there is an indemnity provision in the contract (as there usually is in tandem with the deeming provision: see e.g. the U.K. Standard Conditions, clauses 3 and 4) be able to recover from the tow in respect of its liability to the third party.

Thus in *The Adriatic and The Wellington* (1914) 30 T.L.R. 699, the owners of a ship claimed damages in respect of a collision by a vessel *Ella* with the barge *Adriatic* which was in tow of the tug *Wellington*. The court said of the towage contract:

"The owners of the *Ella* with which the barge came into collision did not know anything about this contract or its terms. So far as they were concerned all they knew was that by the negligence of those navigating the tug *Wellington* the collision was caused . . . . Whose servants were those who negligently navigated the tug? That was a question of fact . . . . It was admitted by the tug master that he was employed and paid by the Alexandra Towing Co. Ltd, and that he was subject to dismissal by them, and them alone. It was also undisputed, and indeed indisputable, that the sole control of the navigation of the tug and tow was with the tug. No one in the barge in tow had in fact any control over those in charge of the tug or any control over or any voice in the navigation of the tug, any more than a casual onlooker on the riverside would have. In these circumstances . . . the tug master and his crew were the servants of the tug owners. Whatever might be the legal rights of the tug owners and barge owners *inter se* under the towage contract, the owners of the *Ella*, who suffered injury by the negligence of those in charge of the tug, were strangers to that contract, and had a right to recover against the masters of the servants whose negligence caused the injury."

Subsequently the tug claimed an indemnity from the tow under the contract. The court held in *The Adriatic* (1915) 85 L.J.P. 12, that the indemnity in favour of the tug covered negligence, and the tug owners were entitled to be indemnified in respect of the damage and costs awarded against them in the collision action and of their own costs in that action.

The question of which of the tug and tow is in control of the manoeuvre or aspect of navigation complained of by the third party as being negligent is, as has been seen above, a question of fact. To determine this question of fact, the Admiralty Court has applied the "control" test laid down by the House of Lords in *Mersey Docks & Harbour Board* v. *Coggins & Griffith* [1947] A.C. 1 in relation to an employee or servant who has two masters. That test can be summarised as follows: when an employee or servant has two masters, which master has control over the employee or servant in the doing of the act which leads to the commission of the tort? As it was put by Lord Porter in that case at p. 17:

"Many factors have a bearing on the result. Who is paymaster, who can dismiss, how long the alternative service lasts, what machinery is employed, have all to be kept in mind. The expressions used in any individual case must always be considered in regard to the subject-matter under discussion but amongst the many tests suggested I think that the most satisfactory, by which to ascertain who is the employer at any particular time, is to ask who is entitled to tell the employee the way in which he is to do the work upon which he is engaged. If someone other than his general employer is authorised to do this he will, as a rule, be the person liable for the employee's negligence. But it is not enough that the task to be performed should be under his control, he must also control the method of performing it."

Thus in *The Polartank* (1948) 82 Ll. L. Rep. 108 the claim arose out of a collision in the Manchester Ship Canal between a tug, the *Rixton*, acting as stern tug to a vessel, the *Polartank*, proceeding downstream, and a dumb barge, the *Lynn* being towed upstream. The *Lynn* collided with both the *Polartank* and the *Rixton* due to the fault equally of the tug towing the *Lynn* and of the *Polartank*. A deckhand on the *Rixton* was injured and sued both vessels. The *Polartank* had contracted on a standard Ship Canal tug contract which deemed the crew of the tug towing her to be the servants of the tow during the towage. It was argued that the deckhand was accordingly the servant of the *Polartank*. Willmer J. rejected this argument on two grounds. First " . . . the fact that there was an agreement between the plaintiff's normal employers [the Ship Canal] and the owners of the *Polartank* is, so far as the plaintiff is concerned, *res inter alios acta*." Secondly, he considered the *Mersey Docks & Harbour Board* v. *Coggins* test as formulated by Lord Porter and stated (at p. 125):

"Now let me apply that test to the facts of this case. The evidence in this case is that the orders given by the ship to the tugs (orders it is true, which the tug has to obey) are confined to such orders as to start or stop towing and as to the direction in which to tow. These orders are normally conveyed to the tug from the ship by whistle signal, the practice being, I understand, to use a pea whistle to convey orders to the head tug and the ship's whistle to convey orders to the stern tug. But I wish to make it quite clear, having regard to the evidence which I have heard, that the only orders which the tug expects to receive in practice are general orders of the character that I have mentioned. It is not suggested that anybody in authority on board the ship has any possible right, even if he had the wish, to control the manner in which any individual member of the tug's crew should go about his individual share of the tug's work. It would, for instance, be no business of the master of the ship to instruct a deckhand of the tug as to how he, the deckhand, ought to make a particular rope fast, how to coil or uncoil a particular rope, or anything of that sort. So far as the details of the work of the plaintiff are concerned, it is quite clear on the evidence that he was solely under the control of his own superiors on board the tug, that is to say, the person who alone had authority to control the manner in which the plaintiff did his work was his own general master, the owner of the tug, through his appointed officers. In those circumstances applying as best as I can the test laid down . . . to the facts of this case, I feel that I must come to the conclusion that on no possible view could the plaintiff be regarded as a servant of the owner of the *Polartank*."

Willmer J., adopted the same approach in *The M.S.C. Panther and The Ericbank* [1957] 1 Lloyd's Rep. 57. In this case the *Panther* was towing the *Ericbank* in the Manchester Ship Canal; she was stern tug. The towage contract provided that the crew of the tug were deemed to be the servants of the tow. The *Panther* collided with a third vessel. All three of the vessels involved were, in part, to blame. The third vessel sued the tug and the tow invoking the deeming provision. Willmer J. again referred to *Mersey Docks & Harbour Board* v. *Coggins* and to Lord Porter's test in that case and stated (at p. 67):

"It seems to me that what applies to a crane and its driver should apply equally to a tug and its master or officer in charge. Accordingly applying the principles there stated to the facts of this case, I find myself quite unable to hold that the crew of the *Panther* become in law the servants of the owners of the *Ericbank*, so as to render the latter, and not the former, liable for a faulty manoeuvre within the province of the man in charge of the tug. The position would, I apprehend, be different if the faulty manoeuvre were one within the province of the pilot or officer in charge of the tow, e.g. if the tug failed to carry out an order or negligently executed without orders a manoeuvre which it was within the province of those in charge of the tow to order. Here, however, the faulty manoeuvre of failing to stop the port propeller in time was a matter which concerned the tug alone and not the tow, and in such circumstances I hold that the liability for the negligence of the mate of the *Panther* rests with his regular employers, the owners of the *Panther*."

It is therefore submitted that the present approach of the Court, following *The Polartank* and *The M.S.C. Panther and The Ericbank*, will be to ignore the agreement between the tug and the tow as to the responsibility of the tow for the tug's servants where a claim is made against either by a third party and will be to apply a factual test, on the *Mersey Docks & Harbour Board* v. *Coggins* model, to ascertain who was in actual control of the servant at the relevant time. This approach may provoke criticism.

It may be said that, while the question who in law is to be liable for an employee's acts should depend upon the contract between the employer and the employee, nevertheless if a third party, for example the tow, contractually assumes the responsibility for that employee's acts as between himself and the employer, then, though that person be not his employee, that third party and not the employer is vicariously liable for the employee's acts. It is submitted that such criticism fails to recognise that the terms of the contract between tug and tow cannot bind third parties and that vicarious liability does not depend necessarily upon the existence of an employer–employee (or, as it is put in the parlance of the older cases, master and servant) relationship, although it most commonly does so. The liability for an employee's acts usually derives from the existence of a contract between the employer and the employee; it is this which ordinarily gives rise to the liability of the master for the acts of his servant. However, vicarious liability may also exist in the absence of a contract of employment, if the person whose acts are in issue is in a special relationship with another person, this being so usually where the other person controls his acts in such a way that the law regards him as liable for them (see e.g. Atiyah, *Vicarious Liability* (1967) Butterworths, p. 1). Where a servant serves in effect two masters, as an officer or deckhand on the tug may, employed as he is by the tug owner but being under the direct orders of the tow as to what he is to do and deemed by a clause, such as Clause 3 of the U.K. Standard Conditions, to be the tow's servant, it will be a question of fact as to whether the general master or the temporary master is in control at any given time and in relation to any given operation (see generally Atiyah, *op. cit.*, Chapter 18). The situation is by no means peculiar to the relationship of tug and tow (see the many different examples considered by Atiyah, *op. cit.*). While a contractor to whom the master provides the services of his servants may agree that the servants are to be deemed to be his during the service, a third party is entitled to look to the real position as to the responsibility for the servant's acts and to the real employer in relation to a particular operation: see Atiyah, *op. cit.*, at p. 167.

4. Clause 4: The exemption clause

"4. Whilst towing, or whilst at the request, either expressed or implied, of the Hirer rendering any service of whatsoever nature other than towing:

    (a) The Tugowner shall not (except as provided in Clauses 4(c) and (e) hereof) be responsible for or be liable for

        (i) damage or any description done by or to the tug or tender; or done by or to the Hirer's vessel or done by or to any cargo or other thing on board or being loaded on board or intended to be loaded on board the Hirer's vessel or the tug or tender or to or by any other object or property; or

        (ii) loss of the tug or tender or the Hirer's vessel or of any cargo or other thing on board or being loaded on board or intended to be loaded on board the Hirer's vessel or the tug or tender or any other object or property; or

        (iii) any claim by a person not a party to this agreement for loss or damage of any description whatsoever;

    arising from any cause whatsoever, including (without prejudice to the generality of the foregoing) negligence at any time of the Tugowner his servants or agents, unseaworthiness, unfitness or breakdown of the tug or tender, its machinery, boilers, towing gear, equipment, lines, ropes or wires, lack of fuel, stores, speed or otherwise and . . . "

(1) Period of application and scheme of the clause

The period during which clause 4 is to apply is the same as that under clause 3 deeming the servants of the tug to be those of the tow: see above. The clause is structured in the following way. Paragraph (a) provides for the exemption of the tug from liability and paragraph (b) confers an indemnity by the hirer or tow in favour of the tug; both of these provisions are subordinate to paragraph (c), which renders the tug liable in certain circumstances, and paragraph (e), which imposes liability for death and personal injury. Paragraph (d) deals with delay and consequential loss.

Given the dependence of the application of the U.K. Standard Conditions upon the parameters of the "towing" and "other service" laid down respectively in clause 1(b)(iv) and (v), most disputes and reported cases have turned on whether the U.K. Standard Conditions applied at the time of the loss or damage covered by the exemption clause, see e.g. *G.W. Rly Co.* v. *Royal Norwegian Government* [1945] 1 All E.R. 324, rather than upon the exact parameters and application of the exemption clauses, which have been regarded as tolerably clear.

What if the tug abandons the tow by slipping her lines and sailing away? It is submitted that the exemption clause would be ineffective in such a case. Pursuant to clause 1(b)(iv) the "towing" would have ended on the slipping once the tug is safely clear; similarly, pursuant to clause 1(b)(iv), "the service for which the tug . . . has been required is ended". Old, pre-*Photo Production* v. *Securicor* cases such as those which restricted the tug's exemption from liability to defaults in the *performance* of the towage rather than in the non-performance of it may still, if treated cautiously, be regarded as offering helpful guidance in applying a "construction" approach to clause 4. For example, in *The Cap Palos* [1921] P. 458 (C.A.) the tug, having been engaged to tow a vessel from Immingham to Hartlepool, abandoned her in a bay off her destination after she had temporarily grounded. The tow tried to leave the bay but, in so doing, was wrecked on rocks. The towage contract exempted the tug from all loss, however caused, "to any vessel being towed, or about to be towed or having been towed". The Court of Appeal, reversing the decision of Hill J. at first instance, held that the clause was not clear enough to cover "not doing the thing contracted for in the way contracted for" (per Atkin L.J.). While the decision is very close to a "fundamental breach" type approach, as a question of construction, it is arguably still correct: see generally pp. 19–21 above.

(2) Paragraph 4(a)

This part of the clause operates as a blanket exemption clause in favour of the tug but it must be read subject to paragraphs 4(c) and 4(e) of the clause. Under the clause, the tug is exempted for all liability in respect of:

(i) any damage done to or by the tug or the tow or done by or to any cargo on board the tow or to "any other object or property" (dock walls, such as bridges and dock gates, for example);

(ii) the loss of the tug or the tow or of any cargo or any other object or property;

(iii) "any claim by a person not a party to this agreement for loss or damage of any description whatsoever". This exclusion is curiously phrased but is sufficient to exclude liability on the part of the tug for liabilities to third parties to which, for example, the tow is exposed by acts or omissions of the tug. As between the tug and the third party, this provision will be ineffective and the tug will be obliged to recover the liability from the tow under the indemnity provisions in paragraph 4(b).

The exemption is in respect of the damage, loss or claims described above "arising from any cause whatsoever". This is a wide exemption. However, as a matter of construction in the old towage cases, such exemption was held to be insufficient to exempt liability for the initial unfitness of the tug, see e.g. *The West Cock* [1911] P. 208. Similarly, the courts have consistently declined to apply wide words of exemption, where the words of the clause can sensibly be construed to exclude liability for acts and omissions otherwise than negligent ones, to exclude liability for negligence (see e.g. *Canada Steamships Lines* v. *The King* [1952] A.C. 192; *Smith* v. *South Wales Switchgear* [1978] 1 W.L.R. 165; and *The Raphael* [1982] 2 Lloyd's Rep. 42; see also *The Forfarshire* [1908] P. 339 ("all transporting at Owners' risk" held to be insufficiently wide to cover tug owner's negligence in equipping the tug with incorrect tackle). Express reference to negligence is usually the safest course to achieve exemption from liability for negligence. Clause 4(a), apart from its wide general words, expressly excludes liability for:

(i) negligence of the tug and of the tug owners' servants "at any time" (this, it is submitted, signifies at any time during the towing or service as defined in Clauses 1(b)(iv) and (v));

(ii) the unseaworthiness or unfitness of the tug in structure, equipment and tackle.

These exemptions will be effective. The dearth of authority on the U.K. Standard Conditions save in relation to the period of application of the exemption (see e.g. *G.W. Rly. Co.* v. *Royal Norwegian Government* [1945] 1 All E.R. 324) is eloquent of the effectiveness of the exemption. In particular, it is very doubtful (although still arguable) whether cases such as *The West Cock* [1911] P. 208 are still good law on the exclusion from the coverage of the exemption clause of instances of unseaworthiness or unfitness of the tug which occurred prior to the towage service. In the latter case, it was held that an exemption clause which provided that the tug owners were "not to be responsible for any damage to the ship they have contracted to tow . . . arising from towing gear (including consequence of defect therein or damage thereto) . . . " did not protect the tug for the poor riveting of the plate to which the towing connection was made on board the tug. Although the Court of Appeal declined to express any view upon that expressed by Sir Samuel Evans P. at first instance that the tug owed a duty corresponding to that of the absolute obligations of seaworthiness in a contract of affreightment at common law, it fully endorsed his view that the clause did not cover pre-existing defects. Vaughan Williams, L.J. stated:

" . . . the more I read this contract, the more I come to the conclusion that it was the intention of both parties to deal only with defects and damage arising in the course of the towage."

Farwell, L.J. agreed and stated that the contract was:

"clearly limited to the period of towage. The liability was an antecedent liability, and it is impossible to read the word 'defect' as extending the protection to a period beyond which governs the whole period. Such a forced rule of construction I think never would be applied, and certainly not in a case like this."

Nothing in the clause itself in this case is apt to confine loss or damage arising from towing gear to cases where it both arises during the towage and where the defect in the gear also occurs during the towage. It is submitted that applying an ordinary construction approach on *Photo Production* v. *Securicor* principles, the clause would now be construed as covering defects in gear whenever they arose.

(3) Paragraph 4(b)

"(b) The Hirer shall (except as provided in Clauses 4(c) and (e)) be responsible for, pay for, and indemnify the Tugowner against and in respect of any loss or damage and any claims of whatsoever nature or howsoever arising or caused, whether covered by the provision of Clause 4(a) hereof or not, suffered by or made against the Tugowner and which shall include, without prejudice to the generality of the foregoing, any loss of or damage to the tug or tender or any property of the Tugowner even if the same arises from or is caused by the negligence of the Tugowner his servants or agents."

This part of the clause provides for an indemnity in favour of the tug by the tow in respect of any and all loss and damage sustained by and any claims made against and liabilities incurred by the tug. It is also subject to paragraphs 4(c) and 4(e). The rationale for the express indemnity is to facilitate the tug owners' recovery from the tow in respect of loss, damage and liability without the need to prove breach and, possibly, without the need to satisfy the common law requirements such as causation and foreseeability as to damages claimed for breach of contract.

As was established in *The Devonshire and The St. Winifred* [1913] P. 23, in order to achieve an indemnity by the tow in favour of the tug, a clear and express provision to this effect is required. Clause 4(b) is, for this reason, explicit. Similarly, in *Det Forenede D.S. Co.* v. *Barry Rly. Co.* (1919) 1 Ll. L. Rep. 658 it was held that an indemnity clause would not support a claim for damage done to the tug owners' property caused by the negligence of the tug's crew. Clause 4(b) is, for this reason, also express in its reference to the indemnity covering "any loss or damage to the tug . . . even if the same arises from or is caused by the negligence of the tug owner, his servants or agents". Accordingly, if in manoeuvring around the tow during the towage, the tug, by navigational negligence unconnected with the tow, collides with a dock wall damaging tug and wall, the tow will be liable to indemnify the tug in respect of its damage and its liability to the dock operator. Thus, by way of example, in *The Riverman* (1927) 29 Ll. L. Rep. 80 the tug passed at an excessive speed and too close to a ship at anchor. This caused the tow to collide with the ship and sink her. The tug admitted liability, but brought in as third party the owners of the tow, claiming an indemnity. The towage contract provided that:

" ... owners or persons interested in the vessel or craft so being towed shall and do undertake, bear, satisfy and indemnify the steam tugowners against all liabilities for the ... negligence of the tugowners' servants."

The court held that the hirer of the tow was bound by the clause and was liable to indemnify the tug notwithstanding the tug's negligence. In *Taylor* v. *Geelong Harbour Trust Commissioners* [1962] 1 Lloyd's Rep. 143 the Supreme Court of Victoria had to consider a provision in similar terms:

"3. The Tugowner shall not, whilst towing, bear or be liable for ... any personal injury ... arising from any cause including negligence at any time of the Tugowner's servants or agents ... and the Hirer shall pay for all ... personal injury ... and shall also indemnify the Tugowner against all consequences thereof ... "

The facts in that case were that a deckhand on board a launch which had been provided with a tug to assist a vessel in berthing was injured while the tow-line was laid over the launch between tug and tow. The accident was solely due to negligence on the part of the tug in tautening the tow-line. The court held that the clause was effective to oblige the tow to indemnify the tug in respect of its liability to the deckhand that the clause covered the liability of the tug for personal injury sustained by any third party, not just a person on board the tug, provided that the cause of the injury was "in some way connected with the tow". The court applied and followed *G.W. Rly. Co.* v. *Royal Norwegian Government* [1945] 1 All E.R. 324 (see above at p. 20).

(4) Paragraph 4(c)

"(c) The provisions of Clauses 4(a) and 4(b) hereof shall not be applicable in respect of any claims which arise in any of the following circumstances:
    (i) All claims which the Hirer shall prove to have resulted directly and solely from the personal failure of the Tugowner to exercise reasonable care to make the tug or tender seaworthy for navigation at the commencement of the towing or other service. For the purpose of this Clause the Tugowner's personal responsibility for exercising reasonable care shall be construed as relating only to the person or persons having the ultimate control and chief management of the Tugowner's business and to any servant (excluding the officers and crew of any tug or tender) to whom the Tugowner has specifically delegated the particular duty of exercising reasonable care and shall not include any other servant of the Tugowner or any agent or independent contractor employed by the Tugowner.
    (ii) All claims which arise when the tug or tender, although towing or rendering some service other than towing, is not in a position of proximity or risk to or from the Hirer's vessel or any other craft attending the Hirer's vessel and is detached from and safely clear of any ropes, lines, wire cables or moorings associated with the Hirer's vessel. Provided always that, notwithstanding the foregoing, the provisions of Clauses 4(a) and 4(b) shall be fully applicable in respect of all claims which arise at any time when the tug or tender is at the request, whether express or implied, of the Hirer, his servants

or his agents, carrying persons or property of whatsoever description (in addition to the Officers and crew and usual equipment of the tug or tender) and which are wholly or partly caused by, or arise out of the presence on board of such persons or property or which arise at any time when the tug or tender is proceeding to or from the Hirer's vessel in hazardous conditions or circumstances."

Paragraph 4(c) provides for the exceptions to the tug's exemptions from liability and the tow's obligation to indemnify the tug. It sets out two sets of circumstances in which claims may arise and provides that paragraphs 4(a) and 4(b) shall not apply to claims arising in those circumstances.

Personal fault of tug owner as to seaworthiness

The first set of "circumstances" is set out in paragraph 4(c)(i). This consists of "a personal failure of the Tugowner" to render the tug "seaworthy for navigation" at the beginning of the service. What does "personal" signify? It is submitted that the same principles will be applied as have been applied to similar wording in Clause 2 of the "Gencon" form of voyage charterparty and Clause 13 of the "Baltime" form of time charterparty (e.g. liability only for "personal want of due diligence on the part of the Owners or their Manager" to render vessel seaworthy). In *The Brabant* [1965] 2 Lloyd's Rep. 546, a case on Clause 13 of the "Baltime" form, McNair J. held that the fault in discharging the particular obligation in question had to be "personal" to the owners themselves and that the fault was not "personal" to the owners themselves if it was the fault of the owners' employees to whom the owners had delegated the performance of that obligation. That this is so in the context of Clause 4(c)(i) is clear as the clause goes on to define what "personal" means for this purpose.

The U.K. Standard Conditions are unusual in that they specifically define those within the tug owners' business who are to have the sufficient "personal responsibility" for the exercise of the seaworthiness obligation; in other words, the clause itself defines who is to be the alter ego of the tug owner. This avoids or, at least, simplifies the enquiry which would have to be undertaken into the alter ego or governing mind of the tug owner corresponding to that which was undertaken and found in the cases in respect of limitation of liability under section 503 of the Merchant Shipping Act 1894 and the test of "actual fault and privity": see e.g. *The Lady Gwendolen* [1965] P. 294; *The Marion* [1984] A.C. 563; *The Ert Stefanie* [1989] 1 Lloyd's Rep. 349; see also the helpful summary given in *Cooke on Voyage Charters* at pp. 166–169 and in *Wilford on Time Charters* (4th Edn.), at pp. 557–559.

Tug not in a position of proximity or risk

The second set of "circumstances" set out in paragraph 4(c)(ii) is less familiar. However, it seeks to introduce a balance between the responsibilities of tug and tow at the time of the towage service and during the "pure towage" aspect of the service. Accordingly, the exemptions from the tug's liability in Clause 4(a) and the indemnity given by the tow to the tug in Clause 4(b) will not apply if the following cumulative conditions are satisfied:

    (i) The tug is "towing" within the meaning of Clause 1(b)(iv) or performing some other service within the period set out in Clause 1(b)(v).

    (ii) Notwithstanding the towing or provision of the other service, the tug is "not in a position of proximity or risk to or from the Hirer's vessel", less inelegantly, is the tug in a position of proximity to or risk from the tow?

    (iii) Additionally, (signified by the conjunctive "and"), the tug must be detached from and safely clear of "any ropes, lines, wire cables or moorings associated with the Hirer's vessel".

    (iv) The tug must not, at the time at which the claim arises, be carrying persons or property for the Hirer, which persons or property wholly or partly cause or are the occasion for the claim.

    (v) The tug must not, at the time at which the claim arises, be proceeding to or from the Hirer's vessel in hazardous conditions or circumstances.

The practical facility of Clause 4(c)(ii) to the tow is very doubtful. The limiting factors from the tow's point of view are the provisos of not being in proximity or at risk and of being detached and clear of the tow's lines. Taking the various stages of an ordinary towage operation, it can be seen how restricted is the situation described by paragraph (c)(ii). In the initial stages of most towage or tug services, the tug is operating in close-quarters to the tow in effecting the towage connection. Such close-quarters will put the tug into "proximity" to the tow. Even when the tug is towing and has the appropriate scope of line out to the tow, is she in a relationship of proximity to the tow? The exclusion from the paragraph of being in a position of risk is potentially far wider. The tug will usually be in a situation of risk from the tow in heavy weather, for example when the tow is surging behind the tug or is shearing during the tow. But the tug is also in a position of risk from the tow when the towing connection is being snatched at by the tow with the risk of a sudden and potentially dangerous (for the tug) parting of the tow-line or hawser. "Proximity" of and "risk" to the tug restrict Clause 4(c)(ii) substantially. A further restriction is achieved by the requirement that the tug shall be detached from and clear of all lines "associated with the Hirer's vessel". The term "associated" here is capable of signifying two meanings: first, that the lines are the tow's; secondly, that the lines are towing lines which the tug has out to the tow or the tow has out to the tug. In the context of an ocean or river towage, the first meaning has no sense but the second has. However, the clause expressly contemplates that the tug may be liable under it when "towing". It is therefore submitted that lines "associated with" the Hirer's vessel do not include the towing line but refer only to the auxiliary lines or mooring lines out from the tow when the tug is alongside the tow.

For these reasons therefore, the situation envisaged by Clause 4(c)(ii) is one where the tug, albeit "towing" within Clause 1(b)(iv) or rendering another service within Clause 1(b)(v), is clear of the tow with no connections to her other than the tow-line and where the tug is sufficiently distant from the tow so as to be unaffected by her movements and not at risk from the tow. Such situations will often arise in towage and may be situations in which the tug causes damage through negligence to some third party. Clause 4(c)(ii) will exclude such situations from the tug's exemption for liability and, more importantly, from the tow's indemnity of the tug. However, the exception from Clause 4(a) and 4(b), under this heading, is an extremely narrow one. The provisions in the latter part of Clause 4(c)(ii) exclude still further its application in various common circumstances (e.g. where a tug is steaming to or from the tow in very bad weather).

(5) Paragraph 4(d)

"(d) Notwithstanding anything hereinbefore contained, the Tugowner shall under no circumstances whatsoever be responsible for or be liable for any loss or damage caused by or contributed to or arising out of any delay or detention of the Hirer's vessel or of the cargo on board or being loaded on board or intended to be loaded on board the Hirer's vessel or of any other object or property or of any person, or any consequence thereof, whether or not the same shall be caused or arise whilst towing or whilst at the request, either express or implied, of the Hirer rendering any service of whatsoever nature other than towing or at any other time whether before, during or after the making of this agreement."

Paragraph 4(d) is a common type exemption clause dealing with liability for loss or damage arising out of delay or detention of the tow or any consequences of such delay or detention. This is an important provision for the tug. One of the major complaints arising in towage cases is that the towage took too long: if the tow is a newbuilding, those responsible for the tow may have incurred penalties to the yard to which she was being towed for fitting out; if the tow is of a vessel for scrapping, the delay may lead to a fall in the scrap market price per ton (or tonne) of the vessel. Clause 4(d) is a wide exemption clause covering delay or detention howsoever caused and whenever arising.

(6) Paragraph 4(e)

"(e) Notwithstanding anything contained in Clauses 4(a) and (b) hereof the liability of the Tugowner for death or personal injury resulting from negligence is not excluded or restricted thereby."

This provision represents an amendment to the previous form (1974 Revision) of the U.K. Standard Conditions to reflect the application of section 2(1) of the Unfair Contract Terms Act 1977 and its prohibition of clauses excluding liability for negligence causing death or personal injury, which prohibition is effective even as regards marine towage contracts (see above, p. 16). The provision by Clause 4(a)(iii) of the 1974 Revision of the U.K. Standard Conditions for the exclusion of liability in such a case is now replaced with an express provision that liability for death or personal injury caused by negligence falls outside the scope of the exemption provisions of Clause 4.

5. Clause 5: Substitution of tug

"5. The Tugowner shall at any time be entitled to substitute one or more tugs or tenders for any other tug or tender or tugs or tenders. The Tugowner shall at any time (whether before or after the making of this agreement between him and the Hirer) be entitled to contract with any other Tugowner (hereinafter referred to as 'the other Tugowner') to hire the other Tugowner's tug or tender and in any such event it is hereby agreed that the Tugowner is acting (or is deemed to have acted) as the agent for the Hirer, notwithstanding that the Tugowner may, in addition, if authorised whether expressly or impliedly by or on behalf of the other Tugowner, act as agent for the other Tugowner at any time and for any purpose including the making of any agreement with the Hirer. In any event should the Tugowner as agent for the Hirer contract with the other Tugowner for any purpose as aforesaid it is hereby agreed that such contract is and shall at all times be subject to the provisions of these conditions so that the other Tugowner is bound by the same and may as a principal sue the Hirer thereon and shall have the full benefit of these conditions in every respect expressed or implied herein."

Clause 5's commercial purpose is to provide for the authorisation by the tow of the tug to enable it to contract with another tug to perform the service and thereby to bind the tow to a contract with the replacement tug but upon the same terms (i.e. the U.K. Standard Conditions). It seeks to achieve, and it is submitted, achieves its purpose by specifically constituting the tug as agent for the tow. In this way the clause remedies the deficiencies in a clause to similar effect considered by the court in *The Conoco Arrow* [1973] 1 Lloyd's Rep. 86. In that case, the Admiralty Court struck out a claim against the tow by the tug owner of a tug which had been substituted by the tug owner who was originally party to the contract of towage on the ground that he had no arguable claim that he was party to or entitled to sue upon the contract of towage. In that case the clause read: "The tug owner may substitute one tug for another and may sublet the work, wholly or in part to other tug owners who shall also have the benefit of and be bound by these conditions." Brandon J. held that the substituted tug could not sue upon the contract between the substituting tug owner and the tow:

"The claim as formulated is a crude claim to obtain rights under a contract between two other persons, without, as I say, any allegation of agency or trusteeship."

6. Clause 6: Reservation of special rights

"6. Nothing contained in these conditions shall limit, prejudice or preclude in any way any legal rights which the Tugowner may have against the Hirer including, but not limited to, any rights which the Tugowner or his servants or agents may have to claim salvage remuneration or special compensation for any extraordinary services rendered to vessels or anything aboard vessels by any tug or tender. Furthermore, nothing contained in these conditions shall limit, prejudice, or preclude in any way any right which the Tugowner may have to limit his liability."

This clause is, for all practical purposes, superfluous. It seeks to preserve (i) the tug's right to claim salvage in a proper case and (ii) the tug's right (and the tug's crew's right) to limit liability. Such rights would not be lost save by very clear and explicit language not present nor, *semble*, intended to be present in the U.K. Standard Conditions.

In so far as the clause seeks to go further and to reserve the tug's right to claim remuneration over and above what has already been agreed because of some "extraordinary services", it is met by the decisions in *The Julia* (1861) Lush. 224; 14 Moo. P.C. 210, and in *The Minnehaha* (1861) Lush. 335; 15 Moo. P.C. 133. The tug is bound, pursuant to its obligation under the towage contract, to continue with the towage even in the event of unforeseen circumstances or difficulties. It will only be entitled to additional, that is extra-contractual or salvage-based, remuneration if it renders services or encounters risk outside the scope of the original contract. Clause 6 merely preserves rights which the tug already has and which the U.K. Standard Conditions do not impinge upon.

7. Clause 7: Further exemption clause

"7. The Tugowner will not in any event be responsible or liable for the consequences of war, riots, civil commotions, acts of terrorism or sabotage, strikes, lockouts, disputes, stoppages or labour disturbances (whether he be a party thereto or not) or anything done in contemplation or furtherance thereof or delays of any description, howsoever caused or arising, including by the negligence of the Tugowner or his servants or agents."

The one-sided nature of the U.K. Standard Conditions is well illustrated by this form of *force majeure* provision which relieves the tug owner alone from his obligations and is not expressed to extend mutually to tug and tow, *cf.* the more balanced position achieved by Clause 20 of the "Towcon" and "Towhire" forms.

The events covered by the clause are commonly found in standard form *force majeure* clauses (although they are much more widely stated in the "Towcon" and "Towhire" forms) and are considered in detail in many authorities. The leading treatments of such clauses in the marine context can be found in *Cooke on Voyage Charters* at pp. 514–534 (dealing particularly with war risks) and *Wilford on Time Charters* (4th Edn.) at pp. 419–426; see also the commentary on laytime and demurrage exceptions in similar terms which is to be found in *Schofield on Laytime and Demurrage* (2nd Edn.), Chapter 4, especially pp. 210–236.

The language and drafting of the clause is not of the clearest. In particular, three matters may be noted.

(i) The clause purports to exempt the tug from the consequences of the stated events and also of "anything done in contemplation or furtherance thereof". It is unclear whether the "thereof" refers to all of the preceding events or only to "stoppages and labour disturbances". It is submitted that the natural reading of the clause is that this phrase is qualified by all of the listed events but the contrary is arguable and the doubt could give rise to a *contra proferentem* construction.

(ii) The clause states "(whether he [i.e., the tug owner] be a party thereto or not)" following the words "stoppages or labour disturbances"; given the punctuation and structure of the clause, it is submitted that on the true construction of the clause, it extends to cover the tug owner whether or not he is party to any strike, lockout, dispute, stoppage or labour disturbance but does not apply if the tug owner is party to any of the other events listed, such as e.g. sabotage.

(iii) The clause extends to "delays of any description". This is not a typical *force majeure* event. It is, however, excluded as a cause of loss and damage even if due to the negligence of the tug. This is a very favourable exemption clause for the tug, since one of the most common complaints on the part of the tow is delay on the part of the tug in performance of the service. The clause is explicit and will, it is submitted, on its construction, exempt the tug from liability for delay even negligent delay on the part of the tug.

8. Clause 8: Non-suit clause

"8. The Hirer of the tug or tender engaged subject to these conditions undertakes not to take or cause to be taken any proceedings against any servant or agent of the Tugowner or other Tugowner, whether or not the tug or tender substituted or hired or the contract of any part thereof has been sublet to the owner of the tug or tender, in respect of any negligence or breach of duty or other wrongful act on the part of such servant or agent which, but for this present provision, it would be competent for the Hirer so to do and the owners of such tug or tender shall hold this undertaking for the benefit of their servants and agents."

To add to the exemption already in place, Clause 8 seeks to prevent the tow from commencing any legal proceedings against the tug or its servants in respect of faults on their part.

9. Clause 9: Jurisdiction clause

"9.(a) The agreement between the Tugowner and the Hirer is and shall be governed by English Law and the Tugowner and the Hirer hereby accept, subject to the proviso contained in sub-clause (b) hereof, the exclusive jurisdiction of the English Courts (save where the registered office of the Tugowner is situated in Scotland when the agreement is and shall be governed by Scottish Law and the Tugowner and the Hirer hereby shall accept the exclusion jurisdiction of the Scottish Courts).
(b) No suit shall be brought in any jurisdiction other than that provided in sub-clause (a) hereof save that either the Tugowner or the Hirer shall have the option to bring proceedings *in rem* to obtain the arrest of or other similar remedy against any vessel or property owned by the other party hereto in any jurisdiction where such vessel or property may be found."

This clause is largely self-explanatory: it provides for English law and jurisdiction (or in appropriate cases, Scottish law and jurisdiction). However, the clause expressly preserves the right of each party to bring *in rem* proceedings in other jurisdictions "to obtain the arrest of or other similar remedy against any vessel or other property owned by" the other party. The object of the clause is clear: that mere security or *saisie conservatoire* type proceedings can be sought in other jurisdictions. However, it is highly questionable whether the clause, by its reference to proceedings *in rem*, would not also permit an action *in rem* in another jurisdiction on the merits of the dispute between tug and tow.

CHAPTER 4

Standard Form Contracts: (II) The BIMCO Forms "Towcon" and "Towhire"

PART A. THE "TOWCON" AND "TOWHIRE" FORMS

1. The genesis of the forms

In the 1980s BIMCO (the Baltic and International Maritime Council) were approached by the International Salvage Union (ISU), whose members comprise the majority of the leading international towage and salvage contractors, with a view to collaborating upon the production of a standard form international towage agreement designed to act as a uniform basis for ocean towage contracts. As a result, a sub-committee of the documentary committee of BIMCO together with representatives of the ISU and of the European Tugowners Association (ETA) debated and produced two standard form contracts for international ocean towage services. The aim of the draftsmen was to produce a more balanced form of contract which did not, as had been the case with standard forms unilaterally prepared by tug owners or tug owners' associations, heavily favour the tug or impose a draconian regime of exemptions to the disfavour of the tow. The U.K. Standard Conditions considered in the previous chapter are a paradigm of such unilateral forms. A significant problem with such forms has been well stated by Mr Lannart Hagbert, legal adviser to the ETA:

" . . . legal developments all over the world authorise courts to overrule or adapt agreement terms which, in the court's opinion, lead to an unreasonable result. The risk of unilaterally prepared standard agreements for the benefit of one party is that a court of law might invalidate or modify such conditions."

Accordingly, BIMCO's aim has been to develop "a balanced and practical document" which, being developed jointly between BIMCO and tug interests, will lead to "a wide international acceptance" of the new form (see BIMCO's explanatory notes to the forms). BIMCO's aim has been rapidly achieved and the forms are "recommended" for use by BIMCO, the ISU and the ETA. It is today uncommon in English legal practice to see ocean towage work or other large-scale ocean tug services being performed under any other forms.

2. The nature of the two forms

The "Towcon" and "Towhire" forms are, in effect, the same form in all substantive provisions save as to the basis upon which the tug is to be remunerated by the tow. The distinction between the tow forms is clear from their full titles:

(i) "Towcon": "International Ocean Towage Agreement (Lump Sum)", i.e., the services of the tug are to be paid for on the basis of a lump sum payment. This basis of payment is that often found in towage contracts where the tow engages the tug to perform a specific service whose features are, in principle, readily ascertainable by both tug and tow in advance such that the price or cost of the service can be estimated by both parties (i.e., "a tow from Walvis Bay to Durban"). In such cases, the parties, especially the tow, will usually wish to contract on the basis of a fixed sum for the service so as to achieve certainty and the tug will be more willing to accept the risks which a fixed sum entails given the specific and determinate nature of the service.

(ii) "Towhire": "International Ocean Towage Agreement (Daily Hire)", i.e., the services of the tug are to be paid for on a daily rate of hire basis. This version of the agreement is closely similar in its form and characteristics to a time charterparty of the "time charter trip" type, i.e., where a vessel is time chartered but in terms of a particular identified voyage or services.

It should be emphasised that the forms were developed for and are used almost exclusively in the context of ocean towage, i.e., large-scale long duration towage. The forms are inapposite for use in respect of smaller-scale towage questions, i.e., in port or short coastal services, or in respect of the rendering of offshore services. So BIMCO states in its explanatory notes to the forms:

"It should be stressed that both Agreements are intended for commercial towage work at sea and have no connection with port towing or salvage."

PART B. THE "TOWCON" FORM

1. The structure and organisation of the form

The "Towcon" form is reproduced in facsimile in Appendix 2. The form, following the usual BIMCO approach, is in two parts.

Part I consists of 39 boxes into which the specific details of the particular agreement concluded between the parties will be entered and by reference to which the standard clauses of the form will come into operation. The matters dealt with by boxes fall into several categories, the most important of which are the following:

(i) Boxes 4 to 12 which deal with the tow and provide for a detailed description of it and its characteristics: its name and type (Box 4) and its flag (Box 7); its tonnage and dimensions including towing draught (Boxes 5 and 6); its classification society and P. & I. insurers (Boxes 9 and 10); details of its "general condition" (Box 11); and any cargo or property on board (Box 12).

(ii) Boxes 13 to 21 which provide for the insertion of like details of the tug in Boxes 13 to 17 and which go on to give the important capabilities of the tug: her bollard pull (Box 18) and indicated horse power (Box 19); her bunker consumption with and without tow (Box 20) and details of her winches and towing gear (Box 21).

(iii) Boxes 22 to 25 covering the nature of the service(s), route and the departure and destination points.
(iv) Boxes 26 to 29 dealing with notices and the delay payments. The notices are those to be given pursuant to Clause 7(c) of the standard terms in Part II. The notice provision is complex providing for four notices in all regarding the readiness and the departure of the tow. This complexity is reflected in the fact that the form is accompanied by "Instructions on how to fill in Box 28 in Part I": see Appendix 2.
(v) Boxes 32 to 34 which provide for the amount of the lump sum and when the same is deemed earned and for interest on a late payment.

Part II consists of the BIMCO standard form terms, 25 clauses in all. These are considered below.

Additionally, the parties are free, as is common, to agree specific *ad hoc* provisions as typed clauses. These are to be indicated in Box 39 of Part I. Apart from any such specially agreed clauses, the order of precedence between the respective provisions of the "Towcon" form is provided for at the conclusion of Part I preceding the signatures of the parties. It is provided that:

"In the event of a conflict of terms and conditions, the provisions of PART I and any additional clauses, if agreed, shall prevail over those of PART II to the extent of such conflict but no further."

As between typed provisions specially agreed upon and those forming part of a printed form, the usual rule of construction is that printed clauses forming part of a standard form yield before specifically agreed and written or typed clauses since these latter clauses represent the "immediate language and terms" which the particular parties have adopted while the printed terms are a formulaic expression of general terms applicable to all those using the form: see e.g. *The Brabant* [1967] 1 Q.B. 588 and *Naviera Amazonica Peruana S.A.* v. *Cia. International de Seguros* [1988] 1 Lloyd's Rep. 116. Compare *Thomas & Co.* v. *Portsea S.S. Co.* [1912] A.C. 1. This common law rule is expressly reflected in the order of precedence in the "Towcon" form.

2. Commentary upon Part II of the form

Part I of the form consisting of boxes in which details are to be entered does not require consideration. However, the concluding words of Part I preceding the space left for signatures contain a general term defining the tug's obligation to the tow. These words state:

"It is mutually agreed between the party mentioned in Box 2 (hereinafter called 'the Tugowner') and the party mentioned in Box 3 (hereinafter called 'the Hirer') that the Tugowner shall, subject to the terms and conditions of this Agreement which consists of PART I including additional clauses, if any agreed and stated in Box 39, and PART II, use his best endeavours to perform the towage or other service(s) as set out herein."

This mirrors the wording of the formulation of the duties of the tug given by Lord Kingsdown in *The Minnehaha* (1861) Lush. 335 discussed above: "when a steamboat is engaged to tow . . . she does engage that she will use her best endeavours for that purpose". For the reasons set out at pp. 29–33 above, it is doubtful whether the use of the term "best endeavours" connotes a higher and more onerous obligation upon the tug to exercise reasonable efforts and care in the execution of the towage service.

(1) Clause 1: "The tow"

"1. The Tow
'The Tow' shall include any vessel, craft or object of whatsoever nature including anything carried thereon as described in PART I to which the Tugowner agrees to render the service(s) as set out in Box 22."

The tow is defined in wide terms by reference to two definitions: the first is that it may be "any vessel, craft, or object of whatsoever nature including anything carried thereon"; the second is that it shall be such vessel, craft or object as is "described in PART I" (i.e., in Box 4) and "to which the Tugowner agrees to render the service(s) . . ." under the contract.

The width of the definition, which is apt to cover any water-borne object, extends the applicability of the form to all types of towage and reflects the breadth of modern towage services and of the possible objects which are required to be transported by towage.

A potential problem may arise in cases where "the Tow" referred to by Clause 1 in the singular is, as described in Box 4 of Part II, made up of more than one water-borne object or of a flotilla of towed objects. Thus if a powerful tug contracts to tow several obsolete warships to a breakers' yard or to tow a number of ocean-going barges (for example, as commonly arises in the towage of barges laden with breakwater or coastal defence materials from Scandinavia to the U.K.), "the Tow" as described in Box 4 will consist of a multiple convoy, e.g., "The hulks of H.M.S. Torrin and H.M.S. Compass Rose" or "Barges C.123; C.56; C.789". If, on the voyage from the place of departure to the place of destination as defined by Box 24 and Box 25, one part of the convoy founders or is lost by stress of weather, difficulties arise when the remainder of the convoy arrives at destination. Has "the Tow" as defined in Box 4 arrived? The question is particularly pertinent where the lump sum is earned, as is not uncommon, in different stages of the towage service, e.g. "25 per cent on the departure of the Tow, 25 per cent on passing Cape Town, 50 per cent on arrival of the Tow in Karachi Roads". If a part of "the Tow" has been lost on passage, has "the Tow" as defined in Box 4 arrived such as to trigger the entitlement to the reserved portion of the lump sum? As a matter of construction it is highly arguable that the lump sum is payable only in the event of the arrival of "the Tow" as described and not for a portion of it. Although Clause 23(b) provides that, for the purposes of the agreement, the singular shall include the plural and vice versa unless the context otherwise requires, where Clause 1 defines the object or objects described in Box 4 as being "the Tow", "the Tow" has been, arguably, defined for the purposes of the contract as comprising all of the objects referred to in Box 4. In such circumstances, Clause 23(b) is of no assistance in resolving this difficulty.

Those providing tugs to perform towage of flotillas or convoys of water-borne objects should be careful to so define "the Tow" in Box 4 as to avoid this complication and, preferably, to append a typed clause clarifying that remuneration is deemed earned upon the happening of a given event or at a given time notwithstanding that any constituent part or parts of "the Tow" were lost or not lost, i.e., a "lost or not lost" clause. The nature of lump sum remuneration is considered in greater detail in subsection 2 below.

(2) Clause 2: "Price and conditions of payment"

Lump sum

"2. Price and Conditions of Payment
(a) The Hirer shall pay the Tugowner the sum set in Box 32 (hereinafter called 'the Lump Sum').
(b) The Lump Sum shall be payable as set out in Boxes 32 and 33.
(c) The Lump Sum and all other sums payable to the Tugowner under this Agreement shall be payable without any discount, deduction, set-off, line, claim or counterclaim, each instalment of the Lump Sum shall be fully and irrevocably earned at the moment it is due as set out in Box 32, Tug and/or Tow lost or not lost, and all other sums shall be fully and irrevocably earned on a daily basis.
(d) All payments by the Hirer shall be made in the currency and to the bank account specified in Box 33."

Paragraphs (a) and (b) provide for the amount of remuneration in the form of a lump sum payment (which is specified in Box 32) and the event upon or time at which the same is to be deemed earned, and paragraph (d) specifies the currency and bank at which the hirer is to make payment (which details are as specified in Box 33).

Mention has already been made of potential difficulties where the earning of the lump sum is to take place upon the happening of events concerning or involving "the Tow" as defined in Box 4. In this connection, a comparison may be made with the principles applicable in relation to lump sum freight payable under a voyage charterparty for the carriage of cargo. These may be summarised as follows:

    (i) A lump sum freight is, on one view, a sum payable for the rent or hire of a vessel for the particular voyage. In *Merchant Shipping Co.* v. *Armitage* (1873) L.R. 9 Q.B. 99 Lord Coleridge C.J. described it thus at p. 107:

        "To avoid all risk and all inconvenience between the parties to the contract, the lump sum was taken to represent that at which the one party was willing to hire and the other was willing to lend the ship for the stipulated voyage."

    This view cannot be taken too far: if a vessel contracts to carry cargo from A to B for a lump sum and gets the cargo to B but by means other than by the vessel herself, e.g. in another bottom or by carts, the cargo interests cannot resist a claim for the lump sum on the basis that the vessel herself was not used and therefore no rent for her is payable: see *Thomas* v. *Harrowing S.S. Co.* [1915] A.C. 57 (where a shipowner who used road carriage rather than the named vessel to get the cargo to destination was held to be entitled to the full lump sum freight).

    (ii) If the lump sum is payable upon the delivery of the cargo and none of the cargo is delivered, the lump sum is not due: see *Merchant Shipping Co.* v. *Armitage* (*op. cit.*) per Bramwell B. at p. 111.

    (iii) However, where the lump sum is payable upon the delivery of the cargo and part of the cargo is lost, if that loss was due to expected perils, the lump sum will be earned in full by the delivery of the remainder of the cargo: see *The Norway (No. 2)* (1865) 3 Moo P.C. (N.S.) 245; *Robinson* v. *Knights* (1873) L.R. 8 C.P. 465 and per Lord Coleridge C.J. in *Merchant Shipping Co.* v. *Armitage* (*op. cit.*) at p. 107:

> "If it were a matter entirely free from authority there might be some ground for saying that 'entire discharge and right delivery of the cargo' meant the entire discharge and right delivery of the cargo originally put on board. But the fair and reasonable construction of it, regard being had to the contract being for a lump sum, seems to me to be that which the courts have already put upon similar contracts, that the cargo is entirely discharged and rightly delivered, if the whole of it not covered by any of the exceptions in the contract itself is delivered."

It is highly arguable that the same reasoning would apply in the case of a tug earning lump sum freight on arrival of "the Tow" where the tow consists of several water-borne objects. The lump sum is payable to the hire of the tug for that service; if "the Tow" is partly lost by excepted causes but is still delivered, the lump sum similarly remains due.

Payment and anti-deduction clause

As seen above, paragraph (c) of Clause 2 provides as follows:

"(c) The Lump Sum and all other sums payable to the Tugowner under this Agreement shall be payable without any discount, deduction, set-off, lien, claim or counterclaim, each instalment of the Lump Sum shall be fully and irrevocably earned at the moment it is due as set out in Box 32, Tug and/or Tow lost or not lost, and all other sums shall be fully and irrevocably earned on a daily basis."

It accordingly deals with two matters: first, when the lump sum is deemed earned and, secondly, how that lump sum shall be paid.

As to the first matter, the clause provides that the sum is "fully and irrevocably earned" at the moment it is said in Box 32 to become due "Tug and/or Tow lost or not lost". These latter words may be inapplicable in certain circumstances, e.g. if the parties stipulate that the sum is due on arrival/or hand-over of the tow at destination, there will be no scope for the question of the "lost or not lost" provision. But very frequently the sum or instalments of it are deemed earned at much earlier stages or in successive stages and the clause protects the tug's right to remuneration notwithstanding a loss of tug or tow or both. It should be noted that, for the reasons discussed above, the "lost or not lost" provision arguably does not address the situation in which not the whole of "the Tow" but part of "the Tow" only is lost.

As to the second matter, the clause seeks to prevent the hirer from making deductions from the lump sum, e.g. in respect of claims which the hirer alleges it has arising from non-performance or poor performance of the contract service. Save in the special case of freight (where it has been long-settled that no right of set-off of claims for damages exists to extinguish or diminish claims for freight: see *The Aries* [1977] 1 W.L.R. 185 (H.L.); *The Dominique* [1989] A.C. 1056 and *The Khian Captain (No. 2)* [1986] 1 Lloyd's Rep. 429; see generally *Cooke on Voyage Charters*, (1993) at pp. 227–229), the claim by the hirer which the hirer seeks to deduct from monies due to the tug will fall into one or more of the following categories:

(a) A pure defence to the claim for the price on the basis that the work is worth less than the price being charged. This is called the defence of abatement: see *Mondel* v. *Steel* (1841) 8 M. & W. 858 also called the right of deduction: see *The Aries* [1977] 1 W.L.R. 185 per Lord Wilberforce discussing *Mondel* v. *Steel* at p. 190 C–F.

(b) A cross-claim which is so closely bound up with the claim for the price and which arises out of the same transaction that it may be set off against it (deriving from the Statutes of Set-off).

(c) A cross-claim which falls outside paragraph (b) above but which courts of Equity would have regarded as being a ground for preventing the claimant for the price from continuing with his claim until the cross-claim was taken into account. This is usually referred to as equitable set-off: see *The Brede* [1974] Q.B. 233 per Lord Denning M.R. at pp. 248–249.

(d) A cross-claim arising out of a different transaction which cannot be set off but which can be raised, in the same proceedings as the claim for the price, as a counterclaim.

Paragraph (c) is a typical "anti deduction" clause. Such provisions are entirely valid in English law: see *Hong Kong and Shanghai Banking Corporation* v. *Kloeckner & Co.* [1990] 2 Q.B. 514; see also *Wood on International Set Off*. However, they will be construed strictly since they take away the fundamental rights of any buyer or cross-claimant. Accordingly, to achieve the barring of set-offs and cross-claims "clear express words" must be used: see *Gilbert Ash Northern Ltd* v. *Modern Engineering (Bristol) Ltd* [1974] A.C. 689, per Lord Diplock at 717. Standard anti set-off clauses usually refer to the price being payable without any set-off or counterclaim being made against it. Such wording may of itself not be sufficient to bar a defence of abatement, although the words "any deduction or diminution in the price" will usually do so.

Paragraph (c) however is widely drawn and specifically covers all possible formulations of the tow's claim thereby effectively barring any deductions whatsoever from the lump sum price and allowing the tug to pursue the hirer by way of summary judgment under R.S.C., Order 14 in respect of any non-payment or under payment.

Bunker adjustment clause

"(e) In the event that the average price per metric tonne of bunkers actually paid by the Tugowner differs from the amounts specified in Box 36, then the Hirer or the Tugowner, as the case may be, shall pay to the other the difference per metric tonne for every metric tonne consumed during the voyage. The average price specified above shall be the average of the prices per metric tonne actually paid by the Tugowner on the basis of quantities purchased at the last bunkering port prior to the voyage, any bunkering port during the voyage, and the first bunkering port after completion of the voyage. The log book of the Tug shall be *prima facie* evidence of the quantity of bunkers consumed."

Paragraph (e) is designed to protect both parties from market fluctuations in the price of bunkers. The parties contract on the basis of the price of the tug's bunkers which is current at the time of contracting; this is set out in Box 36. If the average price of bunkers, as calculated under the clause, is either greater or less than this figure, there is an adjustment under the clause in favour of the tug or the hirer respectively.

"Free time" and "Delay payments"

"(f) Any Delay Payment due under this Agreement shall be paid to the Tugowner as and when earned on presentation of the invoice.
(g) The Free Time specified in Boxes 26 and 27 shall be allowed for the connecting and disconnecting of the Tow and all other purposes relating thereto. Free Time shall commence when the Tug arrives at the pilot station at the place of departure or the Tug and Tow arrives at the pilot station at the place of destination or anchors or arrives at the usual waiting area off such places. Should the Free Time be exceeded Delay Payment(s) at the rate specified in Box 29 shall be payable until the Tug and Tow sail from the place of departure or the tug is free to leave the place of destination."

Since the towage is on lump sum terms with the lump sum having been calculated in part upon the reasonably anticipated duration of the service, some time for connection and disconnection of the tug is already allowed for in the lump sum price by paragraph 2(g). This time, called "free time", is stipulated in Boxes 26 or 27 for connection and disconnection respectively. The moment at which the free time commences is provided for by reference to clear and easily identifiable events: the arrival of the tug at the pilot station for the place of departure for connection free time and the arrival of the tug and tow at either the pilot station or the usual anchorage or waiting place at the place of destination for disconnection free time.

If the free time is exceeded, paragraph 2(g) provides that delay payments will be due at the rate specified in Box 29 . This box envisages the provision of a port rate and a sea rate, presumably, although it is not stated, per day and *pro rata*. This should be specified when filling up Box 29. These payments cover the time from expiry of free time to the sailing of the tug and tow (at the place of departure) or until the tug is free to leave (at the place of destination).

It is submitted that the nature of the delay payment under paragraph 2(g) is equivalent to that of demurrage payable under an ordinary voyage charterparty. While the subject of demurrage is outside the scope of this work and is dealt with in other texts (notably *Schofield on Laytime and Demurrage* (1990), 2nd Edn.), a brief outline of its nature and features in the context of "delay payment" is appropriate.

In an ordinary voyage charterparty there are laytime provisions which usually provide for a period of time within which loading and discharging are to be effected. Although the charterparty will often speak of this period as being time "allowed" to the charterer, the charterer is under an obligation to load or discharge within the permitted laytime. If laytime is exceeded, the charterer is in breach of charterparty. If the charterparty contains a demurrage provision, as it invariably does, the demurrage rate (a sum per day and *pro rata*) will constitute liquidated damages for the breach. The position was succinctly summarised by Hobhouse J. in *The Forum Craftsman* [1991] 1 Lloyd's Rep. 81 at 87:

"A liability for demurrage is a liability for liquidated damages for breach of contract. The breach of contract is the failure to discharge (or load) within the permitted laytime. The obligation has two different aspects: the first is the obligation to discharge and the second is to do so within the limited time. There is no breach before that limited time has expired. Once the limited time has been exceeded there is a continuing breach for which the liability in liquidated damages (that is to say demurrage) continues to accrue minute by minute as the failure to complete discharge continues ... "

The position under paragraph 2(g) is, it is submitted, no different. The hirer is given a certain time, *viz.* that time which is described as "free time", within which the connection or disconnection is to be effected. If this time is exceeded, the hirer is in breach; the hirer's liability in damages is replaced by a liquidated damages provision, being the "delay payment" provided for in Box 29. Significantly, there is no substantial difference in language between common laytime and demurrage provisions under the standard forms of voyage charterparty and paragraph 2(g) of the "Towcon" form.

From the equivalence of "delay payments" to demurrage certain consequences for the tug owner and hirer follow from the general law of demurrage.

(i) The liability of the hirer to pay delay payments will be absolute once the free time has been exceeded and will not depend upon the tow being at fault. That this is so is itself clear from the plain wording of paragraph 2(g): "should Free Time be exceeded, Delay Payment(s) at the rate specified in Box 29 shall be payable until ... ." Thus, whether the connection is not effected within the free time allowed because the hirer has not made the tow ready or because while the tow is ready, the hirer has decided for commercial reasons not to permit connection or because of circumstances beyond her control, for example heavy weather, no connection can be made, the hirer is liable equally to pay the delay payments as provided for in box 29. As Viscount Finlay stated in *William Alexander* v. *Aktiebolaget Hansa* [1920] A.C. 88 at 94:

"If the charterer has agreed to load or unload within a fixed period of time ... he is answerable for the non-performance of that engagement, whatever the nature of the impediments, unless they are covered by exceptions in the charterparty or arise through the fault of the shipowner or those for whom he is responsible."

(ii) It is not necessary for the tug to show that she has suffered any loss as a result of the free time being exceeded in order to be able to recover the delay payment. That fact of the free time having been exceeded is sufficient: see paragraph 2(g); see also generally on liquidated damages provisions *Clydebank Engineering Co.* v. *Don Jose Ramos y Yzquierdo y Castoneda* [1905] A.C. 6.

(iii) The liability to make delay payments will only be excused if the cause of the free time being or having been exceeded is a cause covered by a relevant exceptions clause: see e.g. *Union of India* v. *Cia. Naviera Aeolus* [1964] A.C. 868 at 879. In demurrage cases, the courts have adopted a very strict approach to the construction of exceptions clauses as applying so as to exempt a charterer from his liability to pay demurrage, such that, if the exceptions clause does not expressly refer as such to demurrage or is not a specific "demurrage exceptions" clause, very clear and precise wording will be required so as to extend a general exceptions clause to apply to liability for demurrage (see e.g. *The Johs Stove* [1984] 1 Lloyd's Rep. 38; *The John Michalos* [1987] 2 Lloyd's Rep. 188). It is, however, doubtful whether this particularly strict approach is applicable otherwise than in the field of charterparty demurrage where the absolute nature of the demurrage payment has been long-established and is reflected in the imprecise but striking maxim "once on demurrage, always on demurrage". Provided, therefore, that the exception clause in the towage contract is apt to cover the liability to make delay payments and is not ambiguous in accordance with normal principles of construction (see e.g. *George Mitchell (Chesterhall) Ltd* v. *Finney Lock Seeds Ltd* [1983] 3 W.L.R. 163), the hirer will be excused.

(iv) The tow will be under no liability under paragraph 2(g) if the cause of the free time having been exceeded is a breach of the towage contract on the part of the tug or other wrongful conduct of the tug: see *Schofield (op. cit.)* at pp. 162–168 and pp. 307–313. So, for example, where the tug arrives without her warranted towing gear or with reduced engine power and, as a consequence, free time is exceeded, the hirer will either not be liable for the delay payment or he will be able to cross-claim in respect of any such liability as damages for the tug's breach of contract. This is so perhaps even if the tug's breach is covered by an exceptions clause which exempts it from liability: see *The Union Amsterdam* [1982] 2 Lloyd's Rep. 432 (Parker J.). However, compare the compelling criticism of this case by *Schofield (op. cit.)* at pp. 167–168 and pp. 311–312 and the narrower formulation of this principle in *Cooke on Voyage Charters* at p. 328 as applying where the exception clause does not relieve the owner from the *liabilities* arising out of the breach itself but only relieves the owner from the "liability *in damages* for that breach" (emphasis supplied).

Under paragraph (f) any delay payment is to be paid "as and when earned on the presentation of the invoice". This wording is unclear: if the hirer alleges that no delay payment has been earned because the cause of the delay was a breach of contract on the part of the tug, is the payment still payable upon the presentation of the invoice? It is submitted that the payment is payable upon this event only where there is no *bona fide* dispute as to the payment having been earned.

(3) Clause 3: "Additional charges and extra costs"

"3. Additional Charges and Extra Costs
(a) The Hirer shall appoint his agents at the place of departure and place of destination and ports of all or refuge and shall provide such agents with adequate funds as required.

(b) The Hirer shall bear and pay as and when they fall due:
    (i) All port expenses, pilotage charges, harbour and canal dues and all other expenses of a similar nature levied upon or payable in respect of both the Tug and the Tow.
    (ii) All taxes, (other than those normally payable by the Tugowner in the country where he has his principal place of business and in the country where the Tug is registered) stamp duties or other levies payable in respect of or in connection with this Agreement or the payments of the Lump Sum or other sums payable under this Agreement or the services to be performed under or in pursuance of this Agreement, any Customs or Excise duties and any costs, dues or expenses payable in respect of any necessary permits or licences.
    (iii) The cost of the services of any assisting tugs when deemed necessary by the Tugmaster or prescribed by Port or other Authorities.
    (iv) The cost of insurance of the Tow shall be the sole responsibility of the Hirer to provide.
(c) All taxes, charges, costs, and expenses payable by the Hirer shall be paid by the Hirer direct to those entitled to them. If, however, any such tax, charge, cost or expenses is in fact paid by or on behalf of the Tugowner (notwithstanding that the Tugowner shall under no circumstances be under any obligation to make such payments on behalf of the Hirer), the Hirer shall reimburse the Tugowner on the basis of the actual cost to the Tugowner upon presentation of invoice."

This clause deals with those charges which are to be for the hirer's account in addition to the lump sum payable to the tug.

Paragraph (a) imposes an obligation on the hirer to appoint properly funded agents at the ports or places where the tug and tow will be during the service or where they might call or put into. This is a small but useful provision since a common cause of delays to vessels in charterparty and towage contracts is the temporary inability of local agents to pay locally due expenses which leads to the arrest or *saisie* of the vessel by local claimants and subsequent delays or difficulties in transmitting funds to local agents. This is especially so in less well-organised parts of the world whither the tug and tow may be forced to put in for refuge.

Paragraph (b) deals with the particular heads of expenses and costs which are to be for the account of the hirer. They broadly correspond to the expenses payable by the time charterer under the common forms of "provide and pay for" clauses: see, for example, Clause 2 of the New York Produce Exchange form. Of particular importance are the costs of any assisting tugs deemed necessary by the tug master and all costs and expenses necessary to prepare the tow for the towage which, sensibly, are specifically dealt with.

Paragraph (c) makes it clear that it is for the hirer in the first instance to pay the additional costs and not for the tug to pay them and then reclaim them from the hirer, although the tug has a right to be paid any sums which it does expend in this way upon the presentation to the hirer of the tugs' invoice in respect of such costs.

(4) Clause 4: "War risk escalation clause"

"4. War Risk Escalation Clause
The Lump Sum is based and assessed on all war risk insurance costs applicable to the Tugowner in respect of the contemplated voyage in effect on the date of this Agreement.
In the event of any subsequent increase or decrease in the actual costs due to the Tugowner fulfilling his obligations under this Agreement, the Hirer or the Tugowner, as the case may be,

shall reimburse to the other the amount of any increase or decrease in the war risk, confiscation, deprivation or trapping insurance costs."

Clause 4 implements a similar adjustment procedure for fluctuation in war risk premiums and insurance costs as Clause 2(e) does for fluctuations in bunker prices. Although the clause is headed "Escalation Clause" it covers decreases as well as increases in the costs for the tug of war risk cover. To be recoverable under this adjustment clause, the increase or decrease in war risks must be "due to the Tugowner fulfilling his obligation under this Agreement", i.e., where the tug and tow have to pass or enter a newly arisen war zone, that is, one which has supervened since the conclusion of the contract.

(5) Clause 5: "Interest"

"5. Interest
If any amounts due under this Agreement are not paid when due, then interest shall accrue and shall be paid in accordance with the provisions of Box 34 on all such amounts until payment is received by the Tugowner."

This provision is a standard one to circumvent the absence in English law of a right to recover interest in respect of debts paid late. Usually rates of interest are assessed by reference to ordinary commercial rates, with an additional super-added margin. If, as occasionally occurs, the rate of interest fixed by the tug owner is a punitive rate and designed not simply to reflect the cost to the tug owner of being out of his money but also to act as a penalty provision, the interest provision will fall foul of the general rule against penalty provisions as set out in *Dunlop Pneumatic Tyre Co.* v. *New Garage Co.* [1915] A.C. 79 and will be unenforceable. For a detailed consideration of this rule: see *Macgregor on Damages* (15th Edn.), paragraphs 441 to 497.

(6) Clause 6: "Security"

"6. Security
The Hirer undertakes to provide, if required by the Tugowner, security to the satisfaction of the Tugowner in the form, and in the sum, at the place and at the time indicated in Box 35 as a guarantee for due performance of the Agreement. Such security shall be returned to the guarantor when the Hirer's financial obligations under this Agreement have been met in full.
(Optional, only applicable if Box 35 filled in)."

The "Towcon" form gives an option to include in the towage contract an obligation upon the tow to put up security; if this option is to be exercised the details are to be inserted in Box 35 as to the form and amount of the security and the time at which it is to be put up. The inclusion of this option in the form itself reflects the common situation, especially where the tow consists of a vessel bought by the hirer as scrap and the towage is one to the breaker's yard or where the hirer is a one-ship company or where the company, while the hirer under the towage contract, is not the registered owner of the vessel being towed.

(7) Clause 7: "Place of departure/notices"

The place of departure

"7. Place of Departure/Notices
(a) The Tow shall be tendered to the Tugowner at the place of departure stated in Box 24.
(b) The precise place of departure shall always be safe and accessible for the Tug to enter, to operate in and for the Tug and Tow to leave and shall be a place where such Tug is permitted to commence the towage in accordance with any local or other rules, requirements or regulations and shall always be subject to the approval of the Tugowner which shall not be unreasonably withheld."

The tow is to be tendered to the tug at the "place of departure" named in Box 24, paragraph (a). Paragraph (a) and paragraph (b) contemplate a distinction between the broad "place of departure" at which the tug is to be tendered and the "precise place of departure" within that place where the tug is to make fast and commence operations. Often the two will overlap but not necessarily, e.g., the place of departure of a laid-up vessel might be "Rostock Docks" but the precise place may be dock No. 2 within those docks. By paragraph (b) the precise place of departure must meet three criteria:

(i) It must be safe, both for the tug (i.e., the particular tug named in the contract) to operate in and for the tug and tow to leave. The concept of safety is well developed in the law relating to charterparties. It is perhaps best summarised by Sellers L.J. in *The Eastern City* [1958] 2 Lloyd's Rep. 127 at p. 131:

" . . . a port will not be safe unless, in the relevant period of time, the particular ship can reach it, use it and return from it without, in the absence of some abnormal occurrence, being exposed to danger which cannot be avoided by good navigation and seamanship".

For a detailed account of the cases, see *Wilford* at pp. 177–209 and *Cooke* at pp. 74–91.

Paragraph (b) adds to the requirement of safety a requirement that the place of departure shall be "accessible" for the tug to enter, operate in and leave with the tow. This states expressly what the common law would probably imply as to the accessibility of the tow to the tug: see e.g. *Gamecock Steam Towing Co.* v. *Trader Navigation Co. Ltd* (1937) 59 Ll. L. Rep. 170 and p. 45 above.

(ii) It must be a place where the tug is permitted by any applicable local or other rules and regulations to commence the towage operation. This is an important requirement since many littoral states have enacted detailed rules, usually from the perspective of the avoidance of marine pollution, which in the context of towage, commonly contain powers controlling towage with requirements as to the tow-worthiness of the tow and for the certification of that tow-worthiness by an independent inspection authority. Some countries will require certification by a reputed classification society, others, for example, the United Kingdom, South Africa, the United States and Canada, may require their own departmental inspectorates to be satisfied. Given such rules and that towage is frequently the towage either of old vessels for scrapping or of disabled vessels which present greater potential pollution risks, it is essential for the hirer to undertake that the place of departure will be a place where the towage has been officially permitted and cleared.

In connection with certification of the tow, see also under Clause 11(a) and 12(c) of the "Towcon" form, which are discussed below.

(iii) It must be a place which has received the approval of the tug owner. This requirement allows the tug owner to reject a place of departure proposed by the hirer if the tug owner has reasonable grounds for withholding his approval, for example, on the grounds of exposure which would make connection problematic to heavy swell or of insufficient sea-room in the pick-up area for the proper manoeuvring of the tug.

In the time charterparty context, if the port or berth is named in the charterparty, it is unclear whether the express warranty of safety still applies, since, in such a case, the owner is put on notice of the place to or from which the vessel will be traded and, arguably, can form his own view as to its characteristics and as to whether or not he accepts them as being safe for his vessel. It is submitted that the better view is that where a port is named in a charterparty and the charterparty contains an express warranty of safety, it is a matter of construction whether the express warranty applies to the named port or applies only to unnamed ports to which the charterer can direct the vessel within her trading limits: see *Wilford*, pp. 194–195 and *The Helen Miller* [1980] 2 Lloyd's Rep. 95.

In the context of a towage contract on the "Towcon" form, if the place of departure as stated in Box 24 is co-extensive with and the same as the precise place of departure (e.g. as often occurs, if the place of departure is the grounding place of the vessel at a particular and stated position or if the tow is at a specific place, be it lay-up berth or in the roads), it is submitted that the warranty of safety and accessibility remains applicable as a matter of the construction of paragraphs 7(a) and 7(b). In such cases, the warranty in paragraph 7(b) is made expressly with reference to the named place of departure referred to in paragraph 7(a).

However, if, as is contemplated by the clause, the tug owner has the place of departure presented to him for his approval by the hirer and the tug owner approves it, it is highly arguable that he has waived any objection to proceed to the named place of departure. The position is analogous to that considered in the time charterparty cases as to any owner's loss of his right to reject an uncontractual nomination by the charterer of an unsafe port or berth. In *The Kanchenjunga* [1990] 1 Lloyd's Rep. 391 (H.L.), the vessel was ordered by charterers to Kharg Island, a permissible load port; the vessel proceeded thither and tendered notice of readiness. Due to hostilities, the master then took the vessel away and the owners called upon the charterers to re-nominate a safe port. The charterers refused. The House of Lords held that by the owners' act in sailing for Kharg Island and tendering N.O.R. there, they had elected to comply with the charterers' nomination in circumstances when the owners could have refused to do so and that they were bound by the election. Their sole right was damages for breach of contract in the event that, because of charterers' breach of charter in ordering the vessel to an unsafe place, the vessel was damaged or the owners suffered loss. The separate right to damages was unaffected (but *cf. The Chemical Venture* [1993] 1 Lloyd's Rep.

508 in which very clear conduct on the part of the owners was held to have estopped them from even asserting that the port of Mina-al-Ahmadi was unsafe so as to be able to set up a claim for damages for breach of contract). So, if the particular precise place of departure chosen by the hirer is submitted to the tug and the tug approves it, the tug cannot subsequently refuse to proceed there nor can the tug's approval be withdrawn. The tug's rights against the hirer to claim damages if the place is unsafe or if the towage is not permitted in breach of paragraph 7(b) are probably unaffected by the tug's approval. However, it is always highly advisable for the tug owner to make it very clear in the notice of approval of the place of departure that that approval is made without prejudice to the due performance by the hirer of its obligations under paragraph 7(b).

The notices

"(c)(i) The Tow shall be ready to sail from the Place of Departure between the dates indicated in Box 28(a), hereinafter called the Initial Departure Period.
(ii) The Hirer shall give the Tugowner such notice as is stipulated in Box 28 in respect of Initial Departure Notice (Box 28(b)), Final Departure Period Notice (Box 28(c)) and Final Departure Time and Date Notice (Box 28(d)).
(iii) The Tow shall be offered to the Tugowner, duly certificated and otherwise in accordance with the terms and conditions of this Agreement.
(d) If the Hirer fails to comply strictly with the provisions of Cl. 7(c), the date of departure shall be deemed to be either the last day of the Initial Departure Period or the last day of the Final Departure Period, whichever is earlier, and this date shall be binding for all consequences arising in respect of Delay Payments and any other payments due or charges incurred in the performance of this Agreement."

Paragraphs 7(c) and (d) make provision for the notices to be given by the tug relating to the tendering of the tow to the tug. The chronology of notices contemplated by the sub-clauses, read together with Box 28, is as follows:

  (i) The tow is to be ready to sail from the departure place within a certain period whose limits are defined by the dates specified in Box 28(c) called the "initial departure period", for example 1 to 31 June 1995.
 (ii) The tow is then required within a period stipulated in Box 28(b) to give the tug an "initial departure notice" which is an abbreviated departure period falling within the "initial departure period". So, it may be agreed that the tow shall, 10 days prior to the commencement of the initial departure period of 1 to 31 June 1995, give notice of a period of five days within that period during which the tow will be delivered, for example 10 to 15 June.
(iii) The tow is then required within a stipulated period to give a "Final Departure Period Notice", being a yet further abbreviated departure period falling, this time, within the "initial departure period". So it may be agreed that the tow shall, three days prior to the commencement of the five days' period of 10 to 15 June, give notice of a period of 24 hours within the five-day period previously notified: see Box 28(c).
(iv) Finally, the tow must give a notice stating the specified date and time at which the tow is to leave the departure place within the last identified period

before this final notice must be given within a stipulated period of days (see Box 28(d)).

The importance of the observance of the chronology of notices and the narrowing down of the time at which the tow will be ready for connection lies in paragraph 7(d) which provides that in the event of non-compliance by the tow with the notice provisions contained in paragraph 7(c), the departure date is deemed to be the earlier of the last day of the stated "initial departure period" (Box 28(a)) and of the last day of the "final departure period" (Box 28(c)) for the purposes of "all consequences arising in respect of Delay Payments and any other payments due or charges incurred in the performance of this Agreement".

Box 28(e) in Part I provides for details to be given as to whom the notices in paragraph 7(e) are to be given. This avoids doubts as to the effective receipt of notices.

Certification

Paragraph 7(c)(iii) provides that the tow owner is to tender the tow to the tug "duly certificated" and in accordance with the terms of the agreement, i.e., most importantly having those set characteristics stated in boxes 4 to 12 in Part I. "Duly certificated" is potentially a very wide requirement. However it is submitted that it is limited to:

  (i) certificates necessary for the towage to commence; see paragraph 7(b) of the "Towcon" form;
 (ii) class certificates: see Box 9;
(iii) those certificates specifically referred to in Clause 11 of the "Towcon" form (see below);
 (iv) the certificate of tow-worthiness referred to in Clause 12(c) of the "Towcon" form.

(8) Clause 8: "Place of destination"

"8. Place of Destination
(a) The Tow shall be accepted forthwith and taken over by the Hirer or his duly authorised representative at the place of destination stated in Box 25.
(b) The precise place of destination shall always be safe and accessible for the Tug and Tow to enter, to operate in, and for the Tug to leave and shall be a place where such Tug is permitted to redeliver the Tow in accordance with any local or other rules, requirements or regulations and shall always be subject to the approval of the Tugowner, which approval shall not be unreasonably withheld."

The place of destination is dealt with in the same terms as the place of departure in paragraph 7(b): see the commentary above.

The tow is to be accepted and taken over "forthwith" by the hirer or his representatives. This is, from the tug's perspective, an important obligation upon the hirer. Under a lump sum contract the tug will wish to be free as soon as possible. In the event of delays in the tow being taken over beyond the prescribed "free time" for disconnection specified in Box 27 of Part I, paragraph 2(g) and the scheme of delay payments will become operational.

(9) Clause 9: "Riding crew"

"9. Riding Crew
(a) In the event that the Tugowner provides a Riding Crew for the Tow, such crew and their suitability for the work shall be in the discretion of the Tugowner. All expenses for such personnel shall be for the account of the Tugowner.
(b) In the event that any personnel are placed on board the Tow by the Hirer all expenses for such personnel will be for the account of the Hirer and such personnel shall be at all times under the orders of the Master of the Tug, but shall not be deemed to be the servants or agents of the Tugowner.
(c) The Riding Crew shall be provided at the Hirer's sole expense with suitable accommodation, food, fresh water, life-saving appliances and all other requirements to comply as necessary with the law and regulations of the law of the Flag of the Tug and/or Tow and of the States through the territorial waters of which the Tug will pass or enter. It is a requirement that members of the Riding Crew provided by the Hirer shall be able to speak and understand the English language or any other mutual language."

Where the tow is incapable of independent navigation, such as an unmanned barge, or where the tug is concerned to have a crew aboard her for other reasons, such as the monitoring and adjusting of the towing connection or the trim of the tow, a riding crew may be put on board the tow by the tug owner. Similarly, the hirer may wish to place a crew on board the object being towed; such is commonly the case in the towage of expensive drilling installations or water-borne equipment. Clause 9 makes provision for the case where such a crew is used.

Paragraph (a) deals with a crew put on board by the tug whose discretion as to the choice of the men etc. is expressly stated. Such a crew is at the tug's expense.

Paragraph (b) deals with a crew put on board by the tow. While such a crew is at hirer's expense and the crew members remain the hirer's employees, the crew is to be under the orders of the tug at all times. This will be highly relevant when assessing the question of who is in control of the tug and tow in the event of a collision with a third party under the factual test of control laid down in the *S.S. Devonshire* v. *The Barge Leslie* [1912] A.C. 634 (see pp. 37 *et seq.* above and pp. 189 *et seq.* below).

Whoever provides the riding crew, paragraph (c) places the responsibility for victualling the riding crew and for satisfying any applicable regulatory or statutory requirements as to the crew upon the hirer. If the riding crew is provided to the tow by the hirer under paragraph (b), that crew is required to understand English "or any other mutual language". While this is of importance given the problems caused by the prevalence of different nationalities at different levels of marine service (to take a common example, English or Greek master, Polish officers and Filipino crew), it is doubtful whether the clause addresses such problems satisfactorily by the addition as a permissible alternative to English (as a *lingua franca*) of " . . . any other mutual language". Mutual to whom? If mutual only as between members of the, say, Filipino riding crew, this may not materially assist the tug which may be Dutch- or Scandinavian-crewed. If language and communication is likely to be a problem, the point should be specifically addressed in a typed clause or by an amendment to paragraph 9(c).

(10) Clause 10: "Towing gear and use of tow's gear"

"10. Towing Gear and Use of Tow's Gear
(a) The Tugowner agrees to provide free of cost to the Hirer all towing hawsers, bridles and other towing gear normally carried on board the Tug for the purpose of the towage or other services to be provided under this Agreement. The Tow shall be connected up in a manner within the discretion of the Tugowner.
(b) The Tugowner may make reasonable use at his discretion of the Tow's gear, power, anchors, anchor cables, radio, communication and navigational equipment and all other appurtenances free of cost during and for the purposes of the towage or other services to be provided under this Agreement."

This clause covers the use of the tug's and tow's respective facilities and equipment falling within and included in the lump sum remuneration agreed between the parties.

Paragraph (a) puts all the lines and towing gear "normally carried on the tug" at the disposal of the hirer for the contract service. The main items of these will usually have been defined in Box 21 of Part I and will often be readily identifiable from the tug owners' published particulars or brochures which are commonly available in the market for the very large ocean-going tugs. Notwithstanding the free use of the towing gear, paragraph (a) makes it clear that the manner in which the towing connection is made up and made fast is within the tug's discretion. This is standard practice.

Paragraph (b) offers the tug the like use of the tow's facilities. This will often be highly important: for example, VHF for communications between tug and tow and the tow's power for assistance in line and anchor handling, winches, and for the provision of propulsion and steering.

(11) Clause 11: "Permits and certification"

"11. Permits and Certification
(a) The Hirer shall arrange at his own cost and provide to the Tugowner all necessary licences, authorisations and permits required by the Tug and Tow to undertake and complete the contractual voyage together with all necessary certification for the Tow to enter or leave all or any ports of call or refuge on the contemplated voyage.
(b) Any loss or expense incurred by the Tugowner by reason of the Hirer's failure to comply with this clause shall be reimbursed by the Hirer to the Tugowner and during any delay caused thereby the Tugowner shall receive additional compensation from the Hirer at the Tug's Delay Payment rate specified in Box 29."

As foreshadowed in paragraphs 7(b) and 7(c)(iii), the issue of the certification of the tow and the obtaining of the requisite official permits and licences for the towage service is an important one. Paragraph (a) of clause 11 imposes the obligation to obtain all such permits and certificates upon the hirer. The obligation extends to all such certificates and other documents both in the place of the commencement and of the completion of the towage and in all places and ports of call en route, together with any ports of refuge into which tug and tow may put.

Paragraph (b) specifies expressly that any loss or expense suffered by the tug by the hirer's non-compliance with its paragraph (a) obligation are to be "reimbursed" by the tow. Although it does not use the usual language of indemnity, it is submitted that this provision operates to give the tug an indemnity against such loss and expense; accordingly, the tug is entitled to recover in full indemnity against the same and is not confined to or obliged to satisfy the requirements of a claim for damages for breach of contract.

The usual consequence where a tow's certificates are not in order is merely delay for tug and tow while the necessary authorities are mollified or appeased and while the requisite documents and permissions are obtained. This is reflected in paragraph 11(b) which provides that the tug shall receive "additional compensation" at the rate of the Clause 2(g) delay payments. It is submitted that given the whole of the provisions of Clause 11(b) such "additional compensation" is not akin to demurrage or a delay payment proper and clearly does not prevent the tug from seeking and recovering reimbursement of any other or additional losses and expenses incurred during the delay period as a result of the hirer's failure to have proper certification or permits in place.

(12) Clause 12: "Tow-worthiness of the tow"

"12. Tow-worthiness of the Tow
(a) The Hirer shall exercise due diligence to ensure that the Tow shall at the commencement of the towage be in all respects fit to be towed from the place of departure to the place of destination.
(b) The Hirer undertakes that the Tow will be suitably trimmed and prepared and ready to be towed at the time when the Tug arrives at the place of departure and fitted and equipped with such shapes, signals, navigational and other lights of a type required for the towage."

Fitness of the tow

This clause imposes upon the hirer the obligation to exercise due diligence to ensure that the tow is tow-worthy at the commencement of the tow. It mirrors the common law position considered in Chapter 2 (see pp. 47–48 above).

The central obligation upon the hirer is described in paragraph (a) in the following terms:

"(a) The Hirer shall exercise due diligence to ensure that the Tow shall at the commencement of the towage be in all respects fit to be towed from the place of departure to the place of destination."

The tow-worthiness of the tow is measured by reference to the defined limits of the contractual towage and is assessed only at the commencement of the towage. There is no continuing obligation upon the hirer to ensure that the tow is maintained in a tow-worthy state during the service. Given that the tow may often be unmanned or manned only by a skeleton riding crew, this is a realistic limit upon the obligation and it corresponds to the temporal limit upon the common law warranty of seaworthiness in the field of carriage of goods. The obligation to ensure tow-worthiness is one of due diligence which is equivalent to the same standard imposed by the Hague and Hague-

Visby Rules in relation to seaworthiness, as to which see e.g. *Cooke on Voyage Charters* at pp. 718–722. It should accordingly be noted that:

(i) The obligation upon the hirer to exercise due diligence is not a delegable one. The duty is one upon whoever carries out the work of putting the tow into a fit condition for the service and the hirer will be liable for a failure of any such person even if the hirer himself is not at fault (for example, in the case where the hirer appoints a competent local repairer or welding firm who are to blame for the want of due diligence): see *The Muncaster Castle* [1961] A.C. 807.

(ii) While the term "to exercise due diligence" appears to be more stringent than "to exercise reasonable care", there is no difference between the standard which they impose. The obligation to exercise due diligence is, accordingly, co-extensive and co-terminous with such obligations as are imposed by the ordinary duty of care at common law. As it was put more pithily: "Lack of due diligence is negligence": see *Union of India* v. *N.V. Reederij Amsterdam* [1963] 2 Lloyd's Rep. 223 per Lord Reid at 235.

Paragraph (b) however deals specifically with three particular matters concerning the tow which might be assumed to have been comprised within the overall obligation to ensure tow-worthiness. These matters are matters which "the Hirer undertakes" shall have been done by "the time when the tug arrives at the place of departure". The obligation is an unconditional one upon the hirer and, it is submitted, is unqualified by the lesser standard of due diligence provided for in paragraph (a). Since the three matters are, in principle, ones which should be readily and easily attained on the part of the hirer, this dichotomy of the standard of obligation is perhaps understandable. The three matters which the hirer is to ensure are the following:

(i) The tow is to "be suitably trimmed" (i.e., including proper ballasting).

(ii) "and" the tow is to be "prepared and ready to be towed". While this is potentially a very wide obligation, it follows on from the trimming obligations. It is submitted that the readiness and preparedness relates to matters immediately concerned with the towage, e.g. panama fairleads cleared and bitts made ready; winches tested; anchor chains and windlass in order.

(iii) Lastly, the tow is to have all proper lights and navigational shapes and signals. This addresses specifically the problem which arose in *The Albion* [1952] 1 Lloyd's Rep. 367: see above p. 28.

Certificate of tow-worthiness

"(c) The Hirer shall supply to the Tugowner or the Tugmaster, on the arrival of the Tug at the place of departure an unconditional certificate of tow-worthiness for the Tow issued by a recognised firm of Marine Surveyors or Survey Organisation, provided always that the Tugowner shall not be under any obligation to perform the towage until in his discretion he is satisfied that the Tow is in all respects trimmed, prepared, fit and ready for towage but the Tugowner shall not unreasonably withhold his approval.

(d) No inspection of the Tow by the Tugowner shall constitute approval of the Tow's condition or be deemed a waiver of the foregoing undertakings given by the Hirer."

While the content of the obligations upon the hirer in relation to the fitness of the tow under paragraphs (a) and (b) is clear, the tug not unnaturally requires some tangible proof of the tow-worthiness of the tow before the operation commences. This concern is addressed by paragraph (c) which provides that the tow is, on the tug's arrival at the place of departure, to provide the tug with:

"an unconditional certificate of tow-worthiness issued by a recognised firm of Marine Surveyors or Survey Organisation".

The term "recognised firm" is vague. Even well-known firms may differ greatly in quality and reliability especially when they have, perforce, to appoint a local firm of surveyors to act as their agents to effect a survey in, for example, a far flung location. Paragraph (c) gives the tug the overriding discretion to refuse to start the towage until the tug owner is himself satisfied of the fitness and readiness of the tow. Paragraph (c) requires the refusal to be made on reasonable grounds. It is when such a refusal is made that difficulties commonly arise and lawyers become involved. Often the problem can be resolved by sending out a reputable surveyor or team of joint surveyors acceptable to both parties to address the technical issues in dispute.

Non-waiver clause

In this connection, paragraph (d) expressly provides that no inspection of the tow by the tug shall operate as an approval of the tow or relieve the hirer of its obligation as to tow-worthiness under paragraphs (a) to (c). This makes obvious sense since the inspection on behalf of the tug owner will usually be necessarily limited in scope and duration.

(13) Clause 13: "Seaworthiness of the tug"

"13. Seaworthiness of the Tug
The Tugowner will exercise due diligence to tender the Tug at the place of departure in a seaworthy condition and in all respects ready to perform the towage, but the Tugowner gives no other warranties, express or implied."

While Clause 13 is a pendant provision to Clause 12, it is much briefer and simply provides that the tug owner is to exercise due diligence to provide the tug in a seaworthy condition and in all respects ready to perform the towage. It is submitted this corresponds with the extent of the tug owner's obligation at common law as considered above (p. 28). If those obligations are wider and more absolute (for example, in the way in which they were enunciated in *The West Cock* [1911] P. 23 at first instance by Sir Samuel Evans P., but see the discussion as to this at pp. 29 *et seq*. above), then Clause 13 reduces the obligation to one of reasonable care.

The brevity of the provision compared with the greater detail of Clause 12 reflects the reality that usually the tug will be provided in full operational condition and as a going concern while often the tow is a disabled or unmanned vessel or is a water-borne object of special type which will require special measures to be taken to make her fit for the towage.

(14) Clause 14: "Substitution of tugs"

"14. Substitution of Tugs
The Tugowner shall at all times have the right to substitute any tug or tugs for any other tug or tugs of adequate power (including two or more tugs for one, or one tug for two or more) at any time whether before or after the commencement of the towage or other services and shall be at liberty to employ a tug or tugs belonging to other tugowners for the whole or part of the towage or other service contemplated under this Agreement. Provided, however, that the main particulars of the substituted tug or tugs shall be subject to the Hirer's prior approval, but such approval shall not be unreasonably withheld."

Clause 14 gives the tug owner the right to substitute another tug or combination of tugs for the named tug or tugs at any time before or during the contract service subject to:

    (i) the substituted tug or tugs being of an adequate power;
    (ii) obtaining the hirer's approval (which shall not be unreasonably withheld) of the "main particulars" of the substituted tug or tugs, e.g. flag; g.r.t.; certificated bollard pull; indicated horsepower; bunker consumption details; and details of winches and main towing gear (that is, those details given in Boxes 13 to 21 of Part I).

Clause 14 gives the tug owner the right to sub-contract in tugs owned by others. Unlike the cumbersome provisions of Clause 5 of the U.K. Standard Conditions (above), which deem the tug in such a case to be acting as agent for the tow such that the owner of the substituted tug becomes party to a new contract (on the same terms) with the tow, the "Towcon" contract remains between the original tug owner and the hirer at all times. Any contract relating to the putting in of a substitute tug is a matter between the original tug owner and the owner of the substitute tug. The hirer continues to look to its original contractual counterparty whoever in fact performs the contract service.

(15) Clause 15: "Salvage"

"15. Salvage
(a) Should the Tow break away from the Tug during the course of the towage service, the Tug shall render all reasonable services to re-connect the towline and fulfil this Agreement without making any claim for salvage.
(b) If at any time the Tugowner or the Tugmaster considers it necessary or advisable to seek or accept salvage services from any vessel or person on behalf of the Tug or Tow, or both, the Hirer hereby undertakes and warrants that the Tugowner or his duly authorised servant or agent including the Tugmaster have the full actual authority of the Hirer to accept such services on behalf of the Tow on any reasonable terms."

In *The Minnehaha* (1861) 15 Moo P.C. 133 Lord Kingsdown stated at p. 153:

"When a steam boat engages to tow a vessel . . . she does engage that she will use her best endeavours for that purpose . . . she does not become relieved from her obligations because unforeseen difficulties occur in the completion of her task, because the performance of the task is interrupted . . . as by the breaking of the ship's hawser."

In such circumstances at common law, and as seen above, the tug is under an obligation "to do her duty and to use all reasonable care to protect the ship": see per Bateson J. in *The Refrigerant* (1925) 22 Ll. L. Rep. 492 at 495.

Paragraph (a) of Clause 15 echoes the earlier cases and provides in almost similar vein:

"(a) Should the Tow break away from the Tug during the course of the towage service, the Tug shall render all reasonable services to re-connect the towline and fulfil this Agreement without making any claim for salvage."

Paragraph (a) was the subject of much debate within the BIMCO documentary sub-committee at the drafting stage. The form of the clause which emerged reflects the real difficulty in delineating in advance what services which the tug may render in re-establishing the towage connection will be outside or within the scope of the contract. The clause provides that the tug shall perform all reasonable services without claiming salvage but in so doing does not in reality state any principle which is different from that stated, for example, by Dr Lushington in *The Annapolis* (1861) Lush. 355. In that case, it was held that salvage was only due in circumstances (i) "by reason of unforeseen circumstances in the performance of the contract to tow", (ii) where there have become necessary "new and special services".

Paragraph (b) confers specific actual authority upon the tug owner to enter into salvage contracts with others on behalf of the hirer in circumstances where the tug owner considers the same to be "necessary or advisable". This avoids the need for the tug to establish that it enjoyed an agency of necessity and that it satisfied the four-fold requirements of such an agency (as set out by Slade L.J. in *The Choko Star* [1990] 1 Lloyd's Rep. 516 at 525: see the discussions of this case above at p. 11).

(16) Clause 16: "Cancellation and withdrawal"

"16. Cancellation and Withdrawal
(a) At any time prior to the departure of the Tow from the place of departure the Hirer may cancel this Agreement upon payment of the cancellation fee set out in Box 38. If cancellation takes place whilst the Tug is en route to the place of departure or after the Tug has arrived at or off the place of departure then in addition to the said cancellation fee the Hirer shall pay any additional amounts due under this Agreement.
(c) The Tugowner may without prejudice to any other remedies he may have leave the Tow in place where the Hirer may take repossession of it and be entitled to payment of the Lump Sum less expenses saved by the Tugowner and all other payments due under this Agreement, upon any one or more of the following grounds:
    (i) If there is any delay or delays (other than delay caused by the Tug) at the place of departure exceeding in aggregate 21 running days.
    (ii) If there is any delay or delays (other than a delay caused by the Tug) at any port or place of call or refuge exceeding in aggregate 21 running days.
    (iii) If the security as may be required according to Box 35 is not given within 7 running days of the Tugowner's request to provide security.
    (iv) If the Hirer has not accepted the Tow within 7 running days of arrival at the place of destination.
    (v) If any amount payable under this Agreement has not been paid within 7 running days of the date such sums are due.

(d) Before exercising his option of withdrawing from this Agreement as aforesaid, the Tugowner shall if practicable give the Hirer 48 hours notice (Saturdays, Sundays and Public Holidays excluded) of his intention so to withdraw.

(e) Should the Tug not be ready to commence the towage at the latest at midnight on the date, if any, indicated in Box 37, the Hirer shall have the option of cancelling this Agreement and shall be entitled to claim damages for detention if due to the wilful default of the Tugowner. Should the Tugowner anticipate that the Tug will not be ready, he shall notify the Hirer thereof by telex, cable or otherwise in writing without delay stating the expected date of the Tug's readiness and ask whether the Hirer will exercise his option to cancel. Such option to cancel must be exercised within 48 hours after the receipt of the Tugowner's notice, otherwise the third day after the date stated in the Tugowner's notice shall be deemed to be the new agreed date to commence the towage in accordance with this Agreement."

By the tow

The clause provides for the cancellation of the towage contract or the withdrawal from it by the tow in two circumstances:

(i) Under paragraph (a): "at any time prior to the departure of the Tow from the place of departure" the hirer may cancel the contract upon payment of the cancellation fee in Box 38 of Part I; if the tug has already been mobilised, additional sums may be payable.

(ii) Under paragraph (e): the hirer is given a standard charterparty cancelling clause. If the tug is not ready to commence the towage by the agreed cancelling date (which is set out in Box 37 of Part I), the hirer may cancel the contract; this is so irrespective of whether there has been any breach of contract by the tug. However, while the clause leaves unaffected the common law rule that if the owner is in breach of some other provision of the charterparty, he remains liable in damages for that breach, it provides that if the unreadiness of the tug is due to the "wilful default" of the tug (e.g. where the tug has left the tow so as to service a more lucrative contract), the tow may recover "damages for detention" or damages to reflect the delay to the tow in departing under tow.

In the event that the tug knows in advance that it might not be ready, paragraph (e) provides for a procedure by which the tug can give notice to the tow of this fact and of the tug's new date of readiness. This gives to the hirer an option either to accept the proposed new date or to cancel the contract.

Additionally, paragraph (b) provides that in the event of a termination of the towage operation (whether by the hirer or otherwise) after the service has begun in the absence of fault on the part of the tug, the tug is entitled to be paid the lump sum payments provided for in Box 32 together with any other accrued sums without prejudice to any claim in damages which the tug may have arising out of the premature termination if the termination has arisen from some breach of contract on the part of the hirer.

By the tug

Paragraph (c) confers upon the tug a right of withdrawal from the towage contract and a right to leave the tow in five situations subject only to the tug owner giving 48 hours' notice of withdrawal "if practicable" of his intention to withdraw: see paragraph (d). The five situations are succinctly described in paragraphs 16(c)(i) to (v):

(i) If there is any delay or delays (other than delay caused by the tug) at the place of departure exceeding in aggregate 21 running days.
(ii) If there is any delay or delays (other than a delay caused by the tug) at any port or place of call or refuge exceeding in aggregate 21 running days.
(iii) If the security which may be required according to the stipulation in Box 35 has not been given within seven running days of the tug owner's request to provide security.
(iv) If the hirer has not accepted the tow within seven running days of the arrival of the same at the place of destination.
(v) If any amount payable under the towage contract has not been paid within seven running days of the date when such sums become due.

In the event of such a withdrawal, the tug owner is entitled to be paid the lump sum and any other additional expenses "less expenses saved" by the tug owner.

(17) Clause 17: "Necessary deviation or slow steaming"

"17. Necessary Deviation or Slow Steaming
(a) If the Tug during the course of the towage or other service under this Agreement puts into a port or place or seeks shelter or is detained or deviates from the original route as set out in Box 23, or slow steams because either the Tugowner or Tugmaster reasonably consider
(i) that the Tow is not fit to be towed or
(ii) the Tow is incapable of being towed at the original speed contemplated by the Tugowner or
(iii) the towing connection requires rearrangement, or
(iv) repairs or alterations to or additional equipment for the Tow are required to safeguard the venture and enable the Tow to be towed to destination, or
(v) it would not be prudent to do otherwise on account of weather conditions actual or forecast, or
because of any other good and valid reason outside the control of the Tugowner or Tugmaster, or because of any delay caused by or at the request of the Hirer, this Agreement shall remain in full force and effect, and the Tugowner shall be entitled to receive from the Hirer additional compensation at the appropriate Delay Payment rate as set out in Box 29 for all time spent in such port or place and for all time spent by the Tug at sea in excess of the time which would have been spent had such slow steaming or deviation not taken place.
(b) The Tug shall at all times be at liberty to go to the assistance of any vessel in distress for the purpose of saving life or property or to call at any port or place for bunkers, repairs, supplies, or any other necessaries or to land disabled seamen, but if towing the Tug shall leave the Tow in a safe place and during such period this Agreement shall remain in full force and effect.
(c) The Tug shall have liberty to comply with any orders or directions as to departure, arrival, routes, ports of call, stoppages, destination, delivery, requisition or otherwise howsoever given by the Government of the Nation under whose flag the Tug or Tow sails or any department thereof, or any person acting or purporting to act with the authority for such Government or any department thereof by the committee or person having under the terms of the War Risks Insurance on the Tug the right to give such orders or directions and if by reason of and in compliance with any such orders or directions anything is done or is not done the same shall not be deemed a deviation and delivery in accordance with such orders or directions shall be a fulfilment of this Agreement and the Lump Sum and/or all other sums shall be paid to the Tugowner accordingly.

(d) Any deviation howsoever or whatsoever by the Tug or by the Tugowner not expressly permitted by the terms and conditions of this Agreement shall not amount to a repudiation of thisAgreement and the Agreement shall remain in full force and effect notwithstanding such deviation."

Generally

Clause 17 of the "Towcon" form deals with deviation. Deviation has been well explored in the law of charterparties and carriage of goods by sea: see e.g. *Cooke on Voyage Charters*, pp. 185–202. It consists either of the departure of the vessel, here the tug, from the usual and customary course of the contractual voyage or of the prosecution of the contract voyage by the vessel without exercising all reasonable despatch, for example by slow-steaming or by having idle periods whilst on passage. In the absence of an express liberty to deviate, deviation gives the right to terminate the contract and loss of the protection for the deviating party of any exemption clauses present in the contract.

Since in towage the possibility of deviation is a very real one, Clause 17 has addressed it specifically and has adopted a different regime from that commonly adopted in charterparties, which usually confine themselves to granting a defined and fairly restricted liberty to deviate.

While Clause 17 grants to the tug owner liberties to deviate, it also provides that an unauthorised deviation shall not bring the contract to an end, that is, it leaves the parties confined to a claim in damages and, more importantly, leaves in place the protection of any relevant exemption clauses for the deviating party.

The liberties to deviate

Under Clause 17 there are three categories of permissible deviation (whether by departure from the usual customary route or by delay in the prosecution of the voyage):

(1) In the event of matters connected with or arising out of the towage itself which justify deviation (in which case the tug is entitled to receive "additional compensation" at the delay payment rate provided for by paragraph 2(g) for the extra time taken as a result): see paragraph (a). The matters are three in number:
    (i) either where the tug reasonably considers that:
        (a) the tow is not fit to be towed, or
        (b) the tow is incapable of being towed at the original speed contemplated by the tug owner, or
        (c) the towing connection requires rearrangement, or
        (d) repairs or alterations to or additional equipment for the tow are required to safeguard the venture and enable the tow to be towed to its destination, or
        (e) it would not be prudent to do otherwise than to alter course or delay on account of weather conditions, either actual or forecast;

(ii) or where there is some other good or valid reason outside the control of the tug;

(iii) or where there has been a delay caused by or at the request of the tow.

(2) A standard charterparty-type liberty to deviate in cases of necessity. That is, a liberty to go to vessels in distress for saving life or to take on bunkers or to put off seamen: see paragraph (b). The liberty includes a liberty to deviate to go to vessels for the saving of property. A deviation for this purpose falls outside the common law liberty to deviate which encompasses deviations for the purpose of saving life but excludes those made solely for the purpose of saving property (see e.g. *Scaramanga v. Stamp* (1880) 5 C.P.D. 295 (C.A.)). This extended liberty will be of importance to tug owners, many of whom will be professional salvors whose tugs are often secondarily employed in engaged commercial services in anticipation of salvage service. In such cases the tug may leave the tow in a safe place. This ordinary type of liberty to deviate will be restrictively construed and will be limited, in so far as it is possible to do so upon the language of the clause, so as not to be inconsistent with the main objects of the contract: see e.g. *Hadji v. Anglo-Arabian* (1906) 11 Com. (U.S. 219) and *Stag Line v. Fascolo Mango* [1932] A.C. 328.

(3) Where the deviation arises out of compliance with governmental instructions (paragraph (c)). In the event of a forced termination of the towage under such instructions, the tow is deemed duly delivered and the lump sum and all other sums are deemed earned.

Impermissible deviations

Under paragraph (d) even impermissible deviations are to be treated as not having brought the contract to an end. This leaves unaffected any claim which the hirer may have in damages for breach of the towage contract by the tug.

(18) Clause 18: "Liabilities"

Generally

In place of the blanket exemption of the tug from all liability as adopted by the U.K. Standard Conditions and as widespread in other tug owners' standard forms, the "Towcon" form seeks to achieve a balanced position as between tug and tow which, in broad terms, leaves each party bearing and being responsible for injuries and losses, damage of and to its own employees and equipment. As it is put in the ISU's explanatory notes to the form:

"In accordance with present day practice in the offshore industry, the agreement deals with liabilities as between Tugowner and Hirer on a 'knock-for-knock' basis."

As will be seen, this statement is, perhaps, a rather too sweeping summary of the position under Clause 18.

Injury to or death of those engaged in the towage: Sub-clause (1)

"18. Liabilities

1.(a) The Tugowner will indemnify the Hirer in respect of any liability adjudged due or claim reasonably compromised arising out of injury or death occurring during the towage or other service hereunder to any of the following persons:

    (i) The Master and members of the crew of the Tug and any other servant or agent of the Tugowner;

    (ii) The members of the Riding Crew provided by the Tugowner or any other person whom the Tugowner provides on board the Tow;

    (iii) Any other person on board the Tug who is not a servant or agent of the Hirer or otherwise on board on behalf of or at the request of the Hirer.

(b) The Hirer will indemnify the Tugowner in respect of any liability adjudged due or claim reasonably compromised arising from injury or death occurring during the towage or other service hereunder to any of the following persons:

    (i) The Master and members of the crew of the Tow and any other servant or agents of the Hirer;

    (ii) Any other person on board the Tow for whatever purpose except the members of the Riding Crew or any other persons whom the Tugowner provides on board the Tow pursuant to their obligations under this Agreement."

Clause 18(1) deals with liabilities and settlements in respect of deaths or injuries to those engaged in the towage service.

The clause applies only to such deaths or injuries if "occurring during the towage or other service" under the contract between the parties. The particular bounds of this phrase are not specifically defined and this *lacuna* may give rise to difficulties if the death or injury occurs in the very early or the very late stages of the operation. As has been seen, in the U.K. Standard Conditions *supra* the phrase "whilst towing" which is used in connection with exemptions is given a precise definition. Under the "Towcon" form the service is defined by various provisions in Part I, but not specifically in relation to the operation of Clause 18.

    (i) Boxes 22, 23, 24 and 25 read together with Clauses 7(a) and 8(a) define the nature of the contract service, the places of departure and destination and the contemplated route.

    (ii) Under Clause 2(g) free time for connection starts on the arrival of the tug at the pilot station of the place of departure and, after the expiry of free time, the tug has to be paid for by delay payments until the tug is free to leave the place of destination.

It is submitted that, for the purposes of Clause 18(1), the contract service begins upon the arrival of the tug at the pilot station of the place of departure or upon her being tendered to the tow at the place of departure under Clause 7(a) and extends until either the tow is taken over by the hirer under Clause 8(a) or until the tug is free to leave under Clause 2(g). However, even if the death or injury occurs during this period, it must also occur during the towage or service itself to fall within Clause 18(1). So if the tug, whilst not free from the contract service, suffers a fatality whilst otherwise engaged than in a service to the tow, the clause is inoperative. The same will be true of an accident occurring during a permissible deviation.

The clause provides that the tug shall indemnify the tow in respect of all deaths of or injury to the tug's crew and tug owners' servants or agents, including the riding crew, and to any third person on board the tug (other than the tow's servants). The tow gives a similar indemnity in respect of its own crew and servants and all persons on board the tow (other than the tug's riding crew or servants).

Loss of or damage to or caused by tug and tow: Sub-clause (2)

"2.(a) The following shall be for the sole account of the Tugowner without any recourse to the Hirer, his servants, or agents, whether or not the same is due to breach of contract, negligence or any other fault on the part of the Hirer, his servants or agents:
  (i) Loss or damage of whatsoever nature, howsoever caused to or sustained by the Tug or any property on board the Tug.
  (ii) Loss of damage of whatsoever nature caused to or suffered by third parties or their property by reason of contact with the Tug or obstruction created by the presence of the Tug.
  (iii) Loss or damage of whatsoever nature suffered by the Tugowner or by third parties in consequence of the loss or damage referred to in (i) and (ii) above.
  (iv) Any liability in respect of wreck removal or in respect of the expense of moving or lighting or buoying the Tug or in respect of preventing or abating pollution originating from the Tug.
The Tugowner will indemnify the Hirer in respect of any liability adjudged due to a third party or any claim by a third party reasonably compromised arising out of any such loss or damage. The Tugowner shall not in any circumstances be liable for any loss or damage suffered by the Hirer or caused to or sustained by the Tow in consequence of loss or damage howsoever caused to or sustained by the Tug or any property on board the Tug.
(b) The following shall be for the sole account of the Hirer without any recourse to the Tugowner, his servants or agents, whether or not the same is due to breach of contract, negligence or any fault on the part of the Tugowner, his servants or agents:
  (i) Loss or damage of whatsoever nature, howsoever caused to or sustained by the Tow.
  (ii) Loss or damage of whatsoever nature caused to or suffered by third parties or their property by reason of contact with the Tow or obstruction created by the presence of the Tow.
  (iii) Loss or damage of whatsoever nature suffered by the Hirer or by third parties in consequence of the loss or damage referred to in (i) and (ii) above.
  (iv) Any liability in respect of wreck removal or in respect of the expense of moving or lighting or buoying the Tow or in respect of preventing or abating pollution originating from the Tow.
The Hirer will indemnify the Tugowner in respect of any liability adjudged due to a third party or any claim by a third party reasonably compromised arising out of any such loss or damage but the Hirer shall not in any circumstances be liable for any loss or damage suffered by the Tugowner or caused to or sustained by the Tug in consequence of loss or damage, howsoever caused to or sustained by the Tow."

Under Clause 18(2) the tug and tow each agree to bear certain types of loss, damage and liability in full and without any right of recourse to or upon the other and irrespective of whether that loss, damage or liability has been caused by the other's breach of contract or negligence. Paragraph (a) deals with the losses which the tug will bear and paragraph (b) deals with those to be borne by the tow. The provisions are to identical effect and the losses which each agrees to bear can be summarised. Each party agrees to bear in full the following:

(i) Any loss or damage done to its vessel or to any property on board her.
This covers the most usual type of claim as between tug and tow: that is, for physical damage sustained by either vessel in collision with each other or caused by contact with the towing gear or in collision during the towage with a third vessel or a fixed object (such as a dock wall). Under the clause, each party will bear, for example, all the repair costs and incidental expenses involved arising out of damage sustained however it was caused and even if it was due to the other party's fault.

(ii) Any loss or damage done to third parties or to their property in two circumstances: "by reason of contact with" its vessel or by reason of "obstruction created by the presence of" its vessel.
Thus if a party's vessel collides with a third vessel or a harbour installation, that party will bear the liability for the same. Similarly, as is not uncommon with an unwieldy tow or where a towing connection parts in congested waters or in a port area, if a party's vessel blocks a channel or navigable waterway, that party will bear all liability to third parties for their loss whether or not the other party was actually responsible for causing his vessel to be an obstruction.

(iii) Any loss or damage suffered by that party or by third parties which is consequential upon the loss or damage set out in (i) and (ii) above.
Thus, if the damage to the vessel under (i) or the damage done by the vessel to a third party under (ii) causes consequential losses, such as loss of profit, the party whose vessel it is will bear all claims for such loss also.

(iv) All liability in respect of wreck removal and allied measures and in respect of pollution prevention relating to its vessel.
Thus if the tow founders in a navigable waterway due to the fault of the tug and requires to be buoyed as a wreck, then removed and, in the interim, to undergo an underwater operation to remove her bunkers to prevent pollution, the tow will bear the cost of the same.

In addition to describing the cover which each party is to bear, paragraphs (a) and (b) of Clause 18(2) make it clear that any claims by a third party upon one party to the towage arising out of the loss of or damage to the vessel of the *other* party to the towage are to be the subject of an indemnity by that other party.

Other (financial) losses: Sub-clause (3)

"3. Save for the provisions of Clauses 11, 12, 13 and 16, neither the Tugowner nor the Hirer shall be liable to the other party for loss of profit, loss of use, loss of production or any other indirect or consequential damage for any reason whatsoever."

It is common in standard form contracts to find a clause which excludes liability for "consequential losses". Such a clause was considered in *Croudace Construction Ltd v.*

Cawood's Concrete Products [1978] 2 Lloyd's Rep. 55 and was held only to exclude liability for loss which was not "direct", i.e., which was not loss directly caused by the breach. Since the recovery of loss which has only indirectly been caused by a breach is problematic in any event given the requirement in a claim for damages to demonstrate sufficient causation between the breach and loss, the utility of such a clause is questionable.

Clause 18(3) goes far further and specifically excludes certain heads of loss, that is, loss of profit, loss of use, and loss of production *as well as* "any other indirect or consequential damage". The clause deals effectively with those heads of financial and economic loss which commonly arise such as, for example, when the tow or the tug is damaged during the towage and cannot be used for commercial work thereby occasioning loss of profit and loss of use to the owning party.

This exclusion does not apply to such losses when they arise from breach of the following provisions:

(i) Clause 11: the obligation upon the tow and hirer to arrange for necessary permits and certification.
(ii) Clause 12: the obligation upon the hirer to ensure the tow-worthiness of the tow.
(iii) Clause 13: the obligation upon the tug owner to ensure the seaworthiness of the tug.
(iv) Clause 16: the regime of rights and responsibilities in the event of the wrongful cancellation of the contract or the withdrawal of either tug or tow.

The overall operation of Clause 18

Clause 18 does not purport to exclude *all* liability by a tug or tow for breach of contract or negligence but only where such breach or negligence results in a particular type of loss or damage; where that loss or damage concerns the damaged party's own vessel or men, that party bears the loss. However, save for the general exclusion (with exceptions) of specific types of loss under Clause 18(3), liability for breach of contract otherwise remains at large. If, in breach of contract, the tow is unfit for the towage and this results in extra costs for the tug in terms of bunkers, equipment, crew costs and time, such costs will be recoverable as damages for breach of contract. Similarly, if the tug's gear is deficient, requiring special works on board the tow to enable a connection to be made, and such deficiency constitutes a breach of contract, the cost of such work will be recoverable in damages.

In the most important instances of breach (i.e., Clauses 11, 12, 13 and 16), the full recovery of all losses in damages for breach of contract is unaffected by the "Towcon" terms.

Statutory limitations: Sub-clause (4)

"4. Notwithstanding any provisions of the Agreement to the contrary, the Tugowner shall have the benefit of all limitations of, and exemptions from, liability accorded to the Owners or

Chartered Owners of Vessels by any applicable statute or rule of law for the time being in force and the same benefits are to apply regardless of the form of signatures given to this Agreement."

The tug owner is akin to a carrier, although he is not one in law (see pp. 4–6 above). Clause 18(4) accordingly preserves for the tug owner all statutory rights of limitation, for example limitation of liability, as if the tug owner were a shipowner. In English law, the most important applicable statute will be the Merchant Shipping Act 1979, as to which see Chapter 8 below.

(19) Clause 19: "Himalaya clause"

"19. Himalaya Clause
All exceptions, exemptions, defences, immunities, limitations of liability, indemnities, privileges and conditions granted or provided by this Agreement or by any applicable statute rule or regulation for the benefit of the Tugowner or Hirer shall also apply to and be for the benefit of demise charterers, sub-contractors, operators, master, officers and crew of the Tug or Tow and to and be for the benefit of all bodies corporate parent of, subsidiary to, affiliated with or under the same management as either of them, as well as all directors, officers, servants and agents of the same and to and be for the benefit of all parties performing services within the scope of this Agreement for or on behalf of the Tug or Tugowner or Hirer as servants, agents and sub-contractors of such parties. The Tugowner or Hirer shall be deemed to be acting as agent or trustee of and for the benefit of all such persons, entities and vessels set forth above but only for the limited purpose of contracting for the extension of such benefits to such persons, bodies and vessels."

The clause is a standard one. It deems the tug owner and the hirer to be agents of and trustees for all persons who may be engaged by them to perform services for them within the scope of the towage agreement, so that the exemptions and protections of the towage agreement apply equally to those persons as if they were themselves parties to the towage agreement. Such clauses are commonly found in a wide range of standard form contracts. As to their efficacy and operation: see *The Eurymedon (New Zealand Shipping v. Satterthwaite)* [1975] A.C. 154 and *Midland Silicones v. Scruttons* [1962] A.C. 446.

(20) Clause 20: "War and other difficulties"

"20. War and Other Difficulties
(a) If owing to any Hostilities; War or Civil War; Acts of Terrorism; Acts of Public Enemies; Arrest or Restraint of Princes, Rulers or People; Insurrections; Riots or Civil Commotions; Disturbances; Acts of God; Epidemics; Quarantine; Ice; Labour Troubles; Labour Obstructions; Strikes; Lock-outs; Embargoes; Seizure of the Tow under Legal Process or for any other cause outside the control of the Tugowner it would be impossible or unsafe or commercially impracticable for the Tug or Tow or both to leave or attempt to leave the place of departure or any port or place of call or refuge or to reach or enter or attempt to reach or enter the port or place of destination of the Tow and there deliver the Tow and leave again, all of which safely and without unreasonable delay, the Tug may leave the Tow or any part thereof at the place of departure or any other port or place where the Hirer may take repossession and this shall be deemed a due fulfilment by the Tugowner of this Agreement and any outstanding sums and all extra costs of delivery at such place and any storage costs incurred by the Tugowner shall thereupon become due and payable by the Hirer.

(b) If the performance of this Agreement or the voyage to the place of departure would in the ordinary course of events require the Tug and/or Tow to pass through or near to an area where after this Agreement is made there is or there appears to be danger of such area being blocked or passage through being restricted or made hazardous by reason of War, Acts of Terrorism, Trapping of Vessels, Civil War, Acts of Public Enemies, Arrest or Restraint of Princes, Rulers or People, Insurrection, Riots or Civil Commotions or Disturbances or other dangers of a similar nature then:

   (i) If the Tug has not entered such area en route to the place of departure, or having entered has become trapped therein, the Hirer shall pay a Delay Payment at the rate specified in Box 29 for every day of the resulting delay. Provided that if the delay is for a period of more than 14 days either party hereto shall be entitled to terminate this Agreement by telex, cable or other written notice in which event, save for liabilities already accrued, neither shall be under any further liability to the other but the Tugowner shall not be bound to repay to the Hirer any payments already made and all amounts due shall remain payable.

   (ii) If the Tug and Tow whilst en route to the place of destination have not entered such area during the course of the towage or other service, the Hirer shall pay Delay Payment at the rate indicated in Box 29 for every day by which the towage is prolonged by reason of waiting for such area to become clear and/or safe and/or by reason of proceeding by a longer route to avoid or pass such area in safety.

   (iii) If the Tug and Tow whilst en route to the place of destination have become trapped in such area during the course of the towage or other service, the Hirer shall pay a Delay Payment at the rate specified in Box 29 for every day of the resulting delay. Provided that if the delay is for a period of more than 14 days either party hereto shall be entitled to terminate this Agreement by telex, cable or other written notice in which event, save for liabilities already accrued, neither party shall be under any further liability to the other but the Tugowner shall not be bound to repay to the Hirer any payment already made and all amounts due shall remain payable."

"War and other difficulties" can either prevent the contract from being fulfilled at all or they can delay its performance or render performance more onerous and costly. Paragraph (a) of Clause 20 deals with the former case, paragraph (b) of the clause with the latter.

Paragraph (a)

The list of events falling within Clause 20(a) constitutes a fairly common enumeration of the incidents of war and of other types of *force majeure* event as is found in standard form contracts. All of these have been the subject of considerable authority, especially in the context of charterparty and demurrage exceptions. The list reads:

"Any Hostilities; War or Civil War; Acts of Terrorism; Acts of Public Enemies; Arrest or Restraint of Princes, Rulers or People; Insurrections; Riots or Civil Commotions; Disturbances; Acts of God; Epidemics; Quarantine; Ice; Labour Troubles; Labour Obstructions; Strikes; Lockouts; Embargoes; Seizure of the Tow under Legal Process or for any other cause outside the control of the Tugowner."

For the cases on these general terms reference may be made to *Cooke on Voyage Charters*, pp. 514–534, in particular as to war-like and similar events; to *Wilford on Time Charters* (4th Edn.), pp. 419–426 as to general *force majeure* events. See also *Schofield on Laytime and Demurrage* (2nd Edn.), Chapter 4 and particularly at pp. 210–236.

If an event falling within the clause interferes such as to render it "impossible or unsafe or commercially impracticable" for either the tug or the tow "safely and without unreasonable delay" to leave the place of departure (or any port of call or of refuge) or to reach the place of destination such as to be able to deliver the tow and release the tug there, the towage contract can be abandoned with the tug leaving the tow at any place. It is provided that the contract is to be regarded as fulfilled upon and by this event such that the tug owner is thereby entitled to payment of all sums due under the contract.

Paragraph (b)

The mutability of human fortune may mean that circumstances may arise after the contract has been concluded which result in the fact that the route to be taken by the towage convoy "in the ordinary cause of events" may "pass through or near to an area" of real or reasonably apparent danger to the tug and/or tow or in which they may be exposed to blockade or trapping due to war-like and similar events. It is to this eventuality that paragraph (b) applies. The events covered by paragraph (b) are, however, narrower than those in paragraph (a), being confined purely to war-like ones:

"War, Acts of Terrorism, Trapping of Vessels, Civil War, Acts of Public Enemies, Arrest or Restraint of Princes, Rulers or People, Insurrection, Riots or Civil Commotions or Disturbances or other dangers of a similar nature."

The clause deals separately with the various stages in the towage operation at which the supervening danger or hazard may arise.

  (i) If the tug is delayed or trapped on her way to pick up the tow, the tow shall pay a delay payment at the rate stated in Box 29 of Part I. Delay in excess of 14 days gives to both parties a right to terminate the contract.
 (ii) If tug and tow are delayed en route to destination either by waiting for the danger or hazard to subside or by taking a longer route to avoid the same, then "Delay Payments" are payable by the tow for the extra period. No right of termination is provided for in such a case.
(iii) If tug and tow are trapped whilst en route to destination, then "Delay Payments" are again payable. Both parties have the right to terminate the contract in the event that the period of delay due to trapping exceeds 14 days.

In the event of termination after 14 days under (i) or (iii) above, it is expressly provided that all sums already earned are to remain due and that the tug shall be entitled to retain all payments which have already been made to it under the contract.

(21) Clause 21: "Lien"

"21. Lien
Without prejudice to any other rights which he may have, whether *in rem* or *in personam*, the Tugowner, by himself or his servants or agents or otherwise, shall be entitled to exercise a

possessory lien upon the Tow in respect of any sum howsoever or whatsoever due to the Tugowner under this Agreement and shall for the purpose of exercising such possessory lien be entitled to take and/or keep possession of the Tow; provided always that the Hirer shall pay to the Tugowner all reasonable costs and expenses howsoever or whatsoever incurred by or on behalf of the Tugowner in exercising or attempting or preparing to exercise such lien and the Tugowner shall be entitled to receive from the Hirer the Tug's Delay Payment at the rate specified in Box 29 for any reasonable delay to the Tug resulting therefrom."

This clause gives the tug a possessory lien over the tow in respect of all sums due to the tug under the towage contract. In addition to having the right to retain possession of the tow, the tug has the right to re-take possession. In the event of the tug's exercise of a lien, Clause 21 provides further that:

(i) the tow must bear all expenses of exercising the lien;
(ii) and the tow must pay "Delay Payments" at the Box 29 rate for any delay occasioned to the tug by or as a result of exercising the lien.

(22) Clause 22: "Warranty of authority"

"22. Warranty of Authority
If at the time of making this Agreement or providing any service under this Agreement other than towing at the request, express or implied, of the Hirer, the Hirer is not the Owner of the Tow referred to in Box 4, the Hirer expressly represents that he is authorised to make and does make this Agreement for and on behalf of the Owner of the said Tow subject to each and all of these conditions and agrees that both the Hirer and the Owner of the Tow are bound jointly and severally by these conditions."

This clause is similar in its purported effect to Clause 2 of the U.K. Standard Conditions (above): see the comments on this clause at p. 65 above.

(23) Clauses 23 to 25: General provisions

"23. General
(a) If any one or more of the terms, conditions or provisions in this Agreement or any part thereof shall be held to be invalid, void or of no effect for any reason whatsoever, the same shall not affect the validity of the remaining terms, conditions or provisions which shall remain and subsist in full force and effect.
(b) For the purpose of this Agreement unless the context otherwise requires the singular shall include the plural and vice versa.
(c) Any extension of time granted by the Tugowner to the Hirer or any indulgence shown relating to the time limits set out in this Agreement shall not be a waiver of the Tugowner's right under this Agreement to act upon the Hirer's failure to comply with the time limits.
24. Time for Suit
Save for the indemnity provisions under Clause 18 of this Agreement, any claim which may arise out of or in connection with this Agreement or of any towage or other service to be performed hereunder shall be notified by telex, cable or otherwise in writing within 6 months of delivery of the Tow or of the termination of the towage or other service for any reason whatever, and any suit shall be brought within one year of the time when the cause of action first arose. If either of these conditions is not complied with the claim and all rights whatsoever and howsoever shall be absolutely barred and extinguished.

25. Law and Jurisdiction

This Agreement shall be construed in accordance with and governed by English law. Any dispute or difference which may arise out of or in connection with this Agreement or the services to be performed hereunder shall be referred to the High Court of Justice in London.

No suit shall be brought in any other state or jurisdiction except that either party shall have the option to bring proceedings *in rem* to obtain conservative seizure or other similar remedy against any vessel or property owned by the other party in any state or jurisdiction where such vessel or property may be found."

Clause 23 contains the routine "interpretation", "indulgence not to amount to waiver" and "invalidity" provisions found in almost all standard form contracts.

Clause 24 is a time-bar provision which lays down a time period for the bringing of all claims, other than claims for indemnity under Clause 18. It applies to any claim "arising out of or in connection" with the agreement on the towage services; these words are very wide and are apt to include claims even as to the existence or non-existence of the contract (see the similar wording of arbitration clauses considered in *Mustill and Boyd on Commercial Arbitration* (2nd Edn.), at pp. 117–121). Any claim falling within Clause 24 must:

  (i) be notified to the other party within six months of the delivery of the tow or the date of termination of the service *and*
  (ii) suit must be brought in respect of the claim within one year of the cause of action having arisen.

These two time periods therefore do not necessarily start from the same date and most commonly will not do so. To take an example: under a towage contract, the towage service takes six months from commencement of the service to delivery of the tow; the tow has a claim for faulty towing gear which, it alleges, has caused loss and expense at the end of the third month of the service. Notice must be given within six months of delivery but suit must be brought within three months thereafter, i.e., within 12 months of the cause of action having arisen at the end of the third month of the service.

Clause 25 provides for English law and jurisdiction. This can be amended as necessary to provide for a reference to some other jurisdiction or for the submission of disputes to arbitration. The proper law theoretically can also be changed but given that the form has been drawn up by BIMCO upon the premise of English law as the governing law (as is apparent from many of the provisions and features of the "Towcon" form), it is submitted that this is undesirable.

PART C. THE "TOWHIRE" FORM

1. The structure and organisation of the form

The "Towhire" form is reproduced in facsimile in Appendix 3. It follows the same form as the "Towcon" form save for differences consequent upon the basis of payment under the "Towhire" form, being daily hire rather than a lump sum payable under "Towcon".

The few differences which exist between the two forms are to be found in the following clauses:

   (i) Clause 2: price and payment clause.
  (ii) Clause 7: place of departure.
 (iii) Clause 11: permits and certification.
 (iv) Clause 16: cancellation and withdrawal.
  (v) Clause 17: deviation and slow-steaming.
 (iv) Clause 20: war and *force majeure* clause.
 (vi) Clause 21: lien clause.

Some of these differences are very minor and are merely differences in terminology arising from the absence of the scheme of delay payments in the "Towhire" form. Such a scheme in a daily hire agreement is unnecessary; *cf.* the absence of demurrage provisions in a time charterparty.

2. Commentary on the different provisions in the "Towhire" form

(1) Clause 2: "Price and payment clause"

2. Price and Conditions of Payment
(a) The Hirer shall pay the Tugowner the amount of hire set out in Box 33 per day or *pro rata* for part of a day (hereinafter called the 'Tug's Daily Rate of Hire') from the time stated in Box 36 until the time stated in Box 37.
(b)(i) The Tug's Daily Rate of Hire shall be payable in advance as set out in Box 33; all hire or equivalent compensation hereunder shall be fully and irrevocably earned and non-returnable on a daily basis.
(ii) In the event of the Tug being lost, hire shall cease as of the date of the loss; if the date of the loss cannot be ascertained, then, in addition to any other sums which may be due, half the rate of hire shall be paid, calculated from the date the Tug was last reported until the calculated arrival of the Tug at her destination provided such period does not exceed 14 days.
(iii) In the event of the Tow being lost, hire shall continue until the Tug arrives at its destination or such nearer place, at the Tugowner's discretion, provided such period does not exceed 14 days.
(c) Within 14 days of the termination of the services hereunder by the Tugowner, the Tugowner will if necessary adjust in conformance with the terms of this Agreement hire paid in advance. Any hire paid by the Hirer but not earned under this Agreement and which is refundable thereunder shall be refunded to the Hirer within 14 days thereafter.
(d)(i) In the event that the Daily Rate of Hire includes the cost of bunkers and the average price per metric tonne of bunkers actually paid by the Tugowner differs from the amounts specified in Box 41 then the Hirer or the Tugowner, as the case may be, shall pay to the other the difference per metric tonne for every metric tonne consumed during the voyage. The average price specified above shall be the average of the prices per metric tonne actually paid by the Tugowner on the basis of quantities purchased at the last bunkering port prior to departure on the voyage, any bunkering port during the voyage, and the first bunkering port after completion of the voyage. The log book of the Tug shall be *prima facie* evidence of the quantity of bunkers consumed.
(ii) In the event that the Daily Rate of Hire excludes the cost of bunkers, then the Hirer shall pay to the Tugowner the cost of the bunkers and lubricants consumed by the Tug in fulfilling the terms of this Agreement. The Tug shall be delivered with sufficient bunkers and lubricants on board for the tow to the first bunkering port (if any) or destination and be re-delivered with not less than sufficient bunkers to reach the next bunkering stage en route to the Tug's next port of call. The Hirer upon delivery and the Tugowner upon re-delivery shall pay for the bunkers and lubricants on board at the current contract price at the time at the port of delivery and re-delivery or at the nearest bunkering port.

*(e) If agreed, the Hirer shall pay the sum set out in Box 31 by way of a mobilisation charge. This sum shall be paid on or before the commencement of the Tug's voyage to the place of departure, and shall be non-returnable, Tug and/or Tow lost or not lost.

*(f) If agreed, the Hirer shall pay the sum set out in Box 32 by way of a demobilisation charge. This amount shall be paid tow lost or not lost, on or before the termination by the Tugowner of his services under this Agreement.

(g) The Hire and any other sums payable to the Tugowner under this Agreement (or any part thereof) shall be due, payable and paid without any discount, deduction, set-off, lien, claim or counterclaim.

*Sub-clauses (e) and (f) are optional and shall only apply if agreed and stated in Boxes 31 and 32, respectively."

Hire

The scheme of remuneration for the services of the tug under paragraphs (a) to (c) of Clause 2 is straightforward.

  (i) Hire is payable as a daily rate per day or *pro rata* at the rate stipulated in box 33 between the times set out in Boxes 36 and 37: paragraph (a).

 (ii) The hire is payable in advance as the parties shall agree in Box 37 and is deemed earned on a daily basis: "irrevocably and non-returnable".

(iii) In the event of the loss of the tug, unsurprisingly, hire ceases to be payable. A formula is given for the calculation of when the hire ceased to be payable in the event that the tug is lost but the date of the loss is unknown.

(iv) In the event of the loss of the tow, hire continues to be payable, up to a maximum of 14 days, until the tug arrives at destination or some other place elected by the tug owner.

 (v) Within 14 days of the conclusion of the contract services, there is an adjustment between hire earned and hire paid in advance with any overpayment being refunded to the hirer.

Bunkers

The daily rate of hire may or may not include the cost of the tug's bunkers. If it does, paragraph (d)(i) provides for an adjustment of hire to reflect the difference between the actual cost or bunker to the tug owner and the figure inserted by the parties in Box 41 of Part I as the current rate for bunkers. If the cost of bunkers is not comprised within the hire rate, then under paragraph (d)(ii) these are to be paid for by the hirer at cost.

Mobilisation/demobilisation payment

The clause contains in paragraphs (e) and (f) optional clauses as to mobilisation and demobilisation payments.

Anti-deduction clause

The common law rule as to hire (*cf.* freight) is that the charterer can make an equitable set-off of claims against the owner: see *The Nanfri* [1978] 2 Lloyd's Rep. 132 (C.A.). Clause 2(g) excludes this rule in sweeping terms: see the commentary above as to the similar clause in the "Towcon" form, i.e., Clause 2(c) at pp. 86–87 above.

Absence of "Delay payments" and "Free time"

Since the basis of remuneration of the tug is a daily hire rate from the time of the arrival of the tug until the tug is free again and is not a fixed lump sum, the necessity for a restricted timetable for the connection and disconnection operations and for a system of daily "Delay Payments" for excess time is unnecessary. The "Towhire" form accordingly contains no provisions corresponding to Clauses 2(f) and 2(g) in the "Towcon" form.

(2) Clause 7: "Place of departure"

"7. Place of Departure
(a) The Tow shall be tendered to the Tugowner at the place of departure stated in Box 23.
(b) The precise place of departure shall always be safe and accessible for the Tug to enter, to operate in and for the Tug and Tow to leave and shall be a place where such Tug is permitted to commence the towage in accordance with any local or other rules, requirements or regulations and shall always be subject to the approval of the Tugowner which shall not be unreasonably withheld."

This clause is in very much simpler form than in the "Towcon" form since, given the running of daily hire, there is no need for the provision as to the notices to be given by the tow to the tug as to her readiness.

(3) Other clauses

As has been seen above, under the "Towcon" form any delays due to failure on the part of the tow to put in place the necessary certification for the towage (Clause 22) results in the obligation to pay delay payments. Similarly, Clauses 16, 17, 20 and 21 reflect the fact that, under the "Towcon" form particular provision is made in respect of the recovery of accrued delay payments together with portions of the lump sum earned and in respect of additional time to be paid for by the tow in the form of delay payments (see generally under Part B above). The difference between the "Towcon" and "Towhire" forms in this respect accounts for small drafting differences in respect of these clauses as they appear in the "Towhire" form.

CHAPTER 5

Standard Form Contracts: (III) The BIMCO "Supplytime 89" Form

PART A. THE GENESIS OF THE FORM

The large expansion of offshore activities connected with oil exploration and production in the early 1970s led to an increased demand for supply vessels and other offshore service vessels. Initially, contracts for the provision of the services of such vessels tended to be concluded upon the basis of the in-house form of the larger tug owners or on the basis of an adaptation of one of the standard time charterparty forms. But with the increase in this specialised trade, the need was felt for a uniform contract to form the basis of individual contracts. BIMCO was approached by trade interests and the "Supplytime" form was produced in 1975.

Since that time the offshore industry has become still more sophisticated and the range of services being provided by vessels has become still wider. Major operators of such vessels and the members of the International Support Vessel Owners' Association suggested a revision of the form. A Joint Working Group set up by the Documentary Council of BIMCO set to work on a revision of the form with the following objectives:

> "— To prepare a document which strikes a fair balance between owners and charterers;
> — To prepare a document which would be as 'timeless' as possible and, therefore, to be written 'up-market' thereby, hopefully, avoiding the need for rider clauses;
> — To ensure that the document be as internationally applicable as possible;
> — To try to clarify the document by use of apt words and trade terminology so as to, hopefully, obviate or reduce the possibility of disputes on interpretation of clauses;
> — During the preparatory drafting work to invite trade interests to comment on this project with a view to obtaining the broadest possible support from users in the trade".

The result was the "Supplytime 89" form. The major change to the old form was the adoption of a regime of liability between owner and hirer on the same "knock-for-knock" basis as that adopted by BIMCO under the "Towcon" and "Towhire" forms (*cf.* Clause 15 of the former "Supplytime" form which represented a more traditional charterparty exceptions clause in favour of the owners).

PART B. THE "SUPPLYTIME 89" FORM

1. A species of time charterparty

As its long title denotes, the BIMCO "Supplytime 89" form is a "Uniform Time Charterparty for Offshore Service Vessels". The regime provided for by the form is one which closely resembles that under the well-established forms of time charterparty such as the "New York Produce Exchange" form and the "Baltime form". It provides for a form of time charterparty for the chartering in of tugs and offshore service and supply vessels under which the tug or other vessel can be placed at the disposal of the charterer for a particular service or range of services for a particular period.

As such, much of the law and commentary which has developed in relation to time charterparties *simpliciter* will apply equally to the "Supplytime 89" form. Space does not permit a consideration of the law relating to time charterparties in general. This chapter is accordingly confined to a commentary on those provisions or aspects of provisions in the "Supplytime 89" form which specifically concern questions as between tug and tow rather than generally as between owner and time charterer. As to such general questions, see *passim Wilford on Time Charters* (1995) 4th Edn. For convenience, and as part of the commentary upon the "Supplytime 89" form, reference is made to the relevant passages in *Wilford* (and where appropriate to those in *Cooke on Voyage Charters* (1993)) which touch upon the matters dealt with by those provisions of the BIMCO form which correspond to general time charterparty provisions.

A facsimile of the "Supplytime 89" form is set out in Appendix 4 to this book.

2. The structure and organisation of the "Supplytime 89" form

As with the "Towcon" and "Towhire" forms, the "Supplytime 89" form is divided into two main parts:

Part I consists of 36 boxes into which the parties will enter the specifically agreed features of the employment contemplated. Of the most important of these are:

    (i) Box 7: port or place of delivery.

    (ii) Box 8: port or place of re-delivery.

    (iii) Box 9: period of hire (together with Box 10, optional provision for extensions and Box 11, automatic provision for extension to complete voyage).

    (iv) Box 12: the lump sum mobilisation charge.

    (v) Box 17: the tug's or offshore supply or service vessel's trading limits described as the "area of operation".

    (vi) Box 18: the description and definition of and restrictions upon the service(s) to be rendered by the tug or vessel.

(vii) Box 19–23: dealing with hire payments.

Part II consists of the standard form BIMCO provisions, 36 in number. As has been indicated above, these are broadly similar in their purport to those present in the standard forms of charterparty, albeit coupled with special provisions reflecting the relationship of tug and tow between the offshore service vessel and her charterer or employer, e.g. Clause 12 with a "knock-for-knock" regime of liability between owner and charterer similar to that adopted in the "Towhire" and "Towcon" forms.

There are three Annexes to the charterparty as follows:

(i) Annex "A": which consists of a "Vessel Specification". This is in the form of a questionnaire as to the details and features of the vessel being chartered. This, when completed, will give a very full and complete statement of the attributes of the vessel being chartered covering her machinery, b.h.p., towing- and anchor-handling equipment and fire-fighting equipment. The specific statement of these attributes greatly reduces the scope of the implied term as to the efficiency in general terms of the tug for the service. This is largely replaced by a detailed statement of the tug's mechanical capacity and of her tackle and gear leaving it to the tow to judge whether these warranted attributes are sufficient for and commensurate with the services being requested of her.

(ii) Annex "B": which sets out details of the insurance policies to be procured by the tug owner during the service under Clause 14 of Part II. The insurances cover the standard risks: hull, P. & I., and third party and employers' liability insurance.

(iii) Annex "C": which provides, together with Clause 12(f) of Part II and box 28 of Part I, for a special regime as between the parties to the contract for liability for damage to property and injury and loss of life. The regime is an optional one and has to be specifically agreed and indicated as having been opted for in Box 28.

As with the other BIMCO forms, the "Supplytime 89" form provides for its order of precedence between its various parts. This is set out at the conclusion of Part I and preceding the space left for the signatures of the parties, and is as follows:

"It is mutually agreed that this Contract shall be performed subject to the conditions contained in the Charter consisting of PART I, including additional clauses if any agreed and stated on Box 34, and PART II as well as ANNEX 'A' and ANNEX 'B' as annexed to this Charter. In the event of a conflict of conditions, the provisions of PART I shall prevail over those of PART II and ANNEX 'A' and ANNEX 'B' to the extent of such conflict but no further. ANNEX 'C' as annexed to this Charter is *optional* and shall only apply if expressly agreed and stated in Box 28."

Similarly, specific *ad hoc* provisions can be agreed in addition to and in variation of the "Supplytime 89" form standard provisions. Such provisions will usually prevail over the standard provisions in the event of conflict on ordinary common law principles (see p. 83 above).

PART C. COMMENTARY ON THE FORM

1. Clause 1: "Period"

"1. Period
(a) The Owners stated in Box 2 let and the Charterers stated in Box 3 hire the Vessel named in Box 4, as specified in ANNEX 'A' (hereinafter referred to as 'the Vessel'), for the period as stated in Box 9 from the time the Vessel is delivered to the Charterers.
(b) Subject to Clause 10(b), the Charterers have the option to extend the Charter Period in direct continuation for the period stated in Box 10(i), but such an option must be declared in accordance with Box 10(ii).
(c) The Charter Period shall automatically be extended for the time required to complete the voyage or well (whichever is stated in Box 11(i)) in progress, such time not to exceed the period stated in Box 11(ii)."

Under paragraph (a) of this clause, the basic elements of the parties' agreement are provided for.

(i) *The description of the parties to the contract*. In accordance with the charterparty cases, the general principle is that it is a question of the construction of the contract as a whole as to who is party to the contract: see e.g. *The Swan* [1968] 1 Lloyd's Rep. 5 and *Brandt* v. *Morris* [1917] 2 K.B. 784. The problem most commonly arises where an agent signs for his principal and the real principal seeks to intervene in the contract or the other contracting party seeks to render the agent liable as principal. The description of a named party as "owner" coupled with the signature of the charterparty by that person in an unqualified manner, i.e., in the signature box, "(Owners)", may bind the person signing even if only an agent and may prevent the real principal from suing: see *Humble* v. *Hunter* (1848) 12 Q.B. 310. The description of a person as "Charterer" and his signature under that title is less definitive and has been held not to prevent the true principal from suing or being sued: see *Drughorn* v. *Rederieaktiebolaget Transatlantic* [1919] A.C. 203, *cf.* if the word "charterer" is qualified when signing by the word "as": *Rederieaktiebolaget Argonaut* v. *Hani* [1918] 2 K.B. 247. See generally *Cooke* at pp. 28–33.

(ii) *The identity and name of the vessel chartered* (as stated in Box 4). Albeit that the contract is usually for a named tug or vessel, given the specific provisions of the charter (e.g. as to the provisions to be made by the owners, stipulated for in Clause 7, and as to the detailed specification of the vessel set out in Annex "A"), the "named tug" line of authority in cases such as *Robertson* v. *Amazon Tug and Lighterage Co.* (1881) 7 Q.B.D. 598 (see above at pp. 33 *et seq.*) will not apply.

(iii) *The period of the charter service* (as defined in Box 9).

Paragraphs (b) and (c) provide for extensions of the period of charter service which has been stipulated in Box 9. Under paragraph (b), the charterers may be given a facultative option to extend the charter for such period as the parties agree in Box 10(i), provided that any such advance notice period for the declaration of the extension as they agree (and as is set out in Box 10(ii)) is observed. Paragraph (c) deals with the case where the offshore service vessel is chartered for a voyage or for a rig or a well service and provides for the automatic extension of the charter to complete the voyage or well service defined in Box 11(i) up to the maximum period of time allowed for in Box 11(ii).

2. Clause 2: "Delivery and redelivery"

"2. Delivery and Redelivery
(a) *Delivery*—Subject to sub-clause (b) to this Clause the Vessel shall be delivered by the Owners free of cargo and with clean tanks at any time between the date stated in Box 5 and the date stated in Box 6 at the port or place stated in Box 7 where the Vessel can safely lie always afloat.
(b) *Mobilisation*—(i) The Charterers shall pay a lump sum as stated in Box 12 without discount by way of mobilisation charge in consideration of the Owners giving delivery at the port or place stated in Box 7. The mobilisation charge shall not be affected by any change in the port or place of mobilisation from that stated in Box 13.
(ii) Should the Owners agree to the Vessel loading and transporting cargo and/or undertaking any other service for the Charterers en route to the port of delivery or from the port of redelivery, then all terms and conditions of this Charter Party shall apply to such loading and transporting and/or other service exactly as if performed during the Charter Period excepting only that any lump sum freight agreed in respect thereof shall be payable on shipment or commencement of the service as the case may be, the Vessel and/or goods lost or not lost.
(c) *Cancelling*—If the Vessel is not delivered by midnight local time on the cancelling date stated in Box 6, the Charterers shall be entitled to cancel this Charter Party. However, if despite the exercise of due diligence by the Owners, the Owners will be unable to deliver the Vessel by the cancelling date, they may give notice in writing to the Charterers at any time prior to the delivery date as stated in Box 5; and shall state in such notice the date by which they will be able to deliver the Vessel. The Charterers may within 24 hours of receipt of such notice give notice in writing to the Owners cancelling this Charter Party. If the Charterers do not give such notice, then the later date specified in the Owners' notice shall be substituted for the cancelling date for all the purposes of this Charter Party. In the event the Charterers cancel the Charter Party, it shall terminate on terms that neither party shall be liable to the other for any losses incurred by reason of the non-delivery of the Vessel or the cancellation of the Charter Party.
(d) *Redelivery*—The Vessel shall be redelivered on the expiration or earlier termination of this Charter Party free of cargo and with clean tanks at the port or place as stated in Box 8(i) or such other port or place as may be mutually agreed. The Charterers shall give not less than the number of days notice in writing of their intention to redeliver the Vessel, as stated in Box 8(ii).
(e) *Demobilisation*—The Charterers shall pay a lump sum without discount in the amount as stated in Box 16 by way of demobilisation charge which amount shall be paid on the expiration or on earlier termination of this Charter Party."

Paragraphs (a) and (d) deal with delivery and redelivery respectively. These are very similar to standard time charterparty delivery and redelivery provisions: see *Wilford* at pp. 121–131. Paragraph (c) contains a cancelling clause: as to this standard feature of a time charter, see *Wilford* at pp. 355–360.

A special and not uncommon feature of the employment of a large tug or offshore service vessel is that, at the time at which the charterparty is concluded, she may be laid-up or be on stand-by with a skeleton crew and equipment. The "Supplytime 89" form reflects this with provision for a lump sum mobilisation charge in paragraph (b), payable irrespective of the place of delivery: *viz.* the words " . . . shall not be affected by any change in the port or place of mobilisation . . . ". A corresponding demobilisation charge is provided for by paragraph (e); this is to be payable upon the completion of the service. Clause 2 reflects the similar BIMCO approach adopted in the "Towhire" form as to mobilisation and demobilisation.

3. Clause 3: "Condition of vessel"

"3. Condition of Vessel
(a) The Owners undertake that at the date of delivery under this Charter Party the Vessel shall be of the description and classification as specified in ANNEX 'A', attached hereto, and undertake to so maintain the Vessel during the period of service under this Charter Party.
(b) The Owners shall before and at the date of delivery of the Vessel and throughout the Charter Period exercise due diligence to make and maintain the Vessel tight, staunch, strong, in good order and condition and, without prejudice to the generality of the foregoing, in every way fit to operate effectively at all times for the services as stated in Clause 5."

Clause 3 imposes two separate obligations upon the owner of the vessel being chartered in relation to her condition.

(1) Description and classification

Under paragraph (a) the owner undertakes that the vessel will be of the description and classification set out in Annex "A" to the charterparty at the date of the vessel's delivery and that that description and classification will be maintained during the service. This is an absolute obligation and is not qualified by a requirement to exercise due diligence only. Since the undertaking relates to the fixed characteristics and capabilities of the vessel upon which the charterer is often relying and which can readily be ascertained by the owner, the absolute nature of the owner's warranty is sensible.

However, the owner will usually protect himself, as far as he is able, by qualifying the specific statements of the vessel's characteristics and attributes by a suitable term of dilution such as "about" or "approximately". Such terms are common in descriptions of vessels under time charterparties, especially in relation to speed and consumption, and have been the subject of numerous decisions: as to these, see *Wilford*, pp. 102 *et seq.* and pp. 114 *et seq.*

(2) Seaworthiness

In addition to the obligation set out above, under paragraph (b) there is imposed upon the owner an ordinary obligation to exercise due diligence so as to ensure that the vessel is seaworthy, that is, "tight, staunch, strong, in good order and condition and . . . in every way fit to operate effectively at all times for the services". Similar words to these have been held in the time charter context to amount to a full warranty of the physical seaworthiness of the vessel (see e.g. *The Madeleine* [1967] 2 Lloyd's Rep. 224) and to the requirement that the vessel shall be efficient as a going concern, that is, with a competent crew and with proper documents, such as charts, on board her (see e.g. *The Derby* [1985] 2 Lloyd's Rep. 325). See generally *Wilford*, pp. 153–161. The obligation extends to the condition of the vessel both at the time of delivery and at all times during the service.

In very many cases of the under-performance of the chartered offshore service vessel, the charterer will have a claim under paragraph (a) of Clause 3 and will not need to establish a failure to exercise due diligence. Thus, if, for example, the drill water discharge rate is inferior to that which has been stipulated in Clause 3(d) of Annex "A" to the charterparty making the vessel unfit for the service, the charterer has a claim under paragraph (a) in addition to a possible claim under paragraph (b).

4. Clause 4: "Survey"

"4. Survey
The Owners and the Charterers shall jointly appoint an independent surveyor for the purpose of determining and agreeing in writing the condition of the Vessel, any anchor handling and towing equipment specified in Section 5 of ANNEX 'A', and the quality and quantity of fuel, lubricants and water at the time of delivery and redelivery hereunder. The Owners and the Charterers shall jointly share the time and expense of such surveys."

The parties are to appoint a joint surveyor who is to determine for their agreement the condition of the vessel and, as is common in time charterparties, to determine the quantities of bunkers and oils on board. Such surveys correspond to the usual "on hire" and "off-hire" surveys.

5. Clause 5: "Employment and area of operation"

(1) Scope of vessel's employment

"5. Employment and Area of Operation
(a) The Vessel shall be employed in offshore activities which are lawful in accordance with the law of the place of the Vessel's flag and/or registration and of the place of operation. Such activities shall be restricted to the service(s) as stated in Box 18, and to voyage between any good and safe port or place and any place or offshore unit where the Vessel can safely lie always afloat within the Area of Operation as stated in Box 17, which shall always be within Institute Warranty Limits and which shall in no circumstances be exceeded without prior agreement and adjustment of the Hire and in accordance with such other terms as appropriate to be agreed; provided always that the Charterers do not warrant the safety of any such port or place or offshore unit but shall exercise due diligence in issuing their orders to the Vessel as if the Vessel were their own property and having regard to her capabilities and the nature of her employment. Unless otherwise agreed, the Vessel shall not be employed as a diving platform."

Paragraph (a) of Clause 5 provides that "the vessel shall be employed in offshore activities". These services are subject to various requirements which are cumulative.

(i) The services must be lawful under the law of the vessel's flag and of the place of the performance of the services.

(ii) The services are confined to those set out in the definition of the services which is given in Box 18. Given the wide range of services and the possible temptation for a charterer of an offshore vessel under charter to use her for other services than were discussed, Box 18 requires the parties to agree that "employment of the Vessel [is] restricted to" those services which are to be named or described in that box. These services may be specific, e.g. "transportation of drilling bits to Rig X", or general, "attendance upon drilling platform to provide supply and assistance services". The more general the definition, the more potential ground for dispute there may be as to whether a particular service is or is not comprised within the bounds of the defined service. So, for example, if a vessel is engaged "to assist in the towage/escort of the 'Brent Spar' oil installation to her sinking position", does this service include the vessel being detailed off to shadow and douse with fire hoses a Greenpeace protestors' supply craft which is following and harassing the convoy? To avoid such problems, the fullest definition of the service is often the most prudent course.

(iii) The services must engage the vessel only between safe places where she can lie always afloat: as to the obligation upon a charterer to employ the chartered vessel between safe places see *Wilford*, pp. 177–198 and *Cooke*, pp. 79–91, and see above, p. 93. The charterers do not give an absolute warranty of safety, as is found for example in the "New York Produce Exchange" form or the "Baltime" form. Under the "Supplytime 89" form, the charterers only undertake to exercise due diligence to ensure the vessel is used at and between safe places as if she were their own property; compare the similar approach adopted in the "Shelltime" form of tanker time charterparty. In practice, it is often very difficult to establish a breach of such an undertaking, for example where the unsafety of a place lies in something unexpected which could not have been learned of by the charterers (or the owners) in advance.

(iv) The services must engage the vessel only within the geographical area stipulated in Box 17 as being the contractual "Area of Operation" which is itself to be within the Institute Warranty Limits. As to "trading limits" clauses in charterparties see generally *Wilford*, pp. 141–143.

Provision is made for the not infrequent case of the charterer asking for permission to breach Institute Warranty Limits or the trading limits defined in Box 17. In such a case the owner may accede to the request on terms to be agreed including adjustment of hire.

(v) The services must not involve the vessel in being used as a diving platform. Given the special nature of diving operations and the particular hazards involved in diving work, the ordinary type of offshore service vessel is less well-suited to diving work than a dedicated diving support vessel. The BIMCO form reflects this.

(2) Certificates

"(b) Relevant permission and licences from responsible authorities for the Vessel to enter, work in and leave the Area of Operation shall be obtained by the Charterers and the Owners shall assist, if necessary, in every way possible to secure such permission and licences."

The obtaining of all necessary certification and permission for the services is, as under the "Towcon" and "Towhire" forms, the charterer's responsibility. However, an obligation is also imposed on the owners to give to the charterers their assistance in respect of such matters, if the same be necessary: see paragraph (b).

(3) The vessel's space

"(c) *The Vessel's Space*—The whole reach and burden and decks of the Vessel shall throughout the Charter Period be at the Charterers' disposal reserving proper and sufficient space for the Vessel's Master, Officers, Crew, tackle, apparel, furniture, provisions and stores. The Charterers shall be entitled to carry, so far as space is available and for their purposes in connection with their operations:

    (i) Persons other than crew members, other than fare paying, and for such purposes to make use of the Vessel's available accommodation not being used on the voyage by the Vessel's Crew. The Owners shall provide suitable provisions and requisites for such persons for which the Charterers shall pay at the rate as stated in Box 26 per meal and at the rate as stated in Box 27 per day for the provision of bedding and services for persons using berth accommodation.

    (ii) Lawful cargo whether carried on or under deck.

    (iii) Explosives and dangerous cargo, whether in bulk or packaged, provided proper notification has been given and such cargo is marked and packed in accordance with the national regulations of the Vessel and/or the International Maritime Dangerous Goods Code and/or other pertinent regulations. Failing such proper notification, marking or packing the Charterers shall indemnify the Owners in respect of any loss, damage or liability, whatsoever and howsoever arising therefrom. The Charterers accept responsibility for any additional expenses (including reinstatement expenses) incurred by the Owners in relation to the carriage of explosives and dangerous cargo.

    (iv) Hazardous and noxious substances, subject to Clause 12(g), proper notification and any pertinent regulations."

As to paragraph (c), compare the typical "whole reach and burthen" clauses in time charterparties such as Clause 7 of the "New York Produce Exchange" form or Clause 8 of the "Baltime" form: as to these, see *Wilford*, p. 550. Paragraph (c) also confers upon the charterer the right to use the vessel's space for the carriage of personnel, cargo, and explosive and noxious substances (subject in the case of the latter to proper notification and procedures being carried out and to the granting of an express indemnity in respect of the consequences of the carriage of any dangerous or hazardous cargo). This reflects the common use of such vessels to ferry men and supplies (including dangerous chemicals and explosive charges) to and from the platform or drilling areas being serviced.

(4) Lay-up clause

"(d) *Laying-up of Vessel*—The Charterers shall have the option of laying-up the Vessel at an agreed safe port or place for all or any portion of the Charter Period in which case the Hire hereunder shall continue to be paid but, if the period of such lay-up exceeds 30 consecutive days, there shall be credited against such Hire the amount which the Owners shall reasonably have saved by way of reduction in expenses and overheads as a result of the lay-up of the Vessel."

The charterer may, due to changes in his operational requirements offshore, have no employment for the vessel at all times during the service period. Paragraph (d) allows him to lay-up the vessel during the period of the charterparty, paying full hire for the vessel. After 30 days' lay-up, although hire is payable in full, the saving of expenses to the owners of the vessel is credited against the hire.

6. Clause 6: "Master and crew"

"6. Master and Crew

(a)(i) The Master shall carry out his duties promptly and the Vessel shall render all reasonable services within her capabilities by day and by night and at such times and on such schedules as the Charterers may reasonably require without any obligations on the Charterers to pay to the Owners or the Master, Officers or the Crew of the Vessel any expenses or overtime payments. The Charterers shall furnish the Master with all instructions and sailing directions and the Master and Engineer shall keep full and correct logs accessible to the Charterers or their agents.

(ii) The Master shall sign cargo documents as and in the form presented, the same, however, not to be Bills of Lading, but receipts which shall be non-negotiable documents and shall be marked as such. The Charterers shall indemnify the Owners against all consequences and liabilities arising from the Master, Officers or agents signing, under the direction of the Charterers, those cargo documents or other documents inconsistent with this Charter Party or from any irregularity in the papers supplied by the Charterers or their agents.

(b) The Vessel's Crew, if required by Charterers, will connect and disconnect electric cables, fuel, water and pneumatic hoses when placed on board the Vessel in port as well as alongside the offshore units; will operate the machinery on board the Vessel for loading and unloading cargoes; and will hook and unhook cargo on board the Vessel when loading or discharging alongside offshore units. If the port regulations or the seamen and/or labour unions do not permit the Crew of the Vessel to carry out any of this work, then the Charterers shall make, at their own expense, whatever other arrangements may be necessary, always under the direction of the Master.

(c) If the Charterers have reason to be dissatisfied with the conduct of the Master or any Officer or member of the Crew, the Owners on receiving particulars of the complaint shall promptly investigate the matter and if the complaint proves to be well founded, the Owners shall as soon as reasonably possible make appropriate changes in the appointment."

(1) Ordinary features

This clause corresponds to the usual time charterparty "employment" clause, although it has certain special features to reflect the nature of offshore service. As to the ordinary time charter clauses, see Clause 8 of the "New York Produce Exchange" form and Clause 9 of the "Baltime" form (commented upon in *Wilford*, pp. 291-299 and pp. 550–553 respectively). Thus:

(i) Under paragraph (a)(i) the master of the vessel is under the charterers' orders.

(ii) Under paragraph (a)(ii) the master is to sign cargo documents and the charterers are to indemnify the owners against all consequences of the same. The "cargo documents" referred to expressly exclude bills of lading. This reflects the reality that, in practice, while the vessel may be carrying spares and equipment to and from the rig or well-head, such items will either be the charterers' or will be items which the charterer has himself contracted with the rig-operator to provide and carry. The offshore service vessel will not be acting as the carrier of such goods and the vessel's operators will not enter into any separate contractual relationship with those who may be interested in the goods.

(iii) Under paragraph (b) the crew of the vessel is put at the disposal of the charterer for certain specific works and operations. This list of operations clarifies, in particular, that it is the crew who are to carry out all cargo operations on board the vessel.

(iv) Under paragraph (c) the customary right of the time charterer to complain in the event of dissatisfaction with the vessel's personnel is provided for.

(2) Paragraph (d): Compliance with orders

Paragraph (d) of Clause 6 is of importance to the tug owner or offshore vessel operator. It reads as follows:

"(d) The entire operation, navigation, and management of the Vessel shall be in the exclusive control and command of the Owners, their Master, Officers and Crew. The Vessel will be operated and the services hereunder will be rendered as requested by the Charterers, subject always to the exclusive right of the Owners or the Master of the Vessel to determine whether operation of the Vessel may be safely undertaken. In the performance of the Charter Party, the Owners are deemed to be an independent contractor, the Charterers being concerned only with the results of the services performed."

Given the nature of the operations which the owner's vessel will be called upon by the charterers to perform, it will frequently be the case that the vessel is required to perform hazardous operations, such as a close-quarter manoeuvring around an oil platform in poor weather, as part of its employment. Such services will be far removed from those comprised within ordinary time charterparty service. Under the ordinary forms of time charterparty, the right of the vessel to question the orders given to her by charterers is of very uncertain extent. In *Portsmouth S.S. Co.* v. *Liverpool & Glasgow Salvage Association* (1929) 34 Ll. L. Rep. 459, Roche J. held that it was not for the master to question unduly his orders "within the limits of obviously grave danger". However, in *Midwest Shipping* v. *Henry* [1971] 1 Lloyd's Rep. 375, where a vessel was ordered to tell the authorities at Chalna that she was bound for Singapore (whereas in fact she was bound for Europe), the court held that the master was entitled to query a subsequent order given to the vessel to return to Chalna which would have involved the authorities in learning of the deception. Donaldson J. stated in a passage which has, perhaps, been more often cited than applied:

"It seems to me that against that background it must be the duty of the master to act reasonably upon receipt of orders. Some orders are of their nature such that they would, if the master were to act reasonably, require immediate compliance. Others would require a great deal of thought and consideration before a reasonable master would comply with them."

This broad statement of principle must now be reconsidered in the light of the judgment given by Phillips J. in *The Houda* [1993] 1 Lloyd's Rep. 333. In this case, the owners were held to be in breach of the charterparty in "delaying compliance" with an order by the charterers to discharge cargo at Mina-al-Ahmadi without the production of bills of lading. Phillips J. considered the distinction between non-compliance and delayed compliance at pp. 343–344 as follows:

"I have found the distinction between delay in complying with an order and a refusal to comply with that order elusive if not illusory.

An unequivocal renunciatory refusal to comply with an order is, of course, easy to recognize, but there is no question of such a refusal in this case. Short of that it seems to me that a failure to comply with an order that persists beyond the period for which it is reasonable to delay becomes tantamount to a refusal to obey the order. Thus one cannot sensibly divorce the question of whether there has been a refusal to obey an order from the question of whether there has been unreasonable delay in obeying the order. What, I believe, is really in issue between the owners and the charterers is the right to pause before obeying an order and whether [the] owners' conduct in this case could possibly fall within that right."

He considered the cases including *Midwest Shipping*, and as to these said the following (p. 345):

"In each of these cases the orders given which the master delayed in executing were orders which threatened to expose ship and cargo to potential peril. In such a situation one can readily understand why the courts held that there was no breach of contract if a master paused for a reasonable period to consider the implications of the order. The paramount duty of a master is to exercise reasonable care for the safety of ship and cargo—a duty that will arise out of the contract of carriage and exist independently of the contract. That paramount duty may make it necessary for him to delay before complying with an order from the charterers. The statement of Mr Justice Donaldson that it must be the duty of the master to act reasonably upon receipt of orders must, in my judgment, be read in that context."

He summarised the position as to the extent to which the law recognised a qualification on the duty of the owners to comply with lawful orders as follows (p. 345):

"As a matter of business efficacy—and on the authorities—I can see justification for the right of [the] owners and their master to delay in obeying an order when this is reasonably necessary in the interest of the safety of ship, cargo and crew. I can see scope, as a matter of business efficacy, for the requirement of some term—express or implied—as to the manner in which [the] charterers' orders are to be conveyed to [the] owners. But I do not consider that any principle of law or business efficacy requires that [the] owners be entitled to delay in obeying a lawful order so long as is reasonably necessary to satisfy themselves that the order is authorised, or lawful under the charterparty, or that in discharging the cargo pursuant to that order they are not infringing the rights of the owners of that cargo. It is for the charterparty to provide what orders the charterers can lawfully give and for the charterers to ensure that their orders are lawful. If they give a lawful order, but the owners have doubts about its legality, it seems to me that the owners' delay in complying with that order must be at their own peril."

Paragraph (d) of Clause 6 addresses this important question expressly. While the vessel is at all times to be under the charterers' orders, her navigation and command are to remain under the exclusive control of the vessel's owners who are to "have the exclusive right ... to determine whether operation of the vessel may be safely undertaken". This gives the operator of the tug or other vessel the right to override an order given to his vessel by the charterer in the event that he, *bona fide*, considers the same be too unsafe or to involve the vessel or her crew in too hazardous an operation.

7. Clauses 7 and 8: "Provide and pay for" clauses

"7. Owners to Provide
(a) The Owners shall provide and pay for all provisions, wages and all other expenses of the Master, Officers and Crew; all maintenance and repair of the Vessel's hull, machinery and equipment as specified in ANNEX 'A'; also, except as otherwise provided in this Charter Party,

for all insurance on the Vessel, all dues and charges directly related to the Vessel's flag and/or registration, all deck, cabin and engine room stores, cordage required for ordinary ship's purposes mooring alongside in harbour, and all fumigation expenses and de-ratisation certificates. The Owners' obligations under this Clause extend to cover all liabilities for consular charges appertaining to the Master, Officers and Crew, customs or import duties arising at any time during the performance of this Charter Party in relation to the personal effects of the Master, Officers and Crew, and in relation to the stores, provisions and other matters as aforesaid which the Owners are to provide and/or pay for and the Owners shall refund to the Charterers any sums they or their agents may have paid or been compelled to pay in respect of such liability.
(b) On delivery the Vessel shall be equipped, if appropriate, at the Owners' expense with any towing and anchor handling equipment specified in Section 5(b) of ANNEX 'A'. If during the Charter Period any such equipment becomes lost, damaged or unserviceable, other than as a result of the Owners' negligence, the Charterers shall either provide, or direct the Owners to provide, an equivalent replacement at the Charterers' expense.

8. Charterers to Provide
(a) While the Vessel is on hire the Charterers shall provide and pay for all fuel, lubricants, water, dispersants, fire-fighting foam and transport thereof, port charges, pilotage and boatmen and canal steersmen (whether compulsory or not), launch hire (unless incurred in connection with the Owners' business), light dues, tug assistance, canal, dock, harbour, tonnage and other dues and charges, agencies and commissions incurred on the Charterers' business, costs for security or other watchmen, and of quarantine (if occasioned by the nature of the cargo carried or the ports visited whilst employed under this Charter Party but not otherwise).
(b) At all times the Charterers shall provide and pay for the loading and unloading of cargoes so far as not done by the Vessel's crew, cleaning of cargo tanks, all necessary dunnage, uprights and shoring equipment for securing deck cargo, all cordage except as to be provided by the Owners, all ropes, slings and special runners (including bulk cargo discharge hoses) actually used for loading and discharging, inert gas required for the protection of cargo, and electrodes used for offshore works, and shall reimburse the Owners for the actual cost of replacement of special mooring lines to offshore units, wires, nylon spring lines, etc. used for offshore works, all hose connections and adapters, and, further, shall refill oxygen/acetylene bottles used for offshore works.
(c) The Charterers shall pay for customs duties, all permits, import duties (including costs involved in establishing temporary or permanent importation bonds), and clearance expenses, both for the Vessel and/or equipment required for or arising out of this Charter Party."

These clauses set out in the usual time charterparty form the particular items and services which the charterer and the owner are to provide and pay for and to the vessel for the charterparty service. Clause 7 deals with the owners' responsibilities in this regard and Clause 8 with the charterers' responsibilities. The items and services referred to in Clauses 7 and 8 reflect the typical charterparty division between "ship-side" and "shore-side" in the special context of the special features of the offshore industry.

On such clauses generally, see *Wilford* on Clauses 1 and 2 of the "New York Produce Exchange" form and Clauses 3 and 4 of the "Baltime" form at pp. 211–226 and 547–548 respectively.

8. Clause 9: "Bunkers"

"9. Bunkers
Unless otherwise agreed, the Vessel shall be delivered with bunkers and lubricants as on board and redelivered with sufficient bunkers to reach the next bunkering stage en route to her next port of call. The Charterers upon delivery and the Owners upon redelivery shall take over and pay for

the bunkers and lubricants on board at the prices prevailing at the times and ports of delivery and redelivery."

This clause is materially identical to Clause 3 of the "New York Produce Exchange" form save that no minimum delivery and re-delivery quantities are provided for as they are in Clause 3 of that form. See generally: *Wilford*, pp. 227–228.

9. Clause 10: "Hire and payments"

"10. Hire and Payments

(a) *Hire*—The Charterers shall pay Hire for the Vessel at the rate stated in Box 19 per day or *pro rata* for part thereof from the time that the Vessel is delivered to the Charterers until the expiration or earlier termination of this Charter Party.

(b) *Extension Hire*—If the option to extend the Charter Period under Clause 1(b) is exercised, Hire for such extension shall, unless stated in Box 20, be mutually agreed between the Owners and the Charterers.

(c) *Adjustment of Hire*—The rate of Hire shall be adjusted to reflect documented changes, after the date of entering into the Charter Party or the date of commencement of employment, whichever is earlier, in the Owners' cost arising from changes in the Charterers' requirements or regulations governing the Vessel and/or its Crew or this Charter Party.

(d) *Invoicing*—All invoices shall be issued in the contract currency stated in Box 19. In respect of reimbursable expenses incurred in currencies other than the contract currency, the rate of exchange into the contract currency shall be that quoted by the Central Bank of the country of such other currency as at the date of the Owners' invoice. Invoices covering Hire and any other payments due shall be issued monthly as stated in Box 21(i) or at the expiration or earlier termination of this Charter Party. Notwithstanding the foregoing, bunkers and lubricants on board at delivery shall be invoiced at the time of delivery.

(e) *Payments*—Payments of Hire, bunker invoices and disbursements for the Charterers' account shall be received within the number of days stated in Box 23 from the date of receipt of the invoice. Payment shall be made in the contract currency in full without discount to the account stated in Box 22. However any advances for disbursements made on behalf of and approved by the Owners may be deducted from Hire due.

If payment is not received by the Owners within 5 banking days following the due date the Owners are entitled to charge interest at the rate stated in Box 24 on the amount outstanding from and including the due date until payment is received.

Where an invoice is disputed, the Charterers shall in any event pay the undisputed portion of the invoice but shall be entitled to withhold payment of the disputed portion provided that such portion is reasonably disputed and the Charterers specify such reason. Interest will be chargeable at the rate stated in Box 24 on such disputed amounts where resolved in favour of the Owners. Should the Owners prove the validity of the disputed portion of the invoice, balance payment shall be received by the Owners within 5 banking days after the dispute is resolved. Should the Charterers' claim be valid, a corrected invoice shall be issued by the Owners.

In default of payment as herein specified, the Owners may require the Charterers to make payment of the amount due within 5 banking days of receipt of notification from the Owners; failing which the Owners shall have the right to withdraw the Vessel without prejudice to any claim the Owners may have against the Charterers under this Charter Party.

While payment remains due the Owners shall be entitled to suspend the performance of any and all of their obligations hereunder and shall have no responsibility whatsoever for any consequences thereof, in respect of which the Charterers hereby indemnify the Owners, and Hire shall continue to accrue and any extra expenses resulting from such suspension shall be for the Charterers' account.

(f) *Audit*—The Charterers shall have the right to appoint an independent chartered accountant to audit the Owners' books directly related to work performed under this Charter Party at any time after the conclusion of the Charter Party, up to the expiry of the period stated in Box 25, to determine the validity of the Owners' charges hereunder. The Owners undertake to make their records available for such purposes at their principal place of business during normal working hours. Any discrepancies discovered in payments made shall be promptly resolved by invoice or credit as appropriate."

The clause provides for the common mechanism of daily hire payments. As to these, see, for example, *Wilford*, pp. 231–232 and pp. 243–255. The following features of the "Supplytime 89" form's approach to hire and payment of hire may be noted:

(i) Provision is made by paragraph (c) for the adjustment of the rate of hire after the charter has been concluded or the service has been begun so as "to reflect documented changes . . . in the Owners' costs arising from changes in the Charterers' requirements" or due to changes in applicable regulations. This addresses a potential source of dispute. Often the contract service will be made more onerous by reason of operational changes at the well-head or oil platform; similarly governmental regulations, particularly in relation to safety at work or environmental protection, may be introduced or may become more restrictive. This paragraph allows a proper adjustment in the rate of hire to be made to reflect this. This change in the owners' costs must be documented. To hold the balance between owner and charterer, paragraph (f) allows the charterers to carry out an independent audit of the owners' books to verify the financial background to the changes in costs contended for by the owners.

(ii) Payments due to the owners under the charter are not made subject to an "anti-deduction" clause as they are in the "Towcon" and "Towhire" forms. While paragraph (e) provides that payments are to be made "in full without discount", it is submitted that this wording is ineffective to prevent the charterers from exercising their right of equitable set-off in respect of payment of hire as they can under an ordinary time charterparty (see *Wilford*, pp. 248–251; see also *The Nanfri* [1978] 2 Lloyd's Rep. 132 (C.A.)). As was stated by the House of Lords in *Gilbert Ash Northern Ltd* v. *Modern Engineering (Bristol) Ltd* [1974] A.C. 689, to achieve an effective exclusion of the ordinary rights of set-off "clear express words" must be used. The words "in full without discount" are, it is submitted, insufficiently clear to bar a right of set-off. *Cf.* the words of Clause 2(c) of the "Towcon" and "Towhire" forms ("payable without any discount, deduction, set-off, lien, claim or counterclaim") and see generally pp. 86–87 above.

Indeed, paragraph (e) itself expressly provides for the charterer to have the right to withhold payment of any invoice which is disputed in whole or in part, provided that payment is reasonably disputed and that the charterers can give a reasoned explanation for disputing payment. This reflects the approach of the courts to deductions made under lines 99 and 100 of the "New York Produce Exchange" form: see *The Nanfri* (*op. cit.*) and *The Kostas Melas* [1981] 1 Lloyd's Rep. 18.

(iii) In the event of default of payment or while payment remains due, the owners have the right under paragraph (e):

   (a) to suspend performance of their obligations under the charterparty with the charterers being liable to indemnify them for all consequences of so doing; and

   (b) to withdraw the vessel after failure to pay within five days of the owners giving notice to the charterers.

The express right of withdrawal is common in time charterparties (see *Wilford*, pp. 256–258). However, paragraph (e) fills a *lacuna* which is present in most time charter forms: the right to withdraw under the ordinary forms of time charterparty gives an owner only the right to withdraw completely but does not give him the right to suspend services or to withdraw temporarily. In *The Mihalios Xilas* [1978] 2 Lloyd's Rep. 186, it was held that such a right of suspension would have to be expressly conferred by the charterparty on the owner in clear terms. Paragraph (e) does precisely this. This gives the tug owner a valuable method of putting pressure upon a hirer to make payment of outstanding sums due.

10. Clause 11: "Suspension of hire"

"11. Suspension of Hire

(a) If as a result of any deficiency of Crew or of the Owners' stores, strike of Master, Officers and Crew, breakdown of machinery, damage to hull or other accidents to the Vessel, the Vessel is prevented from working, no Hire shall be payable in respect of any time lost and any Hire paid in advance shall be adjusted accordingly provided always however that Hire shall not cease in the event of the Vessel being prevented from working as aforesaid as a result of:

   (i) the carriage of cargo as noted in Clause 5(c)(iii) and (iv):

   (ii) quarantine or risk of quarantine unless caused by the Master, Officers or Crew having communication with the shore at any infected area not in connection with the employment of the Vessel without the consent or the instructions of the Charterers;

   (iii) deviation from her Charter Party duties or exposure to abnormal risks at the request of the Charterers;

   (iv) detention in consequence of being driven into port or to anchorage through stress of weather or trading to shallow harbours or to river or ports with bars or suffering an accident to her cargo, when the expenses resulting from detention shall be for the Charterers' account howsoever incurred;

   (v) detention or damage by ice;

   (vi) any act or omission of the Charterers, their servants or agents.

(b) *Liability for Vessel not Working*—The Owners' liability for any loss, damage or delay sustained by the Charterers as a result of the Vessel being prevented from working by any cause whatsoever shall be limited to suspension of hire.

(c) *Maintenance and Drydocking*—Notwithstanding sub-clause (a) hereof, the Charterers shall grant the Owners a maximum of 24 hours on Hire, which shall be cumulative, per month or *pro rata* for part of a month from the commencement of the Charter Period for maintenance and repairs, including drydocking (hereinafter referred to as 'maintenance allowance').

The Vessel shall be drydocked at regular intervals. The Charterers shall place the Vessel at the Owners' disposal clean of cargo, at a port (to be nominated by the Owners at a later date) having facilities suitable to the Owners for the purpose of such drydocking.

During reasonable voyage time taken in transits between such port and Area of Operation the

Vessel shall be on Hire and such time shall not be counted against the accumulated maintenance allowance.

Hire shall be suspended during any time taken in maintenance repairs and drydocking in excess of the accumulated maintenance allowance.

In the event of less time being taken by the Owners for repairs and drydocking or, alternatively, the Charterers not making the Vessel available for all or part of this time, the Charterers shall, upon expiration or earlier termination of the Charter Party, pay the equivalent of the daily rate of Hire then prevailing in addition to Hire otherwise due under this Charter Party in respect of all such time not so taken or made available.

Upon commencement of the Charter Period, the Owners agree to furnish the Charterers with the Owners' proposed drydocking schedule and the Charterers agree to make every reasonable effort to assist the Owners in adhering to such pre-determined drydocking schedule for the Vessel."

Clause 11 is an off-hire clause, as to which in general see *Wilford*, pp. 363–379. The features of the "Supplytime 89" form's version of this clause are as follows:

(i) The clause puts the vessel off-hire in a slightly narrower but more clearly defined set of circumstances than, for example, Clause 15 of the "New York Produce Exchange" form. Thus:

" ... any deficiency of Crew or of the Owners' stores, strike of Master, Officers and Crew, breakdown of machinery, damage to hull or other accidents to the vessel ... "

Those events (as to which see *Wilford, op. cit.*) only put the vessel off-hire if she is "prevented from working". The clause is accordingly one under which the charterer must show that time was lost as a consequence of the specified event. If, therefore, the vessel while engaged in loading supplies has a main engine breakdown but loading, that is the working which the vessel is actually engaged upon, is unaffected, the vessel is not off-hire: see *Hogarth* v. *Miller* [1891] A.C. 48. The charterer need not show any breach on the part of the owner in relation to any of the events to trigger the suspension of hire. It is sufficient that the working of the vessel is prevented by one or more of the named events.

The clause is a "net loss of time clause" as is indicated by the words "no hire shall be payable in respect of any time lost"; this means that what is to be allowed to the charterer is the net overall time lost as a result of the specified event or circumstance: see generally as to such clauses *Wilford*, pp. 364–365.

(ii) The vessel is not off-hire if her working is prevented by various events within the charterers' control or for which the charterer is made responsible. These events are listed in Clause 11(a) as follows: the carriage of dangerous or noxious substances; quarantine (unless not due to the employment of the vessel); deviation; detention due to being driven into port by heavy weather; ice; and acts or omissions of the charterers.

(iii) Under paragraph (b) the owners' liability and the charterers' remedy for loss or damage sustained by the charterers arising out of an off-hire event is purportedly limited to suspension of hire.

The ordinary position under a time charter is that if the charterers can prove that the off-hire event occurred as a result of the owners' breach of charterparty (even though, as seen above, the charterer need not establish this merely so as to put the vessel off-hire) and that he has suffered loss over and above wasted hire, the charterer can recover damages irrespective of the off-hire clause: see *The Democritos* [1975] 1 Lloyd's Rep. 386. It is doubtful whether the words "by any cause whatsoever" are wide enough to exclude the charterers' rights in respect of breach of contract; they will certainly not be apt by themselves to exclude the owners' liability for negligence: see *The Raphael* [1982] 2 Lloyd's Rep. 42.

(iv) Paragraph (c) deals specifically and in some detail with drydocking and maintenance. This is usually an off-hire event *per se* (as in Clause 15 of the "New York Produce Exchange" form). This ordinary approach typically adopted in ordinary time charterparties may be unrealistic and undesirable given the type of engagement which will be concluded under the "Supplytime 89" form; the offshore vessel will often require regular maintenance and drydocking during the period of the service which will frequently be long-term. The clause, therefore, provides for "windows" for a proper maintenance and drydocking schedule, which schedule is to be notified to the charterers at the commencement of the charter service. It further provides for an allowed time for such purposes of 24 hours on hire per month or *pro rata*, which allowed time is cumulative and can, therefore, be aggregated by the owner as necessary.

11. Clause 12: "Liabilities"

(1) "Knock-for-knock"

"12. Liabilities and Indemnities

(a) *Owners*—Notwithstanding anything else contained in this Charter Party excepting Clauses 5(c)(iii), 7(b), 8(b), 12(g), 15(c) and 21, the Charterers shall not be responsible for loss of or damage to the property of the Owners or of their contractors and sub-contractors, including the Vessel, or for personal injury or death of the employees of the Owners or of their contractors and sub-contractors, arising out of or in any way connected with the performance of this Charter Party, even if such loss, damage, injury or death is caused wholly or partially by the act, neglect, or default of the Charterers, their employees, contractors or sub-charterers, and even if such loss, damage, injury or death is caused wholly or partially by unseaworthiness of any vessel; and the Owners shall indemnify, protect, defend and hold harmless the Charterers from any and against all claims, costs, expenses, actions, proceedings, suits, demands and liabilities whatsoever arising out of or in connection with such loss, damage, personal injury or death.

(b) *Charterers*—Notwithstanding anything else contained in this Charter Party excepting Clause 21, the Owners shall not be responsible for loss of, damage to, or any liability arising out of anything towed by the Vessel, any cargo laden upon or carried by the Vessel or her tow, the property of the Charterers or of their contractors and sub-contractors, including their offshore units, or for personal injury or death of the employees of the Charterers or of their contractors and sub-contractors (other than the Owners and their contractors and sub-contractors) or of anyone on board anything towed by the Vessel, arising out of or in any way connected with the performance of this Charter Party, even if such loss, damage, liability, injury or death is caused wholly or partially by the act, neglect or default of the Owners, their employees, contractors or sub-contractors, and even if such loss, damage, liability, injury or death is caused wholly or partially by the unseaworthiness of any vessel; and the Charterers shall indemnify, protect, defend and hold harmless the Owners from any and against all claims, costs, expenses, actions, proceedings, suits, demands and liabilities whatsoever arising out of or in connection with such loss, damage, liability, personal injury or death."

Paragraph (a) exempts the charterer in wide terms from liability for loss or damage suffered by the owner. Paragraph (b) does the same on the part of the owner in respect of loss or damage suffered by the charterer. It should be noted that although BIMCO in their "Explanatory Notes" to the "Supplytime 89" form equate the "knock-for-knock" concept used in this form with that used in the "Towcon" and "Towhire" forms, there are significant differences. Unlike the other BIMCO forms, "Supplytime 89" consists of exemption clauses in standard form rather than clauses under which the parties agree to bear certain types of loss. The scope of the exemption for each party is narrower under this approach than in the analogous provisions in "Towcon" and "Towhire".

The most important features of the protection offered to each party under Clause 12(a) and (b) are as follows:

(i) The exemption of the charterers from responsibility and the "hold harmless" or indemnity against suit provision under paragraph (a) is only in respect of loss of or damage to the property of the owners, including their contractors and sub-contractors, and in respect of death or injury to the owners' employees or servants. Importantly, there is no exemption in respect of liabilities which the owners may incur to third parties by reason of the charterers' breach of contract or negligence.

(ii) The owners' exemption from responsibility and the "hold harmless" provision in paragraph (b) is wide. It extends to loss of or damage to any of the charterers' property whether under tow or not, including cargo carried and any offshore unit, and to death or personal injury of the charterers' personnel and, thus far, mirrors the exemption given to the charterers under paragraph (a). However, the clause goes on to exempt the owners from extending to "any liability arising out of" the charterers' property whether or not caused by breach of contract or negligence on the part of the owners. This will cover, for example, liability for wreck removal of the tow and for collision between the tow and a third party vessel.

(iii) In both cases, the exemption of the owners and the charterers applies only to loss or damage, death or injury, and in the case of paragraph (b) to liabilities "arising out of or in any way connected with the performance of this Charter Party".

Generally reference should be made to pp. 107 *et seq.* above in relation to Clause 18 of the "Towcon" and "Towhire" forms.

(2) "Consequential damages"

"(c) *Consequential Damages*—Neither party shall be liable to the other for, and each party hereby agrees to protect, defend and indemnify the other against, any consequential damages whatsoever arising out of or in connection with the performance or non-performance of this Charter Party, including, but not limited to, loss of use, loss of profits, shut-in or loss of production and cost of insurance."

Paragraph (c) is the equivalent of Clause 18(3) in the "Towcon" and "Towhire" forms. It includes two further items in the list of specific forms of consequential damage for which liability is excluded. These additional items are, first, "shut-in", plainly of importance in the context of services being provided for the drilling industry where an accident may lead to suspension of drilling or well-head pumping, and, secondly, "cost of insurance", which is for the owners' account under Clause 14 of the form and which may prove to be a significant cost item.

(3) "Mutual waiver of recourse"

"(f) *Mutual Waiver of Recourse (Optional only applicable if stated in Box 28, but regardless of whether this option is exercised the other provisions of Clause 12 shall apply and shall be paramount)*
In order to avoid disputes regarding liability for personal injury or death of employees or for loss of or damage to property, the Owners and the Charterers have entered into, or by this Charter Party agree to enter into, an Agreement for Mutual Indemnity and Waiver of Recourse (in a form substantially similar to that specified in ANNEX 'C') between the Owners, the Charterers and the various contractors and sub-contractors of the Charterers."

A novel feature of the "Supplytime 89" form is the option granted to the parties by paragraph (f) to enter into an "Agreement for Mutual Indemnity and Waiver of Recourse". If this option is exercised, the agreement is recommended to be in the form of "Annex 'C'" to the form. This recommendation is questionable. While the aim and stated objective of such an agreement is "to avoid entirely disputes as to their liabilities" between the parties and their sub-contractors "for damage or injuries to their respective property or employees", Annex "C" is curiously drafted. (Annex "C" appears in full in facsimile in Appendix 4).

First, even if it is adopted, Annex "C" has no effect on the position as between the charterers and the owners which remains that under Clause 12. This is made clear by the introductory and italicised words of paragraph (f):

" . . . regardless of whether this option is exercised the other provisions of Clause 12 shall apply and shall be paramount."

Secondly, while the preamble to the Annex states that the Annex "C" agreement is premised upon the modification of the relationships which *the parties'* sub-contractors have at common law so as to avoid disputes and liabilities as set out above, the clauses deal chiefly with the position of the owners and their sub-contractors and do not apply to the sub-contractors of the charterers. For convenience of reference, the relevant provisions of Annex "C" are reproduced here:

"This Agreement is made between the Owners and the Charterers and is premised on the following:
    (a) The Charterers and the Owners have entered into a contract or agreement dated as above regarding the performance of work or service in connection with the Charterers' operations offshore ('Operations');
    (b) The Charterers and the Owners have entered into, or shall enter into, contracts or agreements with other contractors for the performance of work or service in connection with the Operations;
    (c) Certain of such other contractors have signed, or may sign, counterparts of this Agreement or substantially similar agreements relating to the Operations ('Signatory' or collectively 'Signatories'); and
    (d) The Signatories wish to modify their relationship at common law and avoid entirely disputes as to their liabilities for damage or injuries to their respective property or employees.
In consideration of the premises and of execution of reciprocal covenants by the other Signatories, the Owners agree that:

1. The Owners shall hold harmless, defend, indemnify and waive all rights of recourse against the other Signatories and their respective subsidiary and affiliate companies, employees, directors, officers, servants, agents, invitees, vessel(s), and insurers, from and against any and all claims, demands, liabilities or causes of action of every kind and character, in favour of any person or party, for injury to, illness or death of any employee of or for damage to or loss of property owned by the Owners (or in possession of the Owners by virtue of an arrangement made with an entity which is not a Signatory) which injury, illness, death, damage or loss arises out of the Operations, and regardless of the cause of such injury, illness, death, damage or loss even though caused in whole or in part by a pre-existing defect, the negligence, strict liability or other legal fault of other Signatories.

2. The Owners (including the Vessel) shall have no liability whatsoever for injury, illness or death of any employee of another Signatory under the Owners' direction by virtue of an arrangement made with such other Signatory, or for damage to or loss of property of another Signatory in the Owners' possession by virtue of an arrangement made with such other Signatory. In no event shall the Owner (including the Vessel) be liable to another Signatory for any consequential damages whatsoever arising out of or in connection with the performance or non-performance of this Agreement, including, but not limited to, loss of use, loss of profits, shut-in or loss of production and cost of insurance.

   . . .

4. The Owners shall attempt to have those of their sub-contractors which are involved in the Operations become Signatories and shall promptly furnish the Charterers with an original counterpart of this Agreement or of a substantially similar agreement executed by its sub-contractors."

Thus, it can be seen from those provisions that:

(i) by Clause 1, *the owners* agree to hold harmless and indemnify those sub-contractors who sign the agreement (called "the Signatories") in respect of all loss and damages, injury and death to the owners' property or employees;

(ii) by Clause 2, *the owners* agree that they shall have no liability in respect of loss or damage or death or injury to a signatory's property or employees;

(iii) by Clause 4, *the owners* agree to attempt to have all of their sub-contractors become signatories to the agreement.

If the purpose of the form of agreement set out as Annex "C" is to cover solely the position of the owners' sub-contractors so as to remove all claims and potential liability with which the owners may be faced from their sub-contractors, then the Annex "C" agreement is effective; however, it leaves untouched the position between the charterers and their sub-contractors and the potential claims which the latter may have against the charterers (or against the owners). If the "waiver of recourse" is intended to be mutual the achievement of that mutuality by Annex "C" is significantly restricted.

(4) "Hazardous and noxious substances"

"(g) *Hazardous and Noxious Substances*—Notwithstanding any other provision of this Charter Party to the contrary, the Charterers shall always be responsible for any losses, damages or liabilities suffered by the Owners, their employees, contractors or sub-contractors, by the Charterers, or by third parties, with respect to the Vessel or other property, personal injury or death, pollution or otherwise, which losses, damages or liabilities are caused, directly or indirectly, as a result of the Vessel's carriage of any hazardous and noxious substances in whatever form as ordered by the Charterers, and the Charterers shall defend, indemnify the Owners and hold the Owners harmless for any expense, loss or liability whatsoever or howsoever arising with respect to the carriage of hazardous or noxious substances."

Paragraph (g) provides for an overriding liability on the part of charterers and for an indemnity to be given by them to owners in respect of any losses, damages or liabilities incurred by owners or any third parties in respect of loss, damage, death, injury, pollution or otherwise arising directly or indirectly from the carriage on the vessel of hazardous or noxious substances at the charterers' request. The carriage of such substances is envisaged by Clause 5(c)(iii) and (iv) of the form and Clause 12(g) makes it clear that such carriage is to be solely for the risk and the responsibility of the charterers.

This clause will apply in respect of pollution due to the carriage on the vessel of hazardous or noxious substances and operates as an exception in this regard to the general pollution clause, Clause 13 (as to which, see below).

(5) Other matters

"(d) *Limitations*—Nothing contained in this Charter Party shall be construed or held to deprive the Owners or the Charterers, as against any person or party, including as against each other, of any right to claim limitation of liability provided by any applicable law, statute or convention, save that nothing in this Charter Party shall create any right to limit liability. Where the Owners or the Charterers may seek an indemnity under the provisions of this Charter Party or against each other in respect of a claim brought by a third party, the Owners or the Charterers shall seek to limit their liability against such third party.

(e) *Himalaya Clause*

    (i) All exceptions, exemptions, defences, immunities, limitations of liability, indemnities, privileges and conditions granted or provided by this Charter Party or by any applicable statute, rule or regulation for the benefit of the Charterers shall also apply to and be for the benefit of the Charterers' parent, affiliated, related and subsidiary companies; the Charterers' contractors, sub-contractors, clients, joint ventures and joint interest owners (always with respect to the job or project on which the Vessel is employed); their respective employees and their respective underwriters.

    (ii) All exceptions, exemptions, defences, immunities, limitations of liability, indemnities, privileges and conditions granted or provided by this Charter Party or by any applicable statute, rule or regulation for the benefit of the Owners shall also apply to and be for the benefit of the Owners' sub-contractors, the Vessel, its Master, Officers and Crew, its registered owner, its operator, its demise charterer(s), their respective employees and their respective underwriters.

    (iii) The Owners or the Charterers shall be deemed to be acting as agent or trustee of and for the benefit of all such persons and parties set forth above, but only for the limited purpose of contracting for the extension of such benefits to such persons and parties."

Paragraphs (d) and (e) deal respectively with the preservation of any applicable statutory and other limitations and with the provision of a "Himalaya" clause; as to these, see p. 112 above, in relation to the corresponding provisions in the "Towcon" form.

12. Clause 13: "Pollution"

"13. Pollution
(a) Except as otherwise provided for in Clause 15(c)(iii), the Charterers shall be liable for, and agree to indemnify, defend and hold harmless the Charterers against, all claims, costs, expenses, actions, proceedings, suits, demands and liabilities whatsoever arising out of actual or potential pollution damage and the cost of cleanup or control thereof arising from acts or omissions of the Owners or their personnel which cause or allow discharge, spills or leaks from the Vessel, except as may emanate from cargo thereon or therein.
(b) The Charterers shall be liable for and agree to indemnify, defend and hold harmless the Owners from all claims, costs, expenses, actions, proceedings, suits, demands, liabilities, loss or damage whatsoever arising out of or resulting from any other actual or potential pollution damage, even where caused wholly or partially by the act, neglect or default of the Owners, their employees, contractors or sub-contractors or by the unseaworthiness of the Vessel."

Given the typical nature of the offshore services rendered under this form to drilling installations and offshore platforms, liability for pollution damage is a matter which, necessarily, the "Supplytime 89" form specifically addresses. Clause 13 apportions liability for pollution between the owners and the charterers on a straightforward basis which involves a simple factual enquiry into the source of the pollution and which reflects, in very rough terms, the concept that the risk of pollution should chiefly be upon the charterer at whose request and for whose purposes the tug or vessel comes into close proximity with rigs, platforms and drilling installations. Under paragraph (a), if the pollution is due to the act or omission of the owners or their personnel which act or omission causes or allows a discharge or leak from the vessel, then the owner is liable unless either the discharge or leak emanates from cargo on or in the vessel or the pollution is covered by the provision of Clause 12(g), i.e. it results from the carriage on the vessel of hazardous or noxious substances at the charterers' request.

In all other cases, even where the cause of the pollution is the breach of contract or the negligence of the owners or of those on board the vessel, the charterers are liable for the same and are to indemnify the owners in respect of the same: see paragraph (b).

13. Clause 14: "Insurance"

"14. Insurance
(a) (i) The Owners shall procure and maintain in effect for the duration of this Charter Party, with reputable insurers, the insurances set forth in ANNEX 'B'. Policy limits shall not be less than those indicated. Reasonable deductibles are acceptable and shall be for the account of the Owners.
(ii) The Charterers shall upon request be named as co-insured. The Owners shall upon request cause insurers to waive subrogation rights against the Charterers (as encompassed in Clause 12(e)(i)). Co-insurance and/or waivers of subrogation shall be given only insofar as these relate to liabilities which are properly the responsibility of the Owners under the terms of this Charter Party.
(b) The Owners shall upon request furnish the Charterers with certificates of insurance which provide sufficient information to verify that the Owners have complied with the insurance requirements of this Charter Party.

(c) If the Owners fail to comply with the aforesaid insurance requirements, the Charterers may, without prejudice to any other rights or remedies under this Charter Party, purchase similar coverage and deduct the cost thereof from any payment due to the Owners under this Charter Party."

In Annex "B" to the form, the owners are to give full details of their insurance in respect of the vessel including hull, P. & I. and third party liabilities. Under Clause 14, the owners are required to maintain such insurance in place and to this end charterers have a right to the production and inspection of the relevant certificates. In the event of breach of this clause, in addition to any rights in damages, the charterers may effect the requisite insurance themselves and deduct the cost of so doing from any sums due to owners.

14. Clause 15: "Saving of life and salvage"

Just as for those owners providing towage services, salvage will be an important aspect of commercial operations for those who provide the services of offshore vessels. Very commonly, large ocean-going salvage tugs are employed in the provision of offshore services and to the greatest extent possible the owners of such vessels will want to keep open the possibility of providing salvage services while under time charter commitments, both so as to maintain their established reputations for commitment to salvage and their "status" as professional salvors and because of the obvious economic considerations. The clause deals with three matters.

(1) Liberty to deviate

"(a) The Vessel shall be permitted to deviate for the purpose of saving life at sea without prior approval of or notice to the Charterers and without loss of Hire provided however that notice of such deviation is given as soon as possible."

Paragraph (a) contains the standard liberty to deviate for the purpose of saving life (but not property) at sea which reflects the common law position (*Scaramanga* v. *Stamp* (1880) 5 C.P.D. 295). The vessel remains on hire under the contract only if the vessel gives notice of the deviation as soon as possible.

(2) Liberty to perform salvage

"(b) Subject to the Charterers' consent, which shall not be unreasonably withheld, the Vessel shall be at liberty to undertake attempts at salvage. It being understood that the Vessel shall be off hire from the time she leaves port or commences to deviate and she shall remain off-hire until she is again in every way ready to resume the Charterers' service at a position which is not less favourable to the Charterers than the position at the time of leaving port or deviating for the salvage services. All salvage monies earned by the Vessel shall be divided equally between the Owners and the Charterers, after deducting the Master's Officers' and Crew's share, legal expenses, value of fuel and lubricants consumed, Hire of the Vessel lost by the Owners during the salvage, repairs to damage sustained, if any, and any other extraordinary loss or expense sustained as a result of the salvage. The Charterers shall be bound by all measures taken by the Owners in order to secure payment of salvage and to fix its amount."

Of more importance is paragraph (b) which gives the vessel a liberty to depart from the service to perform or attempt a salvage service with the consent of the charterer. Such a service is defined in paragraph (b) simply as "salvage", and thus is apt to include the salvage of goods and property as well as of life salvage. If this liberty is exercised by the owners:

(i) the vessel is off hire during her time away from the charter service;

(ii) if the salvage is successful and the vessel becomes entitled to salvage remuneration, that salvage remuneration is to be shared equally between the owners and the charterers after various deductions have been made to cover any costs or expenses incurred by owners in earning the salvage.

The common law approach to such clauses where the items of cost and expense which were to be deductible from the shared remuneration were not specified (see e.g. Clause 19 of the NYPE form which refers only to "after deducting Owner's and Charterers' expenses") was to look at the "net pecuniary result of the salvage operations" arrived at by deducting "what each has contributed towards securing the benefit": see *Booker* v. *S.S. Pocklington* [1899] 2 Q.B. 690. Other forms of time charter (see e.g. Clause 19 of the "Baltime" form) for the avoidance of doubt particularised certain of the more controversial or doubtful heads of loss and expense as being deductible items. Clause 15(b) of the "Supplytime 89" form adopts the same approach as Clause 19 of the "Baltime" form in specifying the deductions which owners can make. These will include the hire of the vessel which has been lost by the owners during the salvage due to the off-hire provision in paragraph (b) and the cost of any repairs to damage sustained by their vessel as a result of the salvage.

(3) *Salvage rendered to the charterer's property*

"(c) The Owners shall waive their right to claim any award for salvage performed on property owned by or contracted to the Charterers, always provided such property was the object of the operation the Vessel was chartered for, and the Vessel shall remain on hire when rendering salvage services to such property. This waiver is without prejudice to any right the Vessel's Master, Officers and Crew may have under any title.

If the Owners render assistance to such property in distress on the basis of 'no claim for salvage', then, notwithstanding any other provisions contained in this Charter Party and even in the event of neglect or default of the Owners, Master, Officers or Crew:

(i) The Charterers shall be responsible for and shall indemnify the Owners against payments made, under any legal rights, to the Master, Officers and Crew in relation to such assistance.

(ii) The Charterers shall be responsible for and shall reimburse the Owners for any loss or damage sustained by the Vessel or her equipment by reason of giving such assistance and shall also pay the Owners' additional expenses thereby incurred.

(iii) The Charterers shall be responsible for any actual or potential spill, seepage and/or emission of any pollutant howsoever caused occurring within the offshore site and any pollution resulting therefrom, wheresoever it may occur and including but not limited to the cost of such measures as are reasonably necessary to prevent or mitigate pollution damage, and the Charterers shall indemnify the Owners against any liability, cost or expense arising by reason of such actual or potential spill, seepage and/or emission.

(iv) The Vessel shall not be off-hire as a consequence of giving such assistance, or effecting repairs under sub-paragraph (ii) of this sub-clause, and time taken for such repairs shall not count against time granted under Clause 11(c).

(v) The Charterers shall indemnify the Owners against any liability, cost and/or expense whatsoever in respect of any loss of life, injury, damage or other loss to person or property howsoever arising from such assistance."

If the vessel renders salvage to property of the charterer which "was the object of the operation" under the charterparty, the vessel under paragraph (c) waives its claim to salvage and performs the salvage upon a contractual basis. This basis is as follows:

(i) The vessel remains on hire.

(ii) The charterers are to be responsible for: (a) any payments which the owners have to make to their master and crew in connection with the service; (b) for any damage sustained by the vessel; (c) for any spillages and emissions of pollutants "however caused within the offshore site" (which is defined in Clause 35 as being a zone of three miles around the charterers' "offshore unit" to which the vessel is rendering services) and any pollution resulting from the same wherever occurring; and, lastly (d) any loss or damage to property or injury or death to personnel.

(iii) The vessel will not be off-hire "as a consequence of giving such assistance" and during the effecting of any repairs to damage to the vessel resulting from such salvage. Such repairs are not to count in connection with the vessel's drydocking and maintenance time provided for by Clause 11(c).

The matters set out in (i) to (iii) above remain unaffected by any neglect or default by the owners or their personnel.

15. Clause 16: "Lien"

"16. Lien

The Owners shall have a lien upon all cargoes for all claims against the Charterers under this Charter Party and the Charterers shall have a lien on the Vessel for all monies paid in advance and not earned. The Charterers will not suffer, nor permit to be continued, any lien or encumbrance incurred by them or their agents, which might have priority over the title and interest of the Owners in the Vessel. Except as provided in Clause 12, the Charterers shall indemnify and hold the Owners harmless against any lien of whatsoever nature arising upon the Vessel during the Charter Period while she is under the control of the Charterers, and against any claims against the Owners arising out of the operation of the Vessel by the Charterers or out of any neglect of the Charterers in relation to the Vessel or the operation thereof. Should the Vessel be arrested by reason of claims or liens arising out of her operation hereunder, unless brought about by the act or neglect of the Owners, the Charterers shall at their own expense take all reasonable steps to secure that within a reasonable time the Vessel is released and at their own expense put up bail to secure release of the Vessel."

This clause is wider than the "Towcon" and "Towhire" lien and reflects the fact that the vessel may have on board cargoes belonging to the charterer or being shipped by him to others. For such clauses generally: see *Wilford*, pp. 479 *et seq.*

16. Clause 17: "Sublet and assignment"

This clause (which is reproduced in the full text of the charter in Appendix 4 below) gives the charterers the right to sub-charter the vessel subject to the owners' consent. The owners have a similar right to assign or transfer the charter.

17. Clause 18: "Substitute vessel"

"18. Substitute Vessel
The Owners shall be entitled at any time, whether before delivery or at any other time during the Charter Period, to provide a substitute vessel, subject to the Charterers' prior approval which shall not be unreasonably withheld."

Cf. Clause 14 of the "Towcon" form (see p. 102 above).

18. Clause 19: "War"

This is a war (and similar perils) clause in fairly common form. It is reproduced in the full text of the charter in Appendix 4 below. It prevents the vessel from being employed in war or similar danger zones without the owners' consent: paragraph (a). If such consent is granted, the owners are entitled to charge the additional insurance premiums to the charterers: paragraphs (b) and (c). Paragraph (e) deals with an outbreak of war (in the broad sense, whether there is formal declaration or not) between countries named in Box 30 or involving the country of the vessel's flag. See generally *Cooke* at pp. 515–535 and pp. 681–682.

19. Clause 20: "Excluded ports"

"20. Excluded Ports
(a) The Vessel shall not be ordered to nor bound to enter without the Owners' written permission (a) any place where fever or epidemics are prevalent or to which the Master, Officers and Crew by law are not bound to follow the Vessel; (b) any ice-bound place or any place where lights, lightships, marks and buoys are or are likely to be withdrawn by reason of ice on the Vessel's arrival or where there is risk that ordinarily the Vessel will not be able on account of ice to reach the place or to get out after having completed her operations. The Vessel shall not be obliged to force ice nor to follow an icebreaker. If, on account of ice, the Master considers it dangerous to remain at the loading or discharging place for fear of the Vessel being frozen in and/or damaged, he has liberty to sail to a convenient open place and await the Charterers' fresh instructions.
(b) Should the Vessel approach or be brought or ordered within such place, or be exposed in any way to the said risks, the Owners shall be entitled from time to time to insure their interest in the Vessel and/or Hire against any of the risk likely to be involved thereby on such terms as they shall think fit, the Charterers to make a refund to the Owners of the premium on demand. Notwithstanding the terms of Clause 11 Hire shall be paid for all time lost including any lost owing to loss of or sickness or injury to the Master, Officers, Crew or passengers or to the action of the Crew in refusing to proceed to such place or to be exposed to such risks."

Such ports are ports affected by fever or epidemic, by legal impediments on the vessel's personnel and, principally, see paragraph (b), ice-bound or ice-affected ports.

They are dealt with in the same way as war or similar danger zones under Clause 18. *Cf.* the General Ice Clause in the Gencon charter form, as to which see *Cooke*, pp. 536–543.

20. Clauses 21 to 36: General provisions

The concluding provisions are largely typical time charterparty provisions or standard form provisions and appear in the full text of the charter in Appendix 4 below:

(i) *Clause 21: "General Average and New Jason Clause"*: see *Cooke*, pp. 675–676. It should be noted that the clause refers to adjustment of general average being in accordance with the York-Antwerp Rules of 1974. The Rules have recently been revised as the York-Antwerp Rules 1994 in aspects which touch directly on the interest of tug and tow. See Chapter 9 below.

(ii) *Clause 22: "Both-to-blame collision clause"*: see *Cooke* pp. 679–680.

(iii) *Clause 23: "Structural Alterations and Additional Equipment"*. The charterer may need to fit the vessel with some dedicated structure such as a platform, or with some special equipment, for the performance of the service to be carried out by the vessel. He may do so with the owner's consent but he must remove the same at the end of the charterparty and is responsible for the maintenance of it during the charter. Such structure or equipment will fall outside the owners' warranty as to the condition of the vessel as set out in Clause 3.

(iv) *Clause 24: "Health and Safety"*, i.e., of vessel's crew; this is to be maintained by the owners in accordance with all applicable regulations.

(v) *Clause 25: "Taxes"*. These are to be borne by each party. However, if the "area of operation" of the vessel as originally fixed by the parties in Box 17 is changed resulting in a documented increase in owners' tax liability, there shall be an adjustment of hire accordingly. *Cf.* the similar approach found in Clause 10(c) to adjustment of hire.

(vi) *Clause 26: "Early Termination"*. This allows the charterers to terminate the charterparty on notice and upon the payment of a sum, called "the settlement sum" which is fixed and stated in Box 14. An automatic right of termination subject to notice provisions exists in the case of the requisition, confiscation, loss or long-term (what is meant by "long term" is to be specified by the parties in Box 32) breakdown of the vessel; the bankruptcy or repudiatory breach of any party or *force majeure* conditions exceeding 15 days.

(vii) *Clause 27: "Force Majeure"*. This is a *force majeure* provision in classical form. As to such clauses generally, see *Lebeaupin* v. *Crispin* [1920] 2 K.B. 714 and *Chitty on Contracts* (27th Edn.), Vol. I, paras. 14–121 *et seq.*

(viii) *Clause 28: "Notices and Invoices"*: the addresses for communications of these between the parties are identified in Boxes 21, 35 and 36.

(ix) *Clause 29: "Wreck Removal"*. The owners remain responsible, as is usual under a time charterparty, for all matters connected with the wreck of the chartered vessel.

(x) *Clause 30: "Confidentiality"*. This is a special provision particular to the "Supplytime 89" form.

"30. Confidentiality
All information or data obtained by the Owners in the performance of this Charter Party is the property of the Charterers, is confidential and shall not be disclosed without the prior written consent of the Charterers. The Owners shall use their best efforts to ensure that the Owners, any of their sub-contractors, and employees and agents thereof shall not disclose any such information or data."

It deals with the situation where because of the vessel's involvement in particular services for the charterers, the owners become aware of confidential information pertaining to the charterers' operations, for example, the location of test bore holes for a potential new oil or gas deposit. An enforceable obligation of confidentiality is imposed upon the owners; this will permit the hirer in a suitable case to restrain by injunctive relief any possible breach of confidence by the owners relating to the hirer's operations.

(xi) *Clause 31: "Law and Arbitration"*. Alternatives are given between London, New York and a specifically chosen place. If no alternative is chosen it is submitted that the arbitration clause becomes unenforceable: see *Lovelock (E.J.R.) Ltd* v. *Exportles* [1968] 1 Lloyd's Rep. 163 (C.A.) and the parties are thrown back, in the event of a dispute, upon the necessity of establishing the jurisdiction of a particular country's courts.

(xii) *Clause 32: "Entire Agreement"* clause.

(xiii) *Clause 33: "Severability Clause"*. *Cf.* Clause 23(a) of the "Towcon" and "Towhire" forms.

(xiv) *Clause 34: "Demise"*. The charterparty like any time charterparty is merely a contract for services and gives the charterer no possession of or possessory right in the vessel: see *Wilford*, pp. 529 *et seq.*, on the similar provision in Clause 26 of the NYPE form.

(xv) *Clause 35: "Definitions"*. This clause defines terms used frequently in the other clauses of the charterparty. Of particular importance are the following:

"'Offshore unit' is defined for the purposes of this Charter Party as any vessel, offshore installation, structure and/or mobile unit used in offshore exploration, construction, pipelaying or repair, exploitation or production.
'Offshore site' is defined for the purposes of this Charter Party as the area within three nautical miles of an 'offshore unit' from or to which the Owners are requested to take their Vessel by the Charterers."

Thus, in connection with the charterers' obligations as to the safety of the places of operation of the vessel under Clause 4(a) of Part II of the form, the charterers are to exercise due diligence in employing the vessel at a safe "offshore unit" as well as in a safe port or place. Similarly, in rendering salvage assistance to the charterers' property, the charterers are responsible for all pollution ensuing within the "offshore site" pursuant to Clause 15(c)(iii) of Part III of the form.

CHAPTER 6

Towage and Salvage

PART A. PRELIMINARY CONSIDERATIONS

1. The historical relationship between towage and salvage

Before the advent of the steam tug, towage of one vessel by another as the rendering of a commercial service by a vessel dedicated to towage was all but unknown. All vessels were sailing ships and want of wind or the awkward set of the wind would affect all such vessels equally. While in port some small towage and manoeuvring would be carried out by oarsmen, towage in the sense in which it is understood today, and as has been considered in Chapter 1 above, did not exist.

This is not to say that towage as an operation did not exist. The towing of one vessel by another commonly arose, but it arose in the context of one vessel rendering assistance to another vessel which was in distress, for example a vessel which had become stranded or which had lost her sails or her rudder. Towage rendered in such a context was usually simply a form, albeit perhaps the commonest form, of salvage assistance. Accordingly, towage when considered at law was considered in the context of a claim for salvage by one vessel in the respect of a salvage service rendered to another vessel; the issues between the parties were whether the service satisfied the requirements for such a claim and what was the appropriate level of remuneration.

With the coming of the steam tug, towage as a commercial operation became possible and tug owners built up their businesses in ports and in the great rivers. Their tugs could be engaged by vessels for towage in all circumstances, the towage being constrained only by the initially limited boiler power of the early paddle tugs. The size and power of the tugs grew and tugs became involved in long ocean tows. The owners of the vessel towed were usually anxious to keep the tug within the terms of the contract which had been concluded between them, especially those as to remuneration. Equally, the tug owner would often be faced with weather and towing conditions which he had not anticipated and which made the bargain less advantageous; in such a case, he often sought to contend that the service which he had rendered was one which fell outside the contract and which entitled him to additional salvage remuneration.

With the development of the steam tug in the early part of the nineteenth century, the operations in which such tugs became engaged expanded from the mere expediting of the progress through the water of the sailing vessel under tow (*cf.* the definition given of towage by Dr Lushington in *The Princess Alice* (1849) 3 Wm. Rob. 138) to wider services concerning the handling of vessels. Historically, the emergence of the professional salvor, that is to say, a person who keeps tugs and other vessels adapted for salvage work and ready for salvage work, followed the development of the large-scale towing companies. Such companies soon grew up in the large ports or where there were navigable waterways in which the sailing vessels particularly required handling and towing. By the end of the century, certain tug owners and operators had large fleets of tugs and such tugs were often very powerful. The tug operators were able to respond to requests for assistance from disabled vessels or vessels in distress and, indeed, to solicit salvage work from such vessels. Such salvage assistance was a useful adjunct to their usual field of operations and provided employment for tugs which might otherwise be idle. Where the largest tug operators were situated there grew up a commitment to and an experience in salvage which soon established their status as "professional". In Dutch and Scandinavian waters the tugs of three or four companies became established as the leaders in the provision of towage and salvage. The development of the salvage industry out of but as a part of the towage industry meant that increasingly towage and salvage contracts were kept separate. It also led to the growth of towage sub-contracts within the context of salvage as tug owners performing a salvage operation contracted in additional tugs from other operators.

2. The nature of salvage

Something as to the nature of salvage has been said above in Chapter 1. Salvage, unlike towage, has never been the subject of precise or satisfactory judicial definition. Indeed, it was stated by Lord Stowell in *The Governor Raffles* (1818) 2 Dods. 14 at p. 17 that:

"It has been said that no exact definition of salvage is given in any of the books. I do not know that it has, and I should be sorry to limit it by any definition now."

However, the underlying principle upon which it operates has frequently been the subject of judicial comment. In *The Calypso* (1828) 2 Hagg. 209 at pp. 217–218 Sir Christopher Robinson declared salvage "to be founded on the equity of remunerating private and individual services", while the distinguished American admiralty judge, Story J. stated in *The Henry Ewbank* (1883) 11 Fed. Cas. (Case No. 6376) 1166, at p. 1170:

"Salvage, it is true, is not a question of compensation *pro opera et labore* . . . it offers a premium by way of honorary reward, for a prompt and ready assistance to human sufferings; for a bold and fearless intrepidity; and for that affecting chivalry, which forgets itself in anxiety to save property, as well as life . . . a mixed question of public policy and private right, . . . "

The principal feature of salvage and its main point of distinction with towage is that salvage exists independently of any contract (although today commonly a form of contract is employed by salvor and salved such as the Lloyd's Open Form or LOF) and depends upon the satisfaction of various criteria before any claim to remuneration will lie. Notably, and in contrast with the concept of towage, the obligation of the vessel which is the subject of a salvage service to remunerate for that service is imposed by law irrespective of any contract. The rights of the salvor are, therefore, independent of any agreement while those of the tug-provider arise solely *ex contractu*. The distinction between the two concepts was well-described in *The Troilus* [1950] P. 92 by Denning L.J. who, at p. 110, stated:

"The obligation on ship and cargo to pay for salvage services is imposed by law irrespective of any contract, express or implied, to that effect; whereas the obligation to pay for towage services arises, if at all, from a contract, express or implied, to pay for them. This difference points the way to the true distinction between the nature of the services. Salvage services arise when the ship is in such danger that the master has no real choice in the matter but must, as a reasonable man, accept them from somebody or lose his ship, or leave it in some remote place; whereas towage services arise when the ship has reached such a position of safety that the shipowner has a freedom of choice either to refuse the service or to have repairs done locally or to contract for towage to get his ship home."

The non-contractual nature of the salvor's rights was also addressed by Sir James Hannen P. in *The Five Steel Barges* (1890) 15 P.D. 142 at p. 146 in the following terms:

"The jurisdiction which the court exercises in salvage cases is of a peculiarly equitable character. The right to salvage may arise out of an actual contract; but it does not necessarily do so. It is a legal liability arising out of the fact that property has been saved, that the owner of the property has had the benefit of it shall make remuneration to those who have conferred the benefit upon him, notwithstanding that he has not entered into any contract on the subject."

See also *The Hestia* [1895] P. 193 per Bruce J. at pp. 199 to 200 and *The Tojo Maru* [1972] A.C. 242 per Lord Diplock at p. 292.

3. The 1989 Salvage Convention

The English law of salvage has been considerably affected by the recent enactment of the 1989 Salvage Convention by section 1(1) of the Merchant Shipping (Salvage and Pollution) Act 1994. That Act has been repealed and replaced by the new codification statute, the Merchant Shipping Act 1995. Pursuant to section 224(1) of the 1995 Act (corresponding to section 1(1) of the 1994 Act), the Convention is to have the force of law in the United Kingdom. The Convention represents a codification of the traditional English law principles of salvage together with the implementation of changes which have been adopted piecemeal over the decade since the revision of the Lloyd's Open Form of salvage agreement in 1980 relating principally to the remuneration of salvors in respect of services rendered in connection with environmental hazards. The Convention was brought into force on 1 January 1995 by the Merchant Shipping (Salvage and Pollution) Act 1994 (Commencement No. 2) Order 1994 (S.I. 1994 No. 2971). It is now the starting point in considering salvage questions.

4. The essential criteria for salvage

The law of salvage and the application of salvage principles is beyond the scope of this book; the leading texts are *Kennedy on the Law of Salvage* (5th Edn.), Stevens, edited by David Steel Q.C. and Dr Francis Rose, and *The Maritime Law of Salvage* (2nd Edn.) by Geoffrey Brice Q.C. The most up-to-date, compendious and authoritative guide to the 1989 Salvage Convention and to the inter-relationship between the Convention and the English law of salvage before 1 January 1995 is the commentary of Professor Nicholas Gaskell on the Merchant Shipping Act 1994 in *Current Law Statutes*, 1994, Volume II; see also by Gaskell [1990] L.M.C.L.Q. 352 and (1991) 16 *Tulane Maritime Law Journal* 1; see too G. Brice Q.C. [1990] L.M.C.L.Q. 32. However, a brief account of the general principles is necessary to put the relationship between towage and salvage service into context.

The principles of salvage will apply only where four essential requirements are met. From these requirements the differences between towage and salvage are readily apparent.

(1) Subject of salvage

There must be a recognised subject of salvage. Salvage can only arise if the service is rendered to an object or property which the law recognises as having to contribute salvage remuneration, whereas, as has been seen above, towage can be and frequently is performed in respect of a wide variety of water-borne objects. The most common objects recognised as proper subjects of salvage are ships and cargo. Following the enactment of the 1989 Salvage Convention, these subjects have been restated: vessel means any ship or craft or structure capable of navigation, and property means any property not permanently and intentionally attached to the shoreline: see e.g. Articles 1(b) and (c). The older cases on the subject of salvage must be read with considerable caution in the light of these changes.

This requirement gives rise to a potential problem in the field of towage where the tug may seek to assert salvage in relation to a service rendered to a water-borne object which does not correspond to a ship, vessel or boat, take for example a caisson or floating piece of machinery or a rig-part. The potential difficulties are exemplified by the case of *The Gas Float Whitton* [1897] A.C. 337 (H.L.), but see especially the judgment of Lord Esher M.R. in the Court of Appeal, [1896] P. 42 at pp. 63–64, which was approved by the House of Lords. In that case, the courts had to consider a service rendered to a gas float used as a fixed navigational aid which, while having a ship-shaped hull, was never intended for and was very ill-suited for navigation. It was held that the float was not a ship and therefore a service rendered to it was not salvage. Lord Esher M.R. stated that "whether salvage could be granted for the saving of what is called a lightship may be doubtful". This case must be of doubtful guidance following the definitions now given by the 1989 Salvage Convention. It may be noted that in *The North Goodwin No. 16* [1980] 1 Lloyd's Rep. 71, it was not contested between the parties and the court accepted that a lightship under tow under the U.K. Standard Conditions was capable of being a subject in salvage; for the facts of this case, see above at p. 64. *Cf.* also *The Boiler ex The Elephant* (1891) 64 L.T. 543 where salvage was recovered by a default judgment in respect of the saving of a ship's boiler found floating in open seas, although this case may have turned on the fact that wreck and derelict is a recognised object of salvage.

The problem arose acutely in the towage of objects used in the offshore industry, many of which corresponded with difficulty to inclusion in the recognised classes of salvage subject. It is submitted that many of the potential problems have been removed by the width of the definitions given by Article 1, especially that of "property" given by Article 1(c) which will be wide enough to cover almost all water-borne objects. However, a very important exclusion from subjects of salvage provided for by the 1989 Salvage Convention should be noted. By Article 3 it is stated that the Convention does not apply to "fixed or floating platforms or to mobile offshore drilling units" when the same "are on location engaged in the exploration, exploitation or production of sea-bed mineral resources". This will leave unaffected their status either as vessels or property when the same are under tow.

(2) Danger

The subject of salvage must have encountered a marine peril or found itself in a position of danger which requires a salvage service in order to preserve it from loss or damage and bring it to a position of safety: see *The Wilhelmine* (1842) 1 Notes of Cases 376. In that case, Dr Lushington described (at p. 378) the presence of danger as one of the foundations of the existence of a right to salvage. The requirement of danger is not that the danger should be absolute or immediate although it must be real and sensible (see *Kennedy, op. cit.*, at paragraph 303; see also *The Mount Cythnos* (1937) 58 Ll. L. Rep. 18, in which Sir Boyd Merriman P. stated that, for danger to be operative for salvage purposes, it must not be "fanciful but a real possibility", see p. 25). As was confirmed in *The Charlotte* (1848) 3 W. Rob. 68 at p. 71 by Dr Lushington, it is sufficient that the subject of the service is facing or has encountered a state of affairs which might possibly expose it to loss or damage if the service in question were not rendered. In that case, a tow, en route from Bombay to Liverpool, became caught up amongst breakers during a violent gale with fog, rain and heavy seas. She began to drift toward the rocks. The anchors were let go but did not hold. The masts, sails and rigging were cut as a last resort. A vessel was launched from the shore and those on board tried to board the tow without success. As the gale moderated, a second boat was launched and the tow was boarded. Subsequently, four boats took her in tow and, keeping her clear of the breakers, towed her to safety. Although she was in no immediate danger of being wrecked, Dr Lushington had no hesitation in finding that the service was one of salvage, stating at p. 71:

"It is not necessary, I conceive, that the distress should be actual or immediate, or that the danger should be imminent and absolute; it will be sufficient if, at the time the assistance is rendered, the ship has encountered any damage or misfortune which might possibly expose her to destruction if the services were not rendered."

The danger can range from the risk of total loss to the risk of damage or even capture. As Dr Lushington went on to put it in *The Phantom* (1866) L.R. 1 A. & E. 58 at p. 60:

"It is not necessary that there should be absolute danger in order to constitute a salvage service, it is sufficient if there is a state of difficulty and reasonable apprehension."

(3) Voluntariness

To constitute a salvage service, the service must be performed by a volunteer, that is to say, by a person who is not under a pre-existing contractual or other legally recognised duty to perform that service: see *Brice* (*op. cit.*), at paragraph 1–169. As Lord Stowell expressed it in a celebrated dictum in *The Neptune* (1824) 1 Hagg. 227 at p. 236, for a person to be capable of being recognised by the court as a salvor that person must be:

"A person who, without any particular relation to a ship in distress, proffers any useful service, and gives it as a volunteer adventurer, without any pre-existing covenant that connected him with the duty of employing himself for the preservation of that ship."

It is this requirement which marks the great dividing line and difference between salvage and towage. Given that a tug can easily perform the same service either in the context of a salvage operation or in the context of a contract for services, the question has often arisen as to whether a particular service rendered by the tug is a service which it was obliged to render pursuant to or which fell within the scope of what the tug had agreed to do under the tug's "pre-existing covenant". The importance of the question most commonly lies in the difference in remuneration: if the service is a contractual rate, the tug is entitled only to the contract rate or, if none has been agreed, to a *quantum meruit* assessed by reference to the value of the services, but if the service is salvage then the tug will be entitled to a usually enhanced level of remuneration.

The dividing line between what *Bucknill on Tug and Tow*, 2nd Edn. at p. 1 described as "work done under a towage contract as distinguished from towage work done by a salvor" is a difficult but important question. It is considered below in Part B.

(4) Success

To entitle the salvor to recover salvage remuneration the service must succeed in, or at least meritoriously contribute to, the preserving of the subject of the service from the danger or peril: see *Owners of the S.S. Melanie* v. *Owners of the S.S. San Onofre* [1925] A.C. 246 and the famous speech of Lord Phillimore at pp. 262–263. As it was put by the 1910 Brussels Convention on Salvage, the service had to have had "a useful result" or "a beneficial result"; the 1989 Salvage Convention in its Articles 12.1 and 12.2 uses simply the term "a useful result". While this requirement has received some qualification in the field of services rendered for the attempted prevention of pollution or for the protection of the marine environment, in particular under Article 14 of the 1989 Salvage Convention, the requirement remains a critical one in ordinary cases of salvage.

The contrast with towage is clear: under a towage contract the tug is entitled to be paid for the service rendered under and in accordance with the terms of the contract. Whether the service has been successful or has achieved the aim of the contract is not of itself decisive. So, where as may occur, the contract provides for the payment of a lump sum to be earned at a particular stage in the towage service, the fact that the tow is lost or the contract is not performed thereafter will not affect the right to that payment, albeit that the tow may have a cross-claim. Remuneration for the towage service will ordinarily be made according to the terms of the contract or at a reasonable rate for the service on the basis of *quantum meruit*: see *The Glaisdale* (1945) 78 Ll. L.

Rep. 477, in which a tug was engaged to tow a steamer and encountered difficulties which necessitated the services of a second tug; both tugs claimed salvage and, in dismissing their claims, Scott L.J. noted at p. 478:

" . . . had the tugs asked for towage remuneration, the second tug would certainly have got a fair *quantum meruit* . . . "

On a simple contractual basis, it follows that the towage service will be fully remunerated provided that it is properly performed and regardless of any success or failure in bringing the tow to safety: see *Anderson* v. *Ocean Steamship Co.* (1883) 13 Q.B.D. 651, at pp. 660 to 661 per Brett M.R. Notwithstanding the view of Dr Lushington in *The Reward* (1841) 1 Wm. Rob. at 177, it is clear that a tug may conclude and perform a simple towage contract without giving rise to a claim for salvage, notwithstanding that the tow has suffered injury or damage and is faced with some danger: see again *Anderson* v. *Ocean Steamship Co.* (1883) 13 Q.B.D. 651.

Connected with the typical towage contract is the case where salvage services are rendered under a contract which is a hybrid towage/salvage contract; such services are usually referred to as "engaged services" and special considerations apply as to them: see for example the special equitable jurisdiction of the Admiralty Court referred to in Chapter 1 above. One such consideration flowing from the hybrid nature of such services is the absence of a requirement that the service be successful. This question and whether the concept of "engaged services" has survived the enactment of the 1989 Salvage Convention is considered further below in Part C.

PART B. FROM TOWAGE SERVICE TO SALVAGE SERVICE

The circumstances in which a towage service is converted into a salvage service can only be broadly defined. It is often very difficult to isolate the precise moment at which a salvage entitlement arises. As was stated by Lord Cranworth L.C. in *Boyse* v. *Rossborough* (1857) 6 H.L.C. 3 at p. 45 (in a passage worthy of A. P. Herbert's Lord Mildew), cited by Gorell Barnes J. in *The Liverpool* [1893] P. 154 at p. 161 on the question of the change from towage to salvage:

"There is no possibility of mistaking midnight for noon; but at what precise moment twilight becomes darkness is hard to determine."

1. The issues and questions arising

Where a tug is engaged to tow a vessel, the extent of its obligations to perform the contract service will be defined by the contract, either by the express terms and conditions used by the parties or incorporated by them from one of the standard forms or, alternatively, in the absence of such express terms by the terms implied at common law and as discussed in the cases already considered above in Chapter 2, such as *The Minnehaha* and *The Julia*. However, the very nature of towage is such that very often the tug and tow will encounter conditions rather different from what was contemplated at the time the contract was made; these may require the tug to perform services of a different kind from those envisaged as being involved in the contract work. In such circumstances, the tug will wish to seek additional remuneration. From the perspective of the tow, the contract must necessarily be taken to cover all ordinary eventualities and to have some latitude in the services which the tug may have to perform. Similarly, as has been seen, when a supervening peril occurs, the tug is under an obligation, by reason of the contractual relationship which already exists between the parties, to stand by and to assist the tow.

The Admiralty Court from the earliest days of its jurisdiction over towage cases sought to strike a balance between the interest of the tug to be properly remunerated for extra-contractual services and that of the tow to be sufficiently protected from attempts by the tug to escape from the confines of the towage contract. As it was put by Gorell Barnes J. in *The Liverpool* [1893] P. 154 at p. 164:

"I ought to say that, while it is the duty of the court to take care to adequately remunerate all salvors for salvage services, in order to encourage those services to be performed, and in this spirit salvage services are always looked upon in this Court, it is equally the duty of the court to see, where a towing contract has been made, that a little departure from the exact mode in which that contract is to be performed is not magnified so as to convert towage into salvage services."

2. The approach in *The Minnehaha*

The relationship between these issues was first considered in *The Minnehaha* (1861) 15 Moo. P.C. 133 in the speech of Lord Kingsdown, part of which has already been referred to in Chapter 2. In that case, a contract of towage was held by the Privy Council to have been terminated by reason of the extreme weather conditions prevailing, the ebb tide and the breaking of the tug's hawser. The Privy Council's statement at pp. 152 to 154 of the law as to the test for the conversion of towage into salvage and as to the circumstances which are to be regarded as within and outside the original towage contract is definitive and exhaustive and it merits citation in full.

"When a steam-boat engages to tow a vessel for a certain remuneration from one point to another, she does not warrant that she will be able to do so and will do so under all circumstances and at all hazards; but she does engage that she will use her best endeavours for that purpose, and will bring to the task competent skill, and such a crew, tackle and equipments, as are reasonably to be expected in a vessel of her class.

She may be prevented from fulfilling her contract by a *vis major*, by accidents which were not contemplated, and which may render the fulfilment of her contract impossible, and in such case, by the general rule of law, she is relieved from her obligations.

But she does not become relieved from her obligations because unforeseen difficulties occur in the completion of her task; because the performance of the task is interrupted, or cannot be completed in the mode in which it was originally intended, as by the breaking of the ship's hawser. But if in the discharge of this task, by sudden violence of wind or waves, or other accidents, the ship in tow is placed in danger, and the towing-vessel incurs risks and performs duties which were not within the scope of her original engagement, she is entitled to additional remuneration for additional services if the ship be saved, and may claim as a salvor, instead of being restricted to the sum stipulated to be paid for mere towage. Whether this larger remuneration is to be considered as in addition to, or in substitution for, the price of towage is of little consequence practically. The measure of the sum to be allowed as salvage would, of course, be increased or diminished according as to whether the price of towage was or was not included in it. In the cases on this subject, the towage contract is generally spoken of as superseded by the right to salvage.

It is not disputed that these are the rules which are acted upon in the Court of Admiralty, and they appear to their Lordships to be founded in reason and in public policy, and to be not inconsistent with legal principles.

The tug is relieved from the performance of her contract by the impossibility of performing it, but if the performance of it be possible, and in the course of it in the ship in her charge is exposed, by unavoidable accident, to dangers which require from the tug services of a different class and bearing a higher rate of payment, it is held to be implied in the contract that she shall be paid at such higher rate.

To hold, on the one hand, that a tug, having contracted to tow, is bound, whatever happens after the contract, though not in the contemplation of the parties, and at all hazards to herself, to take the ship to her destination; or, on the other, that the moment the performance of the contract is interrupted, or its completion in the mode originally intended becomes impossible, the tug is relieved from all further duty, and at liberty to abandon the ship in her charge to her fate, would be alike inconsistent with the public interest.

The rule as it is established guards against both inconveniences, and provides at the same time for the safety of the ship and the just remuneration of the tug. The rule has been long settled: parties enter into towage contracts on the faith of it; and we should be extremely sorry that any doubt should be supposed to exist upon it.

It is said that it has never been brought before us for decision. If so, considering how often the rule has been acted upon, the necessary inference is that it has never been made the subject of appeal because it has been universally acquiesced in."

From this judgment came the first articulation of a two-fold requirement for the circumstances in which a tug owner would be able to claim salvage, notwithstanding the existence of a towage contract: *first*, unforeseen difficulties in the completion of the tug's task which place the tow in danger and, *secondly*, the incurring of risks and the performing of duties which were "not within the scope of the original engagement" or, as it was put later, the requirement from the tug of "services of a different class and bearing a higher rate of payment".

3. Its re-statement in the later cases

In the later cases, while the test for the conversion of a towage service into a salvage service has been restated and rephrased, the two-fold requirement laid down by Lord Kingsdown and as summarised above has been faithfully followed.

The test for the entitlement of a tug already bound under a towage contract to claim a salvage award in respect of services rendered by it to the tow was certainly more succinctly set out by Hill J. in *The Homewood* (1928) 31 Ll. L. Rep. 336. In that case, a tug was engaged to tow a steamer under a contract which provided that if the tug became separated from the tow and was prevented from completing the contract, the tug would be paid *pro rata* for the distance towed. In the course of the voyage, the wind blew up and the hawser parted, causing the steamer to come adrift with no propulsion. She dropped her anchors and her master and crew were taken off by lifeboat. The weather then deteriorated to such a degree that nothing could be done to assist her. The tug nevertheless kept her under observation and, when the conditions eased, came alongside and put two men aboard. Hill J. held that, in a towage of the kind in question, there must always be a risk of interruption and delay by bad weather, a risk that the hawser may part, and a risk that the tow may have to anchor. They were all matters within the scope of the contract. However, the contract did not contemplate that the crew of the tow would be taken off and that she would be left at anchor unmanned, nor that she would have to be towed without anchors, which it had been necessary to slip. Nor, it was said, did the contract contemplate that the tug would be used to put the crew of the steamer back aboard, as in fact occurred, and thereby incur risk of damage to the tug. In the circumstances, it was held that a salvage claim was appropriate. At p. 339 Hill J. stated the applicable test in the following terms:

"To constitute a salvage service by a tug under contract to tow two elements are necessary: (1) that the tow is in danger by reason of circumstances which could not reasonably have been contemplated by the parties; and (2) that risks are incurred or duties performed by the tug which could not reasonably be held to be within the scope of the contract."

The test laid down by Hill J. in *The Homewood* (1928) 31 Ll. L. Rep. 336 was applied by Langton J. in three leading cases in 1940 and 1941. In the first, *The Trevorian* (1940) 66 Ll. L. Rep. 45, Langton J. restated the test in this way at p. 49:

"The questions I have to ask myself are these: first, was the service which the [tug] undertook turned into a salvage service by reason of the fact that it differed in quality from the service she had originally undertaken?; and, secondly, as regards [the second tug], was she called upon to assist *The Trevorian* when *The Trevorian* was in a position of danger? . . . it has been said times without number that every incident or mishap that may take place in a towage service does not necessarily turn that towage service into anything else."

In the second, *The Glenbeg* (1940) 67 Ll. L. Rep. 437, two tugs had been engaged to tow a vessel but in the course of the operation the vessel fouled her propeller on a buoy as a result of going too slowly. Accordingly, she was in an "uncomfortable and unpleasant position", although not one which was critical or imminently dangerous. However, she risked drifting against a nearby wall if her propeller came free. Langton J. put the question at p. 441 in these terms, following Lord Kingsdown's alternative formulation of services falling outside the towage contract because they were services different due to "bearing a higher rate of payment":

"Is a ship in that condition, when tugs take her in tow, in a position which requires from the tugs services of a different class and therefore bearing a higher rate of payment than for ordinary towage? In other words, assuming that a contract had to be made to deal with the vessel in that condition, would the tug owner be ready to render services at the ordinary towage rate? The answer to that would obviously be 'No'."

The tug masters agreed that the services which they had rendered did not really differ from what they would have done in the normal way. Langton J. nevertheless felt obliged to ask himself the further question:

" . . . were they called upon to exert skill of a character which would not be necessary at all, and is not, therefore, contemplated in the ordinary service of a tug to a ship going up river?"

In answering this question in the affirmative, he awarded salvage on the basis that the tugs had exerted such skill both smartly and properly in rescuing the vessel from its position.

The last case in the trilogy is the decision in *The Domby* (1941) 69 Ll. L. Rep. 161 in which the owners of a tug alleged that the tow grounded during performance of the towage contract. Langton J. noted at p. 163:

"It has been laid down over and over again in this court that the work of contract tugs cannot be changed from that of contract into a matter of salvage merely because some unexpected incident happened to have taken place in the course of the towage. The whole of the circumstances must have changed in order to effect such a metamorphosis as to convert a contract of towage into salvage. If a vessel, which is being brought in by tugs under contract in circumstances of ordinary navigation, in fact gets into a position of real danger, and the services the tugs are called upon to perform are something quite different, not merely in quantity, but in quality, from what they were engaged to do, then it is proper that a claim of salvage should be admitted. But not every incident which happens to take place in the course of navigation can be admitted to bring a contract service into the far different realm of salvage."

On the facts, Langton J. held that the tow was never aground, that the conditions were calm with an ordinary tide, and that she had room to manoeuvre. Accordingly, he held that the tow was in no danger and the claims of the tug owners to an entitlement to salvage were dismissed.

More recently, the two-fold requirement for conversion of towage into salvage was applied in *The North Goodwin No. 16* [1980] 1 Lloyd's Rep. 71 by Sheen J. In that case, a light vessel was in the tow of a tug and was to be passed to two other tugs in order to be towed on to a berth. The two tugs were engaged under the U.K. Standard Conditions. At the time at which the tugs were due to take over the tow there was a gale blowing and a swell estimated at between three and four metres. One tug took the view that the conditions were too poor to take over the tow. The original, therefore, proceeded to tow the light vessel into shore where it was hoped that the change-over could be effected with the benefit of shelter. The tug was manoeuvred accordingly, but her master realised that he was too close to the shoreline and therefore swung to starboard. In the course of the turn, the hawser parted and the light vessel began to drift down wind. One of the other tugs went to the assistance of the light vessel, got a line aboard her, and towed her to an anchorage. That tug claimed a salvage reward in respect of that service. This was rejected by the court on the basis, first, that the light ship was not in danger despite the unforeseen circumstance since she had sufficient anchors to put out and, secondly, because in simply putting a line out to the light ship and towing her clear, the tug had not incurred risks or performed duties outside the scope of those contemplated by the contract. As Sheen J. stated:

"*Northsider* came out on a towage contract. It is implied in all such contracts that the tug will do her duty in case of accident and do all she can to take care of and protect the ship. From time to time towing ropes do part. If *Northsider* had already taken the light vessel in tow and the tow rope had parted in precisely the same position as that in which it parted, and thereafter *Northsider* had made fast again, I do not think it would have been arguable that the tow was in danger by reason of circumstances which could not reasonably have been contemplated by the parties, or that risks were incurred or duties performed by the tug which could not reasonably be held to be within the scope of the contract. In these circumstances, it being conceded that *Northsider* had come out of the protection of the piers pursuant to the terms of her contract, I do not think it can properly be said that risk were incurred or duties performed which were not within the scope of the contract."

In concluding his judgment, Sheen J. compendiously wrapped up the question in the following pragmatic test:

"The matter can be tested in another way. If, when *Northsider* came up with the light vessel, [the master] had offered the services of his tug on salvage terms, would that offer have been declined by [the captain of the light ship]? I have no doubt that it would have been declined."

It is clear from the decision of Hill J. in *The Homewood* that the courts will examine the nature of the danger with which the tow is faced and the nature of the services contemplated by the parties at the time of making the contract as compared with those in fact rendered not separately but in combination, or as it is put by the editors of *Kennedy* (*op. cit.*) at paragraph 513, the two elements of the test will be "judged cumulatively". Nevertheless, it is helpful to consider how the content of each limb of the two-fold test has been approached by the courts.

4. The test as expressed in the Salvage Conventions

The common law approach was largely embodied in the Brussels Convention on Salvage 1910 which, by Article 4, provided:

"A tug has no right to remuneration for assistance to or salvage of the vessel she is towing or of the vessel's cargo, except where she has rendered exceptional services which cannot be considered as rendered in fulfilment of the contract of towage."

Although the Brussels Convention did not expressly in this Article refer to the requirement of danger to the tow, given its general requirement of danger to the subject of salvage, this can be taken as implicit. The reflection of the English common law by the Brussels Convention rendered its formal incorporation in English law largely superfluous and unnecessary, although Articles 6, 10 and 11 were given statutory effect in sections 6 to 8 of the Maritime Conventions Act 1911. The common law principle is similarly reflected in the 1989 Salvage Convention whose Article 17 states:

"Article 17: Services rendered under existing contracts.
No payment is due under the provisions of this Convention unless the services rendered exceed what can be reasonably considered as due performance of a contract entered into before the danger arose."

It is submitted that the legal principles and the approach of the Admiralty Court in salvage and towage cases before the enactment are unaffected by Article 17 of the 1989 Salvage Convention and that this merely codifies the principle which the court has followed since the decision in *The Minnehaha*.

5. *The first requirement*: Unforeseen circumstances putting tow in danger

The conversion of towage into salvage depends firstly on the tug encountering operating conditions or circumstances affecting those conditions which are outside the contemplation of the parties at the time of contracting. However, it is not enough that there are unforeseen circumstances which arise in the course of the towage contract, those circumstances must be such as to put the tow in danger; in common with all salvage cases, the subject of the salvage (here the tow) must be in danger. As to the parameters of the requirement of danger in salvage, see in outline p. 155 above and the commentaries in *Kennedy* and *Brice*.

(1) Unforeseen circumstances

In assessing whether or not the conditions or circumstances are unforeseen, regard must be had to the contract of towage. The scope of the service which the tug undertakes to provide under the contract will be derived both from the express and implied terms of the contract and it will extend to cover all those services and to accept the risk of all of those eventualities which fall within the normal scope of operations which a tug will usually and reasonably supply and incur given the particular definition of the engagement. Thus, the circumstances which will be deemed to be within the contemplation of the parties will be different in the case of a contract for the towage of a vessel without the use of her main engines from Ushant to Santander via the Bay of Biscay in January from those in the case of a contract for the towage of a fully manned and powered V.L.C.C. from a berth at Fos to the roads in the clement weather and sea conditions of mid-August. The provisions of the contract are taken to extend to all problems or difficulties which might arise ordinarily in the course of its performance, for example interruptions during the towage: see *The Refrigerant* [1925] P. 130, in which, at p. 140, Bateson J. noted:

"In all these contracts it must be implied that the parties contemplate an interruption of the service. The price would be prohibitive if there was a guarantee that the towage would be without incident, and business could not be carried on on such terms."

Greater contractual remuneration *qua* salvage is therefore not available simply by reason of unforeseen difficulties alone: see *The Aboukir* (1905) 21 T.L.R. 200 and *The Domby* (1941) 69 Ll. L. Rep. 161. In the latter case, the tow grounded during the service but was in no danger and, as a consequence, Langton J. held, at p. 163, that:

" . . . the work of contract tugs cannot be changed from that of contract into a matter of salvage merely because some unexpected incident happens to take place in the course of the towage."

Nor is it available merely by reason of unexpected delay during the towage service. A good illustration of this is to be found in *The Lampas* (1933) 45 Ll. L. Rep. 259 in which three tugs were engaged to turn a vessel at an oil jetty as she made to go alongside. The owners of the tugs claimed that in the course of the manoeuvre the vessel took the ground. Bateson J. found as a fact that she was only smelling the ground and possibly sticking with her keel. The vessel was, he held, never in any real danger. Accordingly, at p. 262, he stated:

"I do not think in this case that the tugs did any more than could be expected from them according to their contract. They have got to keep the ship out of trouble—that is what they are taken for in narrow waters like this—and the slightly extra time (I think perhaps half an hour) they were engaged on this ship does not amount to anything more than what they could naturally be asked to do in taking a ship to her berth in this way. I do not think they rendered any extra services; I do not think they ran any extra risk, and, even if the ship was in a little danger, it was not sufficient to support a claim for salvage."

In respect of delay, see also *The Hjemmett* (1880) 5 P.D. 227, in which the tug owner's claim for detention or demurrage, arising out of delay to the towage operation caused by the refusal of the master of the towage operation to proceed with it until certain collision wreckage and damage to his vessel had been cleared and repaired, was dismissed by Sir Robert Phillimore. In *The Five Steel Barges* (1890) 15 P.D. 142, Sir James Hannen P. remarked, at p. 144, of the tug owners:

"They must also have taken into consideration that they were liable to delays, . . . No doubt it was somewhat longer than could have been expected; but I do not attach great importance to the delay . . . "

   Other operational difficulties will not normally affect the nature of the service which is performed: see, for example, *The Liverpool* [1893] P. 154 in which the tow smelled the ground with a consequent risk of grounding and bottom damage, and in which the towing-hawser parted, without giving rise to salvage remuneration; similarly, *The Annapolis* (1861) Lush. 355 in which the tow became entangled with a third vessel. For the same reasons, a deterioration in weather conditions will not normally or without more take the service rendered in such conditions outside the ambit of the contract. Thus, in *The Slaney* [1951] 2 Lloyd's Rep. 538, the tow had lost the use of her engines, was at anchor in a wind which rose temporarily from a force two to a force six gusting seven, and required to be towed into port. Lord Merriman P. found that, although the weather had deteriorated, there was nothing in that deterioration which was not expected or to be expected at that time of the year; and that there was no service or duty performed by the tug which could not reasonably be held to be within the scope of the contract. In holding that the services of the tugs were "mere towage", he stated with characteristic terseness, at p. 543:

"We have all looked at the relevant passages . . . of the well-known textbook by the late Lord Justice Kennedy [i.e. *Kennedy on Salvage*], and bearing in mind that under the heading 'Principles by which the right to salvage is governed', it is stipulated that, because fair or moderate weather changes to ordinary bad weather—ordinary bad weather—or because there is some damage to the tow, even that does not change towage into salvage, I am asked nevertheless to consider that this case comes within the proposition stated by the late Mr Justice Hill in *The Homewood* (1928) 31 Ll. L. Rep. 336 at p. 339 . . . . In my opinion, neither the one proposition nor the other is within measurable distance of being satisfied."

See also *The Galatea* (1858) Swab. 349, and *The I.C. Potter* (1870) L.R. 3 A. & E. 292, in both of which good weather conditions rapidly deteriorated, although only to such an extent as to be no worse than might ordinarily be anticipated given the nature of the contract service being carried out. Similarly, ordinary difficulties in the service due to the condition of the tow or to the ordinary hazards of the operation, such as, typically, the parting of tow-lines, are difficulties which the tug owner is to be taken as having accepted. As Lord Kingsdown said in *The Minnehaha* (1861) 15 Moo. P.C. 133 at p. 153:

"[The towing-vessel] does not become relieved from her obligations because unforeseen difficulties occur in the completion of her task, because the performance of the task is interrupted, or cannot be completed in the mode in which it was originally intended, as by the breaking of the ship's hawser."

It follows that what is required in order to be able to set up the most basic claim for greater remuneration than that for which the contract provides on the basis of salvage is a significant change in the operating conditions of the towage service.

(2) Circumstances creative of danger for the tow

As to the requirement that the unforeseen circumstances should put the tow in danger, the cases are clear, even if the expression of the requirement of danger is not express in the salvage conventions, as seen above. In *The I.C. Potter* (1870) L.R. 3 A. & E. 292, the tug *Retriever* was engaged to tow the *I.C. Potter* into Liverpool for £45. During the operation a hurricane blew up and the vessels were placed in serious danger. The tug continued to tow and thereby prevented the tow from drifting upon a lee-shore. The wind soon moderated and the tug brought her tow to safety in Liverpool. The tug owner was awarded salvage in the sum of £500. In the course of his judgment, Sir Robert Phillimore stated at pp. 298–299:

" . . . a contract once entered into cannot be broken merely because a change of weather or other supervening circumstances have rendered the execution of it more onerous than was antici- pated . . . there must be among the supervening circumstances an element of serious danger, not in contemplation of the parties to the contract, in order to justify the abandonment of that contract and to found a salvage service . . . . The continuance of the towage, therefore, in these circumstances, which placed both life and property in danger, became . . . a salvage service."

It was made clear by the judge that, in order to give rise to a salvage award, it was not necessary that the towage service for which the tug was engaged be interrupted but that it was necessary for the tow to be placed in danger by the new circumstances. Similarly, clear authority for this proposition that the unforeseen circumstance must be one productive of danger for the tow is provided by the decision in *The Dimitrios N. Bogiazides* (1930) 37 Ll. L. Rep. 27. In that case, the claim of the owners of a tug to an entitlement to salvage failed on the ground that the tow was in no substantial danger and that the services were no more than towage services. The tow was at anchor in heavy gusts and squalls which affected her to some extent. However, the pilot on board used her engines to keep her in position and used the anchor to keep her head into the wind. The master nevertheless wished to engage the services of a tug and thus the tug was sent out in response to the vessel's signals. The tug made fast with no real difficulty and proceeded to tow the vessel to a better position. The tug was assisted by the engines of the tow. In the course of his judgment, Bateson J. commented at page 32:

"In these circumstances, I cannot myself see how it can be said that this is a salvage service at all. It does not seem to me that this ship was in any real or apprehended danger either in herself or from her master's excitability . . . the Pilot had full control of the ship . . . it is a little difficult to say what [danger she was in], except that she had trouble in getting herself head to wind and had got her port anchor leading out behind her and could not very well get it up without some assistance from the tug at the time when she did get it up, and that was a position which might develop into danger if there had been a squall hard enough to overcome a sound ship with helm and engines . . . . It seems to me a very remote possibility in order to say that something should be given by way of salvage award."

A similar approach to the requirement of danger was adopted by Hill J. in *The Matina* (1920) 2 Ll. L. Rep. 360. Two tugs were ordered to assist a steamer in docking, but during the towage operation the tow-rope upon which one tug was heaving parted and fouled the propeller of the steamer. The steamer then drifted and grounded. The tug then came to the westward of the steamer and began to push the starboard side in an attempt to free her, whilst the second tug continued to hold her bows steady. The steamer nonetheless remained aground. The tug then moved to the stern of the steamer and began to pull. After some minutes, with their engines full ahead, the tugs succeeded in pulling the steamer clear. On the basis that she had been rescued from a position of great danger by well and properly rendered services, the crew of the tugs claimed an entitlement to salvage. Hill J., applying the principles laid down in *The Minnehaha* (1861) 15 Moo. P.C. 133 and *The Liverpool* [1893] P. 154, asked the following questions (at p. 363):

" . . . was the *Matina* in any immediate danger? . . . Did either of the tugs incur any risk or render any services beyond what was reasonably to be expected of her in the performance of the towage contract?"

On the facts, Hill J. held that there was no danger to her until, after some hours, the tide fell, and held also that she might have been got away by ropes carried out to the pier or by the ebb tide setting her off. Accordingly, he held that there was no immediate danger. As regards any risk of danger to the tugs, Hill J. found that the second tug, in holding the steamer, did nothing beyond what was required in an ordinary docking; in respect of the other tug, a dictum from *The Liverpool* [1893] P. 154, was applied:

"The tug is engaged for the purpose of avoiding dangers which a vessel of this size must to some extent run in entering a dock."

Hill J. added:

"One of those dangers is that a hawser may part and that the ship may be set out of position. In such an event, it is clearly the duty of the tug to make fast again and bring the ship back into position. I am not prepared to say that it is not her duty, if occasion calls for it, to push as well as to tow . . . "

Accordingly, he found that the first tug did nothing beyond what would normally be expected of a docking operation, and that neither tug had performed in such a way as to convert the towage contract into a salvage service.

A further illustration of the principle which must be applied in determining the effect of a particular danger and the approach which must be adopted by the court is provided in *The Lolin* (1931) 39 Ll. L. Rep.182 in which three tugs came to the aid of a vessel. The vessel, in the tow of two tugs was alleged to have grounded. The plaintiff tug owners claimed that, with the additional assistance of the third tug, the vessel was refloated. Langton J. found as a fact that the vessel did not ground as alleged, but that she may have touched the bottom. He commented at p. 184:

" . . . one has to bear in mind that tugs engaged on an ordinary contract of towage service cannot in the performance of that service be debarred from claiming salvage where a real and unexpected danger has confronted the ship, and where they have been instrumental in saving her from that new, real and unexpected danger . . . in the first instance the court scrutinises narrowly the claim of vessels who are engaged upon towage services to be ranked as salvors, and having scrutinised it narrowly the court then goes on to consider, 'was there in the circumstances a really new and unexpected danger'."

In applying this statement of law to his findings of fact, Langton J. went on to say at p. 188:

" . . . is that [i.e. the touching] a danger, a new danger and a real danger, and is it such a change of circumstances as could not have been reasonably contemplated by the parties when they made the towage contract, and does it turn the case from towage into salvage? . . . I am quite satisfied that it does not."

However, in common with the ordinary salvage cases and the principles laid down in the cases of *The Charlotte* and *The Strathnaver* referred to above, the danger need not be immediate or absolute. In the towage case of *The Aztecs* (1870) 3 Asp. M.L.C. 326, the crew of a steamer found a casualty at anchor in a heavy breeze and were hailed by the captain. The casualty had suffered damage as a result of a collision and had lost much of her equipment, but was still able to steer. An agreement was reached that the steamer would tow the casualty into Harwich harbour, weather permitting. Every effort was made to bring the casualty in, but a sudden change of the wind to the North-East made the voyage impossible. The casualty was brought to an anchorage not far from where she was found. When the weather moderated, the casualty proceeded to safety. It was submitted by the owners of the casualty that the agreement had not been fulfilled and that the steamer could not therefore claim salvage. Sir Robert Phillimore held that fulfilment of the agreement was rendered impossible by a change in the weather, an Act of God, and that, accordingly, the services were in the nature of salvage. He held at p. 329:

"It is certainly a mistake as to the law of salvage to suppose that in order to constitute a salvage service a vessel must be in actual danger at the time when the services are rendered to her. The danger may be probable or imminent . . . "

(3) Danger to tow not of itself sufficient

However, the requirement is a dual one. A danger to the tow will not of itself necessarily entitle the tug to salvage remuneration or to abandon the towage contract in the absence of the circumstances unforeseen by the towage contract and the parties thereto. In *The Liverpool* [1893] P. 154 at p. 160 Gorell Barnes J. commented:

" . . . I do not think that the argument . . . can be placed quite so high as counsel endeavoured to put it, namely, that in all cases of danger to the salved property, the tug is entitled to a salvage award . . . "

In many cases, the dual aspect of the requirement of unforeseen circumstances creating danger for the tow has been subsumed in a reference to the presence of supervening danger which renders the contract incapable of performance in the contemplated way. While supervening danger as a term is of some utility, it should not be taken to replace the need both for the new circumstances and for the resultant danger. See the following instances where this type of approach has been adopted: "supervening circumstances" (per Sir Robert Phillimore in *The I.C. Potter* (1870) L.R. 3 A. & E. 292 at pp. 298–299), "an unforeseen and extraordinary peril" (per Dr Lushington in *The Saratoga* (1861) Lush. 318), and a "superior danger and service superior to towing" (again, per Dr Lushington, at first instance, in *The Minnehaha* (1861) Lush. 335), which causes the duty under the towage agreement to be "abandoned" (see again *The I.C. Potter* (1870) L.R. 3 A. & E. 292), "vacated" (see again *The Minnehaha* (1861) Lush. 335 per Dr Lushington), or "supervened" (see again *The Saratoga* (1861) Lush. 318 per Dr Lushington).

(4) No need for danger to the tug

It should be noted that while the unforeseen circumstances must be such as to put the tow into a situation of danger, it is not necessary that there be any danger presented thereby to *the tug* in order for salvage to be earned. This was made clear in *The Pericles* (1863) Br. & L. 80. In that case, a tug was engaged to tow a steamer and to dock her. During the course of the operation the steamer stuck in a basin and needed to be towed out again. In the course of towing her out, the tow-rope broke. Accordingly, she remained jammed with the tide falling. Along with other tugs, the original tug succeeded in freeing the steamer. Dr Lushington awarded salvage and stated that it is not a necessary element of salvage that there be risk to the salvor.

6. The second requirement: Service or services outside the scope of the contract

Even if the tug and tow encounter unforeseen circumstances and even if these are such as to put the tow in danger, the tug will still not be entitled to salvage and will be confined to the contract if the services which the tug renders are within the scope of the contract. To take an example: the tow-line unexpectedly parts while tug and tow are navigating in a channel; there is an unforeseen current caused by an outfall pipe which pushes the tow towards the shore; the tug goes about and re-connects without danger or difficulty. The service is entirely what one would expect the tug to be ready routinely to perform under the contract. In such an event, the tug will have no claim in salvage. In Lord Kingsdown's words in *The Minnehaha* (1861) 15 Moo. P.C. 133 cited above, was the service one "of a different class and bearing a higher rate of payment". In Langton J.'s formulation in *The Trevorian* (1940) 66 Ll. L. Rep. 45, did the service differ in quality from the service which the tug had originally undertaken?

It follows that, in determining whether or not the services provided actually differ in their nature from those which are required under the contract of towage, the contractual services must be carefully defined and compared with those in fact provided, as is suggested by Dr Lushington in *The White Star* (1866) L.R. 1 A. & E. 68. In that case, a tow dragged and slipped from both anchors during a break in the performance of a towage contract. This was the result of a heavy gale. The tug went to the assistance of the tow and put the master ashore to bring off further anchors. Dr Lushington held that putting the master ashore was an extra service, not connected in any way with the towage, and which merited a salvage award. He stated at pp. 70–71:

"The real question is, what are the contracting parties reasonably supposed to have intended by the engagement, and what degree of alteration had they a right to expect, because to suppose that the performance of the service would always be of the same character would be absurd. I apprehend that, when a master of a vessel contracts with the master of a tug, it is upon the supposition that the wind and weather, and the time for performing the service, will be what are ordinary at the time of year, and that the sum contracted for is that which is supposed to be a sufficient remuneration for the ordinary performance of the voyage. It may be a short voyage if all the circumstances are favourable, and it may be a long one if they are unfavourable. I shall submit to you that when an engagement is made, a contract, for a specific time, that contract must be adhered to, and is not to be broken hastily, unless it be shown that circumstances have occurred which could not have been within the contemplation of the parties, and that, such is the state of circumstances, that to insist upon the contract and hold it binding would be contrary to all principles of justice and equity. It should be utterly impossible to define all such circumstances, but I think we should never have any doubt in saying in any particular case what they were, which would give a right to abandon the contract . . . . If the tugs were merely ordinarily delayed in performing the service they must not have additional remuneration; but if the delay was unexpected, and beyond all contemplation, they must have something additional."

Sometimes the question of whether or not a service is within the scope of the contract may be answered by the express terms. If the contract provides that the tug shall tow from A to B and that she will hold the tow up on arrival as necessary, the holding up will be within the service. Contrast a contract which simply provides for the towage as was considered in *The Albion* (1861) Lush. 282, in which a tug was engaged to tow a steamer. Mid-way through the service, the vessels anchored. A gale arose and blew the steamer to sea, with loss of anchors and equipment. The tug was forced to shelter nearby. Once the weather had moderated, the tug put to sea to search for and to locate the steamer which, after considerable endeavour, she did. The steamer was then towed to London. The tug was awarded salvage for her efforts, including those in respect of the search and location of the steamer.

The situation is the same in the United States. In *Sinclair* v. *Cooper* 108 U.S. 352, a cargo vessel loaded with cotton engaged a tug to tow her down the Mississippi River. After towing for approximately 26 miles, tug and tow laid up at an anchorage for the night. Later in the evening, a fire was found to have started aboard the tow. With some speed, officers and crew of the tug, with the assistance of others, succeeded in extinguishing the blaze. Those aboard the tug claimed a salvage award on the ground that, in extinguishing the fire, they had performed a service which went beyond and was different in nature from that contemplated by the parties when the tug was initially engaged. In the course of the judgment, the court noted that:

"The contract . . . was to tow the ship, and did not include the rendering of any salvage service, by putting out fire or otherwise. Such a service, which . . . rescued the ship from an unforeseen and extraordinary peril, gave the owner, as well as the officers and crew of the towboat, a right to salvage."

See also *The Driade* [1959] 2 Lloyd's Rep. 311 (an engaged tug employed to tow held up a vessel and thereby became entitled to salvage remuneration) and *The Mount Cythnos* (1937) 58 Ll. L. Rep. 18 at p. 25, in which it was found that a tug which had in tow a vessel which subsequently became jammed in a dock entrance, and which succeeded in freeing the tow, was entitled to a salvage award. More recently, in *The*

North Goodwin No. 16 [1980] 1 Lloyd's Rep. 71, a light vessel was in the tow of a tug bound for the River Tyne. She was to be passed to two tugs which were engaged under the U.K. Standard Conditions (above), which provide at Clause 1(b)(v):

"Any service of whatsoever nature to be performed by the tug owner other than towing shall be deemed to cover the period commencing when the tug ... is placed physically at the disposal of the liner ... or if such be at a vessel when the tug ... is in a position to receive and forthwith carry out orders to come alongside and shall continue until the employment for which the tug ... has been engaged is ended ... "

At the time at which one of the tugs was due to take over the tow there was a gale blowing. Accordingly, the tow was brought closer in to facilitate the pick-up but the line parted. The waiting tug came out in rough conditions and pulled the light ship clear. She claimed a salvage reward in respect of that service. Sheen J. held, *inter alia*, that the service was entirely within the terms of the towage contract and that under the clause towing and the towage service had begun.

   More typically, the contract will not cover the matter expressly. In such a case, just as with a question of foreseeability in damages, in examining the nature of the services in fact provided, it is necessary to ask what was in the reasonable contemplation of the parties when the agreement to tow was concluded. As it was put in *The Liverpool* [1893] P. 154 by Gorell Barnes J., citing *The Pericles* (1863) Br. & L. 80 at p. 160:

"there must be ... something done either in the nature of risk run or extra services performed by the tug, beyond that which is included in the contemplation of the parties in the services which she is engaged to perform."

The operation of the reasonable contemplation test is well demonstrated in the decision of Sir James Hannen P. in *The Five Steel Barges* (1890) 15 P.D. 142. In that case, a steam-tug took five steel barges in tow. The towage contract provided that if any of the barges broke adrift and were lost, the tug was still entitled to the full sum. In the course of the voyage, the wind blew so fiercely as to force the tug and barges to anchor. When the vessels left anchor, heavy seas were encountered and four of the barges broke adrift. The tug took the remaining barge back to the anchorage and then returned to search for the others. With much difficulty, the barges were brought back. Towage recommenced but the barges again broke adrift and three men were drowned. In the final event, three of the barges were towed to port by a second tug and the other two to their destination by the original tug. The President held that, notwithstanding that it was obvious at the time of making the contract that the towage was of a peculiar character, would be difficult at that time of year and would be carried out in exposed and dangerous waters, and despite the fact that some delay would be anticipated, the parties could not have contemplated a delay as long as that which occurred due to the violence of the weather, nor could they have contemplated the additional operations which were required to be performed. Accordingly, a salvage award was made independently of the towage contract. At p. 144 he stated:

" ... it is not necessary, in order to become entitled to salvage, that the supervening danger should be of such a character as to actually put an end to the towage contract. It is sufficient if the services rendered are beyond what can be reasonably supposed to have been contemplated by the parties entering into such a contract. It depends on the circumstances of each case whether or not the services are advanced in this way to a higher degree, so as to establish a right to salvage . . . . The character of the contract is, of course, to be looked at, and the circumstances to which it related . . . ".

7. The burden and standard of proof

It is clear from these cases that the burden of proving the conversion of a service from one of towage to one of salvage lies upon the tug. The Admiralty Court has traditionally viewed claims to convert with, as the old cases put it, "extreme jealousy". Thus, in the *locus classicus* of *The Minnehaha* (1861) 15 Moo. P.C. 133, in which the tug claimed that the services rendered by it fell outside the contract, Lord Kingsdown commented at p. 155 that:

" . . . their Lordships are of opinion that such cases require to be watched with the closest attention, and not without some degree of jealousy."

While the policy reasons behind imposing a stringent burden upon the tug were sound at the mid-point of the nineteenth century when the reported cases reflect an unscrupulousness on the part of certain tug owners and a willingness to take advantage of their tows, whether today the standard of proof is so exacting is highly questionable (*cf.* the comments of Captain Kovats, *The Law of Tugs and Towage* (1980), at p. 131).

Irrespective of the heaviness of the burden upon the tug, in proving their case and in discharging the burden upon him, the tug claiming as aspirant salvor must, as was made clear by Lord Kingsdown in *The Minnehaha* (1861) 15 Moo. P.C. 133 at 158, establish three essential elements:

" . . . they must show that, the ship being in danger from no fault of theirs, they performed services which were not covered by their towage contract, and did all they could to prevent the danger."

In *The Marechal Suchet* [1911] P. 1, the position was summarised by Sir Samuel Evans P., who at p. 12 stated:

"The burden of proof is upon the plaintiff. It is a two-fold burden. They must show that they were not wanting in the performance of the obligations resting upon them under the towage contract; and they must also account for [the casualty] by showing something like *vis major*, or an inevitable accident."

In that judgment, the President had relied upon the decision of the Court of Appeal in *The Robert Dixon* (1879) 5 P.D. 54, where it was observed by Brett L.J. that:

" . . . it lies on [the plaintiffs] to show that the change occurred without any want of skill on their part, but by mere accident over which they had no control. The burden of proof on both the affirmative and the negative issues is on the plaintiffs, that is, both that there was an inevitable accident beyond their control, and that they showed no want of skill."

The approach of Brett L.J. most succinctly explains the burden of proof in respect of the conversion from towage to salvage. The same approach is expressly approved in the judgment of Gorell Barnes J. in *The Duc d'Aumale (No. 2)* [1904] P. 60 at p. 71, and in the judgment of Bateson J. in *The St. Patrick* (1929) 35 Ll. L. Rep. 231 at p. 238.

8. The effect of "conversion into salvage" upon the towage contract

The common law is not entirely clear as to the precise effect of the circumstances which give rise to a salvage service upon the subsisting towage contract. As has been demonstrated above, a tug performing under a towage contract will normally be required unconditionally to complete it: see *The Minnehaha* (1861) 15 Moo. P.C. 133. However, it is accepted that the emergence of a supervening circumstance may render the performance of the contract of towage impossible and will, arguably, bring it to an end. In *The Minnehaha* (*op. cit.*) Lord Kingsdown stated (at p. 153), in a passage already cited:

" . . . if in the discharge of [the towage obligations], by sudden violence of wind or waves, or other accidents, the ship in tow is placed in danger, and the towing vessel incurs risks and performs duties which were not within the scope of her original engagement . . . the towage contract is generally spoken of as superseded by the right to salvage . . . . The tug is relieved from the performance of her contract by the impossibility of performing it; but if the performance of it be possible, but in the course of it the ship in her charge is exposed by unavoidable accident to dangers which require from the tug services of a different class, and bearing a higher rate of payment, it is held to be implied in the contract that she shall be paid at such higher rate."

See also *The Liverpool* [1893] P. 154 at pp. 159–160 where Lord Kingsdown's speech to this effect was approved by the Court of Appeal as accurately representing the law.

In this context, the law of frustration and the Law Reform (Frustrated Contracts) Act 1943 will apply as normal. To this extent, charges payable under the agreement prior to the frustrating event are no longer payable. However, the common approach taken by the courts is that where, as a result of any performance by the tug under the contract of towage, the casualty has obtained a valuable benefit prior to the frustrating event, the court may exercise its discretion in ordering the tow to pay what is considered to be a reasonable sum by the tug. This approach is contained within section 1(3) of the 1943 Act. Modern towage contracts not infrequently include a provision to the effect that the terms of the contract are to apply notwithstanding any frustrating event and any inconsistency with the terms of the Act.

Where a towage service is subsequently converted to a salvage service, payment for each of the services will normally be separately assessed and remunerated. The difficulty arises in the way in which the operation of the contract is to be approached by the courts. The older authorities cited above suggest that the occurrence of a supervening event which gives rise to a salvage service justifies the abandonment of the towage contract. However, the prevailing view is well-settled, and is that the conversion to a salvage service may, though not necessarily, justify the abandonment of the towage contract but will often only give rise to its temporary "suspension", "vacation" or "supersession". However, despite the plethora of different terms used, it seems clear that where supervening circumstances occur which do not permanently alter the contemplated and foreseen operating conditions, the towage contract is effectively suspended while the supervening circumstances operate, but that it is not actually superseded or terminated. Accordingly, upon the termination of the special circumstances, the towage contract will recommence and the tug is obliged to recommence its contractual towage obligations in so far as that is possible in the post-salvage circumstances.

In the leading case of *The Leon Blum* [1915] P. 90; [1915] P. 290 (C.A.), Sir Samuel Evans P., after reviewing the leading authorities in the area (see [1915] P. 90), distilled the various dicta and decisions as follows at p. 101:

"The right conclusion to draw from the authorities, I think, is that where salvage services (which must be voluntary) supervene upon towage services (which are under contract) the two kinds of service cannot co-exist during the same space of time. There must be a moment when the towage service ceases and the salvage service begins; and, if the tug remains at her post of duty, there may come a moment when the special and unexpected danger is over, and then the salvage service would end, and the towage service would be resumed. These moments of time may be difficult to fix, but have to be, and are, fixed in practice. During the intervening time the towage contract, in so far as the actual work of towing is concerned, is suspended. I prefer the word 'suspended' to some of the other words which have been used, such as 'superseded', 'vacated', 'abandoned', &c."

Similarly, in *The Five Steel Barges* (1890) 15 P.D. 142 at p. 144, Sir James Hannen P. noted that:

" . . . it appears to me that it is not necessary, in order to become entitled to salvage, that the supervening danger should be of such a character as to actually put an end to the towage contract. It is sufficient if the services rendered are beyond what can be reasonably supposed to have been contemplated by the parties entering into such a contract."

However, where the towage contract is actually frustrated because of some permanent change in circumstances and all further (contemplated) performance is brought to an end, a new contract may arise, giving effect to new rights. This issue was addressed by Sir Francis Jeune P. in *The Madras* [1898] P. 90 where at p. 94 he noted:

" . . . [in the case of] an indivisible contract which cannot be fulfilled owing to circumstances for which neither party is to blame . . . I think there could be no question that the law holds neither party liable to fulfil that contract, or liable to consequences for not fulfilling it . . . . Subject, of course, to this, that if there is a new contract to be implied by the acts of the parties, that gives rise to new rights."

Alternatively, however, it was suggested in *The Massalia* [1961] 2 Q.B. 278 by Pearson J. at pp. 312 to 314 that, in similar circumstances, the tow may be liable to pay for towage following the supervening circumstances on a *quantum meruit* basis. In appropriate circumstances it may be the case that, albeit that the resumed towage operation takes place on the basis of the original terms, higher remuneration is due than would earlier have been the case by reason of the more arduous circumstances which prevail. Although the court would not have jurisdiction to raise the contractual rate for this reason, it may nonetheless be open to the court to recognise an implied obligation requiring higher remuneration for additional services. Such remuneration would be made either on the basis of *quantum meruit* or, perhaps, on a basis of quasi-contract or restitution by reason of the fact that the tow might otherwise be unjustly enriched to the detriment of the tug.

9. The relationship with salvage under the common forms of contract

The relevance and application of these common law principles may be qualified by the specific terms of the towage contract. The provisions of the standard form contracts which frequently govern the performance of a modern towage service are considered in detail in Chapters 3, 4 and 5 above. However, the relationship between contracts on such forms and the conversion into salvage may be briefly noted here.

The United Kingdom Standard Conditions for Towage and Other Services (1986) (discussed in Chapter 3 above) preserve the tug owner's common law entitlement to claim salvage and therefore leave the common law principles untouched, providing in Clause 6 that:

"Nothing contained in these conditions shall limit, prejudice or preclude in any way any legal rights which the Tugowner may have against the Hirer, including, but not limited to, any rights which the Tugowner or his servants or agents have to claim salvage remuneration or special compensation for any extraordinary services rendered to vessels or anything aboard the vessels by any tug or tender . . . ".

Similarly, the BIMCO standard form contracts and conditions, "Towcon" and "Towhire", while expressly covering the question of salvage, leave unaffected the common law position. In both forms, the relevant provision is clause 15 which provides that:

"(a) Should the tow break away from the tug during the course of the towage service, the tug shall render all reasonable services to reconnect the tow-line and fulfil this agreement without making any claim for salvage.

(b) If at any time the Tugowner or the Tugmaster considers it necessary or advisable to seek or accept salvage services from any person or vessel on behalf of the tug or tow, or both, the Hirer hereby undertakes and warrants that the Tugowner or his duly authorised servant or agent including the Tugmaster shall have the full actual authority of the Hirer to accept such services on behalf of the tow on reasonable terms."

Clause 15(a) accordingly does little more than to re-phrase the obligation upon the tug to render all reasonable services as enshrined in the decisions of *The Minnehaha* and *The Julia* and of which Dr Lushington stated in *The Galatea* (1858) Swab. 349:

" . . . the [tug] is bound by [the] engagement to do all that is necessary to facilitate the safe voyage of the ship from the one place to the other; and she is to take the chance of bad weather, which may occasion delay and inconvenience."

Clause 15(b) deals merely with the question of conferring upon the tug by the tow of sufficient express authority to enter into salvage contracts with third parties on behalf of tug and/or tow in appropriate circumstances. *Cf.* the different interpretation of this clause by Brice Q.C. in his *Maritime Law of Salvage* (2nd Edn.), at pp. 92–97.

As has been seen above, ordinary principles of contractual construction will be applied in determining the precise requirements of contractual performance. Thus, where the contract grants an express right to claim salvage, it is submitted that the principles of construction at common law must be applied with rigour if the term amounts not merely to a clause preserving the right of the tug to claim salvage in a proper case, but to one which in effect operates as a clause allowing the tug to deem certain services to be salvage, whether or not the criteria for salvage are in fact made out. Such provisions are rare but it is submitted that where the same fall to be construed they should be strictly construed. It is not, it is submitted, open to imply into the contract a wider entitlement to claim salvage unless the same is clearly and expressly suggested by the words of the agreement. An example of such a provision has been considered in South Africa. In *The Manchester* [1981] (2) S.A. 798 (C), a vessel became immobilised 300 miles north-west of Walvis Bay. Repairs were effected at sea by the vessel's engineers, but the engines were finally stopped when it was thought to be dangerous to proceed any further. A tug was engaged to tow the vessel to Walvis Bay, which it duly did. The towage contract provided that the tug owners:

" have the right to claim . . . salvage, if the services rendered to the said vessel should be such as to warrant a salvage award".

Burger J. in, it is submitted, an unusual judgment, held the contract to entitle the tug owner to salvage "if justified by the circumstances". This was so, notwithstanding that the South African courts apply English case law principles in determining whether salvage is to be awarded. In the event, salvage was awarded despite the fact that only those services called for by the towage contract were performed. It is respectfully submitted that the approach adopted by Burger J. is not in line with the established tests for construction and for the conversion of towage service into salvage.

10. Towage contracts providing for "no salvage charges"

Occasionally towage contracts provide for the exclusion of any right on the part of the tug owner to claim salvage. Such clauses are more common where the tug is engaged by the tow in circumstances where the tow is already in danger and where she seeks to avoid a salvage contract and prefers rather to bind the tug to a fixed-price contract. In such a case, the services of the tug are usually referred to as "engaged services" (as to which see in greater detail below).

Where the towage contract contains no express or implied exclusion of the recovery of a salvage award, the court may forthwith treat any service rendered under the contract as one of salvage if the necessary requirements discussed above are made out. In *The Charles Adolphe* (1856) Swab. 153, in which a vessel was disabled and in distress from the moment at which the towage contract was agreed, Dr Lushington commented at p. 157 that, in the absence of an express exclusion clause or implied prohibition on the recovery of salvage, the service "cannot by possibility be compared to an ordinary towage service". However, the *prima facie* right to salvage may be expressly excluded, although the court will usually adopt a strict approach to construction requiring clear terms to achieve such an exclusion. It was stated by Lord Stowell in *The Waterloo* (1820) 2 Dods. 433 at pp. 435–436 that:

" . . . where the exemption is claimed from a right otherwise universally allowed, and highly favoured in law, for the protection of those who are subjected to it; . . . it is for their benefit that it exists under that favour of the law. It is what the law calls *jus liquidissimum*, the cleanest right that they who have saved lives and property at sea should be rewarded for such salutary exertions; and those who say that they are not bound to reward ought to prove their exemption in very definite terms, and by arguments of irresistible cogency."

However, assuming that a clear exclusion can be demonstrated and shown to be in accordance with public policy, recovery of a salvage award may properly be excluded. This was acknowledged by Lord Salvesen in *Clan Steam Trawling Co. Ltd* v. *Aberdeen Steam Trawling and Fishing Co. Ltd* 1908 S.C. 651 at p. 655 where he noted an agreement to exclude the payment of salvage charges:

"Such an agreement might conceivably be objected to as being contrary to public policy. But, assuming its validity, I think it must be clear, from the agreement, that the rendering of assistance to a vessel in distress shall not found a claim for remuneration. The right to obtain salvage remuneration is one very much favoured in law, and therefore cannot be excluded unless by express words or by very clear implication from the language used."

Similarly, and more recently, the High Court of Australia has made it clear that the exclusion of a right to salvage is very unlikely to operate by way of implication. Accordingly, express agreement will be required: see *Fisher* v. *The Oceanic Grandeur* [1972] 2 Lloyd's Rep. 396 per Stephen J. at p. 407.

Nevertheless, an agreement which *prima facie* appears effectively to exclude a right to salvage may fail to have the desired effect if the agreement is intended to have effect only in certain circumstances and those circumstances alter. A classic illustration of the way in which an exclusion will fail to operate is to be found in *The Glenmorven* [1913] P. 141, in which tug owners agreed to tow a vessel on a basis of "no cure, no pay, no claim to be made for salvage". This was treated by Sir Samuel Evans P. as a contract to provide towage services to a partly-disabled vessel manned by officers and crew. It was held that the abandonment of the vessel by the officers and crew without reasonable cause served to bring to an end the agreement as a whole, and that thereafter the tug owner's services were provided as salvage. Accordingly, £1,400 was awarded as salvage and £300 provided on a *quantum meruit* for the earlier service as towage. It is submitted that the principle which emerges is the normal common law principle that an express exclusion will only be effective in the precise event to which it is stated to apply. This principle received further confirmation in *The Queen Elizabeth* (1949) 82 Ll. L. Rep. 803.

Effect upon the rights of the tug crew. It should be noted that the mere fact of a tug owner entering into a contract excluding salvage will not exclude claims by the crew and officers of the tug for salvage in a proper case; the owner has no authority to contract out of their individual rights: see *The Margery* [1902] P. 157 and *The Leon Blum* [1915] P. 90 (Sir Samuel Evans P.).

11. The sub-contracting in of tugs in salvage services

With the retrenchment of the modern salvage industry and the rationalisation of many salvage operators' fleets, it is increasingly common for a salvor who engages in a salvage service and who has entered into an LOF contract to engage tugs under sub-contracts to assist him in performing the service. Thus a salvor may offer his services to a vessel in distress but, because he has no tug handy or because he needs more pulling power than he can readily dispose of, the salvor hires in the services of the necessary vessels from another tug owner.

In such a case, whether or not the sub-contractor can claim salvage will depend upon the nature and terms of the sub-contract. It is submitted that, where a tug is engaged by a salvor to perform a particular service as part of a salvage operation in circumstances in which it is the common understanding of the parties that the tug is assisting in the performance of the salvor's salvage of the vessel but on ordinary terms, such as a daily rate of hire or a lump sum (whether on "no cure, no pay" terms or not), it will be a rare case in which the sub-contracted tug can assert a claim to salvage. While there is no contractual relationship between the sub-contracted tug and the vessel in distress, which is the position considered in the cases such as *The Homewood*, the tug is not rendering the services voluntarily, but rendering its normal services pursuant to the sub-contract. Just as a port authority may be under an obligation to provide a tug under its statutory constitution and is thereby unable to claim salvage in respect of services which it renders pursuant to that constitution (see e.g. *The Mars and other Barges* (1948) 81 Ll. L. Rep. 452 and *The Gregerso* [1973] Q.B. 274), similarly a tug which is rendering a service to another vessel pursuant to and in accordance with the terms of a contract entered into by it with another tug, albeit a salvor, is not acting as a volunteer. Certain circumstances may alter the position. Thus, if a tug is engaged by a salvor under a sub-contract on a fixed daily rate to hold up a vessel in distress while the salvor performs the salvage service, and the tug is called upon to render very different services such as fire-fighting or emergency pumping out, a claim for salvage may lie against the vessel unless the sub-contract expressly prohibits such a claim in terms which are enforceable by the salvor.

The question has not been specifically addressed in any English case. However, the New South Wales Court of Appeal in *The Texaco Southampton* [1983] 1 Lloyd's Rep. 94 touched upon the question. In that case, a vessel was disabled. Her owners contacted their usual tug supplier and requested a tug; no mention of salvage was made. The supplier, having no tugs available, engaged another tug under a sub-contract. The crew of the tug claimed salvage but the court rejected the claim. It stated that in accordance with normal principles where a tug is engaged under a towage contract and does no more than perform what she was engaged to, she is not entitled to claim salvage. Here the court relied upon the existence of the sub-contract between the sub-contracted tug and the other tug supplier as barring the claim to salvage against the disabled vessel. This follows the approach set out above. A similar approach was adopted in the American case of *Nunley* v. *The Dauntless* 863 F. 2d. 1190 (1989).

The terms of Article 17 of the 1989 Salvage Convention do not appear to change this analysis. Article 17 provides that no salvage payment is due "unless the services . . . exceed what can be reasonably considered as due performance of a contract entered into before the danger arose". This provision applies equally to the case where the service rendered for which it is desired to claim salvage is one rendered under a contract with the vessel salved or under a sub-contract with a salvor already engaged by that vessel.

In practical terms, a sub-contracted tug, if provided by a tug owner who himself has salvor status, will often enter into an agreement under which she becomes a joint salvor. In this connection, the standard form ISU sub-contract or "International Salvage Union Sub-contract (Award Sharing) 1991" form is frequently used; this enables the award obtained by the salvor to be shared with the sub-contracted tug on the basis of a determination before a salvage arbitrator of the contribution made by the sub-contractor to the success of the service and the remuneration awarded to the salvor as a result of it.

12. The effect of misconduct by the tug

As has been seen in above, in *The Minnehaha* (1861) 15 Moo. P.C. 133, Lord Kingsdown commented (at p. 155) that one of the matters to which the court had to have regard when considering the claim of the tug as aspirant salvor was whether the court would be warranted in finding that the danger and unforeseen conditions facing the tow were due to the tug. The effect of misconduct on the part of a salvor is fully considered in the leading salvage texts. In the special context of tug and tow, the effect of causative misconduct by the tug upon any subsequent salvage service which it may perform has been closely examined by the courts.

(1) The early authorities

The position under earlier authority was well-summarised in the speech of Lord Kingsdown in *The Minnehaha* (1861) 15 Moo. P.C. 133, who at p. 155 observed:

"If the danger from which the ship has been rescued is attributable to the fault of the tug; if the tug, whether by wilful misconduct, or by negligence, or by the want of that reasonable skill or equipments which are implied in the towage contract, has occasioned or materially contributed to the danger, we can have no hesitation in stating our opinion that she can have no claim to salvage. She can never be permitted to profit by her own wrong or default."

The early authorities largely stand for the proposition that misconduct on the part of the tug, which gives rise to the need for the salvage service which is eventually performed by the wrongdoing tug, will debar the tug from recovering any salvage award. In *The Cargo ex Capella* (1867) L.R. 1 A. & E. 356, two vessels collided and one subsequently effected a salvage service for the other. Dr Lushington held at p. 357:

" . . . I look to the principle which ought to govern the case. In my mind, the principle is this, that no man can profit by his own wrong. This is a rule founded in justice and equity . . . The asserted salvors were the original wrongdoers; it was by their fault that the property was placed in jeopardy. The rule would bar any claim by them for services rendered to the other ship which was a co-delinquent in the collision; . . . ."

Similarly, in *The Duc d'Aumale (No 2)* [1904] P. 60, Gorell Barnes J. commented at pp. 74–75:

"Both on principle and as a matter of good policy . . . it would not be desirable to encourage a crew to recover a salvage reward in such cases of tug and tow where the master of the tug has been one of the causes of the disaster from which the ship to which salvage services has been rendered is rescued . . . it would be bad policy to encourage sailors, as it were, to hope and expect that their master might get the ship he was towing into danger, so that they would have to render services for which they could recover."

The soundness of the earlier authorities must now be doubted in the light of the more recent authorities on the effect generally, and not just in the context of tug and tow, of misconduct on the part of the salvor which is causative of the need for salvage assistance.

(2) The modern approach

The modern approach is found in the decision of the House of Lords in *The Beaverford* v. *The Kafiristan* [1938] A.C. 136, which has been subsequently applied in *The Susan V. Luckenbach* [1951] P. 197 (C.A.). The speech of Lord Wright in the former case at pp. 141 to 154 sets out the prevailing view, founded upon the approach adopted by Sir Robert Phillimore in *The Glengaber* (1872) L.R. 3 A. & E. 534, that there is no principle of law which prevents a ship which has rendered a salvage service from obtaining a salvage award simply on the ground that she caused or, at least, was partly responsible for the damage which gave rise to the need for the salvage service. Accordingly, a tug which, by its own misconduct, gives rise to a danger which puts the tow in need of a salvage service which, in the final event, is rendered by that same tug, is not necessarily deprived of the opportunity to claim a salvage award. Lord Wright stated at p. 148:

"There does not seem to be any reason in equity why the salved vessel . . . should not pay the appropriate salvage remuneration merely because the salving vessel belongs to the same owners as the other colliding vessel. That fact seems to be irrelevant so far as concerns the usefulness and meritorious character of the actual services rendered. This is not less true when the possibility of the other colliding vessel being held to blame in whole or in part is taken into account."

Lord Wright went on to say, at pp. 148–149, that the maxim "that no man can profit by his own wrong" was wholly inapplicable. Although the decision in this case concerned a claim for salvage by a salving vessel in the same ownership as the wrongdoing vessel, and might therefore be distinguished from the position where the salving vessel is itself the wrongdoing vessel, the speech of Lord Wright appears not to support such a distinction. He commented *obiter* at p. 149:

"It is, however, said that if the principle that no man can profit by his own wrong excludes a claim for salvage where the salving vessel is the colliding vessel, as was held in *The Cargo ex Capella*, and other cases, the same principle should apply where the salving and the negligently colliding vessel belong to the same owner, because the wrong is committed by the person who salves, acting in either case by his servants. I shall assume that the principle there is established. I am doubtful of the logic or equity of it . . . if the rule laid down in *The Cargo ex Capella* is at all sound."

Further, at p. 153 he added:

"It is only when the salving vessel is to blame for the collision that it seems that not only the members of the crew actually in fault, but the whole crew, however meritorious their services, are debarred. I feel doubt about the equity or policy of so sweeping a rule . . . "

Similarly, it appears that the principle of circuity of action has no direct application. The approach to be taken by the courts is, first, to determine and assess any salvage award, and, secondly to ascertain the responsibility for the collision or danger. Thus, it may be that the salvor is liable in damages to the owner of the casualty for his proportion of the responsibility. Accordingly, any salvage award would be reduced by the level of damages. Of course, were the damages to equal the quantum of the salvage award, nothing would be recoverable: see *The Beaverford* v. *The Kafiristan* [1938] A.C. 136 per Lord Wright at pp. 148 and 152–153.

The principle upon which Gorell Barnes J. relied in *The Duc d'Aumale (No. 2)* [1904] P. 60 was described by Lord Wright (at p. 151) as being "of dubious soundness".

The provisions of Article 18 of the 1989 Salvage Convention confirm the approach of the court in *The Beaverford*. Article 18 provides, albeit in relation to a salvor, that:

"A salvor may be deprived of the whole or part of payment due under this Convention to the extent that the salvage operations have become necessary or more difficult because of fault or neglect on his part or if the salvor has been guilty of fraud or other dishonest conduct."

It is interesting to note that the effect of misconduct as determined in *The Beaverford* v. *The Kafiristan* is not reflected in the approach of the United States courts which continue to follow the earlier English authorities so that misconduct of a towage service which leads to the need for a salvage service will normally result in the tug being debarred from recovering salvage as a matter of principle. One of the earliest U.S. cases on the issue is *The Homely* Fed. Cas. No. 661 (1876), in which a tug, in towing the vessel, caused her to ground by reason of the tug's negligence. A second tug was engaged to assist in the refloating of the vessel. Together, the two tugs succeeded in refloating the vessel and towing her to her destination. Both tugs claimed a salvage award. It was held that the second tug was entitled to an award, but that the first tug was not, by reason of the fact that the salvage service had been necessitated by the negligence of the first tug. The United States courts have also, interestingly, held that where a towage service is rendered by tugs in common ownership, but a salvage service becomes necessary by reason of the misconduct of one, the other will not be debarred from recovering a salvage award. In *Hendry Corporation* v. *Aircraft Rescue Vessels* 113 F. Supp. 198 (1953), a number of aircraft rescue vessels were in the tow of two tugs in common ownership. Some of the tows went aground as a result of the negligence of one of the tugs. The second tug, still with its tows, provided assistance in refloating the stranded tows. The court awarded salvage to the second tug.

PART C. CONTRACTS FOR "ENGAGED SERVICES"

1. The nature of "engaged services"

A further category of services which falls neither into the category of towage nor, strictly, salvage, is that generally referred to as "engaged services" or services at request. This category is exceptional in that success is not a requirement. The nature of "engaged services" is well-illustrated by the decision in *The Undaunted* (1860) Lush. 90 in which a vessel summoned assistance in terrible conditions having lost her anchors. She was approached by a second vessel and it was agreed that assistance would be provided. However, prior to the assistance being provided, the vessel was secured, partly by her own endeavours and partly with the efforts of a third vessel. Notwithstanding, the second vessel advanced a claim for salvage. In awarding salvage to the second vessel, Dr Lushington commented at p. 92:

" ... if men are engaged by a ship in distress, whether generally or particularly, they are to be paid according to their efforts made, even though the labour and service may not prove beneficial to the vessel. Take the case of a vessel at anchor in a gale of wind, hailing a steamer to lie by and be ready to take her in tow if required; the steamer does so, the ship rides out of the gale safely without the assistance of the steamer. I should undoubtedly hold in such a case that the steamer was entitled to a salvage reward ... "

Thus, salvage awards were made in *The Helvetia* (1894) 8 Asp. M.C. 264, in which a request to tow was met without any tangible benefit, and in *The Cambrian* (1897) 8 Asp. 263, in which a vessel was requested to stand by in circumstances in which it was anticipated that the crew on board the casualty would require imminent rescue although, in the event, no such rescue was necessary. In *The Helvetia* (1894) 8 Asp. M.C. 264 Barnes J. stated at p. 265:

" ... speaking for myself, it seems to me that if there is in fact a request to render assistance ... a request to attempt to tow the ship, and the service requested is in fact performed as far as it is possible to do it, and the ship is afterwards saved by other means, then the persons who rendered the services are ... entitled to some salvage remuneration ... it is almost obvious that in rendering these services they may be unsuccessful and may incur a great loss of time and much risk. I think it would deter them in such circumstances from attempting to render assistance if it were held that on rendering them at the request of the master of the ship they were not entitled to any reward at all unless the services proved actually beneficial to the ship."

However, in *The Renpor* (1883) 3 P.D. 115 it was held by the Court of Appeal that a vessel which stood by another at its express request, but which conferred no obvious benefit, recovered nothing by way of salvage. Brett M.R. commented at pp. 117–118:

" ... in order to found an action for salvage, there must be something saved more than life, which will form a fund from which salvage may be paid ... It is said that under some circumstances if life is saved after the services of the salvors have been requested by the master of the ship which is in danger, the shipowner is bound to pay salvage, although there is no res saved, *The Undaunted* has been cited in support of this proposition ... But *The Undaunted* is really no authority in favour of the plaintiffs' contention, because in that case the ship was saved, and therefore there was a fund from which payment could be made. ... something must be saved in order to give valid grounds for a salvage action ... there are two circumstances necessary in order to make an agreement binding on an owner; first, the contract must be made under a necessity; and, secondly, it must be made for his benefit."

Thus, it is submitted, that the principle of "engaged services" has only a limited ambit. Following the decision in *The Renpor* (1883) 3 P.D. 115, it was held by Phillimore J. in *The Dart* (1889) 8 Asp. 481 that a vessel which was engaged to tow a casualty would not recover salvage in the absence of any benefit. In qualifying the principle in *The Undaunted*, Phillimore J. noted that a vessel would get no award:

" . . . unless she gets it under the doctrine that she was engaged. If she had been engaged to stand by, or if she had been engaged to try and tow, then I should have been able to give her some award."

At p. 483 he again commented:

" . . . she was engaged to tow. I construe that to mean to tow into a port of safety, and she failed in doing that."

It would seem to follow that a salvage award will be earned where the vessel completes or fulfils the task for which she is engaged, albeit not, in doing so, conferring the success necessary at common law for a salvage award. In the absence of completing the task, it seems that no award is merited; an attempt at the engaged task will not suffice. The position is aptly illustrated in *The Marechal Suchet* [1911] P. 1. However, in *The Benlarig* (1888) 14 P.D. 3, in which a casualty requested another vessel to tow her to Gibraltar and which the latter agreed to attempt to do although, in the event, leaving the casualty in a more dangerous position than before, Butt J. held that no salvage award was payable, but that adequate remuneration was due for what had been done in fulfilment of the agreement. He stated at p. 6 that the contract between the parties was:

" . . . not a contract merely to render salvage service, and certainly not a contract to take the vessel into Gibraltar; but a contract . . . [to] attempt to do so."

Accordingly, the precise terms and nature of the agreement will be crucial to the determination of whether or not the contract is one for "engaged services".

2. Have "engaged services" survived the 1989 Salvage Convention?

Article 12 of the 1989 Salvage Convention, in so far as material, provides as follows:

"1. Salvage operations which have had a useful result give right to a reward.
2. Except as otherwise provided, no payment is due under this Convention if the salvage operations have had no useful result."

The Article represents the ordinary position that a salvage service to earn remuneration must be successful or, put another way, must confer a benefit upon the object of the salvage service. The only exception to this principle provided for by the 1989 Salvage Convention is found in Article 14 which relates to environmental protection.

As has been seen above, the concept of "engaged services" represents a half-way house between pure salvage and pure towage; in circumstances of danger to a vessel which would qualify services rendered to her as salvage services, a tug is requested by the vessel to do or to perform a particular service, rather than the whole salvage itself. Thus a tug (or other vessel) might be engaged by a vessel with flooded holds to proceed at full speed to the nearest harbour to pick up some submersible pumps or materials with which to staunch an ingress of water. By virtue of the request (which is, perhaps, the essential feature of services which have been "engaged" see e.g. *Kennedy on Salvage* (5th Edn.) at para. 629, pp. 279–280), the tug is entitled to remuneration upon a salvage basis. As Professor Gaskell has crisply put it (*Current Law Statutes*, 1994, Vol. II, 29–12) "entitlement depends on the making of a request for services, even though they may not be of any use".

This species of a hybrid towage/salvage service may or may not fall within Article 12(1) of the 1989 Convention. If the engaged services have a useful result, then they will fall within the definition of "salvage operations which have had a useful result". But if they have not had a useful result because their performance has not proved possible (for example, no submersible pumps were available) or because, even though performed in full pursuant to the request, they have conferred no benefit or have "had no useful result" (for example, where the pumps, although obtained, were inoperable because of the suspension of cargo in the water which clogged the pump filters), then such services are, *prima facie*, within Article 12(2) of the 1989 Convention and entitle the provider of them to "no payment".

It is submitted that the combined effect of the provisions of the 1989 Convention and of the Merchant Shipping Act 1995 is that the legal concept of "engaged services" and the cases which have developed that concept are probably no longer good law. The material provisions are the following:

   (i) Article 6(1) of the 1989 Convention provides that:

> "This Convention shall apply to any salvage operations save to the extent that a contract otherwise provides expressly or by implication."

   (ii) Article 1(a) of the 1989 Convention defines "salvage operations" as follows:

> "Salvage operation means any act or activity undertaken to assist a vessel or any other property in danger in navigable waters or in any other waters whatsoever."

   (iii) By section 224(1) of the 1995 Act:

> "The provisions of [the 1989 Convention] as set out in Part I of Schedule 11 to this Act . . . shall have the force of law in the United Kingdom."

The combined effect of these provisions is that the terms of the 1989 Convention will apply as a matter of law to all salvage operations, as defined, unless the salvage operation in question is performed under a contract which either specifically, or implicitly "contracts out" of the 1989 Convention.

"Engaged services" are, by their nature, acts or activities undertaken to assist a vessel or property in danger on navigable or other waters; accordingly they are comprised within Article 1(a) of the 1989 Convention. As "salvage operations", "engaged services" fall within the scope of the 1989 Convention under Article 6(1). Unless, therefore, they can be regarded as being rendered under an engagement which expressly or impliedly excludes the operation of the 1989 Convention, such services will have to satisfy the requirement of success or "useful result" if they are to qualify for any reward: see Article 12 of the 1989 Convention cited above.

Where the "engaged services" are rendered upon a clear contractual basis which addresses the issue of salvage and remuneration, little difficulty arises since the services will be rendered under a contract which excludes the 1989 Convention. So, if a vessel in distress hires a tug to ferry essential supplies on a daily hire basis with a clause excluding the right to claim salvage, the tug will be entitled to remuneration as agreed. However, the usual case of "engaged services" is where a vessel is engaged to render specific assistance without terms being agreed. On one view since the services are "engaged", it could be argued that the request carries with it a sufficient "implication" so as to exclude the 1989 Convention. The difficulty with such an argument is that it ignores the fact that the entitlement to remuneration for "engaged services" has never been recognised by the court as being contractual in any way (see e.g. *The Hestia* [1895] P. 193) and that the court has always stressed the close affinity between pure salvage remuneration and remuneration for "engaged services". Thus remuneration for "engaged services" is not on a *quantum meruit* basis, as might be expected of a service done at request, but has always been assessed on a salvage basis (*The Undaunted* (1860) Lush. 90; *The Maude* (1876) 3 Asp. 338; see also *The Melpomene* (1873) L.R. 4 A. & E. 129).

Since "engaged services" represent a hybrid or special category of salvage service or of services treated as salvage and rewarded as such, they fall within the provisions of Articles 6(1) and 1(a). Unless the engagement is very clear in its terms, if the services are unsuccessful, under the codified law as set out under Article 12 of the 1989 Convention, no remuneration is payable.

The effect of the 1989 Convention upon "engaged services" (and upon other aspects of English salvage law) was the subject of debate in the House of Lords during the passage of the Merchant Shipping (Salvage and Pollution) Bill, in particular in relation to the re-phrasing of the jurisdiction of the Admiralty Court in salvage matters as provided for by section 20(2)(j) of the Supreme Court Act 1981. That section was amended by paragraph 6 of Schedule 2 to the Merchant Shipping (Salvage and Pollution) Act 1994 to read as follows so as to give the Admiralty Court jurisdiction to hear and determine:

"(j) any claim–
    (i) under the Salvage Convention 1989;
    (ii) under any contract for or in relation to salvage services; or
    (iii) in the nature of salvage not falling within (i) or (ii) above;
. . . "

Certain speakers in the House of Lords plainly regarded this provision as preserving the additional features of the old law of salvage, such as that of "engaged services". However, it is submitted that all that it achieves is to preserve the jurisdiction of the Admiralty Court to hear and determine heads of salvage additional to those arising under the 1989 Convention if, but only if, those heads of salvage are not inconsistent with and are not to be treated as having been superseded by the new codification of the law which the 1989 Convention effects. This was the view of Lord Donaldson of Lymington who stated (*Hansard*, H.L., Vol. 555, col. 697) that paragraph 6 of Schedule 2 was jurisdictional: "it neither adds to or subtracts from the Salvage Convention or anything else". If, therefore, the view above is correct and "engaged services" are inconsistent with the Salvage Convention, paragraph 2 of Schedule 2 by itself is insufficient to modify the Salvage Convention by engrafting on to it the concept of such services as an additional head of salvage.

The question of the survival of the concept of "engaged services" is one of the interesting questions arising out of the enactment of the 1989 Salvage Convention which will have to be addressed by the Admiralty Court.

PART D. SALVAGE OF A TUG AND TOW

Where a towage convoy is itself collectively the subject of a salvage service, ordinary principles of salvage law and practice will apply. The only particular area of potential difficulty is in relation to the identification of those vessels which are to contribute in salvage. Similar problems arise in the field of contribution in general average. The question which arises is whether the tug and tow are to be treated on a unitary basis as one contributing interest in salvage (or general average). In relation to general average, the matter has been the subject of discussion in particular cases and is addressed by the new York-Antwerp Rules of 1994: as to this, see below in Chapter 9.

In salvage, there is no rule or principle by which tug and tow are to be treated as one in all cases. The question of contribution is answered by identifying which of the constituent parts of the towage convoy were in danger and whether, and, if so, in what circumstances and to what extent, salvage services were rendered to those constituent parts. To give some examples:

(i) A tug tows an unmanned water-borne object such as a dumb barge or a floating piece of equipment which is owned by the tug owner. Due to an engine failure both are in danger of stranding. They are salved. *Result*: the tug owner contributes in salvage on the basis of the salved value of the tug and the barge.

See e.g. *The Rilland* [1979] 1 Lloyd's Rep. 455 in which a tug towing a barge laden with a bucket-dredger owned by the tug owner were taken together to arrive at a salved value in respect of salvage services rendered to the whole convoy.

(ii) Take the previous example but with the barge or equipment under tow being owned by a different party. *Result*: the tug owner and the tow owner separately contribute in salvage on the basis of the value of their own property taken separately.

(iii) A tug tows a barge or piece of equipment owned by the tug-owner. Due to an engine failure both are in danger of stranding. The tow-line parts (or is slipped). As a result the barge is pushed towards the shore but the tug succeeds in anchoring herself and in arresting her drift. The barge alone is salved, the tug being in no danger. *Result*: the tug owner is liable to contribute in salvage as owner of the barge but only in respect of the property at risk, the barge, whose salved value alone is relevant.

(iv) A tug tows a barge owned by a third party. Due to an engine failure both are in danger of stranding. The tow-line parts. Both tug and tow require to be

salved. However, due to the windage of the barge, the services rendered to
the barge are dangerous and difficult, while those to the tug merely consist
of holding-up. *Result*: both tug and tow are liable to contribute in salvage.
Their respective contributions will be assessed separately both by reference
to the different services provided to each and in relation to the separate value
of each as the salved property.

CHAPTER 7

Collisions Involving Tug and Tow

PART A. PRELIMINARY REMARKS

1. The scope of the chapter

This chapter considers the relationship between the tug and her tow in the event of a collision and how the question of the liability of each, both for its own acts and for those of the other, is addressed by the courts. In the ordinary course of events, a collision at sea between two or more vessels will give rise to a cause of action in negligence in the event of navigational fault or omission on the part of one or more vessels which results in loss or damage to another vessel. Physical contact between vessels is not the only instance where a vessel may sue another for negligence in navigation: a vessel may proceed too fast and cause a wash which damages another vessel; a vessel by its negligent navigation may force another vessel to take evasive action which results in that vessel colliding or stranding.

The special features in the case of tug and tow are, first, the contract of towage which regulates duties, obligations and liabilities between tug and tow (as seen in Chapter 2 above), secondly, the immateriality of that contract to a third vessel which is involved in a collision with tug and/or tow in determining which of tug and/or tow is liable, thirdly, the question of the apportionment of liability which arises where tug, tow and third party vessels are in collision and, lastly, the special navigational considerations which a towage convoy or flotilla will often present to other vessels under way.

A general treatment of collision law and practice is beyond the scope of this book. See for a detailed treatment of the subject Marsden: *Collisions at Sea* (4th Edn.) Stevens; Sturt: *The Collision Regulations* (2nd Edn.), LLP; for the general regime of collision liabilities and apportionment of liability, see the lucid account in *Meeson on Admiralty Jurisdiction and Practice* (2nd Edn.), LLP.

2. Navigation and the Collision Regulations

(1) Navigation and navigational rules

The duties upon a vessel in relation to navigation arise from two sources: first, from the ordinary duty to exercise reasonable care and skill, in other words, the duties of good seamanship; secondly, from the Collision Regulations which lay down navigational "Rules". The history of the formal regulation of the rules of the road at sea dates back to 1840 when five rules of seamanship, three for sailing vessels and two for steamships were promulgated by Trinity House. Increased regulation by the Board of Trade followed, with new codifications in 1863 and 1910. Following World War II, international agreement was reached on rules of navigation in 1948.

The current position is that the International Regulations for Preventing Collisions at Sea adopted at the Inter-Governmental Maritime Consultative Organisation, or IMCO, conference in London in 1972 have had force of law in the United Kingdom since 1983. In their present form, the Regulations have force of law pursuant to the Merchant Shipping (Distress Signals and Prevention of Collisions) Regulations 1989 (S.I. 1989 No. 1798). The Secretary of State for Transport has a general power under Section 85 of the Merchant Shipping Act 1995 to make regulations for safety at sea; this power is used to effect change to the Collision Regulations where necessary.

(2) *The role of the Collision Regulations*

The inter-relationship between the ordinary dictates of good seamanship and the Collision Regulations is a pragmatic one. As was said by Sheen J. in *The Roseline* [1981] 2 Lloyd's Rep. 410 at 411, the Regulations very often state in codified form what has long been recognised as a rule of good seamanship and of commonsense. For present purposes, the position can be summarised as follows:

(i) Failure to comply with the Collision Regulations in circumstances which mean that the Regulations have been wrongfully contravened (see sub-paragraph (iii) below) is a criminal offence and the owner of the vessel, the master and any person having the conduct of the vessel may be detained by the Department of Transport.

(ii) A contravention of the Regulations formerly resulted in the vessel in contravention being deemed to be at fault in the event of a collision, irrespective of whether the breach of the Regulations played any causative part in the collision (per section 17 of the Merchant Shipping Act 1873). This statutory presumption of fault was abolished by section 4 of the Maritime Conventions Act 1911. However, while proof of a breach of the Regulations is of itself now neutral in a civil collision action until the plaintiff proves that the vessel was thereby at fault and that the fault caused or contributed to the collision or other loss or damage, a strong inference of fault or of negligent conduct will usually arise if it is shown that the Regulations were breached, leaving the plaintiff to establish causation. *Cf.* the position in America which still corresponds to that in the U.K. between 1873 and 1911: the leading case is *The Philadelphia* 86 U.S. 125 (1873) under which, once a breach of the Regulations is made out, the rule is laid down that "the burden rests upon the ship of showing not merely that her fault might not have been one of the causes or that it was probably not, but that it could not have been".

(iii) The Collision Regulations, while laying down rules of navigation, provide also for the impact of special circumstances to which the rules may not adequately apply and to which they may not properly be applicable. The 1972 Regulations themselves, state, by Rule 2(b) that "in construing and complying with these Rules due regard is to be had to all dangers of navigation and collision and to any special circumstances, including the limitations of the vessels involved, which may make a departure from these Rules necessary to avoid immediate danger".

(iv) As already noted, the Collision Regulations co-exist with the ordinary duty of good seamanship. Accordingly, as has been succinctly stated (see *Sturt, op. cit.* at p. 24, para. 1.14): "Nothing in the 1972 Rules exonerates any vessel, or its owner, master or crew, from the consequences of any neglect to comply with the Rules or of the neglect of any precaution which may be required by the ordinary practice of seamen or by the special circumstances of the case."

3. The general scheme for apportioning liability in collisions between vessels

Where two or more vessels collide and more than one vessel is at fault in some respect which is causative of the collision and of the resultant damage sustained, their liability in respect of the collision will be apportioned in accordance with section 187(1) of the Merchant Shipping Act 1995 (replacing section 1(1) of the Maritime Conventions Act 1911) which requires the court to assess "the proportion of the degree to which each vessel was at fault". If no assessment is possible, then the liability is to be apportioned equally (see section 187(2) of the 1995 Act, a relic of the old pre-1911 law). In practice, the court approaches apportionment in the same way as it approaches the question of contributory negligence under the Law Reform (Contributory Negligence) Act 1945: see e.g. *Davies* v. *Swan Motor Co. Ltd* [1949] 2 K.B. 291 (C.A.) at 319 and *The Miraflores and Abadesa* [1966] P. 18 (C.A.) at 33E.

Where two or more vessels are at fault they may seek contribution from the other vessel or vessels at fault so as to reduce the proportion to be borne in money terms of the whole claim to a proportion which is equivalent to the degree to which the particular vessel was herself at fault. Section 189(1) of the Merchant Shipping Act 1995 provides:

"Where loss of life or personal injuries are suffered by any person on board a ship owing to the fault of that ship and any other ship or ships, and a proportion of the damages is recovered against the owners of one of the ships which exceeds the proportion in which she was in fault, they may recover by way of contribution the amount of the excess from the owners of the other ship or ships to the extent to which those ships were respectively at fault."

PART B. NAVIGATION BY TUG AND TOW

1. The role of the towage contract

As seen above in Chapter 2, pursuant to the terms implied at common law which found their most detailed exposition in the decisions of the Privy Council in *The Julia* (1861) 14 Moo. P.C. 210 and *The Minnehaha* (1861) 15 Moo. P.C. 133, the tug owes a duty to the tow to exercise all reasonable care and skill in and about the towage operation, including the navigation of the tow. Similarly, the tow owes a duty to the tug so to dispose herself in navigational matters as not to prevent the fulfilment of the towage operation by the tug. Very often, there will be a considerable overlap between the duties owed by tug and tow *inter se* in the performance of the towage contract and those owed to others in the navigation of the towage convoy. Thus, as part of its duty to the tow, the tug is required to proceed at a proper and safe speed. That duty is usually co-extensive with that owed to other vessels. Similarly, the tow, if directing the navigation, is required to stop the tug proceeding either at all or at an inappropriate speed in fog or where there are obstacles to navigation. The duty is owed both to the tug and to other vessels who may be encountered by tug and tow. However, while the implied duties on tug and tow are framed in terms of the proper fulfilment of the contract (or as Lord Kingsdown put it in *The Julia*, "an engagement that each vessel would perform its duty in completing it" and, in *The Minnehaha*, "[the tug] does engage that she will use her best endeavours" for that purpose [i.e. the contract "to tow a vessel from one point to another"]), the duty of care upon each vessel which is owed to other vessels and owners of other maritime property will extend wider and will be defined by the requirement upon each vessel to exercise care not just towards each other but also to third parties.

The statement by Lord Sterndale M.R. in *The Francis Batey* (1921) 8 Ll. L. Rep. 247 in relation to the position of the tow is equally applicable as regards the tug's and tow's individual duties to third parties in respect of their joint activities.

"I think it is very important to maintain what I think is the law as laid down by all the cases, that although the tug may be in charge of the navigation, that does not dispense the tow from taking the ordinary precautions that ought to be taken, and that a tow has no right to go about without any look-out and to allow herself to run blindly into danger, simply because the tug is in charge of the navigation."

2. The duties upon the tug

The general incidents of the duty of the tug to navigate herself and her tow safely have been considered above in the context of the tug's contractual obligations (see Chapter 2). From the perspective of third party vessels, the essential features of the duty of good seamanship and prudent and skilful navigation as it impinges upon a tug with a tow are the following.

  (i) Notwithstanding that the tug may receive her orders as to navigation from the tow, the tug is under a separate duty to take such course as will carry her tow and herself clear of collision and avoid other damage: see *The Sinquasi* (1889) 5 P.D. 241 and *Spaight* v. *Tedcastle* (1881) 6 App. Cas. 217.

  (ii) This is especially so in waters which present special difficulties for a towage convoy such as narrow channels or other waters which are confined in sea-room or which are made so by press of other shipping. In such waters, the tug will usually have the special burden of deciding upon course and speed changes and of responding to sudden difficulties: see *The Isca* (1886) 12 P.D. 34 and *The Sinquasi* (1880) 5 P.D. 241.

(iii) The separate duty upon the tug to take care both for herself, her tow and other vessels encountered will, where necessary, require the tug to make her own appreciation of the situation where the tow gives an order to the tug. If that order is incorrect or if it is an improper or negligent order and this can be appreciated by the tug exercising reasonable care and seamanship, then the order should be refused and the tug should take her own course as she sees fit. As Dr Lushington crisply put in *The Duke of Manchester* (1846) 4 Notes of Cases 575 at 582:

> "The vessel and the lives of the crew are not to be risked because there is a law which imposes the ordinary responsibility upon one individual . . . . It is not for [the tug], knowing the danger, to maintain, as it were, a sulky silence, and make herself, as it were, instrumental in the destruction of life and property."

(iv) The tug's separate duty will most often be particularly acute in questions of speed. See, for example, *The American* and *Syria* (1874) L.R. 6 P.C. 127 in which the *American*, towing the *Syria*, saw another vessel shortly ahead. The towing vessel should have reduced speed but instead attempted to cross in front of the other vessel. She collided with her and then the *Syria* under tow was pulled into collision with her and sank her. The tug was held solely to blame. This is especially so in conditions of reduced visibility such as fog (see *The Challenge and Duc d'Aumale* [1905] P. 198).

(v) It is also acute in questions of look-out where the tug is under a duty to keep a good look-out not only for herself but also for her tow, even when the same is manned, since the latter cannot always see ahead or do so in the same way. In *The Jane Bacon* (1878) 27 W.R. 35 (C.A.), it was stated that it was the duty of the vessel towing to keep a look-out for both herself and the tow.

(vi) As for the tug's duties as to lights being burned on the tow: see below at p. 192.

3. The duties upon the tow

As the dicta by Buckley L.J. in *The S.S. Devonshire* [1912] P. 21 (C.A.) (cited at pp. 48–49 above) and by Lord Sterndale M.R. in *The Francis Batey* (1921) 8 Ll. L. Rep. 247 (p. 190 above) make clear, the tow, even though she may be completely under the impulsion and direction of the tug, is not thereby relieved of her own separate duty to exercise reasonable care and good seamanship in the navigation of the towage convoy, so far as she is able. The extent of her duty will vary according to her own capabilities. The following examples may be considered:

(i) If the tow is fully manned and capable of independent propulsion and steerage, she will often be required to give orders as to the navigation both of herself and the tug, at least when the towage convoy is in open sea: see e.g. *The Niobe* (1888) 13 P.D. 55 and *The Energy* (1870) L.R. 3. A. & E. 48 (*cf.* where the convoy is in crowded waters: as to which see above).

(ii) If the tow is a vessel not capable of such independent means of navigation, such as a dumb barge, she will still be required to exercise care in all matters which she can influence, such as her lights (see *The Albion* [1952] 1 Lloyd's Rep. 38) and the keeping of a proper look-out on board her both for herself and the tug (see: *The Francis Batey* (1921) 6 Ll. L. Rep. 389).

An interesting example of the way in which the duty of seamanship will be dependent upon the state and condition of the tow is given by the case of *The Marmion* (1913) 29 T.L.R. 646. In this case, a vessel was under tow by two tugs. She collided with another vessel; the tow had no steam up on her main engine; the head tug was blowing a signal indicating that she was about to turn; there was no signal from the tow. The court held that it was good seamanship not to blow the whistle on board the tow when there was no steam on the main engine as the whistle would indicate the existence of such steam and the consequent inference would be that the tow could work her main engines.

Whatever the state or condition of the tow, provided that she is manned (and if she is of a type of vessel which should be manned when under tow, such as a dumb barge upon a busy river, then failure to man her may, of itself, amount to a failure to exercise good seamanship: see *The Harlow* [1922] P. 175), then certain paramount duties will always be imposed upon her. *First*, it is her duty to warn the tug of any navigational dangers which she perceives to threaten either the tug, herself or both tug and tow: see the colourful if antique method of warning the tug by "girting the tug" which it was held that the tow should have used in *The Niobe* (1888) 13 P.D. 55. *Secondly*, the tow must follow the tug faithfully in her course and, in the absence of an obviously ill-considered improper movement by the tug, be diligent in altering course to follow that of the tug (see, for example, *The Jane Bacon* (1878) 27 W.R. 35). *Thirdly*, and often very importantly, the tow must always be alert as to the possibility of having to slip the tow-line: see *The Energy* (1870) L.R. 3 A. & E. 48.

4. Special aspects of the Collision Regulations

The Collision Regulations lay down navigational rules and requirements which are of general application. However, certain provisions specifically applicable to tug and tow and some general provisions which arise in a towage context should be noted. These provisions fall into three categories.

(1) Lights and shapes

Rule 24 makes specific and detailed provision for the lights and shapes to be exhibited by vessels towing and being towed (or pushing and being pushed) where the towing or pushing vessel is a power-driven vessel. It is set out in Appendix 5.

Special questions have arisen in the past in relation to the respective obligation of tug and tow as to lights.

One such question arises as to the circumstances in which it is the responsibility of the tug to burn towing lights, but that of the tow to burn such lights to show she is at anchor. In *The Romance* [1901] P. 15, a pair of tugs had in tow a vessel which was being taken to a nearby anchorage. The tugs carried their towing and side lights, but the tow carried lights indicating that she was at anchor. In the course of the towage operation, a collision took place between the tow and a fourth vessel, necessitating a salvage service eventually being performed by one of the tugs for the benefit of the tow. In defence to the claim of the tug to a salvage award, the tow contended that the collision which gave rise to the alleged salvage service occurred only by reason of the negligence of the tugs in exhibiting inappropriate and misleading light configurations. In holding that the contention failed, Gorell Barnes J. stated that the lights displayed by each of the vessels were appropriate and correct, including those of the tow itself. In a similar case, *The Devonian* [1901] P. 221, a vessel lay at anchor in the River Mersey. She carried appropriate lights, and a tug to which she was made fast and which, albeit not towing, was standing by on her starboard side, burned its masthead and side lights as opposed to its towing lights. The *Devonian* collided with the vessel at anchor. The latter brought proceedings against the *Devonian*, which argued that the collision had resulted from a misleading light display by the tug standing by the casualty. In line with the decision in *The Romance*, Sir Francis Jeune P., with the subsequent approval of the Court of Appeal, held that the tug, albeit not actually in the process of towing, was "attached for the purpose of towing" and, accordingly, by not burning towing lights had displayed inappropriate lights. This was so, notwithstanding that there was no tension on the towing hawser at the time of the collision.

A further issue which arose in *The Devonian* [1901] P. 221, was the extent to which a tow owes a duty to a third party to ensure that its tug is exhibiting appropriate lights. The Court of Appeal, affirming the decision of Sir Francis Jeune P., held that the failure of the tug standing by the casualty to display appropriate lights barred recovery against the *Devonian*. In setting out the test, Sir Francis Jeune P. stated ([1901] P. 221):

"Were the two (the tug and the tow) in such a position towards one another that the control of the tow over the tug was practicable and possible? ... I should say that in all those cases where liability has been established, it has been because the tow was in a position to exercise control, and that control over the tug ought to have been applied."

The position is the same in reverse, it may be noted. A tug or towing vessel will be liable for damage resulting from the display of improper lights by its tow, as was held in *The Mary Hounsell* (1879) 4 P.D. 204. See also *The Albion* [1953] 2 Lloyd's Rep. 82.

(2) Sound signals

Rule 35, which makes provision for sound signals in restricted visibility whether by day or night, makes specific provision for the sound signals to be made by tug and tow in such visibility. The signals to be sounded are the following:

(i) *By the tug*: pursuant to Rule 35(c), a vessel engaged in towing or pushing another vessel shall, instead of sounding the usual signals, "sound at intervals of not more than two minutes three blasts in succession, namely, one prolonged followed by two short blasts".

(ii) *By the tow*: pursuant to Rule 35(e), a vessel towed (or if there is a flotilla of more than one towed vessel, the last of the towed vessels) if she is manned is to sound "at intervals of not more than two minutes four blasts in succession, namely, one prolonged followed by three short blasts". To promote the avoidance of confusion in dissonance between tug and tow, Rule 35(e) further provides that:

> "When practicable, this signal shall be made immediately after the signal made by the towing vessel."

Where tug and tow are acting as pushing and pushed vessels and "are rigidly connected in a composite unit", then they are to be treated as an ordinary power-driven vessel and are to obey the ordinary sound signals in restricted visibility set out in Rules 35(a) and (b).

(3) Navigational rules

How are tug and tow to be treated as regards the body of the Rules regulating navigation? The towage convoy, at its least numerous, will comprise two vessels or one vessel (the tug) and one other type of water-borne object. Are the vessels to be treated as one or as separate vessels? How is the water-borne object to be treated?

(a) Application to water-borne objects

To take the latter case first: the Rules "apply to all vessels upon the high seas and in all waters connected therewith navigable by seagoing vessels": Rule 1(a). Rule 3(a) defines "vessel" in the following manner:

> "(a) The word 'vessel' includes every description of water craft, including non-displacement craft and sea planes, used or capable of being used as a means of transportation on water."

A tug will, accordingly, be treated as sea-going within the meaning of the Rules if upon the high seas or waters connected therewith. While the Rules will also apply to the tow if the tow is a "water craft used or capable of being used as a means of transportation on water", if the tow consists of a water-borne object, such as a caisson or other object which does not resemble a "water craft", the Rules will not apply to her (or it).

However, the application of the Rules to the tug in such a case will mean that the Rules will have to be observed by the tug, both on her own behalf and that of the tow, and that third party vessels encountering tug and tow in navigation may have to adapt their navigation to the special constraints imposed by an unwieldy towage convoy. In particular, the Rules make special provision for a vessel restricted in her ability to manoeuvre "being a vessel which from the nature of her work is restricted in her ability to manoeuvre as required by these Rules and is therefore unable to keep out of the way of another vessel": see Rule 3(g), which by sub-paragraph (vi) includes within the non-definitive list of instances of such vessels the case of:

> "(vi) a vessel engaged in a towing operation which severely restricts the towing vessel and her tow in their ability to deviate from their course."

(b) Tug and tow: How treated

As to the first case: are tug and tow to be treated as one (composite) vessel or two separate vessels? In the earliest days of towage, a tug and tow under way were treated as a composite unit and as one (extended) vessel for the purposes of collision regulations. The rule was put pithily by the Privy Council in *The Cleadon* (1860) 14 Moo. P.C. 97. In that case, a tug and tow collided with a third vessel at night. The decision of the Privy Council was summarised by Dr Lushington in this report of the decision (at (1860) Lush. 158) as follows:

"The vessel towed and the vessel towing are to be considered as one long steamer for the conduct of which the vessel towed is responsible and the vessel being so towed at night is bound to avoid other vessels"

(see also *The American and The Syria* (1874) L.R. 6 P.C. 127 at 132). From Dr Lushington's summary of the rule, it is evident that the rule sprang from two different sources. First, from the practical considerations of two vessels under way together which, so long as the towage was maintained, were incapable of independent navigation; in other words, a composite of vessels but essentially acting as one single vessel. Secondly, and unsupportable since 1912, from the presumption (largely fostered by Dr Lushington) that the tow is presumed to be responsible for the acts of the tug and that the command of the towage convoy should not be treated as a divided command but as one single command, with that command or "control" reposing in the tow.

While this presumption received its long overdue *quietus* in the decision of the House of Lords in *The S.S. Devonshire* v. *The Barge Leslie* [1912] A.C. 634, for the purposes of the Collision Regulations the tug and tow convoy are frequently treated as one vessel. But it will be a question of fact in each case dependent upon the circumstances of the towage. Thus, if the tow is unmanned, the tug and tow will often be one navigational unit in practice and treated as such under the Regulations. In such a case, the tug will for many purposes not be mistress of her own movements and will be severely limited in her power and ability to stop or to reduce the tow's speed or to make sudden changes in the course which either of them follow through the water. In *The Lord Bangor* [1898] P. 28, a barque was in tow of a tug in St. George's Channel. A steamship crossed and the tug and tow heard her whistle signals (as the steamship heard their signals). It was held that the tug and tow could not have stopped or gone slower than they did and were not to blame for the ensuing collision. Sir Francis Jeune P. summarised the findings of the Trinity Masters sitting as assessors as follows (at p. 33):

"Now, no one can doubt that the case of *The Knarwater* shews that many of the ordinary obligations of a steamer are shared by a tug and her tow, because to a great extent the tow and tug together partake of the nature of a steamer. They are bound in many cases by the same rules, and there are a great many things which a steamer ought to do which a tow and tug can and ought to do. Is that true in this particular case? Assume that the obligation on a steamer was to stop, is there anything in the nature of things in the case of a tow and tug which makes a modification of that rule essential? On this point I have consulted the Trinity Masters, and they tell me that they think there is. Of course a tug can do a good many things with her tow in the way of stopping and altering her course. If she is approaching another vessel she can tow ahead or astern, or a variety of things of that kind, but where it is a matter of stopping, apart from the question of casting off, is it practicable for a tug and tow to reduce themselves to a condition of absolute standstill? The Trinity Masters tell me that in their judgment it is not, and one can see that that is the commonsense of the matter. If a tug absolutely stops what happens? The weight of the wire rope will draw the tow up to the tug, and if it be a screw there will be risk of fouling the propeller. Then it becomes necessary for the tug to go ahead a little bit, and she must draw the tow after her, and so you cannot obtain a position of absolute standstill. In this case was the movement of the tug and tow more than was necessary, they being a tug and tow? The facts appear clear that it was about as slow as it possibly could be."

Compare *The Challenge and Duc d'Aumale* [1905] P. 198 in which, on similar facts, it was found that the tug could have stopped and taken way off the tow and that she was to blame for the collision. If on the other hand, the tow is well able to respond herself and can shape her own course, then the factual classification of both as one vessel may be less appropriate. Similarly, the sea-room available to the towage convoy may well bear on whether they are to be treated as one or two vessels: on the open sea, it may be convenient and practical to treat them as one (large) navigational unit; this may be unrealistic in the narrow confines of a harbour or channel.

Even when treated as "one long steamer" for the purposes of the Collision Regulations, tug and tow will often be treated as a special sort of steamer to which particular considerations apply. In *The Arthur Gordon* (1861) Lush. 270, the Privy Council qualified the position of tug and tow as a single navigational unit by stating that in the ordinary course it was nevertheless inappropriate to treat the unit as if a free vessel under way; a third vessel owed a duty to have regard to her special features and to keep out of the way of tug and tow. Similarly in *The La Plata* (1857) Swa. 220, Dr Lushington held that in applying the starboard hand rule in a narrow channel, while tug and tow were to be treated as if one vessel, some latitude was appropriate and the rule should be applied more flexibly than in the case of a single free vessel navigating alone. See also *The Kingston-By-Sea* (1850) 3 W. Rob. 155.

PART C. COLLISION BETWEEN TUG AND TOW

1. The relevance of the contract

In almost all modern cases of collision between tug and tow, the position is covered by the express provisions of the contract. Section 187(5) of the Merchant Shipping Act 1995 (replacing section 1(1)(c) of the Maritime Conventions Act 1911) expressly preserves the right of parties to contract out of the regime for the apportionment of liability laid down by the Act. Various possible solutions, usually at the expense of the tow, are adopted by the standard forms of contract as have been seen above. The most common are:

(i) A provision which deems the crew of the tug to be the servants of the tow with the result that no claim based on the negligence of such crew can be brought by the tow, since, as between tug and tow, the tow is their employer, not the tug.

(ii) A provision which renders the tow liable to indemnify the tug for all damage sustained by the tug, however caused and whether or not by the tug's own negligence; this is often coupled with a provision by which the tow agrees to hold the tug harmless in respect of loss or damage sustained by the tow or for any liabilities which the tug may incur in respect of the same.

(iii) Under the more balanced regime adopted in the BIMCO standard forms of contract, the tug or tow each agree alone to bear the risk of loss and damage to their respective vessels even if caused by the other and to indemnify each other in respect of any liabilities which each may incur in respect of loss or damage to the other's property.

2. Where the contract is silent

Where the contract is silent and where the collision is due to negligent navigation rather than to some separate and distinct breach of contract (such as an unseaworthy tug or one with defective towing gear), then in the event that the tug is alone at fault, it will be liable and, in the event that tug and tow are both to blame, then the ordinary rules of apportionment and of cross-actions or counterclaims will apply. See section D below where these rules are considered in relation to collision with their vessels.

PART D. COLLISIONS DURING THE TOWAGE WHICH INVOLVE A THIRD VESSEL

1. The irrelevance of the contract

As has been seen above, when considering the respective liabilities of tug and tow in the case of a collision involving a third vessel, while any contractual provisions such as those just considered above which render the tow (or the tug) responsible or liable for the acts of tug (or the tow) in respect of negligent navigation are binding as between tug and tow, they are of no effect between tug and tow and the third vessel. The third vessel is entitled (and obliged) to identify, first, the actual wrongdoer whose acts or omissions caused the collision and, secondly, the person who in law is responsible for that person's acts. As the court remarked in *The M.S.C. Panther and The Ericbank* [1957] 1 Lloyd's Rep. 57 at pp. 63–64:

"In all the circumstances I agree with counsel for the plaintiffs that it is necessary to decide, first, whether anyone was to blame, and, if so, who, for the fact that the *Trishna* and the *M.S.C. Panther* came into contact, and secondly, whether the failure to stop the propeller of the *M.S.C. Panther* was blameworthy and, if so, to whom the blame is to be imputed. It clearly required the combination of contact between the vessels with the fact of the propeller being in motion to bring about the major part of the damage."

This results from the straightforward application of the rule of privity of contract; while the towage contract regulates the mutual rights and responsibilities of tug and tow, as regards a third party the contract is irrelevant as a *res inter alios acta*. An example of this principle can be seen in *The Socrates and The Champion* [1923] P. 76. In that case, a vessel sued the owners of a tow and its tug for collision damage resulting from the tug's negligence. Hill J. held that it was not open to the tug to contend that, by reason of the fact that the crew of the tug were contractually obliged to, and did, obey the commands of the tow, it bore no responsibility and that it was not itself negligent.

"The tug was co-operating in an operation which was negligent as regards the [casualty] or any other ships in the river. The master [of the tug] was the servant of the owners [of the tug]. He was, it is true, under a contractual obligation to obey the orders received from the [tow]. He may have been under a legal obligation to obey the orders of the pilot of the [tow] if, as I suppose, pilotage was compulsory, ... If he co-operates in an operation which is negligent as regards the rest of the world, is it any answer to say 'I did it because I had voluntarily put myself under the orders of another person'? I think not. *Qua* the [casualty], the [tug] cannot be regarded as an innocent ship."

2. The doctrine of control

The factual question as to the identity of the individual person or persons who are at fault in navigation is often straightforward, but it leaves unanswered the question of which of tug and tow is to be regarded as responsible for their actions *vis-à-vis* a third party involved in the collision.

   This question is usually answered by identifying which of tug and tow was in control of the navigation of the towage convoy at the relevant time. The question of control arises between tug and tow and is often to be answered by a consideration of the practical consequences of the contract. Even though the contract cannot of itself bind the third party, the factual state of affairs as to navigation of the towage convoy which results from it will often be an important factor in the assessment to be carried out by the third party as to which of tug and tow was in control at the time of the collision.

(a) The old law

The cases before the turn of the nineteenth century adopted a fairly absolute presumption that the tug was the servant of the tow in all cases. In *The Ticonderoga* (1857) Swa. 215, Dr Lushington dealt with the position of a vessel which, pursuant to the terms of a governing charterparty, was bound to engage the services of a tug. In the course of the towing operation the vessel came into contact with and damaged a third vessel by reason of fault on the part of the towing vessel. Dr Lushington set out a broad statement of principle:

"In cases of one vessel coming into collision with another, and the vessel proceeded against having been in charge of a steamer, there can be no doubt whatever that the vessel which has the steamer in her employ is responsible both for her own acts and those of the steamer."

Similarly, in *The Sinquasi* (1880) 5 P.D. 241, a tug, which was officially in the charge of the tow, improperly and without warning or approval altered course. The sudden alteration brought the tow into collision with a pier head at the opening to the Regent's Canal Basin. Sir Robert Phillimore, in line with the decision in *The Ticonderoga*, held that the tow was liable for the damage to the pier, stating at p. 244:

"The tug was the servant of the *Sinquasi* and the *Sinquasi* is responsible for what the tug did."

Doubts as to the validity of this approach came to be expressed from about 1885. In *The Stormcock* (1885) 5 Asp. M.L.C. 470, in which a tug towing at night collided with a third vessel, Sir James Hannen P., who found that the tow was in no respect negligent, notwithstanding that both counsel admitted that the tow was liable for the actions of the tug, commented in relation to the "presumption":

"I confess I have been somewhat astonished to find to what extent that principle has been carried by my learned predecessors. But for those decisions, apparently based, according to Dr Lushington, on considerations of expediency, that there should not be divided command, I myself should have been inclined to think that the decisions of the American courts establish a rule more in conformity with my own ideas of justice; that is, that the particular circumstances should be looked at in each case to see whether the tug or the tow, or both, are liable."

Despite this obvious inclination toward what is now the prevailing approach to the doctrine of control, the President abided by the earlier decisions of Dr Lushington. However, further progress was made in his decision in *The Niobe* (1888) 13 P.D. 55 which concerned a tug which, while towing, collided with a third vessel which proceeded to sue the tow. The tug admitted liability but both tug and tow were held to be liable, the tow on the basis that it had failed to keep a good look-out and had failed to check the speed of the tug. Sir James Hannen P. stated that:

"I agree that in a towage at sea with a long scope it is more difficult for the tow to communicate with the tug, and if it had been shown that the *Flying Serpent* (the tug), by some sudden manoeuvre which those on board the *Niobe* (the tow) could not control, had brought about the collision, I should have held the *Niobe* blameless."

This general implied acknowledgement that a tow is not always liable for the acts of its tug also gained the approval of the Court of Appeal in *The Morgengry and Blackcock* [1900] P. 1, where at p. 10 it was observed by A.L. Smith L.J.:

" . . . a tow is not always responsible for the acts of its tug, though in many cases it is."

Further recognition came with the decision of Sir Francis Jeune P. in *The Devonian* [1901] P. 221 where, at p. 229, the emphasis upon the circumstances of the case in contrast with a supposed intendment of liability was expressed as the question:

"Were the two (the tug and tow) in such a position towards one another that the control of the tow over the tug was practicable and possible?",

while Lord Alverstone C.J. observed at p. 237:

"Speaking for myself, I think that if two vessels are so attached, and are under such management and control that they move practically as one vessel, the tow is responsible for the action of the tug."

(b) The test in The Devonshire

This principle of fixing the tow with responsibility for the fault of the tug regardless of which vessel actually had control of the navigation of the convoy was overruled by the decision of the House of Lords in *S.S. Devonshire (Owners)* v. *The Barge Leslie (Owners)* [1912] A.C. 634, which held that the tow will not be held liable for the acts and omissions of her tug unless those on board and in charge of the tug, who were responsible for the wrongful acts, were actually acting under the control of the tow. This is not a question of law, as once it was considered, but an issue of fact, to be determined in each case according to its own circumstances: see per Lord Ashbourne at p. 648 and Lord Atkinson at p. 656 (and note also Lord Atkinson's reference at p. 655 to the question of which vessel possessed the "governing power").

While the pre-*Devonshire* cases must now be treated with caution, often the factual circumstances considered in those cases and the result arrived at offer useful guidance in identifying where control for the navigation lies. Examples of these cases are referred to in Chapter 2.

(c) "Control" not necessarily decisive

The mere fact of the tug or the tow having control over the navigation will not of itself be necessarily decisive of liability for the collision. No vessel is a passive spectator. Each vessel remains always under an obligation to exercise reasonable care in and about her navigation simply as a matter of self-help and of a duty owed to others: see Buckley L.J.'s dictum in *The Devonshire* [1912] P. 21, cited above (pp. 48–49). Thus if a tug is in control of the navigation of a dumb barge manned by a lighterman and she proceeds too fast causing the barge to bear down on another vessel, the barge may be solely at fault, irrespective of the question of control, if the collision could have been avoided by merely slipping the tow-line in good time. Similarly, where a tug is under the orders of the tow which is directing navigation and has control of the same, the tug will still be solely to blame if she negligently manoeuvres in executing an otherwise proper order given to her by the tow. The tug may also be liable if the order given by the tow is one which, if the tug had exercised its own seamanlike appreciation of the position, was patently negligent and should not have been followed, but which the tug nevertheless heedlessly obeys.

3. Liabilities between tug, tow and third party vessel

(1) Third party vessel not to blame

Where a collision occurs between tug and/or tow and a third party vessel and the third party vessel is innocent of blame, the possible liabilities of tug and tow, depending upon the allocation of fault and the incidence of control, can be summarised as follows:

> (i) Where a tow collides with a third vessel and is solely to blame, the tow will be solely liable.
>
> (ii) Where a tug, with a vessel in tow, collides with a third vessel and is solely to blame, the tug will be solely liable.
>
> (iii) Where a tug and tow are in collision with an innocent third vessel by reason of fault on the part of the tow:

(a) the tow owners will be liable;

(b) the tug owners may also be liable if the collision resulted, even in part, from an error on the part of the tug in directing the course of the tug or, in the case of the example, referred to above, the tug being negligent in its navigation by its obedience to the unseamanlike orders of the tow.

(iv) Where a tow collides with a third vessel by reason only of the fault of the tug:

(a) the tug owners will be liable;

(b) the tow owners may be liable also if it is demonstrated that, in all the circumstances, the tow retained control of the navigation of both tug and tow (see, for example, *The Umona* [1914] P. 141).

(v) Where a tug and/or its tow collide with a third vessel and both tug and tow are to blame, both will be jointly and severally liable.

(2) Third party vessel also to blame

Where a tug and/or tow collide with a third vessel which is also to blame, liability between the vessels will be apportioned according to the relative gravity of their respective faults pursuant to section 187 of the Merchant Shipping Act 1995 (replacing section 1 of the Maritime Conventions Act 1911) in the ordinary way. This provides in so far as material:

"187(1) Where, by the fault of tow or more ships, damage or loss is caused to one or more of those ships, to their cargoes or freight, or to any property on board, the liability to make good the damage or loss shall be in proportion to the degree in which each ship was in fault.

(2) If, in any such case, it is not possible to establish different degrees of fault, the liability shall be apportioned equally.

(4) Nothing in this section shall operate so as to render any ship liable for any loss or damage to which the fault of the ship has not contributed."

The rule now contained within section 187 of the 1995 Act has been held to apply in circumstances where, notwithstanding its wording, the vessels at fault were not themselves in collision. This will often be very material in the case of a collision involving an innocent barge and a tug and third vessel at fault. In *The Cairnbahn* [1914] P. 25, a hopper barge collided with a steamship, the *Cairnbahn*, while being towed. The owners of the barge brought proceedings against the tug which towed them and the steamship. The steamship, at the same time, brought a counterclaim against the tug. On the facts, the steamship and the tug were held to be equally to blame for the collision. The steamship satisfied the entire claim of the barge and then sought to recover half of its payment from the wrongdoing tug relying on section 1 of the Maritime Conventions Act 1911 (corresponding now to section 187 of the Merchant Shipping Act 1995). The owners of the tug contended that section 1 was not applicable because the actual vessels in collision in their case were not both wrongdoers. The Court of Appeal held that the Act was applicable. At pp. 32–33 Lord Sumner observed:

"Why does not s.1, sub-s.1, of the Maritime Conventions Act 1911 [i.e. see now section 187(1) of the Merchant Shipping Act 1995] apply to this case? Though damage may be caused to a vessel, loss cannot be, nor is the phrase 'damage is caused to a vessel' apt to express simply that the vessel is damaged. Loss is caused to the owners and charterers of the vessel, and damage is caused to them too when the vessel is damaged. I think the section regulates rights and liabilities between parties in fault and extends to pecuniary prejudice, which may accrue, legally and not too remotely, to persons interested in vessels by reason of the faulty navigation of persons for whom they are responsible. The word 'loss' is wide enough to include that form of pecuniary prejudice which consists in compensating third parties for wrong done to them by the fault of persons for whose misconduct the party prejudiced must answer. It covers the sum recovered by the owners of the hopper against the owners of the *Cairnbahn*. To say that damage to the hopper is not loss to the *Cairnbahn* so as to be loss or damage caused to one or more of 'those vessels', namely, those vessels which are at fault, is to make this remedial legislation unexpectedly one-sided. Is the jurisdiction to apportion the consequences between the vessels in fault to stop short at the consequences to the vessel and not to extend to the consequences to the owners? I cannot doubt that where the jurisdiction to apportion such consequences applies it is meant to apply widely."

At p. 38 Warrington J. put the matter more shortly:

"I am, therefore, of opinion that, according to the true construction of the Act, all damage or loss to one or more of the vessels in fault is to be apportioned between those vessels, whether it arises from collision between them or not."

The section will also apply to a claim by a tow against her tug for loss or damage which the tow has suffered by reason of the joint negligence of both tug and tow, for both of these are wrongdoing vessels within the ambit of the provision: see *The Francis Batey* (1921) 8 Ll. L. Rep. 247.

CHAPTER 8

Towage and Limitation of Liability

PART A. LIMITING LIABILITY: GENERAL PRINCIPLES

1. Historical background

(1) A question of policy

The right in English law of a shipowner to limit his liability to a fixed sum calculated by reference to the tonnage of his vessel in the event of loss or damage caused to others by his vessel or his crew, rather than by his personal fault or omission, is of considerable antiquity (the first statute of limitation of liability was in 1734, 7 Geo. 2, c. 15). The right is a creature of statute and, although it may appear to work injustice in certain cases, it is well-settled as a matter of public policy and is (arguably) defensible upon these grounds (see e.g. a recent critique by D.W. Steel Q.C.: *Ships are different* [1995] LMCLQ 77). As Lord Denning M.R. summarised the position in *The Bramley Moore* [1964] P. 200 at 220:

" . . . but limitation of liability is not a matter of justice. It is a rule of public policy which has its origin in history and its justification in convenience."

A detailed consideration of the law relating to limitation of liability is outside the scope of this book. For a detailed account, see *Limitation of Shipowners' Liability: The New Law*, ed. Professor N. Gaskell, (1986) Sweet and Maxwell; for a basic summary, see Griggs and Williams, *Limitation of Liability* (2nd Edn.), LLP.

However, a consideration of the historical development of the statutory limitation of a shipowner's liability is necessary in order to put into context the decisions of the English courts on certain important limitation questions touching upon tug and tow.

(2) The English approach

The English statutory approach to limitation of liability became gradually defined during the eighteenth and nineteenth centuries (see e.g. the Responsibility of Ship-owners Act 1813 and the Merchant Shipping Act 1854). Certain features of that approach set it apart from corresponding developments in the law of the United States and of other ship-owning nations, such as the Scandinavian states. The features of the

English approach were five-fold: (i) the shipowner was entitled to limit his liability to a sum of money calculated by reference to a fixed sum multiplied by the tonnage of the offending vessel rather than upon the value of the ship after the casualty; (ii) the claims in respect of which the shipowner could invoke limitation were confined, at first, to claims in respect of damage to property with, thereafter, a special limitation category for claims for death and personal injury; (iii) the "fund" produced by the tonnage calculation was to be distributed between the claimants *pro rata* in proportion to the size of their claims one to another (*cf.* the approach in other jurisdictions which adopted a gradation of claimants on principles akin to those regulating priorities *in rem*); (iv) the English approach restricted the application of limitation of liability to claims arising on any one distinct occasion rather than permitting its application to a simple aggregation of all claims which had accrued at the date of the casualty; (v) the right to limit liability was lost in the event that the loss and damage or casualty resulted from personal fault on the part of the shipowner himself rather than from the negligence or default of his crew.

(3) Section 503 of the Merchant Shipping Act 1894

These principles were reflected in the first of the modern statutes dealing with limitation of liability, the Merchant Shipping Act 1894 in its section 503. As originally enacted, section 503 of the Act provided for a system of limitation based on a fixed sum per ton of the vessel's tonnage, calculated in accordance with the Act. The right to limit granted to shipowners was lost in the event that the relevant "occurrence" took place "with their actual fault or privity".

The English law of limitation of liability remained that enacted in the 1894 Act. In 1924 the Comité Maritime International was prominent in the adoption and promotion of an International Convention on Limitation which allowed the shipowner the right to choose between limiting on the basis of a sum per ton (corresponding closely to the English system) and the value of the vessel and its freight. The United Kingdom did not accede to the Convention which remained, consequently, of limited effect, although it was adopted by several important ship-owning nations.

Following World War II, further progress was made at the international and conventional level. The 1957 Convention Relating to the Limitation of Liability of Owners of Sea-going Ships was the result. This Convention marked the international recognition and adoption of the English statutory approach set out in the 1894 Act, coupled with a much wider application of the right of limit to cover, in practice, all liabilities in respect of loss and damage occasioned by the shipowner's operation of a vessel. The close correspondence between the 1957 Convention and the English statutory system led to the amendment of the 1894 Act by the Merchant Shipping (Liability of Shipowners and Others) Act 1958 to implement the 1957 Convention.

The Merchant Shipping Acts 1979, 1981 and 1984 made further changes to the 1894 Act, principally to change the limitation figures to Special Drawing Right figures and to increase the limitation fund.

(4) The Merchant Shipping Act 1979 (replaced by the Merchant Shipping Act 1995): The new regime

The limitation figures adopted by the Convention were little higher than those used in the nineteenth-century United Kingdom statutes. The inadequacy and insufficiency of these rapidly became apparent in the 1960s. The growing awareness of oil pollution risks and the consequent adoption in 1969 of the Convention on Civil Liability for Oil Pollution Damage with a greatly increased limitation figure for oil pollution damage led the CMI to start work on the revision of the 1957 Convention.

The 1976 Convention which resulted made a radical change to the approach of the 1957 Convention. While liability was still to be limited by reference to a limitation figure or "fund" calculated on the basis of the defendant vessel's tonnage, that limit was greatly increased. (Although the increase did little more than to reflect what was, in 1976, the level of limit used in the 1924 Convention, scaled up for the change in money values). In return for the increase in the level of the limitation fund, the Convention abandoned the test of "actual fault or privity" on the part of the owner seeking to limit liability as the test for conduct which removed the right to limit and replaced it with a much more exacting test from the point of view of the claimant seeking to break the limit. In the words of Article 4:

"A person shall not be entitled to limit his liability if it is proved that the loss resulted from his personal act or omission, committed with the intent to cause such loss or recklessly and with knowledge that such loss would probably result."

The change in the test for conduct barring limitation has resulted in a change in the burden of proof in the ordinary limitation action. Whereas, under the old 1894 and 1958 Merchant Shipping Acts, the burden was on the shipowner asserting his right to limit to establish that the casualty had occurred without his actual fault or privity, under the 1976 Convention, the burden is on the claimant to establish intention or recklessness on the part of the shipowner under Article 4, see e.g. *The Bowbelle* [1990] 1 Lloyd's Rep. 532 (Sheen J.). In practice, in all but the rarest cases it will be extremely difficult for a claimant to discharge the burden, notwithstanding that under the amended Rules of the Supreme Court he may seek discovery before deciding whether or not to contest the owner's limitation action: see R.S.C., Order 75, rules 37 to 40.

The 1976 Convention was enacted by the Merchant Shipping Act 1979. That Act, in so far as material, has been repealed and replaced by the new codification statute, the Merchant Shipping Act 1995.

2. The framework of the 1976 Convention and the Merchant Shipping Act 1995

For present purposes, the relevant provisions of the 1976 Convention in addition to Article 4 may be noted.

(i) *Who can limit liability?* By Article 1 of the Convention "shipowners and salvors" as defined in the Convention may limit liability. "Shipowner" means "the owners, charterer, manager and operator of a sea-going ship" and "salvor" means "any person rendering services in direct connection with salvage operators": see Articles 1(2) and 1(3). The express inclusion of salvors as persons entitled to limit remedies the deficiency in the 1957 Convention identified in *The Tojo Maru* [1972] A.C. 242.

(ii) *In respect of what claims can limitation be invoked?* Articles 2 and 3 define those claims for which limitation may and may not be invoked. Claims for salvage, general average and oil pollution damage are excluded (see Article 3(a) and (b)). In practice, claims arising out of towage will fall under Article 2(2)(a) as:

> "Claims in respect of loss of life or personal injury or loss of or damage to property (including damage to harbour works, basins and waterways and aids to navigation), occurring on board or in direct connection with the operation of the ship or with salvage operations, and consequential loss resulting therefrom."

(iii) *What is the limit?* Article 6 sets out the limitation figures in "Units of Account" defined in Article 8 as IMF Special Drawing Rights or "SDRs". The limit is in respect of "liability for claims" (other than passenger claims) and is calculated by reference to the tonnage of the ship. Article 9 deals with the aggregation of claims and provides, by paragraph (1), that the limit of liability is to be applied "to the aggregate of all claims which arise on any distinct occasion".

(iv) *How does one limit?* Chapter III of the Convention (Articles 11 to 14) makes provision for the constitution and operation of the "Limitation Fund".

3. Special questions arising in relation to tug and tow

In the field of towage, limitation of liability raises three particular questions:

(i) Can limitation be invoked at all in respect of the tug and tow, i.e., is the tug and is the tow a "sea-going ship" within Article 1(2)?

(ii) Assuming both tug and tow to be ships for the purposes of the Convention, are they to be treated as one ship for the purposes of limitation, so that their tonnages are aggregated to make a bigger fund?

(iii) How is the test of "any distinct occasion" to be operated in respect of tug and tow and damage occurring at various stages during the towage service?

PART B. APPLICATION OF THE LIMITATION CONVENTION TO "SHIPS"

1. The relevant wording of the 1976 Convention

Under Article 1(1) of the 1976 Convention, shipowners (and salvors) as defined in the Convention may limit their liability in accordance with the rules set out in it. A "shipowner" is defined by Article 1(2) as meaning "the owner, charterer, manager or operator of a sea-going ship". Under Article 2 of the Convention, which defines those claims in respect of which a person is entitled to invoke limitation, such claims are defined as being claims "in respect of loss of life or personal injury or loss of or damage to property", which loss of life, injury or other loss or damage occurs "on board or in direct connection with the ship".

Accordingly, the person entitled to invoke the limit must be a "shipowner" and, in most cases, the claim in respect of which the limit is invoked must be a claim arising out of the operation and/or arising in connection with "the ship". The Convention gives no definition of "ship" other than that it is to be "sea-going".

2. The position in English law

The Merchant Shipping Act 1995 (and its predecessor the Merchant Shipping Act 1979) in enacting the 1976 Convention extends and defines its application to "shipowners".

(a) Pursuant to paragraph 2 of Part II of Schedule 7 to the Merchant Shipping Act 1995, which sets out special provisions having effect in connection with the Convention, "the right to limit liability" under the Convention is to apply "in relation to any ship whether sea-going or not and the definition of 'shipowner' in paragraph 2 of Article 1 shall be construed accordingly". This extends the right to limit, for example, to small non sea-going vessels, such as small river or harbour tugs.

(b) Paragraph 12 of Part II of Schedule 7 states that references to "ship" in the Convention are to "include" (the definition given is, accordingly, not comprehensive or definitive):

" ... any structure (whether completed or not or in the course of completion) launched and intended for use in navigation as a ship or part of a ship."

This definition should be read together with those given in the Merchant Shipping Act of 1894 and in following Acts, in relation to which a considerable body of authority has grown up. This is referred to in greater detail in Chapter 10 below. While the definition directly addresses the question of incomplete newbuildings (*cf. The Andalusian* (1878) 3 P.D. 182 in which the court held that a newly launched vessel not yet fully fitted out and not yet registered was not a "ship"), the definition leaves unaffected decisions such as *The Gas Float Whitton* [1897] A.C. 337 which held that an unmanned gas float shaped like a ship but fixed in position as a navigational aid was not a ship. It is submitted that floating structures such as rigs or platforms as well as large objects which are capable of flotation and being water-borne (such as drydocks or caissons) will not be "ships" for the purposes of limitation under the 1976 Convention and the Merchant Shipping Act 1995.

PART C. THE AGGREGATION OF TUG AND TOW FOR THE PURPOSES OF THE LIMITATION FUND

1. The question of aggregation: The "flotilla issue"

A towage convoy or "flotilla" will usually consist of a small but powerful tug, or a combination of such tugs, and a much larger vessel under tow. The tonnage of the tug or tugs, while often not negligible, will for the purposes of the limitation of liability usually tend to produce a very small limitation fund. This was especially so under the regime of the Merchant Shipping Acts in which the limitation figures had long been rendered nugatory by the erosion of inflation. While this erosion was intended to be addressed by the 1976 Convention, the position today is largely unchanged. The tonnage of the tow may often present a much more attractive tonnage to be applied in the calculation of the limitation fund than the tug.

The disparity between tug and tow in their respective potential limitation funds if approached separately has encouraged attempts to apply the same approach as has been seen in the context of the collision liabilities, namely, to treat tug and tow as "one long steamer" and to aggregate their respective tonnages for limitation purposes. The issue of whether or not a towage convoy is to be treated as one unit for limitation purposes is usually referred to in the books and cases as "the flotilla issue". The issue may be shortly stated: are the tonnages of tug and tow to be treated as one aggregate tonnage for limitation purposes and, if so, in what circumstances?

Compared with other jurisdictions, the resolution of this issue by the English courts has proved pragmatic and straightforward. Nevertheless, since the court has often professed itself to be reaching the result it does by reference to the language of the limitation statute and since there is no modern English authority on the position under the 1976 Convention and the Merchant Shipping Act 1995 or its predecessor the Merchant Shipping Act 1979, it is necessary to have in mind the sequence of the authorities and the different statutory provisions being considered. A helpful composition of the various incarnations of section 503 of the 1894 Act can be found in *Limitation of Shipowners' Liability: The New Law, op. cit.*, pp. 333 to 341.

2. The cases before the Merchant Shipping Act 1958

(1) The wording of the 1894 Act

Taking the case of damage done by a ship to another as an example, section 503(1) of the Merchant Shipping Act 1894 provided, in so far as material, as follows:

"The owners of a ship ... shall not, where all or any of the following occurrences take place without their actual fault or privity; (that is to say,)

  ...

   (d) Where any loss damage is caused to any other vessel ... by reason of the improper navigation of the ship;
   be liable to damages beyond the following amounts; (that is to say,)
   ...
      (ii) In respect of loss of or damage to vessels ... an aggregate amount ... for each ton of their ship's tonnage."

The wording of the section plainly sought to achieve the result that an owner of a ship which had caused loss or damage to another by her improper navigation was entitled to limit his liability by reference to the tonnage of that ship.

(2) The cases

The question of aggregation specifically arose in two cases.

However, it is first necessary to consider the decision in *The Ran; The Graygarth* [1922] P. 80 which has given rise to much debate. In that case, a tug *Graygarth* towed a flotilla of barges. One barge, the *Ran*, was owned by the tug owner. The tug negligently navigated the barge which collided with a third vessel. That vessel brought an action *in rem* against the *Ran* alleging "wrongful navigation of the *Ran* by the servants of the defendants", i.e., those on board the tug. The Court of Appeal held that the allegation was made out and that, accordingly, the relevant vessel, that is "the ship" which improperly navigated, was the *Ran* and not the *Graygarth*. Atkin L.J. (with whom Younger L.J. appears to have agreed) dealt with the case simply as one of whether negligence in towing could be attributed to the tow as a question of the operation of the doctrine of "control". As he put it at p. 20:

" . . . there may be circumstances in which the tow, whether or not she has got persons on board her, is being navigated by the tug, and under those circumstances if she is navigated so as negligently to damage another vessel, then it seems to me that it is the tow that is being improperly navigated, and the only question then arising is whether the defendants, the owners of the tow, are responsible for that improper navigation. That will depend on whether or not those on board the tug are or are not the servants of the owners of the tow to navigate the tow, and they may be so because they are in the ordinary position in which there are a skilled crew on the tow and the tug has to obey their orders. But the facts may be otherwise. There may be nobody on the tow to direct her, but the tug is provided by the owners of the tow under such circumstances that the crew of the tug are in fact the servants of the owners of the tow. Under those circumstances it appears to follow logically and necessarily that the improper navigation, which, *ex hypothesi*, is that of those on board the tug who are improperly navigating the tow, is the improper navigation of the servants of the owners of the tow for which the owners of the tow are responsible. That seems to me to establish the liability."

Lord Sterndale M.R. put it similarly at p. 86:

"The question of the liability of tug and tow always raises the issue as to whether the persons on the tug where the tug is negligent were the servants of the owners of the tow."

Having reached a decision on "control" and on the liability of the *tow* (which may or may not have been sound on the facts), the decision of the Court of Appeal that limitation was therefore to be calculated by reference to the tow's and not the tug's towage was unexceptional. As the tow was found to be the vessel liable and as the action lay against the tow, the tow was the vessel whose tonnage was to be used for limitation. Despite the complications which arose in relation to this decision in *The Bramley Moore* [1964] P. 200 (see below), it is submitted that this case is more a "control" case than one which assists on the question of aggregation (see also *Bucknill on Tug and Tow* (2nd Edn.), at p. 81).

This interpretation of the decision was adopted by Sir Henry Duke P. in *The Harlow* [1922] P. 175, the first true aggregation case. A tug *Harlow* towed five dumb barges; tug and tow were all owned by the same person. A vessel was struck by the tug and one of the barges, the *Silver*; another barge, the *Sokoto*, was lashed to the colliding barge and by her weight and momentum contributed to the damage. It was found as a fact that all of the vessels had been negligent in navigation (they had been on the wrong side of the channel) but that only the *Harlow*, *Silver* and *Sokoto* were held to have caused (or in the case of the *Sokoto* to have contributed to) the damage done. The owners of the flotilla relied on *The Ran* to justify limitation by reference to the tonnage of the barge *Silver only*. They did so on the basis of a common ownership argument. The President rejected this view of *The Ran* and relied upon the following words of Lord Sterndale in that case (p. 186):

"The Master of the Rolls, it will be seen, said this, 'the action having been brought against the owners of the *Ran*, they, as represented by their bail, could only be responsible if the *Ran* was improperly navigated and such improper navigation caused the collision. As owners of the *Graygarth* they might be liable also, but in the action in which they were sued as owners of the *Ran* they could only be responsible if the *Ran* was improperly navigated.' The *Ran* was found to have been improperly navigated, and judgment went against her owners accordingly. To say that this decision proceeded upon a rule that the vessel in collision can alone be involved in liability is directly contrary to the statement of the Master of the Rolls with regard to the owners, that 'as owners of the *Graygarth* they might be liable also.' "

The court held that limitation was to be calculated by reference to the aggregate tonnage of those units of the flotilla which were at fault and which had played a part in the damage: the *Harlow* and the two barges, *Silver* and *Sokoto*.

See also the second true aggregation case: *The Freden* (1950) 83 Ll. L. Rep. 427 in which *The Harlow* was applied (tug and three barges in common ownership; all negligently navigated; one barge collided with a vessel; it was held that the tonnage of the tug and of that barge were to be taken but not the tonnage of the other barges which did not cause or contribute to the damage).

It will be seen that the critical questions for the court, which apply whether or not tug and tow are in common ownership, were: (i) which vessel or vessels was or were at fault; (ii) which of those vessels at fault caused or contributed to the damage.

3. The cases following the Merchant Shipping Act 1958

(1) The wording of the 1894 Act as amended by the 1958 Act

Section 503(1) of the Merchant Shipping Act 1894 was amended by the Merchant Shipping Act (Liability of Shipowners and Others) Act 1958. For present purposes, the only material change was in paragraph (d) which was amended to define an occurrence in respect of which limitation could be inserted:

"Where any loss or damage is caused to any property . . . through the act or omission of any person (whether on board the ship or not) in the navigation or management of the ship."

This replaced the 1894 wording of loss or damage caused "by reason of the improper navigation of the ship".

(2) The decision in The Bramley Moore (1964)

This slight change in the wording effected by the 1958 Act was heavily relied upon by the Court of Appeal in the case of *Alexandra Towing* v. *Millet (Owners) and Egret (Owners), The Bramley Moore* [1964] P. 200. A tug, the *Bramley Moore* had two barges (*Millet* and *Buckwheat*), owned by third parties, in tow on the River Mersey. One of the barges, *Millet* collided with another vessel, the *Egret*, and sank. The *Millet* sued the *Egret* and the *Bramley Moore* and, both of these vessels being held to blame, judgment was given in the barge's favour against the tug and in favour of the *Egret* on her counterclaim against the tug. The *Bramley Moore* commenced a limitation action against the barge *Millet* and the *Egret* and contended that her limit of liability should be calculated by reference to the tonnage of the tug alone. Cairns J. upheld that claim and rejected the argument that the tug's limitation was to be assessed by reference to the aggregate tonnage of the tug and the two barges even though the barges were separately owned. The Court of Appeal upheld that decision.

Lord Denning M.R., giving the judgment of the Court of Appeal, considered what the law was prior to the 1958 Act. He summarised the applicable principles as they appeared to be, absent the decision in *The Ran; The Graygarth* [1922] P. 80, as follows at p. 217:

"But the section requires you also to look at the cause of the damage. That is clear from the words 'by reason of'. And in a case where those on the tug are negligent, and those on the barge are not, the cause of the damage is in truth the improper navigation of the tug, not the improper navigation of the barge. It is the tug which is the cause of all the trouble. That is, at any rate, the way in which these cases have been regarded in the past. Take first the case of tug and tow where those on board the tug are negligent and those on the tow are not, and the negligence of those on the tug causes the tow to come into collision with another vessel. Tug and tow belong to different owners. No one has ever suggested that the owners of the tug cannot limit their liability at all. On the contrary, it has been generally assumed that liability is limited to the tonnage of the tug: see *The Vigilant* and *The Ant*. This must be on the assumption that the damage is 'by reason of the improper navigation of' the tug, but not 'by reason of the improper navigation of' the tow. Take next the cases where those on the tug are negligent and also those on the tow, and their combined negligence causes the tow to come into collision with another vessel. In such cases, the owners of the tug can limit their liability according to the tonnage of the tug and the owners of the tow can limit their liability according to the tonnage of the tow. When the damaged vessel makes claims against both, the limit is the combined limit. If both tug and tow are in the same ownership, the limit is found by taking the aggregate tonnage of those vessels whose negligence caused the collision: see *The Harlow*. No one has ever suggested in any such case that the owners of the tug cannot limit their liability at all."

He then dealt with the troublesome decision in *The Ran*. At first instance, Cairns J., at [1964] P. 205, had analysed this case as being a decision that where an action had been commenced *in rem* against *the tow* for negligent navigation, and where the negligent navigation, being the navigation of the tow by the tug, was attributable to the tow, then the tug (as the person liable *in personam* for the acts of the tow) could limit by reference to the tonnage of the offending vessel, that is, the tow. Notwithstanding the rather strained nature of the exercise performed by the Court of Appeal in *The Ran*, it is submitted (see above) that this analysis is formally correct. Perhaps in reaction to the forceful argument based on *The Ran* advanced before the Court of Appeal by Henry

Brandon Q.C. (as he then was) in support of the argument for aggregating tonnage of tug and tow, the Court of Appeal chose a different route: to explain *The Ran* as a "special case" on common ownership of tug and tow. As Lord Denning M.R. put it at p. 218:

"Viewing the cases as they stood before 1958, I think that the general rule in these tug and tow cases was that the owners of the tug could limit their liability by reference to the tonnage of the tug, but that, in cases where tug and tow were in the same ownership, there was a special exception, based on no logical ground, whereby the limit was to be found by taking the tonnage of the tow."

This ignored the fact that no aggregation was performed by the Court of Appeal in *The Ran*. Oddly, Lord Denning isolated the relevant features of the decision in *The Ran*, but, in reaching his conclusion on the pre-1958 law, did not base his analysis of what exactly *The Ran* had decided upon them. As he put it (p. 218):

"The decision seems to have depended on two factors: (i) the fact that tug and barge were both in the same ownership; (ii) the fact that the action by the owners of the damaged vessel was an action *in rem* against the owners of the barge. I cannot myself see the relevance of either of those factors."

The Court of Appeal then distinguished *The Ran* on the basis that the decision was no longer applicable given the different wording of the 1958 Act:

"Since the Act of 1958, Mr Brandon's argument cannot hold water. The logical difficulty [i.e., the decision in *The Ran* as interpreted by the Court of Appeal] has been dispelled. Section 503 has been amended by the Act of 1958 ... "

The Court of Appeal then stated the position under the amended section 503 (it is submitted, considerably overstating the importance of *The Ran*):

"Let me apply this to a tug and tow case such as we have been considering. If those on board the tug are negligent and those on board the tow are not, and the tow comes into collision with another vessel, then clearly the damage is caused through an 'act or omission of any person on board the tug'. If you insert the appropriate words into the section as now amended, it reads in this way: 'The owners of a tug shall not, where damage "is caused through any act or omission of any person on board" the tug, be liable in damages' beyond an amount calculated on the tonnage of the tug. So read, it seems clearly to cover the case where those on the tug are negligent and those on the tow are not. It shows that the owners of the tug can limit their liability according to the tonnage of the tug.
    The amendment of 1958 therefore makes it clear that the previous practice was right and makes it doubtful whether *The Ran* is any longer good law."

(3) *The decision in* The Sir Joseph Rawlinson *(1972) and later cases*

In *The Bramley Moore*, the victim of the collision had sought to argue that although the tug and tow were separately owned, these should be aggregated on the basis of *one* "ship" having caused the collision. The decision in that case was considered in a case of common ownership of tug and tow in *London Dredging Co.* v. *Greater London Council (The Sir Joseph Rawlinson)* [1972] 2 Lloyd's Rep. 437. The limitation action was brought by London Dredging Co. as owner of the tug and a dumb barge. The tug and tow collided with a G.L.C. dredger which sank. Of the tug and tow, the tug was negligent but there was no negligence on the part of anyone on board the tow. The tug applied to limit on the basis of her tonnage alone; the G.L.C. contended that the tonnage of both tug and tow should be the basis of limitation.

"The issue is on what basis the owners of a tug and tow can limit their liability for collision damage where there was negligence for which they are liable on the part of the person in charge of the tug but no negligence on the part of anyone on the tow. More particularly the issue is whether the present case, although one of common ownership of tug and tow, is covered by the decision ... in a case called *The Bramley Moore*."

It was argued on behalf of the dredger that the tonnages of tug and tow should be aggregated. The argument rested on two propositions: first, that the word "ship" in section 503 could apply to more than one ship on the basis that, under the Interpretation Act 1889, the singular includes the plural and that the context of section 503 requires no different result; secondly, and more importantly, that where a person in charge of a tug with a tow attached is negligent in his navigation and if the tug and the tow thereby cause damage to the property of a third party, then it is in accordance with the authorities to refer to that negligent person as having been negligent in the navigation *not only* of the tug *but also* of the tow. Reliance was placed on *The Ran*, *The Harlow* and *The Freden*.

Kerr J. was impressed by the logical cogency of the argument that common ownership was to be distinguished from the separate ownership considered in *The Bramley Moore*. As he put it (at p. 440):

"Thirdly, Mr Thomas submitted that there is nothing intrinsically anomalous in a result which distinguishes between cases of common ownership and cases where the tug and tow are in different ownerships. He said that when an owner is employing (to use a neutral term) more than one of his ships in circumstances in which more than one is involved in one collision, then there is nothing anomalous in a result whereby his liability is higher than if only one ship had been involved.

Here again it seems to me that Mr Thomas is correct in principle. The section is based on the tonnage of a ship, which is intended to reflect her value and size, so that it follows that the greater the tonnage, the greater the potential limited liability. It therefore seems to me that there is nothing anomalous in a result whereby an owner is under a greater liability, albeit limited, if two of his ships are involved in a collision than one if only one is involved. Indeed, in the present case by far the greater amount of the damage was done by the barge."

And at p. 445:

"In my view, he is right in saying that there is nothing in *The Bramley Moore* standing in the way of the correctness of the view taken in *The Ran* that a person on a tug can be negligent in navigating both the tug and the tow, because Lord Denning himself recognises this."

However, he considered himself to be bound by the decision of the Court of Appeal in that case, i.e. that the position pre-1958 (either under *The Ran* or otherwise) had been changed by the 1958 Act. Referring to the passage in Lord Denning M.R.'s judgment cited above, Kerr J. stated (at p. 445):

"It seems to me that on the basis of that passage the only causative negligence, which is the negligence to which one must look, must in cases such as this be regarded as negligence in the navigation of the tug, and not negligence in the navigation of the tow or negligence in the navigation of both the tug and tow. Accordingly, whilst it is apparently still correct to say that a person who negligently navigates a tug towing something may be negligent in the navigation both of the tug and tow, in particular where the damage is caused wholly or as in the present case partly by the tow, it seems to me that the effect of the decision of the Court of Appeal is that the causative negligence is in such cases to be treated as negligence in the navigation of the tug alone. I also consider that if this is the correct approach to the statutory position before 1958, then one cannot say that this has been altered by the 1958 Act."

He reluctantly (see p. 446, col. 1) held that the London Dredging Co. could limit its liability by reference to the tonnage of the tug alone (circa £5,000), rather than by reference to the aggregated tonnage of tug and barge (circa £27,000).

This approach was followed in *The Smjeli* [1982] 2 Lloyd's Rep. 74. In that case, a tug and a very large dumb barge, the *Transporter III*, were in common ownership. The barge hit groynes at Folkestone. The district council sued the owners. It is important to note that the council not only alleged negligence in the navigation of the tug but that it also alleged specific acts of negligence on the part of the owners in preparing the barge for the voyage (in relation to proper towing-lines of adequate strength). Accordingly, the claim was for negligence within the owning company on the part of *both* "the tug" *and* of "the tow" owned by that company.

Sheen J. considered *The Bramley Moore* and commented that the case concerned negligence on the part of *the tug* alone, i.e., the barge "merely followed in the wake of the tug and if the tug proceeded too fast so did the" barge (p. 80). He then stated (p. 80):

"It seems to me that the first question is: What acts or omissions give rise to liability in damages? Then follows the second question: Has a limit been set upon the damages payable by the tortfeasor? Applying those questions to the 'tug and tow' cases, if a barge has been brought into collision by reason of the negligent conduct of the tug-master (even if he is guilty of several faults), the totality of his negligence gives rise to one cause of action. It does not assist to describe the act or omission in the navigation of the tug also as 'negligent navigation of the tow' because s. 503 does not provide a statutory cause of action, it prescribes a limit to the amount of damages payable. One cause of action gives rise to one (limited) liability. However, this case does not arise out of a collision, and there is more than one distinct cause of action. The defendants are liable in damages for acts of negligence which occurred before the flotilla left Rotterdam, and they are admittedly liable in negligence for negligence which occurred at sea.

The writ is a writ *in rem* against two ships. Two separate writs could have been issued, one against *Transporter III* and the other against *Smjeli*. My judgment does not depend upon any procedural point. I mention this only to give emphasis to the point that the defendants are liable to the plaintiffs on two unconnected causes of action."

He proceeded to deal with the separate claims against the separate vessels and the separate limitation funds which resulted (pp. 80–81).

"The plaintiffs' cause of action against *Transporter III* arises out of negligent acts or omissions which occurred when making the arrangements for the towage of the barge before she left Rotterdam. A claim for damages would have been successful if a servant of the barge owners was guilty of those acts or omissions regardless of who owned the tug. The owners of the barge are not liable to damages beyond an amount calculated by reference to her tonnage, namely £62,078. I can see no reason why that liability should be limited to a lesser sum because the owners of that barge also own the tug.

The plaintiffs also have a cause of action against *Smjeli*. It is admitted in the amended further and better particulars of the fifth and final version of the defence that Captain Vukusic was negligent in his navigation of *Smjeli* in causing or allowing the fuse wire to part and in failing to seek shelter towards North Foreland and instead attempting to hold the tow in the Dover Strait.

For these acts of negligence, the defendants have admitted liability in damages limited to the sum of £23,602.

Accordingly, I give judgment for the plaintiffs for the sum of £85,680 and interest thereon."

(4) A summary of the law before the Merchant Shipping Act 1979 (now the Merchant Shipping Act 1995)

It is submitted that following the decision in *The Bramley Moore*, the position prior to the Merchant Shipping Act 1979 (now re-enacted as part of the Merchant Shipping Act 1995) can be summarised by the following propositions:

(1) The owner of each vessel in the towage flotilla (i.e., tug and tow or each tow if more than one) is entitled to limit his liability by reference to the tonnage of his own vessel.

(2) The question of which vessel is to be taken as the vessel by reference to which the limitation figure is to be calculated depends upon which vessel is alleged to have been at fault and, by that fault, to have caused the casualty in respect of which the right to limit is invoked.

(3) There is no difference in principle between the position where tug and tow are separately owned or are in common ownership.

(4) Thus, in the following examples:

   (a) Tug and tow separately owned; tug (or tow) alone to blame. Tug's (or tow's) tonnage used for limitation (see e.g. *The Bramley Moore* [1964] P. 200).

   (b) Tug and tow in common ownership; tug (or tow) alone to blame. Tonnage of tug (or tow) alone is taken (see e.g. *The Sir Joseph Rawlinson* [1972] 2 Lloyd's Rep. 437).

   (c) Tug and tow separately owned; both to blame. Each owner can limit by reference to the tonnage of his individual vessel alone.

   (d) Tug and tow in common ownership; both to blame. The common owner can limit by reference to the tonnage of both of his vessels (see e.g. *The Smjeli* [1982] 2 Lloyd's Rep. 74).

(5) Where the towage flotilla is made up of several objects under tow, some of which, but not others, are at fault and are involved in the collision, limitation is by reference to those objects which were at fault and whose fault caused the collision: see *The Harlow* [1922] P. 175 (five barges; one at fault with one lashed to her: limitation by reference to the two barges).

(5) A comparison: The Canadian and American cases

The Canadian courts have reached a different result on statutory wording very similar to that of the Merchant Shipping Act 1958.

In *Monarch Towing Co. v. British Columbia Cement Co.* [1957] S.C.R. 816, a tug towed a barge which it had under lease. A cargo of cement was loaded on board the barge which was unmanned. During the towage the barge grounded and sank rendering the cargo a total loss. The tug sought to limit liability. The Supreme Court of Canada aggregated the tonnage of tug and barge on the basis that the correct approach was to take the tonnage of the whole of that part of the flotilla which was at fault. Although there may have been special reasons for this decision on the basis of a finding, based on a concession, that tug and tow were both at fault, the decision reflected the earlier decision in *Pacific Express* v. *Salvage Princess* (1940) Ex. C.R. 230 (see p. 234) and has been followed as laying down a general principle. That principle was summarised in *The Kathy K* [1972] 2 Lloyd's Rep. 36 by Heald J. at first instance at p. 47.

"I hold also that the plaintiffs are entitled to calculate on the basis of the combined tonnage of tug and tow. Liability must be calculated on the aggregate tonnage of the wrongdoing mass: *Pacific Express* ... *Monarch Towing* ... "

The same approach was adopted in the Supreme Court: [1976] 1 Lloyd's Rep. 153 at 164. In *The Kathy K*, a yacht was sunk with loss of life by a barge towed by a tug. The tug had negligently increased the scope of the towing-line and had increased speed also. The relevant statute, the Canada Shipping Act 1970, section 649, was in almost identical terms to the English 1958 Act. Applying English principles, the court should have held that the tug was alone at fault and its tonnage alone was relevant. The English decisions do not appear to have been cited to the Canadian court, or, if they were, the court did not see fit to refer to them.

The American cases have developed in a yet further direction and one of considerable complexity. A distinction is drawn between whether limitation of liability is invoked against a third party with whom there is no contractual relationship (i.e., a pure claim in tort, for example arising out of a collision) or against a claimant in contract, (e.g., where a barge is towed under a contract and if it or its cargo is lost). In the context of a tort claim, the vessel "actively responsible" determines the limit, with any vessel which is merely "a passive instrument" left out of account even if in common ownership. Hence the tug alone is most usually taken as the limitation tonnage: see *Liverpool Brazil and River Plate S.N. Co.* v. *Brooklyn Eastern District Terminal*, 251 U.S. 48 (1919). However, in the context of a contract claim, if tug and tow are in common ownership, they are to be taken together as the "offending vessel": see *The Columbia* 73 F. 226 (9th Cir. 1896) as applied in *Sacramento Navigation Co.* v. *Salz*, 273 U.S. 326 (1927). On this involved question, see further Parks and Cattell, *Law of Tug, Tow and Pilotage* (3rd Edn.) at pp. 337–341.

4. The Merchant Shipping Act 1995 (replacing the Merchant Shipping Act 1979) and the 1976 Limitation Convention

(1) *The relevant wording*

Article 2 of the 1976 Convention defines the claims which are subject to limitation in a wider way than that adopted by the 1894 and 1958 Acts. In respect of a claim for loss of or damage to property, Article 2(1)(a) provides:

"(1). Subject to Articles 3 and 4 the following claims, whatever the basis of liability may be, shall be subject to limitation of liability:
    (a) claims in respect of loss of life or personal injury or loss of or damage to property (including damage to harbour works, basins and waterways and aids to navigation),

occurring on board or in direct connexion with the operation of the ship or with salvage operations, and consequential loss resulting therefrom;"

(2) The current state of the law on aggregation

It is submitted that in the absence of any contrary intention shown by the language of the Merchant Shipping Act 1995 (and its predecessor the 1979 Act) or the 1976 Limitation Convention, the present law will remain that which was applied in *The Bramley Moore*, *The Sir Joseph Rawlinson* and *The Smjeli*.

The only material difference in wording is between the wording of the 1958 Act which restricted limitation to liability in damages for loss or damage to property or for loss of life caused "through the act or omission of any person . . . in the navigation or management of *the ship*" (emphasis supplied) and that of Article 2 of the 1976 Convention which defines the claims in respect of which limitation can be invoked as being claims "whatever the basis of liability may be" in respect of various types of loss and damage, and death and injury "occurring on board or in direct connexion with the operation of *the ship*" (emphasis supplied). Limitation under the 1976 Convention is by reference to the tonnage of that ship: see Article 6.

It is submitted that the 1976 Convention makes no change to the law under the 1958 Act. The causal connection between the fault of the vessel and the liability incurred or claim arising, while expressed in wider terms ("on board or in direct connexion with the operation of the ship"), is still clearly present in the 1976 Convention, hence the adjective "direct". While certain commentators (Davison and Snelson, *The Law of Towage* (1990), p. 87) have suggested that the wider wording of the 1976 Convention enables the court to sidestep the older cases and to aggregate the tonnage of tug and tow, it is difficult to see why this should be so on the language of Article 2(1). The two-stage approach adopted by Sheen J. in *The Smjeli* [1982] 2 Lloyd's Rep. at 80:

"What acts or omissions give rise to liability in damages? . . . Has a limit been set on the damages payable by the tortfeasor?"

is unaffected by the 1976 Convention. To take the example of a tug and tow in common ownership. If the tug alone is negligent and damage is caused as a result to another vessel, that vessel will have a cause of action or claim against the tug owner. That claim will be one which falls within Article 2(a) of the 1976 Convention as a "claim in respect of . . . damage to property . . . occurring in direct connexion with the operation of the ship", i.e., the tug. Limitation under Article 6 will be by reference to the tonnage of "the ship", i.e., the tug. The tonnage of the tow is irrelevant since the claim is one in respect of damage occurring in connection with the operation of *the tug*, since it is the tug's fault which gives rise to the claim. The fact that the tow is involved as well because it forms part of the flotilla is immaterial; the damage, properly regarded, does not "occur in direct connexion with the operation of the tow" which played no part and against which no claim lies.

The importance of the change in the wording in Article 2(1) and, in particular, of the words "whatever the basis of liability may be" (much relied on by Davison and Snelson) is that it addresses and surmounts the problem of decisions such as *The*

Kirknes [1957] P. 51 which excluded limitation in respect of indemnity claims because the liability was not one "in damages" within the 1894 and 1958 Acts. It is not (*cf.* Davison and Snelson) addressing the question of limitation in flotillas of vessels in respect of claims arising in relation to their operation.

5. The special problem of the physical structure of the flotilla

While the decision of the Court of Appeal in *The Bramley Moore* [1964] P. 200 disposed of the apparent principle that negligent navigation by a tug in a towage flotilla in respect of the tow could be treated as the independent negligent navigation of the tow (see *The Sir Joseph Rawlinson* [1972] 2 Lloyd's Rep. 437), in none of the English decisions addressing the flotilla issue has the physical structure of the flotilla been considered. This is understandable in that in none of the decided cases was the flotilla constituted by anything but a standard towing arrangement of a tug towing behind it one or more tows connected only by ropes. It follows that the possible treatment of a tug and tow as a single, purpose-built manoeuvrable unit would raise novel considerations. It is submitted that a tug and tow which are designed to operate together and which have the design, structure and manoeuvrability of one vessel should for limitation purposes be treated as one. To adopt a different approach would be unrealistic. Further, if tug and tow, when operating together, carry the lighting arrangement of a single navigable unit within Rule 24(b) of the International Regulations for the Prevention of Collisions at Sea 1972, this adds greater strength to the argument that they are factually and for limitation purposes to be considered as one and that their tonnages ought to be aggregated. This view gains support from the decision of the Canadian Supreme Court in *The Kathy K* [1976] 1 Lloyd's Rep. 153 (considered above), in which it was held that for the purposes of limitation the relevant tonnage is the aggregate of "the wrongdoing mass" of the vessels contributing to the damage, and from the decision in *The Harlow* [1922] P. 175 where Sir Henry Duke P. considered in a similar way the question of the "massing" of the five barges and their "combined weight and momentum" (see p. 184) and held that the tonnage of a barge which was closely lashed to the barge at fault was to be taken with that barge for the purpose of limitation (both being in common ownership).

PART D. LIMITATION OF CLAIMS "ARISING ON ANY DISTINCT OCCASION"

1. The wording of the 1976 Convention

A frequent problem is where the plaintiff asserts separate claims arising out of several incidents: is he able to recover against a separate limitation fund in respect of each incident? The 1976 Convention follows the approach and wording of the 1958 Act in looking to whether or not the claims can be said to arise "on any distinct occasion". Article 9(1) of the 1976 Convention therefore states:

"1. The limits of liability determined in accordance with Article 6 shall apply to the aggregate of all claims which arise on any distinct occasion:

(a) against the person or persons mentioned in paragraph 2 of Article 1 and any person for whose act, neglect or default he or they are responsible; or ... "

Given the possibility of several incidents causing loss or damage during one towage operation, the meaning of "any distinct occasion" has been specifically considered in towage cases.

2. The cases

In *The Rajah* (1872) L.R. 3 A. & E. 539, a tug was standing by near a steamer preparing to take her in tow. A ship collided with the tow and immediately afterwards with the tug which sank. Sir Robert Phillimore rejected an argument that there were two collisions and hence two distinct occasions. He stated at p. 542:

"In the present case, although the *Rajah* came into collision with two ships, yet the collision with each of these ships took place if not at the same moment of time, yet substantially at the same time and on the same occasion; and the whole damage seems to have been caused by one act of improper navigation ... "

Secondly, in *The Harlow* [1922] P. 175, a tug towing five barges in the same ownership as the tug collided with a vessel as a result of its own negligent navigation. As a result of the collision, the tug's steering gear jammed while she sought to turn in the river, bringing her into collision with another vessel. Sir Henry Duke held that the two collisions occurred on a single and distinct occasion and required that the claims of both plaintiffs be proved against a single limitation fund.

For an illustration in a non-towage case, see *The Lucullite* (1929) 33 Ll. L. Rep. 186. A vessel moored alongside another began to range against her in poor weather. In order to avoid further damage, she cast off but struck a third vessel which she sank. The owners of the wrongdoing vessel contended that both vessels were damaged on a single distinct occasion. The court rejected this argument, holding that the loss of the third vessel was not a necessary consequence of the collision with and casting-off from the second. Accordingly, the two collisions were held to be two separate and distinct events meriting two separate limitation funds.

CHAPTER 9

Tug and Tow and General Average

PART A. THE SPECIAL ISSUES ARISING

1. General average and the York-Antwerp Rules

It is beyond the scope of this book to give any account of the law and practice relating to general average. A basic definition of general average can be taken as follows (see *Cooke on Voyage Charters*, p. 422):

"The principle which underlines general average is that where any property at risk in a maritime adventure is sacrificed where extraordinary expenditure is incurred, for the common safety, the owners of any property at risk should constitute to the loss and expense in proportion to the values of their property which has survived."

(See also: the York-Antwerp Rules 1974, Rule A, and section 66 of the Marine Insurance Act 1906). General average and its principles have been long settled; they are perhaps one of the oldest facets of the law merchant with their origins in the Rhodian law as epitomised by Justinian's digest as the *Lex Rhodia de Iactu* and in the *Rolls of Oleron*, pre-dating the crusades. In the nineteenth century, the principles and practices of general average were codified internationally in sets of rules originally with the "Glasgow Rules" of 1860 and the "York Rules" of 1864 and culminating in the York-Antwerp Rules of 1887. These rules have been revised and amended on frequent occasions (i.e., 1890, 1924 and 1950) and charterparties and maritime contracts frequently contain clauses which specify both where the general average adjustment is to take place (of importance, since the practice of adjusters varies from country to country) and that it shall be adjusted pursuant to a particular version of the York-Antwerp Rules. Until very recently, the revision in current use has been that of the York-Antwerp Rules of 1974. The leading general text on this subject is *Lowndes and Rudolf on General Average on the York-Antwerp Rules* (11th Edn., 1990, Stevens).

In accordance with the usual practice, the York-Antwerp Rules are reviewed, in principle, every quarter-century. The International Convention on Salvage 1989 led to a piecemeal amendment of the 1974 York-Antwerp Rules in 1990 (i.e., Article VI). Since then, the York-Antwerp Rules have been further considered and revised. On 7 October 1994, the plenary session of the Comité Maritime International held in Sydney adopted a further revised text of the York-Antwerp Rules to be designated the York-Antwerp Rules 1994. The Comité further recommended that the 1994 Rules should be applied in all adjustments as soon as practicable after 31 December 1994. An approved text has now been published (see the CMI Yearbook) and the 1994 Rules will rapidly replace the 1974 Rules in current use.

The 1994 Revision is of importance for tug and tow since it specifically addresses the applicability of general average within the relationship of tug and tow.

2. Questions specific to tug and tow

Two questions arise in the law relating to general average which impact upon the relationships between tug and tow:

  (i) First, to what extent are towage expenses incurred by a vessel recoverable as general average expenses?
  (ii) Secondly, to what extent do the principles of general average apply as between tug and tow themselves?

PART B. RECOVERY OF TOWAGE EXPENSES IN GENERAL AVERAGE

1. Summary of the position

Despite some conflicting passages in the cases, it is well-settled that where a vessel, in a time of peril to the common maritime adventure, enters into a towage contract for the common safety, that act is capable of amounting to a general average act provided that the other requirements of general average, and in particular of Rules A and C of the York-Antwerp Rules, are satisfied. The relevant portions of Rules A and C for present purposes are the same in the 1974 Revision and in the new 1994 Revision of the Rules and provide as follows:

"RULE A

There is a general average act when, and only when, any extraordinary sacrifice or expenditure is intentionally and reasonably made or incurred for the common safety for the purpose of preserving from peril the property involved in a common maritime adventure."

"RULE C

Only such losses, damages or expenses which are the direct consequences of the general average act shall be allowed as general average."

Accordingly, in order to be able to recover the expense incurred under the towage contract as a general average expense from the respective contributing interests, the vessel towed which entered into the contract must establish:

  (i) that the entry into the towage contract was a general average act, that is, that the entry into the contract was intentionally and reasonably made for the common safety and for the preservation of the interests in the common maritime adventure;
  (ii) that the expenses incurred under that contract are the direct consequence of the entry into the towage contract.

2. The leading cases

The application of these requirements is usefully demonstrated in the few cases on this topic.

In *Anderson Tritton & Co.* v. *Ocean S.S. Co.* (1884) 10 App. Cas. 107, a laden vessel grounded on a sand bank in the River Yangtse. She engaged another vessel to tow her off under a form of contract used by that vessel in such circumstances pursuant to which the vessel would pay a fixed sum and all costs of repairs to any damage which the towing vessel incurred. The vessel was successfully refloated and sought to recover a proportion of the fixed sum and cost of repairs from cargo interests. The Court of Appeal upheld the general average nature of the expense in principle, but sent the case back to the jury to determine what the reasonable amount of that expense properly chargeable to general average should be. As Lord Blackburn stated (at p.117):

" . . . I think that the disbursement, in so far as it is a disbursement for the salvation of the whole adventure from a common imminent peril, may be properly charged to general average. But I think that there is neither reason nor authority for saying that the whole amount which the owners choose to pay is, as a matter of law, to be charged to general average."

Reliance on this authority did not avail the owners in *Société Nouvelle d'Armement* v. *Spillers & Bakers Ltd* [1917] 1 K.B. 865. A sailing vessel had to sail to Sharpness, Bristol from Queenstown just after the sinking of the *Lusitania* by a submarine and after her crew had seen the corpses from that vessel being brought ashore at Queenstown. To avoid possible torpedo attack by submarine, the vessel engaged a tug to tow her to Bristol so as to speed the passage and make the vessel more able to alter course. She sought to recover the cost in general average. Sankey J. held that the chance peril of being torpedoed was not a sufficiently imminent peril capable of giving rise to general average.

The application of Rules A and C of the York-Antwerp Rules was considered in striking circumstances arising out of two towage contracts each concluded on the U.K. Standard Conditions (considered in Chapter 3 above) in *Australian Coastal Shipping Commission* v. *Green* [1971] 1 Q.B. 456; 1 Q.B. 481 (C.A.). In that case, two separate instances of tug assistance were in issue involving two vessels. The *Bulwarra* lost her moorings in heavy weather and engaged a tug on the U.K. Standard Conditions to hold her up. The tug did so, but due to the tug's unseaworthiness she was wrecked when the tow-line parted and fouled her propeller. The vessel was, however, saved from harm. The owners successfully resisted the tug's claim for an indemnity under the U.K. Standard Conditions and in doing so incurred some irrecoverable costs in defending the tug's claim. The other vessel, the *Wangara*, grounded and engaged another tug on the same Conditions to tow her off. The tug did so, but, once again, the tow-line parted and fouled the tug's propeller. The tug required to be salved and claimed the cost of salvage from the vessel under the U.K. Standard Conditions indemnity provision. The vessel was held liable for the claim in full and had also to pay the tug's costs of the action. The vessel sought to recover these different heads of expense from their insurers as general average losses. The Court of Appeal held that the entry by the vessels in both cases into a towage contract was a general average act. As Lord Denning M.R. put it (at p.481 referring to *Anderson Tritton*):

" . . . I have no doubt that the towage contract is a 'general average act'. It was intentionally and reasonably made for the common safety . . . "

The indemnity provisions of the U.K. Standard Conditions were held to be a reasonable and usual provision in towage contracts such that they did not break the chain of causation from the general average act.

"If the indemnity clause had been unreasonable and such that the master ought never, in justice to the cargo owners, to have agreed to it, then I think that the expenditure would not flow from the general average act. But, seeing that the indemnity clause here was reasonable, then I think the expenditure flowed directly from the general average act. The indemnity was quite reasonable. So was the expenditure under it. It was the direct consequence of the general average act and must be accepted as a general average loss."

As to the well-established reasonableness of such provisions, see also *The Luna* [1920] P. 22.

3. The adjusters' rules of practice

The Association of Average Adjusters have from time to time adopted "Rules of Practice" which in effect form the "customary rules of English average adjusting. These rules were preceded by other rules called "Customs of Lloyd's". These rules can be found in *Lowndes and Rudolf* (*op. cit.*) in Appendix 3. Those touching upon towage or salvage as akin to towage are as follows:

(i) Rule F.12 relating to "Express at a Port of Refuge" (Custom of Lloyd's, amended 1890–1891) which, in so far as material, provides:

"When a ship puts into a port of refuge on account of accident and not in consequence of damage which is itself the subject of general average, then, on the assumption that the ship was seaworthy at the commencement of the voyage, the Custom of Lloyd's is as follows:
(a) All costs of towage, pilotage, harbour dues, and of other extraordinary expenses, incurred in order to bring the ship and cargo into a place of safety, are general average. Under the term 'extraordinary expenses' are not included wages or victuals of crew, coals, or engine stores, or demurrage."

(ii) In connection with Rule F.12 should be read Rule F.14: "Towage from Port of Refuge" (1876). This provides:

"That if a ship be in a port of refuge at which it is practicable to repair her, and if, in order to save expense, she be towed thence to some other port, then the extra cost of such towage shall be divided in proportion to the saving of expense thereby occasioned to the several parties to the adventure."

PART C. GENERAL AVERAGE AS BETWEEN TUG AND TOW

1. The fundamental requirements for general average

As has been seen above, for there to be a general average act, Rule A of the York-Antwerp Rules, reflecting the principles of general average at common law, requires the act to be one in relation to the preservation of a "common maritime adventure" which is threatened by a "peril". The typical example of a common maritime adventure is a laden cargo ship where the interests which make up the common adventure are the ship and the cargo. Even where there exists such a common adventure an act will not amount to a general average act unless it is for the purpose of preserving the *whole* adventure and not just one interest in the same. In other words, the peril referred to in Rule A must be a common peril facing all the interests making up the adventure: see *Lowndes and Rudolf* (*op. cit.*), para. A.41, pp. 80–81.

2. Practical importance for tug and tow

The practical importance of the application of general average principles for tug and tow can be seen in considering a common enough set of facts. A tug is towing a flotilla of two barges or other water-borne objects in different ownership; the weather worsens and the tug is threatened by the barges which are surging forward. The tug disconnects to save herself and as a result the barges collide and both sink. Can both of the tows recover this loss in general average from the tug? Changing the facts, if one of the barges is unaffected by the disconnection but the other barge is driven ashore and wrecked as a result of it, can that tow recover its loss from the tug or from the tug and the surviving barge?

Two separate questions will therefore arise in practice:

(i) Can tug and tow form a "common maritime adventure" for the purposes of general average?

(ii) In the circumstances in which they are to be so regarded, when and upon what basis are the various interests which may be bound up in the adventure (for example the tug; barge no.1; barge no.2; the owners of the cargo laden on board each barge) liable to contribute in general average?

3. The importance of the York-Antwerp Rules 1994

As to the question whether a tug and tow form a "common maritime adventure" for the purposes of the application of general average, this question is differently answered in different jurisdictions. In certain common law jurisdictions, for example the United States, the answer to the question is that tug and tow do not form a common adventure and that, accordingly, general average does not arise between tug and tow either at common law or under the York-Antwerp Rules of 1974 (and earlier). However, other jurisdictions have adopted the contrary view (e.g. Norway). The position in English law later is more uncertain and is considered in more detail below. In order to achieve uniformity of approach and with a view to clarifying the situation, the International Sub-Committee of the Comité Maritime International as part of its revision of the York-Antwerp Rules proposed a specific Rule dealing with tug and tow and clarifying their inclusion within the body of ordinary general average principles. This new Rule was adopted by the CMI's Plenary Session in Sydney in 1994. It is considered in detail below.

The application of the York-Antwerp Rules 1994 depends upon their express incorporation as the basis of the adjustment of general average in the towage contract (or the charterparty or contract of carriage). Since the 1994 Rules are very recent, contracts are likely for some time to refer by way of standard form general average clauses to the York-Antwerp Rules 1974 (see e.g. Clause 21 of the "Supplytime 89" form) or, as is the case in standard form "pure" towage contracts, to make no reference at all to general average. In such a case, the pre-1994 Rules position will continue to apply. For this reason, it is considered below.

Tug owners, tow owners and hirers under towage and offshore service contracts which involve towage should accordingly consider the specific incorporation of the York-Antwerp Rules 1994 in their contracts so as clearly to put themselves within the regime of general average.

4. The position prior to the 1994 Rules

(1) Commonality of adventure

In English law there is no authority which decides that tug and tow are or are not to be treated as a common maritime adventure. It is submitted that there is a good reason for this absence of authority. The question as to what is the nature of the maritime adventure being undertaken by tug and tow is a question which will be one of fact and of the construction of the towage contract in each case. For example, if the towage is one of a fully-manned vessel being conned by her own master who is making his own navigational decisions in tandem with those of the tug, there may be little identity between tug and tow as units in the operation and no commonality of adventure. On the other hand, if the tug is towing a flotilla of dumb barges or an unmanned drilling installation, while the contract is not one of carriage or affreightment, tug and tow are engaged on one common adventure, with the tow under one single control and with both vessels deployed in one series of interlinked and independent operations to bring the tow to its destination. It is very little dissimilar in its commonality of adventure to that of the ordinary situation of the carriage of goods; all that is different is that the goods are being conducted by a vessel rather than carried in one.

The test of whether or not the towage "adventure" is one in the sense of being an adventure where different interests are involved but which are subject to one controlling mind as to the navigation of the tug and tow, at least at the particular stage of the towage when the peril arises, receives tacit support in *Lowndes and Rudolf (op. cit.)* at para. A.62, p. 90 and para. A.66, p. 92. It is submitted that this approach is consistent with principle and accords with commonsense.

Although the question of common adventure has never been addressed by the English courts in the context of tug and tow, it has been the subject of a small body of American cases. These have been described as "of rather doubtful authority" (see *Lowndes and Rudolf (op. cit.)* at para. A.62, p. 90); the doubtfulness, it is submitted, arises from the difficulties in reconciling the authorities both *inter se* and with the general principles of general average.

In *The J.P. Donaldson* 167 U.S. 599, 17 S. Ct. 951 (1897), a tug contracted to tow two barges laden with cargo from Buffalo to Michigan via the Great Lakes. The barges were at all times fully-manned and equipped with separate crew and a barge master who, while subject to the navigational control of the tug, nevertheless had otherwise full control over the cargoes and barges and was able to slip the towing connections when he wanted to do so. A storm arose during the towage and threatened to drive the tug ashore. The tug cut the tow-lines in order to save herself. Subsequently, the barges were washed ashore and they and their cargoes were lost. The barge owners claimed contribution from the tug in general average. The Supreme Court rejected the claim principally upon the basis that the tow was manned and under separate command and that in such circumstances the tug-master had no authority on behalf of the barges as constituent elements of the venture to decide to sacrifice a part of them for the common good. As the court put it:

"And if the question is presented whether the barge should be run ashore for the purpose of saving her cargo . . . the decision of the question whether such stranding or jettison should or should not be made is within the exclusive control of the master of the particular barge, and in no degree under the control of the master of the tug;"

In *Loveland Co. Inc.* v. *United States* 1963 A.M.C. 260, 207 F. Supp. 450, the tug and tow, two laden barges, were in common ownership, which was not the case in *The J.P. Donaldson*. The barges were unmanned. The tug grounded and the two barges collided with her. The tug refloated herself. One of the barges had sustained damage and was leaking. The tug pushed her aground to prevent her from sinking and then continued with the voyage towing the remaining barge. The grounded barge was subsequently pulled off and towed to her destination by another tug. On these facts, it is difficult to see how any question of general average arose since there was no danger threatening the whole venture, just a danger of sinking confronting the holed barge. The court nevertheless held that all were liable to contribute in general average. This case has been regarded by certain U.S. commentators (see *Gilmore and Black on Admiralty* (2nd Edn.) at paragraphs 5–9, pp. 259–260) as establishing the principle that "where . . . the vessel in tow is a mere barge under the control for all purposes of the master of the towing vessel, it would seem that the venture is actually one". While this is one way of distinguishing it from the previous decision, it has to be said that it is difficult to discern what principle guided the court. It relied upon the difference between a contract of towage in *The J.P. Donaldson* and a contract of affreightment in the case before it, but what difference this would make to the commonality of adventure save to treat the latter as, in effect, one contract of carriage to which all were to be regarded as interested to the same extent, is not clear.

It is submitted that these authorities give very little guidance in determining whether or not the tug and tow are to be regarded as a common maritime adventure and that the matter has to be resolved by first principles and by reference to the facts of each case. The origin of general average and the reason why it does not apply in relation to carriage by land or air is the common maritime adventure which the different interests are bound up in when prosecuting a voyage by sea: see e.g. *Morrison Steamship Co.* v. *The Greystoke Castle* [1947] A.C. 265. In most cases, the towage of one object by another where the tow depends upon the tug to be brought to her destination and where the tug seeks to bring her there so as to earn the remuneration under the towage contract will amount to a common adventure on any realistic view.

(2) The basis of contribution between the respective interests

Contribution will arise only when some or all of the units which form part of the towage convoy and which are engaged on the common adventure are threatened by a common peril and are threatened to the same extent by that peril. The principle is easy enough to state in the light of Rule A of the York-Antwerp Rules but the application of it to the case of tug and tow and to the very different factual situations involved from those involved in the ordinary case of carriage of goods by and in a vessel raises difficulties. The different possible results can best be considered by taking various hypothetical examples as was done in relation to contribution in salvage in Chapter 6.

> (i) The simplest case is where a tug towing a barge suffers some mechanical failure whilst on an ocean voyage which prevents her from continuing with the towage. She has to put in for repairs but given the weather and sea conditions or because it is not possible to anchor the tow, the barge cannot be left and has to be taken into the port of refuge. Both tug and tow are faced with the same position, namely, that the towage cannot be continued without putting into the port of refuge. In such a case, the tow would be liable to contribute in general average in respect of the costs of putting in and of repairing the tug.

> (ii) If the example in (i) above is modified slightly by considering the same facts with the towage taking place in confined waters and with it being possible to anchor the barge safely while the tug puts in for the necessary repairs before recommencing, the position is changed. The barge is in no danger and is not concerned by the need to put in for repairs. In such a case, the barge is not liable to contribute in general average to the expenses incurred by the tug.

> (iii) A tug tows a flotilla of five barges. During the towage, two barges collide with each other. One is badly holed and her cargo is at risk of wetting. The other, in ballast, seems unaffected. The tug puts the barge safely aground and continues with the towage. The other barge involved in the collision develops problems and is left at a port of refuge for repairs. In this case, neither the tug nor the three other barges are put in peril and are unaffected by the casualty affecting the two barges. While general average will apply in respect of the first incident as between the barge and her cargo with cargo liable to contribute in respect of salvage or other remedial measures, neither the tug nor the four barges are liable to contribute. In respect of the second incident, since only one interest is imperilled (the barge being empty), general average does not arise.

> (iv) A tug is towing a flotilla of five barges. During the towage which is taking place in a narrow channel, the line to one barge parts and the barge is carried by the current ahead of the flotilla and strands, blocking the channel. She

requires to be lightened and refloated. In this case, all of the vessels making up the flotilla are imperilled in the same way and they, together with cargo, will be liable to contribute in general average in respect of the costs of the operation.

(v) A tug tows a water-borne object. A heavy storm gets up. The tug slips the line so as to be able to manoeuvre more easily and so as to be able to save herself but she thereby effectively dooms the tow to founder or to strand. In this case, there is a clear analogy with the well-established category of general average sacrifice of jettison of cargo. The tow is sacrificed to save the tug and, accordingly, the loss of the tow or the expenses of salving her fall to be treated in general average as expenses to be contributed to by the tug.

(vi) If the example in (v) above is modified so that the tow is a powered-vessel capable of independent navigation and both tug and tow are threatened by the storm to an equal degree with their only chance of survival being to cut the tow-line, the position is different. After their separation, the tug and tow are independent units of navigation and any accident or hazard which happens to them is unconnected with the decision to terminate the towage. In the event of either of them sustaining loss or damage, that loss or damage is not a general average sacrifice.

5. The York-Antwerp Rules 1994 and the new Rule B

The new Rule B introduced by the York-Antwerp Rules 1994 addresses these questions specifically. It provides as follows:

"There is a common maritime adventure when one or more vessels are towing or pushing another vessel or vessels, provided that they are all involved in commercial activities and not in a salvage operation.

When measures are taken to preserve the vessels and their cargoes, if any, from a common peril, these Rules apply.

A vessel is not in common peril with another vessel or vessels if by simply disconnecting from the other vessel or vessels she is in safety; but if the disconnection is itself a general average act, the common maritime adventure continues."

The International Sub-Committee of the Comité Maritime International charged with the revision of the York-Antwerp Rules modelled this rule on a corresponding rule in the Rhine Rules, which Rules make provision for general average in relation to water transport on the River Rhine, following representations from the British Maritime Law Association and the Association Internationale des Dispacheurs Européens. Water transport on the River Rhine by its nature has a considerable volume of barge traffic and problems between tug and tow in relation to the application of the rules of general average commonly arises. The position is now governed by Rule XXV of these Rules, which is in very similar form to the new Rule. Rule XXV has proved to be a useful and pragmatic resolution of the commonest problems to arise.

The Rule is largely self-explanatory but some points arising on the new Rule may be noted.

(i) The first paragraph of the Rule provides specifically for the commonality of maritime adventure in the case of tug and tow (or where the operation is a pushing operation) without differentiation between the possible forms of tow or of the towage operation. Accordingly, in the case of every towage convoy and whether the tow is a dry-dock or a cargo-vessel or the service is a short port tow or a long ocean towage, the convoy is treated for the purposes of general average as one maritime adventure. This provision has the compelling merit of simplicity and realism.

The only limitation upon this provision is that it excludes towage when performed as part of a salvage operation from the concept of a common maritime adventure and confines the Rule to commercial towage operations. This avoids the possibility of a general average within a general average, for example where a salvor's tug working under a salvage contract breaks down and requires repair and thereby imperils tug and tow; in such a case, the salvor will not be able to invoke general average and seek a contribution from the salved interests. There was some opposition to this restriction from Dutch representatives present at the Plenary Session in Sydney.

(ii) The second paragraph sets out the test for whether or not a particular measure is a general average one falling within the Rules. The measure must be one taken to preserve the vessels and their cargoes if any from a common peril. This paragraph adds little to the position as it would have been had such words been absent given the well-settled requirement of a common peril. For this reason, certain representatives argued that the paragraph was superfluous.

(iii) Of more purpose is the third paragraph which deals with the most difficult question of general average between tug and tow, namely, where the tow-line is slipped to save one or other or both vessels. The third paragraph follows Rule XXV of the Rhine Rules fairly closely, except possibly that the requirement that the vessel shall be in safety may be regarded as a lesser one than that under the Rhine Rules that the vessel shall be placed in safety. It is submitted that the Rule's object is clear and that the minor linguistic differences between the two sets of Rules are immaterial. The test is: can the vessel make herself safe by slipping the line?

Under this paragraph, if a vessel can make herself safe by doing so, then there is no common peril. So, if a tug and tow are being driven ashore and by slipping the line the tug can avoid the danger, then there is no common peril. So also, if a tug and tow are on course to strand and the tow can avoid doing so by simply casting off the line, there is no such peril.

The paragraph deals with the position where the act of disconnection itself is a general average act and provides, that if it is, then the common adventure continues. This deals with the position where the line is slipped to save one or more of the elements of the convoy but where the act of doing so does not of itself immediately place the disconnecting vessel in safety. To take an example: a tug and tow are faced with heavy weather and are in danger from the fact of being connected; the line is let go to preserve both tug and tow with the intention of reconnecting later; thereafter, the tow strands or both vessels suffer a casualty. Under the new Rule, the fact of disconnection does not of itself end the common maritime adventure. Although separated, the tug and tow are treated as one adventure still, so that sacrifices incurred by one or other or both fall to be treated in general average.

CHAPTER 10

Admiralty Jurisdiction

1. Historical background

As has been seen above in Chapter 6, before the advent of the steam tug towage, as an operation distinct from a towage service rendered to a vessel in distress in the context of salvage, was exceptionally rare. The Court of Admiralty had long exercised jurisdiction in salvage cases: see the magisterial analysis of the sources and origins of this jurisdiction given by Lord Esher M.R. in *The Gas Float Whitton (No.2)* [1896] P. 42 at p. 47 *et seq*. However, with the development of towage as a separate field of marine operation, quite distinct from salvage, an important lacuna in the jurisdiction of court became apparent: the Admiralty Court had no jurisdiction to deal with ordinary towage cases. As Dr Lushington stated (in *The Wataga* (1856) Swa. 165 at p. 167 adopted by the Court of Appeal in *The Heinrich Bjorn* (1885) 10 P.D. 48 at p. 52):

"The court, prior to the statute, had jurisdiction over salvage and damage but, under limitation as to locality, it had not over simple towage which was only then coming into use . . . "

Accordingly, "all demands for towage . . . were cognisable in the courts of common law alone": per Dr Lushington in *The Ocean* (1845) 2 W. Rob. 368 at p. 370. (*Cf.* the view expressed by Meeson in *Admiralty Jurisdiction and Practice*, 2nd Edn., at p. 39 which, with respect, is submitted to be incorrect. See further Roscoe, *The Admiralty Jurisdiction and Practice*, 5th Edn. (1931), at p. 187, footnote (d); Wiswall, *The Development of Admiralty Jurisdiction and Practice since 1800* (1970) at p. 41.

With the rapid increase in towage work (in 1840, Thomas Carlyle described a night walk by the River Thames as punctuated by tugs "snorting about the river, each with a lantern at its nose"), this lacuna became increasingly important. The matter was considered by a Select Parliamentary Committee charged with considering generally the widening of the Admiralty jurisdiction. This reported in 1833 but initially nothing was done. Jurisdiction was conferred upon the Admiralty Court in respect of towage for the first time by section 6 of the Admiralty Court Act 1840 (3 and 4 Vict., c.65), which reached the statute book largely as a result of the efforts of Dr Lushington.

The first reported decision on towage in the Admiralty Court (or elsewhere) appears to be *The Betsey* (1843) 2 Wm. Rob. 167: see Parks and Cattell, *The Law of Tug, Tow and Pilotage* (3rd Edn.) at p. 6.

2. Present-day Admiralty jurisdiction

The present successor to section 6 of the 1840 Act is section 20 of the Supreme Court Act 1981 which provides as follows:

"20. Admiralty Jurisdiction of High Court.
(1) The Admiralty jurisdiction of the High Court shall be as follows, that is to say:
     (a) jurisdiction to hear and determine any of the questions and claims mentioned in sub-section (2);
. . .
(2) The questions and claims referred to in sub-section (1)(a) are:
. . .
     (k) any claim in the nature of towage in respect of a ship or an aircraft;
. . . "

It is beyond the scope of this book to consider the features of the Admiralty jurisdiction in any detail: for these, see *McGuffie on Admiralty Practice* (1964), Stevens, and the leading modern account by Nigel Meeson: *Admiralty Jurisdiction and Practice*, 2nd Edn., (1993); see also Order 75 of the Rules of the Supreme Court and the accompanying notes in the current *Supreme Court Practice*. However, certain features in respect of the jurisdiction over towage should be noted.

3. Features of the jurisdiction in respect of towage

(1) Jurisdiction in rem

Pursuant to section 21(4) of the Supreme Court Act 1981, provided that the claim in the nature of towage arises in connection with a ship and that the person who would be liable on the claim if it were brought against the person (i.e., *in personam* rather than *in rem*) was at the time the cause of action arose the owner, charterer or someone in possession or control of the ship, then an action *in rem* can be brought either against that ship, if the person who would be liable is, at the time of the action being brought either the owner or demise charterer of the vessel, or against any other ship of which that person is the owner at the time of the action being brought (i.e., any "sister ship").

If an action *in rem* can be brought under section 21(4), the plaintiff has the right to arrest the ship and, in the event of obtaining judgment, can proceed to the sale of the same in satisfaction of his judgment if no security has been put up to obtain the release of the vessel from arrest.

(2) No maritime lien

Certain claims falling within the Admiralty jurisdiction give rise to a maritime lien. The effect of the lien is to allow the action *in rem* to be brought and the right of arrest to be exercised against the ship in connection with which the claim arises irrespective of subsequent changes in ownership: see section 21(3) of the 1981 Act. As Sir John Jervis stated in *The Bold Buccleugh* (1851) 7 Moo. P.C. 267: "This claim or privilege travels with the thing into whosoever's possession it may come" (p. 284).

Although salvage claims give rise to a maritime lien, claims in the nature of towage do not. In *Westrup* v. *Great Yarmouth Steam Carrying Co.* (1889) 43 Ch. Div. 241 it was argued, by reference to some indications in two cases in the 1840s, that towage was to be treated in the same way as salvage. This argument was rejected by Kay J. who applied the following dictum of the Court of Appeal in *The Heinrich Bjorn* (1885) 10 P.D. 48 at 53, a case on necessaries:

"It has been suggested that the way in which necessaries are associated with salvage and damage implies an intention to give in respect of necessaries the same lien as existed in respect of salvage, but the argument is not satisfactory, especially when it is observed that necessaries are more closely associated with towage, which gave no lien, than with salvage or damage."

The point has been treated as decided since that time. See also, per Fry L.J. in *The Heinrich Bjorn* (*op. cit.*) at p. 53; per Lord Bramwell in the House of Lords (1886) 11 App. Cas. 270 and *The Sara* (1889) 14 App. Cas. 209.

(3) "Towage in respect of a ship"

Section 20(2)(k) gives jurisdiction in respect of "any claim in the nature of towage in respect of *a ship*" (emphasis supplied). This effects a potentially significant restriction upon the ambit of the jurisdiction when considering water-borne objects which cannot be described as "a ship". The relevant principles as to the construction of the term "ship" as used in section 20 are as follows:

(i) Section 24(1) of the Supreme Court Act 1981 defines "ship". The definition given is that:

"'Ship' includes every description of vessel used in navigation . . . ",

and includes a hovercraft.

(ii) However, the Merchant Shipping Act 1921 by section 1(1) defined "ship" as including " . . . every description of lighter, barge or like vessel used in navigation in Great Britain however propelled . . . ", except if used in non-tidal waters (except harbours).

(iii) "Vessel" is not defined in the Supreme Court Act 1981 as such but, as a term which was used in and defined by the Merchant Shipping Act 1894, has given rise to a considerable body of authority. Section 742 of the 1894 Act defined "vessel" as including "any ship or boat or other description of vessel used in navigation". In *Steedman* v. *Scofield* [1992] 2 Lloyd's Rep. 163, in which Sheen J. had to consider whether a "jet-ski" was a vessel used in navigation, the learned judge defined a boat as conveying:

" . . . the concept of a structure, whether it be made of wood, steel or fibreglass, which by reason of its concave shape provides buoyancy for the carriage of persons or goods",

and a vessel as being:

" . . . a hollow receptacle for carrying goods or people . . . it includes every description of watercraft used or capable of being used as a means of transportation on water."

(iv) In the enactment of the new codifying statute, the Merchant Shipping Act 1995, the word "vessel" has been replaced throughout by the word "ship". Section 742 of the 1894 Act and its definition is now replaced by section 313(1) of the 1995 Act with the same definition given in section 24(1) of the Supreme Court Act 1981 (see (i) above).

(v) As to the phrase "used in navigation", this connotes both a vessel of the type used in navigation and one used in navigable waters: see for a compendious consideration of the cases *Meeson on Admiralty Jurisdiction and Practice* (2nd Edn.), p. 20.

Examples of what has and has not been held to be a ship or vessel abound in the cases. In the final analysis, it will be a question of fact in each case and often a matter of first impression. As Scrutton L.J. put it with characteristic simplicity in *Merchants Marine Insurance Co.* v. *North of England P. & I.* (1926) 23 Com. Cas. 165 in relation to the question of whether a pontoon crane was a "ship" (it was held not to be so):

"I find myself in the not very courageous position of saying that all the contribution I can make is to say that I am not convinced that the learned judge below was wrong. One might possibly take the position of the gentleman who dealt with the elephant by saying he could not define an elephant but he knew what it was when he saw one; and it may be that this is the foundation of the learned judge's judgment, that he cannot define 'ship or vessel' but he knows this thing is *not* a ship or vessel. I should have liked to have given a definition here because considering that these words are the words in every ordinary marine policy and in every Club policy, and that they are also, with some addition, the words in the Merchant Shipping Act, it is rather a pity that the courts are not able to give a definition of the words, which was constantly turning up in a mercantile transaction."

Thus, held to be a "ship" or "vessel" have been barges incapable of independent propulsion (see e.g. *The Harlow* [1922] P. 175); a floating crane incapable of independent propulsion (see e.g. *R* v. *St. John Shipbuilding* (1981) 126 D.L.R. (3d) 353); a land reclamation dredger vessel-shaped and capable of propulsion but often fixed in one place for long periods (see e.g. *Cook* v. *Dredging & Construction Co. Ltd* [1958] 1 Lloyd's Rep. 334) and, assumed and conceded to have been a ship, a floating light-ship incapable of self-propulsion (see e.g. *The North Goodwin No.16* [1980] 1 Lloyd's Rep. 71).

The following have been held not to be "ships": a gas float anchored in a fixed position and used as a navigational light, rather like a light ship (see e.g. *The Gas Float Whitton (No. 2)* [1897] A.C. 337, H.L., but *cf. The North Goodwin No.16* referred to above); a dismasted vessel used as a coal hulk (see e.g. *European & Australian Royal Mail* v. *P. & O.* (1866) 14 L.T. 704); a newbuilding launched but as yet without means of propulsion having been fitted (see e.g. *The Andalusian* (1878) 3 P.D. 182). A raft of wood, that is, logs lashed together for towage, was held not to be a "ship" by Dr Lushington in *A Raft of Timber* (1844) 2 W. Rob. 251, although this was doubted by Lord Herschell in *The Gas Float Whitton* (*op. cit.*) at p. 345.

Where the subject-matter of the towage is not a "ship", Admiralty *in rem* jurisdiction may still be able to be established under another head of section 20(2) of the Supreme Court Act 1981, such as section 20(2)(h). Some of these other potential heads of jurisdiction are considered under heading (5) below.

(4) "Claims in the nature of towage"

There are very few cases on what is or is not a claim "in the nature of towage". However, it is submitted that certain principles can be discerned.

(i) "Towage" is to be interpreted widely so as to include all usual tug-provided services. In *The Leoborg* [1962] 2 Lloyd's Rep. 146 Hewson J. stated in relation to the corresponding section of the earlier Act:

> "Under Sect. 1(1)(k) of the Administration of Justice Act, 1956, there is Admiralty jurisdiction for any claim in the nature of towage in respect of a ship. It is not claimed that actual towage was performed in respect of this ship, but that escorting services were provided from outside the Hook of Holland to Schiedam.
>
> In my view, such escorting services by a tug from outside a port into a port are services in the nature of towage."

However, the term "towage" will not be wide enough to extend to many common offshore industry services.

(ii) "Claims in the nature of towage" is, *prima facie*, a narrow phrase and is apt to be confined merely to claims for towage remuneration, see, for example, the claim in *Westrup* v. *Great Yarmouth Steam Co.* (1889) 43 Ch. Div. 241. It is submitted that it is uncertain whether jurisdiction under paragraph (k) extends to claims other than those simply brought by the tug for monies due in respect of towage performed by it. The 1840 Act introduced the jurisdiction in respect of towage in conjunction with jurisdiction in respect of claims in respect of necessaries and most authors treat towage claims in a similar way: see e.g. *Roscoe on The Admiralty Jurisdiction and Practice* (5th Edn.) at pp. 187–188 and *Bucknill on Tug and Tow* (2nd Edn.) at p. 72. Cases where the claim is one by the tow against the tug, such as for breach of the contract of towage seem always to have been brought under other heads of Admiralty jurisdiction.

Thus, in *The Isca* (1886) 12 P.D. 34, a claim by a tow against her tug for negligently canting her into a bridge was brought under the head of:

> "any claim arising out of any agreement made in relation to the use or hire of any ship".

which corresponds to section 20(2)(h) of the Supreme Court Act 1981 but *not* as a claim in the nature of towage (*cf. Meeson on Admiralty Jurisdiction and Practice* (2nd Edn.) at p. 40, footnote 174, which appears to be incorrect). It was held that the claim plainly fell within this head of jurisdiction. Similarly, in *The Conoco Britannia* [1972] 1 Lloyd's Rep. 342, a claim was brought by a tug against the tow under a contract on the U.K. Standard Conditions for an indemnity in respect of the loss of the tug in a collision with the tow. The claim was held to be within the same head of Admiralty jurisdiction which provided in the same terms as section 20(2)(h) of the 1981 Act now provides, *viz.*:

> "(h) any claim arising out of any agreement relating to the carriage of goods in a ship or to the use or hire of a ship."

Brandon J. stated (at p. 345):

"For the plaintiffs it was argued that all three claims came within para. (h). It was said that they were claims arising out of an agreement relating to the use or hire of a ship, namely the tug *Hullman*. For the defendants it was argued that the words 'relating to the use or hire of a ship' should be construed *ejusdem generis* with the preceding words in para. (h), namely 'relating to the carriage of goods in a ship' and should accordingly be given a narrow construction which would not cover the case of a towage contract under which a tug is hired to attend on and assist a ship. I am of the opinion that there is no reason for giving a restricted meaning to the words, 'relating to the use or hire of a ship'. It seems to me that the words in their ordinary and natural meaning are amply wide enough to cover the case of the hire of a tug under a towage contract, and, even if this Act stood alone without any history behind it, I should be of that opinion. The point is, however, to my mind, put almost beyond doubt, when one does consider the history of the jurisdiction in this matter."

In relation to the argument that the claim fell equally under the head of jurisdiction in respect of claims "in the nature of towage" Brandon J. declined to pronounce a view but confined himself (at p. 346) to saying this:

"I have, therefore, no hesitation in holding that the first ground relied on by counsel for the defendants is bad. As I am of that opinion, it is not necessary that I should express a conclusion on the question whether the claims would come within certain other paragraphs of sect. 1(1) which have been canvassed, namely, (d), (e) and (k). Since it is unnecessary to express an opinion on those questions, I do not propose to do so. I shall only say that I think that there are arguable points in relation to them."

Contrast the decision in *The Valsesia* [1927] P. 115. In that case, the owners of two tugs brought an action *in rem* against a foreign steamship for the price agreed with the agents of the ship for the performance of a towage job. The tugs were unable to perform the contract owing to the negligence of the crew of the tow. Mr Justice Hill, in awarding damages *in personam* against the owners of the tow, who had appeared to the writ *in rem*, said that it must be a judgment *in personam*, because an action for negligence in the performance of such a contract as this did not give rise to a writ *in rem*.

(5) *Other available heads of jurisdiction*

As the discussion above shows, it is often possible to bring a claim arising in respect of a towage contract under a head of Admiralty jurisdiction other than the "towage" head provided for in section 20(2)(k). This will be useful where the subject-matter of the towage is not "a ship" or where there is doubt as to whether it is or not (for example, a drilling rig or other specialised water-borne object), or where the service rendered by the tug is far removed from "towage" *simpliciter*, or where the claim is not one for monies due under a towage contract in respect of a towage service and it is wished to avoid the potential pitfalls of "a claim in the nature of towage".

In addition to section 20(2)(h) of the Supreme Court Act 1981, considered above, the following other potential heads of jurisdiction should be borne in mind (for a detailed consideration of each, see *Meeson, op. cit.*):

  (i) Section 20(2)(d): "any claim for damage received by a ship" (e.g. tug or tow damaged).
 (ii) Section 20(2)(e): "any claim for damage done by a ship" (e.g. tug or tow damaged).
(iii) Section 20(2)(f) relating to claims for loss of life and personal injury.
(iv) Section 20(2)(g): "any claim for loss of or damage to goods carried in a ship" (e.g. a barge's cargo, or equipment being conveyed by a supply vessel).
 (v) Section 20(2)(q) relating to claims in respect of general average acts (see Chapter 9 above).

APPENDIX 1

U.K. STANDARD CONDITIONS FOR TOWAGE AND OTHER SERVICES (revised 1986)

U.K. STANDARD CONDITIONS FOR TOWAGE AND OTHER SERVICES (Revised 1986)

1. (a) The agreement between the Tugowner and the Hirer is and shall at all times be subject to and include each and all of the conditions herein after set out.

(b) for the purposes of these conditions

(i) "towing" is any operation in connection with the holding, pushing, pulling, moving, escorting or guiding of or standing by the Hirer's vessel, and the expressions "to tow", "being towed" and "towage" shall be defined likewise.

(ii) "vessel" shall include any vessel, craft or object of whatsoever nature (whether or not coming within the usual meaning of the word "vessel") which the Tugowner agrees to tow or to which the Tugowner agrees at the request, express or implied, of the Hirer, to render any service of whatsoever nature other than towing.

(iii) "tender" shall include any vessel, craft or object of whatsoever nature which is not a tug but which is provided by the Tugowner for the performance of any towage or other service.

(iv) The expression "whilst towing" shall cover the period commencing when the tug or tender is in a position to receive orders direct from the Hirer's vessel to commence holding, pushing, pulling, moving, escorting, guiding or standing by the vessel or to pick up ropes, wires or lines, or when the towing line has been passed to or by the tug or tender, whichever is the sooner, and ending when the final orders from the Hirer's vessel to cease holding, pushing, pulling, moving, escorting, guiding or standing by the vessel or to cast off ropes, wires or lines has been carried out, or the towing line has been finally slipped, whichever is the later, and the tug or tender is safely clear of the vessel.

(v) Any service of whatsoever nature to be performed by the Tugowner other than towing shall be deemed to cover the period commencing when the tug or tender is placed physically at the disposal of the Hirer at the place designated by the Hirer, or, if such be at a vessel, when the tug or tender is in a position to receive and forthwith carry out orders to come alongside and shall continue until the employment for which the tug or tender has been engaged is ended. If the service is to be ended at or off a vessel the period of service shall end when the tug or tender is safely clear of the vessel or, if it is to be ended elsewhere, then when any persons or property of whatsoever description have been landed or discharged from the tug or tender and/or the service for which the tug or tender has been required is ended.

(vi) The word "tug" shall include "tugs", the word "tender" shall include "tenders", the word "vessel" shall include "vessels", the word "Tugowner" shall include 'Tugowners', and the word "Hirer" shall include "Hirers".

(vii) The expression "tugowner" shall include any person or body (other than the Hirer or the owner of the vessel on whose behalf the Hirer contracts as provided in Clause 2 hereof) who is a party to this agreement whether or not he in fact owns any tug or tender, and the expression "other Tugowner" contained in Clause 5 hereof shall be construed likewise.

2. If at the time of making this agreement or of performing the towage or of rendering any service other than towing at the request, express or implied, of the Hirer, the Hirer is not the Owner of the vessel referred to herein as "the Hirer's vessel", the Hirer expressly represents that he is authorised to make and does make this agreement for and on behalf of the owner of the said vessel subject to each and all of these conditions and agrees that both the Hirer and the Owner are bound jointly and severally by these conditions.

3. Whilst towing or whilst at the request, express or implied, of the Hirer, rendering any service other than towing, the master and crew of the tug or tender shall be deemed to be the servants of the Hirer and under the control of the Hirer and/or his servants and/or his agents, and anyone on board the Hirer's vessel who may be employed and/or paid by the Tugowner shall likewise be deemed to be the servant of the Hirer and the Hirer shall accordingly be vicariously liable for any act or omission by any such person so deemed to be the servant of the Hirer.

4. Whilst towing, or whilst at the request, either expressed or implied, of the Hirer rendering any service of whatsoever nature other than towing: —

(a) The Tugowner shall not (except as provided in Clauses 4 (c) and (e) hereof) be responsible for or be liable for

(i) damage of any description done by or to the tug or tender; or done by or to the Hirer's vessel or done by or to any cargo or other thing on board or being loaded on board or intended to be loaded on board the Hirer's vessel or the tug or tender or to or by any other object or property

or

(ii) loss of the tug or tender or the Hirer's vessel or of any cargo or other thing on board or being loaded on board or intended to be loaded on board the Hirer's vessel or the tug or tender or any other object or property;

or

(iii) any claim by a person not a party to this agreement for loss or damage of any description whatsoever;

arising from any cause whatsoever, including (without prejudice to the generality of the foregoing) negligence at any time of the Tugowner his servants or agents, unseaworthiness, unfitness or breakdown of the tug or tender, its machinery, boilers, towing gear, equipment, lines, ropes or wires, lack of fuel, stores, speed or otherwise and

(b) The Hirer shall (except as provided in Clauses 4(c) and (e)) be responsible for, pay for and indemnify the Tugowner against and in respect of any loss or damage and any claims of whatsoever nature or howsoever arising or caused, whether covered by the provisions of Clause 4(a) hereof or not, suffered by or made against the Tugowner and which shall include, without prejudice to the generality of the foregoing, any loss of or damage to the tug or tender or any property of the Tugowner even if the same arises from or is caused by the negligence of the Tugowner his servants or agents.

(c) The provisions of Clauses 4(a) and 4(b) hereof shall not be applicable in respect of any claims which arise in any of the following circumstances:—

(i) All claims which the Hirer shall prove to have resulted directly and solely from the personal failure of the Tugowner to exercise reasonable care to make the tug or tender seaworthy for navigation at the commencement of the towing or other service. For the purpose of this Clause the Tugowner's personal responsibility for exercising reasonable care shall be construed as relating only to the person or persons having the ultimate control and chief management of the Tugowner's business and to any servant (excluding the officers and crew of any tug or tender) to whom the Tugowner has specifically delegated the particular duty of exercising reasonable care and shall not include any other servant of the Tugowner or any agent or independent contractor employed by the Tugowner.

(ii) All claims which arise when the tug or tender, although towing or rendering some service other than towing, is not in a position of proximity or risk to or from the Hirer's vessel or any other craft attending the Hirer's vessel and is detached from and safely clear of any ropes, lines, wire cables or moorings associated with the Hirer's vessel. Provided always that, notwithstanding the foregoing, the provisions of Clauses 4(a) and 4(b) shall be fully applicable in respect of all claims which arise at any time when the tug or tender is at the request, whether express or implied, of the Hirer, his servants or his agents, carrying persons or property of whatsoever description (in addition to the Officers and crew and usual equipment of the tug or tender) and which are wholly or partly caused by/or arise out of the presence on board of such persons or property or which arise at anytime when the tug or tender is proceeding to or from the Hirer's vessel in hazardous conditions or circumstances.

(d) Notwithstanding anything hereinbefore contained, the Tugowner shall under no circumstances whatsoever be responsible for or be liable for any loss or damage caused by or contributed to or arising out of any delay or detention of the Hirer's vessel or of the cargo on board or being loaded on board or intended to be loaded on board the Hirer's vessel or of any other object or property or of any person, or any consequence thereof, whether or not the same shall be caused or arise whilst towing or whilst at the request, either express or implied, of the Hirer rendering any service of whatsoever nature other than towing or at any other time whether before during or after the making of this agreement.

(e) Notwithstanding anything contained in Clauses 4 (a) and (b) hereof the liability of the Tugowner for death or personal injury resulting from negligence is not excluded or restricted thereby.

5. The Tugowner shall at any time be entitled to substitute one or more tugs or tenders for any other tug or tender or tugs or tenders. The Tugowner shall at any time (whether before or after the making of this agreement between him and the Hirer) be entitled to contract with any other Tugowner (hereinafter referred to as "the other Tugowner") to hire the other Tugowner's tug or tender and in any such event it is hereby agreed that the Tugowner is acting (or is deemed to have acted) as the agent for the Hirer, notwithstanding that the Tugowner may in addition, if authorised whether expressly or impliedly by or on behalf of the other Tugowner, act as agent for the other Tugowner at any time and for any purpose including the making of any agreement with the Hirer. In any event should the Tugowner as agent for the Hirer contract with the other Tugowner for any purpose as aforesaid it is hereby agreed that such contract is and shall at all times be subject to the provisions of these conditions so that the other Tugowner is bound by the same and may as a principal sue the Hirer thereon and shall have the full benefit of these conditions in every respect expressed or implied herein.

6. Nothing contained in these conditions shall limit, prejudice or preclude in any way any legal rights which the Tugowner may have against the Hirer including, but not limited to, any rights which the Tugowner or his servants or agents may have to claim salvage remuneration or special compensation for any extraordinary services rendered to vessels or anything aboard vessels by any tug or tender. Furthermore, nothing contained in these conditions shall limit, prejudice, or preclude in any way any right which the Tugowner may have to limit his liability.

7. The Tugowner will not in any event be responsible or liable for the consequences of war, riots, civil commotions, acts of terrorism or sabotage, strikes, lockouts, disputes, stoppages or labour disturbances (whether he be a party thereto or not) or anything done in contemplation or furtherance thereof or delays of any description, howsoever caused or arising, including by the negligence of the Tugowner or his servants or agents.

8. The Hirer of the tug or tender engaged subject to these conditions undertakes not to take or cause to be taken any proceedings against any servant or agent of the Tugowner or other Tugowner, whether or not the tug or tender substituted or hired or the contract or any part thereof has been sublet to the owner of the tug or tender, in respect of any negligence or breach of duty or other wrongful act on the part of such servant or agent which, but for this present provision, it would be competent for the Hirer so to do and the owners of such tug or tender shall hold this undertaking for the benefit of their servants and agents.

9. (a) The agreement between the Tugowner and the Hirer is and shall be governed by English Law and the Tugowner and the Hirer hereby accept, subject to the proviso contained in sub-clause (b) hereof, the exclusive jurisdiction of the English Courts (save where the registered office of the Tugowner is situated in Scotland when the agreement is and shall be governed by Scottish Law and the Tugowner and the Hirer hereby shall accept the exclusive jurisdiction of the Scottish Courts).

(b) No suit shall be brought in any jurisdiction other than that provided in sub-clause (a) hereof save that either the Tugowner or the Hirer shall have the option to bring proceedings in rem to obtain the arrest of or other similar remedy against any vessel or property owned by the other party hereto in any jurisdiction where such vessel or property may be found.

APPENDIX 2

TOWCON*

Recommended by
International Salvage Union (ISU)
European Tugowners Association (ETA)
The Baltic and International Maritime Council (BIMCO)

1. Date and place of Agreement	**RECOMMENDED** **INTERNATIONAL OCEAN TOWAGE AGREEMENT (L U M P S U M)** **CODE NAME: "TOWCON"** PART I
2. Tugowner/place of business	3. Hirer/place of business
4. T o w (name and type)	5. Gross tonnage/displacement tonnage
6. Maximum length/maximum breadth & towing draught (fore and aft)	7. Flag and place of registry
8. Registered owners	9. Classification society
10. P. & I. liability insurers	11. General condition of tow
12. Particulars of cargo and/or ballast and/or other property on board the tow	
13. T u g (name and type)	14. Flag and place of registry
15. Gross tonnage	16. Classification Society
17. P. & I. liability insurers	
18. Certificated bollard pull (if any)	19. Indicated horse power
20. Estimated daily average bunker oil consumption in good weather and smooth water	
(a) at full towing power with tow	
(b) at full sea speed without tow	
21. Winches and main towing gear	

(continued)

Copyright, published by
The Baltic and International Maritime Council (BIMCO)

Printed and sold by Fr. G. Knudtzons Bogtrykkeri A/S, 55 Toldbodgade, DK-1253 Copenhagen K
by authority of The Baltic and International Maritime Council (BIMCO), Copenhagen

* Reproduced by kind permission of BIMCO.

243

(continued)   "TOWCON" INTERNATIONAL OCEAN TOWAGE AGREEMENT (LUMP SUM)   PART I

22. Nature of service(s) (Cl. 1)	23. Comtemplated route (Cl. 17)
24. Place of departure (Cl. 7) 25. Place of destination (Cl. 8)	
26. Free time at place of departure (Cl. 2(g))	27. Free time at place of destination (Cl. 2(g))
28. Notices (Place of departure) (Cl. 7(c))	29. Delay payment (Cl. 2(g))
(a) Initial departure period (from/to)	(a) Port rate
(b) Initial departure notice (days notice/days period)	(b) Sea rate
(c) Final departure period and notice (days notice/days period)	30. Riding crew to be provided by (also state number to be provided) (Cl. 9)
(d) Final departure time and date notice (days notice)	
(e) Notices to be given to	31. If riding crew provided by Tugowner state amount per man per day payable by Hirer (Cl. 9)
32. Lump sum towage price (also state when each instalment due and payable) (Cl. 2)	33. Payment of lump sum & other amounts (state currency, mode of payment, place of payment and bank account) (Cl. 2)
(a) Lump sum towage price	
(b) amount due and payable on signing Agreement	
(c) amount due and payable on sailing of tug & tow from place of departure	
(d) amount due and payable on passing of tug and tow off	
(e) amount due and payable on arrival of tug & tow at place of destination	
34. Interest rate (%) per annum to run from (state number of days) after any sum is due (Cl. 5)	35. Security (state sum, by whom to be provided and when) (optional, only to be filled in if expressly agreed) (Cl. 6)
36. Current cost of tug's bunker oil (also state type of bunkers) (Cl. 2(e))	37. Cancelling date, if any agreed (Cl. 16(e))
38. Cancellation fee (Cl. 16)	39. Numbers of additional clauses, covering special provisions, if agreed

It is mutually agreed between the party mentioned in Box 2 (hereinafter called "the Tugowner") and the party mentioned in Box 3 (hereinafter called "the Hirer") that the Tugowner shall, subject to the terms and conditions of this Agreement which consists of PART I including additional clauses, if any agreed and stated in Box 39, and PART II, use his best endeavours to perform the towage or other service(s) as set out herein. In the event of a conflict of terms and conditions, the provisions of PART I and any additional clauses, if agreed, shall prevail over those of PART II to the extent of such conflict but no further.

Signature (Tugowner)	Signature (Hirer)

INSTRUCTIONS ON HOW TO FILL IN BOX 28 in PART I

Notices to be communicated according to Clause 7(c)

Initial Departure Period (Box 28(a))

The Tow shall be ready to sail from the place of departure between the dates indicated.

Initial Departure Notice (Box 28 (b))

The Hirer shall give the Tugowner the number of days notice of the number of days period falling within the initial departure period as to when the Tow will be ready to depart.

Final Departure Period and Notice (Box 28 (c))

The Hirer shall give the Tugowner the number of days notice of the number of days period falling within the initial departure notice period as to when the Tow will be ready to depart.

Final Departure Time and Date Notice (Box 28 (d))

The Hirer shall give the Tugowner the number of days notice of the time and date of sailing of the Tow which day shall fall within the final departure period.

Notices to be given to (Box 28 (e))

The above notices shall be given by the Hirer to the addressee mentioned in Box 28 (e).

PART II
"Towcon" International Ocean Towage Agreement (Lump Sum)

1. The Tow

"The Tow" shall include any vessel, craft or object of whatsoever nature including anything carried thereon as described in PART I to which the Tugowner agrees to render the service(s) as set out in Box 22.

2. Price and Conditions of Payment

(a) The Hirer shall pay the Tugowner the sum set in Box 32 (hereinafter called "the Lump Sum").

(b) The Lump Sum shall be payable as set out in Boxes 32 and 33.

(c) The Lump Sum and all other sums payable to the Tugowner under this Agreement shall be payable without any discount, deduction, set-off, lien, claim or counter-claim, each instalment of the Lump Sum shall be fully and irrevocably earned at the moment it is due as set out in Box 32, Tug and/or Tow lost or not lost, and all other sums shall be fully and irrevocably earned on a daily basis.

(d) All payments by the Hirer shall be made in the currency and to the bank account specified in Box 33.

(e) In the event that the average price per metric tonne of bunkers actually paid by the Tugowner differs from the amounts specified in Box 36 then the Hirer or the Tugowner, as the case may be, shall pay to the other the difference per metric tonne for every metric tonne consumed during the voyage. The average price specified above shall be the average of the prices per metric tonne actually paid by the Tugowner on the basis of quantities purchased at the last bunkering port prior to the voyage, any bunkering port during the voyage, and the first bunkering port after completion of the voyage. The log book of the Tug shall be prima facie evidence of the quantity of bunkers consumed.

(f) Any Delay Payment due under this Agreement shall be paid to the Tugowner as and when earned on presentation of the invoice.

(g) The Free Time specified in Boxes 26 and 27 shall be allowed for the connecting and disconnecting of the Tow and all other purposes relating thereto. Free Time shall commence when the Tug arrives at the pilot station at the place of departure or the Tug and Tow arrives at the pilot station at the place of destination or anchors or arrives at the usual waiting area off such places. Should the Free Time be exceeded, Delay Payment(s) at the rate specified in Box 29 shall be payable until the Tug and Tow sail from the place of departure or the Tug is free to leave the place of destination.

3. Additional Charges and Extra Costs

(a) The Hirer shall appoint his agents at the place of departure and place of destination and ports of call or refuge and shall provide such agents with adequate funds as required.

(b) The Hirer shall bear and pay as and when they fall due:-

(i) All port expenses, pilotage charges, harbour and canal dues and all other expenses of a similar nature levied upon or payable in respect of both the Tug and the Tow.

(ii) All taxes, (other than those normally payable by the Tugowner in the country where he has his principal place of business and in the country where the Tug is registered) stamp duties or other levies payable in respect of or in connection with this Agreement or the payments of the Lump Sum or other sums payable under this Agreement or the services to be performed under or in pursuance of this Agreement, any Customs or Excise duties and other costs, dues or expenses payable in respect of any necessary permits or licences.

(iii) The cost of the services of any assisting tugs when deemed necessary by the Tugmaster or prescribed by Port or other Authorities.

(iv) All costs and expenses necessary for the preparation of the Tow for towing (including such costs or expenses as those of raising the anchor of the Tow or tending or casting off any moorings of the Tow).

(v) The cost of insurance of the Tow shall be the sole responsibility of the Hirer to provide.

(c) All taxes, charges, costs, and expenses payable by the Hirer shall be paid by the Hirer direct to those entitled to them. If, however, any such tax, charge, cost or expense is in fact paid by or on behalf of the Tugowner (notwithstanding that the Tugowner shall under no circumstances be under any obligation to make such payments on behalf of the Hirer) the Hirer shall reimburse the Tugowner on the basis of the actual cost to the Tugowner upon presentation of invoice.

4. War Risk Escalation Clause

The Lump Sum is based and assessed on all war risk insurance costs applicable to the Tugowner in respect of the contemplated voyage in effect on the date of this Agreement.

In the event of any subsequent increase or decrease in the actual costs due to the Tugowner fulfilling his obligations under this Agreement, the Hirer or the Tugowner, as the case may be, shall reimburse the other the amount of any increase or decrease in the war risk, confiscation, deprivation or trapping insurance costs.

5. Interest

If any amounts due under this Agreement are not paid when due, then interest shall accrue and shall be paid in accordance with the provisions of Box 34, on all such amounts until payment is received by the Tugowner.

6. Security

The Hirer undertakes to provide, if required by the Tugowner, security to the satisfaction of the Tugowner in the form and in the sum, at the place and at the time indicated in Box 35 as a guarantee for due performance of the Agreement. Such security shall be returned to the guarantor when the Hirer's financial obligations under this Agreement have been met in full.

(Optional, only applicable if Box 35 filled in).

7. Place of Departure/Notices

(a) The Tow shall be tendered to the Tugowner at the place of departure stated in Box 24.

(b) The precise place of departure shall always be safe and accessible for the Tug to enter, to operate in and for the Tug and Tow to leave and shall be a place where such Tug is permitted to commence the towage in accordance with any local or other rules, requirements or regulations and shall always

be subject to the approval of the Tugowner which shall not be unreasonably withheld.

(c) (i) The Tow shall be ready to sail from the Place of Departure between the dates indicated in Box 28 (a), hereinafter called the Initial Departure Period.

(ii) The Hirer shall give the Tugowner such notice as is stipulated in Box 28 in respect of Initial Departure Notice (Box 28 (b)), Final Departure Period Notice (Box 28 (c)) and Final Departure Time and Date Notice (Box 28 (d)).

(iii) The Tow shall be offered to the Tugowner, duly certificated and otherwise in accordance with the terms and conditions of this Agreement.

(d) If the Hirer fails to comply strictly with the provisions of Cl. 7(c) the date of departure shall be deemed to be either the last day of the Initial Departure Period or the last day of the Final Departure Period, whichever is earlier, and this date shall be binding for all consequences arising in respect of Delay Payments and any other payments due or charges incurred in the performance of this Agreement.

8. Place of Destination

(a) The Tow shall be accepted forthwith and taken over by the Hirer or his duly authorised representative at the place of destination stated in Box 25.

(b) The precise place of destination shall always be safe and accessible for the Tug and Tow to enter, to operate in, and for the Tug to leave and shall be a place where such Tug is permitted to redeliver the Tow in accordance with any local or other rules, requirements or regulations and shall always be subject to the approval of the Tugowner, which approval shall not be unreasonably withheld.

9. Riding Crew

(a) In the event that the Tugowner provides a Riding Crew for the Tow, such crew and their suitability for the work shall be in the discretion of the Tugowner. All expenses for such personnel shall be for the account of the Tugowner.

(b) In the event that any personnel are placed on board the Tow by the Hirer all expenses for such personnel will be for the account of the Hirer and such personnel shall at all times under the orders of the Master of the Tug, but shall not be deemed to be the servants or agents of the Tugowner.

(c) The Riding Crew shall be provided at the Hirer's sole expense with suitable accomodation, food, fresh water, life saving appliances and all other requirements to comply as necessary with the law and regulations of the law of the Flag of the Tug and/or Tow and of the States through the territorial waters of which the Tug will pass or enter. It is a requirement that members of the Riding Crew provided by the Hirer shall be able to speak and understand the English language or any other mutual language.

10. Towing Gear and Use of Tow's Gear

(a) The Tugowner agrees to provide free of cost to the Hirer all towing hawsers, bridles and other towing gear normally carried on board the Tug, for the purpose of the towage or other services to be provided under this Agreement. The Tow shall be connected up in a manner within the discretion of the Tugowner.

(b) The Tugowner may make reasonable use at his discretion of the Tow's gear, power, anchors, anchor cables, radio, communication and navigational equipment and all other appurtenances free of cost during and for the purposes of the towage or other services to be provided under this Agreement.

11. Permits and Certification

(a) The Hirer shall arrange at his own cost and provide to the Tugowner all necessary licenses, authorisations and permits required by the Tug and/or Tow to undertake and complete the contractual voyage together with all necessary certification for the Tow to enter or leave all or any ports of call or refuge on the contemplated voyage.

(b) Any loss or expense incurred by the Tugowner by reason of the Hirer's failure to comply with this Clause shall be reimbursed by the Hirer to the Tugowner and during any delay caused thereby the Tugowner shall receive additional compensation from the Hirer at the Tug's Delay Payment rate specified in Box 29.

12. Tow-worthiness of the Tow

(a) The Hirer shall exercise due diligence to ensure that the Tow shall, at the commencement of the towage, be in all respects fit to be towed from the place of departure to the place of destination.

(b) The Hirer undertakes that the Tow will be suitably trimmed and prepared and ready to be towed at the time when the Tug arrives at the place of departure and fitted and equipped with such shapes, signals, navigational and other lights of a type required for the towage.

(c) The Hirer shall supply to the Tugowner or the Tugmaster, on the arrival of the Tug at the place of departure an unconditional certificate of tow-worthiness for the Tow issued by a recognised firm of Marine Surveyors or Survey Organisation, provided always that the Tugowner shall not be under any obligation to perform the towage until in his discretion he is satisfied that the Tow is in all respects trimmed, prepared, fit and ready for towage but the Tugowner shall not unreasonably withhold his approval.

(d) No inspection of the Tow by the Tugowner shall constitute approval of the Tow's condition or be deemed a waiver of the foregoing undertakings given by the Hirer.

13. Seaworthiness of the Tug

The Tugowner will exercise due diligence to tender the Tug at the place of departure in a seaworthy condition and in all respects ready to perform the towage, but the Tugowner gives no other warranties, express or implied.

14. Substitution of Tugs

The Tugowner shall at all times have the right to substitute any tug or tugs for any other tug or tugs of adequate power (including two or more tugs for one, or one tug for two or more) at any time whether before or after the com-

PART II
"Towcon" International Ocean Towage Agreement (Lump Sum)

mencement of the towage or other services and shall be at liberty to employ 185
a tug or tugs belonging to other tugowners for the whole or part of the tow- 186
age or other service contemplated under this Agreement. Provided how- 187
ever, that the main particulars of the substituted tug or tugs shall be subject 188
to the Hirer's prior approval, but such approval shall not be unreasonably 189
withheld. 190

15. Salvage 191

(a) Should the Tow break away from the Tug during the course of the towa- 192
ge service, the Tug shall render all reasonable services to re-connect the 193
towline and fulfill this Agreement without making any claim for salvage. 194

(b) If at any time the Tugowner or the Tugmaster considers it necessary or 195
advisable to seek or accept salvage services from any vessel or person on 196
behalf of the Tug or Tow, or both, the Hirer hereby undertakes and warrants 197
that the Tugowner or his duly authorised servant or agent including the Tug- 198
master have the full actual authority of the Hirer to accept such services on 199
behalf of the Tow on any reasonable terms. 200

16. Cancellation and Withdrawal 201

(a) At any time prior to the departure of the Tow from the place of departure 202
the Hirer may cancel this Agreement upon payment of the cancellation fee 203
set out in Box 38. If cancellation takes place whilst the Tug is en route to the 204
place of departure or after the Tug has arrived at or off the place of depart- 205
ure then in addition to the said cancellation fee the Hirer shall pay any ad- 206
ditional amounts due under this Agreement. 207

(b) In the event that the towage operation is terminated after departure from 208
the place of departure, but before the Tow arrives at the place of destination 209
without fault on the part of the Tugowner, his servants or agents, the Tugow- 210
ner shall be entitled to be paid, and if already paid to retain all sums payable 211
according to Box 32, accrued Delay Payments and any other amounts due 212
under this Agreement. The above amounts are in addition to any damages 213
the Tugowner may be entitled to claim for breach of this Agreement. 214

(c) The Tugowner may without prejudice to any other remedies he may ha- 215
ve leave the Tow in a place where the Hirer may take repossession of it and 216
be entitled to payment of the Lump Sum less expenses saved by the 217
Tugowner and all other payments due under this Agreement, upon any one 218
or more of the following grounds: 219

(i) If there is any delay or delays (other than delay caused by the Tug) at 220
the place of departure exceeding in aggregate 21 running days. 221

(ii) If there is any delay or delays (other than a delay caused by the Tug) 222
at any port or place of call or refuge exceeding in aggregate 21 running 223
days. 224

(iii) If the security as may be required according to Box 35 is not given 225
within 7 running days of the Tugowner's request to provide security. 226

(iv) If the Hirer has not accepted the Tow within 7 running days of arrival 227
at the place of destination. 228

(v) If any amount payable under this Agreement has not been paid with- 229
in 7 running days of the date such sums are due. 230

(d) Before exercising his option of withdrawing from this Agreement as 231
aforesaid, the Tugowner shall if practicable give the Hirer 48 hours notice 232
(Saturdays, Sundays and public Holidays excluded) of his intention so to 233
withdraw. 234

(e) Should the Tug not be ready to commence the towage at the latest at 235
midnight on the date, if any, indicated in Box 37, the Hirer shall have the op- 236
tion of cancelling this Agreement and shall be entitled to claim damages for 237
detention if due to the wilful default of the Tugowner. Should the Tugowner 238
anticipate that the Tug will not be ready, he shall notify the Hirer thereof by 239
telex, cable or otherwise in writing without delay stating the expected date 240
of the Tug's readiness and ask whether the Hirer will exercise his option to 241
cancel. Such option to cancel must be exercised within 48 hours after the 242
receipt of the Tugowner's notice, otherwise the third day after the date stat- 243
ed in the Tugowner's notice shall be deemed to be the new agreed date to 244
commence the towage in accordance with this Agreement. 245

17. Necessary Deviation or Slow Steaming 246

(a) If the Tug during the course of the towage or other service under this 247
Agreement puts into a port or place or seeks shelter or is detained or devia- 248
tes from the original route as set out in Box 23, or slow steams because 249
either the Tugowner or Tugmaster reasonably consider 250

(i) that the Tow is not fit to be towed or 251

(ii) the Tow is incapable of being towed at the original speed contem- 252
plated by the Tugowner or 253

(iii) the towing connection requires rearrangement, or 254

(iv) repairs or alterations to or additional equipment for the Tow are re- 255
quired to safeguard the venture and enable the Tow to be towed to de- 256
stination, or 257

(v) it would not be prudent to do otherwise on account of weather con- 258
ditions actual or forecast, or 259

because of any other good and valid reason outside the control of the Tug- 260
owner or Tugmaster, or because of any delay caused by or at the request 261
of the Hirer, this Agreement shall remain in full force and effect, and the 262
Tugowner shall be entitled to receive from the Hirer additional compensa- 263
tion at the appropriate Delay Payment rate as set out in Box 29 for all time 264
spent in such port or place and for all time spent by the Tug at sea in excess 265
of the time which would have been spent had such slow steaming or devia- 266
tion not taken place. 267

(b) The Tug shall at all times be at liberty to go to the assistance of any ves- 268
sel in distress for the purpose of saving life or property or to call at any port 269
or place for bunkers, repairs, supplies, or any other necessaries or to land 270
disabled seamen, but if towing the Tug shall leave the Tow in a safe place 271
and during such period this Agreement shall remain in full force and effect. 272

(c) The Tug shall have liberty to comply with any orders or directions as to 273
departure, arrival, routes, ports of call, stoppages, destination, delivery, re- 274
quisition or otherwise howsoever given by the Government of the Nation un- 275
der whose flag the Tug or Tow sails or any department thereof, or any per- 276
son acting or purporting to act with the authority for such Government or 277
any department thereof by the committee or person having under the terms 278
of the War Risks Insurance on the Tug the right to give such orders or direc- 279
tions and if by reason of and in compliance with any such orders or di- 280

rections anything is done or is not done the same shall not be deemed a de- 281
viation and delivery in accordance with such orders or directions shall be a 282
fulfilment of this Agreement and the Lump Sum and/or all other sums shall 283
be paid to the Tugowner accordingly. 284

(d) Any deviation howsoever or whatsoever by the Tug or by the Tugowner 285
not expressly permitted by the terms and conditions of this Agreement shall 286
not amount to a repudiation of this Agreement and the Agreement shall re- 287
main in full force and effect notwithstanding such deviation. 288

18. Liabilities 289

1. (a) The Tugowner will indemnify the Hirer in respect of any liability adjud- 290
ged due or claim reasonably compromised arising out of injury or death oc- 291
curring during the towage or other service hereunder to any of the following 292
persons: 293

(i) The Master and members of the crew of the Tug and any other serv- 294
ant or agent of the Tugowner; 295

(ii) The members of the Riding Crew provided by the Tugowner or any 296
other person whom the Tugowner provides on board the Tow; 297

(iii) Any other person on board the Tug who is not a servant or agent of 298
the Hirer or otherwise on board on behalf of or at the request of the 299
Hirer. 300

(b) The Hirer will indemnify the Tugowner in respect of any liability adjud- 301
ged due or claim reasonably compromised arising from injury or death oc- 302
curring during the towage or other service hereunder to any of the following 303
persons: 304

(i) The Master and members of the crew of the Tow and any other ser- 305
vant or agents of the Hirer; 306

(ii) Any other person on board the Tow for whatever purpose except the 307
members of the Riding Crew or any other persons whom the Tugowner 308
provides on board the Tow pursuant to their obligations under this 309
Agreement. 310

2. (a) The following shall be for the sole account of the Tugowner without any 311
recourse to the Hirer, his servants, or agents, whether or not the same is 312
due to breach of contract, negligence or any other fault on the part of the Hi- 313
rer, his servants or agents: 314

(i) Loss or damage of whatsoever nature, howsoever caused to or sus- 315
tained by the Tug or any property on board the Tug. 316

(ii) Loss or damage of whatsoever nature caused to or suffered by third 317
parties or their property by reason of contact with the Tug or obstruction 318
created by the presence of the Tug. 319

(iii) Loss or damage of whatsoever nature suffered by the Tugowner or 320
by third parties in consequence of the loss or damage referred to in (i) 321
and (ii) above. 322

(iv) Any liability in respect of wreck removal or in respect of the expense 323
of moving or lighting or buoying the Tug or in respect of preventing or 324
abating pollution originating from the Tug. 325

The Tugowner will indemnify the Hirer in respect of any liability adjudged 326
due to a third party or any claim by a third party reasonably compromised 327
arising out of any such loss or damage. The Tugowner shall not in any cir- 328
cumstances be liable for any loss or damage suffered by the Hirer or 329
caused to or sustained by the Tow in consequence of loss or damage how- 330
soever caused to or sustained by the Tug or any property on board the Tug. 331

(b) The following shall be for the sole account of the Hirer without any re- 332
course to the Tugowner, his servants or agents, whether or not the same is 333
due to breach of contract, negligence or any fault on the part of the Tugow- 334
ner, his servants or agents: 335

(i) Loss or damage of whatsoever nature, howsoever caused to or su- 336
stained by the Tow. 337

(ii) Loss or damage of whatsoever nature caused to or suffered by third 338
parties or their property by reason of contact with the Tow or obstruc- 339
tion created by the presence of the Tow. 340

(iii) Loss or damage of whatsoever nature suffered by the Hirer or by 341
third parties in consequence of the loss or damage referred to in (i) and 342
(ii) above. 343

(iv) Any liability in respect of wreck removal or in respect of the expense 344
of moving or lighting or buoying the Tow or in respect of preventing or 345
abating pollution originating from the Tow. 346

The Hirer will indemnify the Tugowner in respect of any liability adjudged 347
due to a third party or any claim by a third party reasonably compromised 348
arising out of any such loss or damage but the Hirer shall not in any circum- 349
stances be liable for any loss or damage suffered by the Tugowner or cau- 350
sed to or sustained by the Tug in consequence of loss or damage, how- 351
soever caused to or sustained by the Tow. 352

3. Save for the provisions of Clauses 11, 12, 13 and 16 neither the Tugow- 353
ner nor the Hirer shall be liable to the other party for loss of profit, loss of 354
use, loss of production or any other indirect or consequential damage for 355
any reason whatsoever. 356

4. Notwithstanding any provisions of this Agreement to the contrary, the 357
Tugowner shall have the benefit of all limitations of, and exemptions from, 358
liability accorded to the Owners or Chartered Owners of Vessels by any ap- 359
plicable statute or rule of law for the time being in force and the same bene- 360
fits are to apply regardless of the form of signatures given to this Agreement. 361

19. Himalaya Clause 362

All exceptions, exemptions, defences, immunities, limitations of liability, 363
indemnities, privileges and conditions granted or provided by this Agree- 364
ment or by any applicable statute rule or regulation for the benefit of the 365
Tugowner or Hirer shall also apply to and be for the benefit of demise char- 366
terers, sub-contractors, operators, master, officers and crew of the Tug or 367
Tow and to and be for the benefit of all bodies corporate parent of, subsidi- 368
ary to, affiliated with or under the same management as either of them, as 369
well as all directors, officers, servants and agents of the same and to and be 370
for the benefit of all parties performing services within the scope of this 371
Agreement for or on behalf of the Tug or Tugowner or Hirer as servants, 372
agents and sub-contractors of such parties. The Tugowner or Hirer shall be 373
deemed to be acting as agent or trustee of and for the benefit of all such per- 374
sons, entities and vessels set forth above but only for the limited purpose of 375
contracting for the extension of such benefits to such persons, bodies and 376
vessels. 377

PART II
"Towcon" International Ocean Towage Agreement (Lump Sum)

20. War and Other Difficulties 378

(a) If owing to any Hostilities; War or Civil War; Acts of Terrorism; Acts of 379
Public Enemies; Arrest or Restraint of Princes, Rulers or People; Insurrec- 380
tions; Riots or Civil Commotions; Disturbances; Acts of God; Epidemics; 381
Quarantine; Ice; Labour Troubles; Labour Obstructions; Strikes; Lock-outs; 382
Embargoes; Seizure of the Tow under Legal Process or for any other cause 383
outside the control of the Tugowner it would be impossible or unsafe or 384
commercially impracticable for the Tug or Tow or both to leave or attempt to 385
leave the place of departure or any port or place of call or refuge or to reach 386
or enter or attempt to reach or enter the port or place of destination of the 387
Tow and there deliver the Tow and leave again, all of which safely and with- 388
out unreasonable delay, the Tug may leave the Tow or any part thereof at the 389
place of departure or any other port or place where the Hirer may take re- 390
possession and this shall be deemed a due fulfilment by the Tugowner of 391
this Agreement and any outstanding sums and all extra costs of delivery at 392
such place and any storage costs incurred by the Tugowner shall thereu- 393
pon become due and payable by the Hirer. 394

(b) If the performance of this Agreement or the voyage to the place of de- 395
parture would in the ordinary course of events require the Tug and/or Tow 396
to pass through or near to an area where after this Agreement is made there 397
is or there appears to be danger of such area being blocked or passage 398
through being restricted or made hazardous by reason of War, Acts of Ter- 399
rorism, Trapping of Vessels, Civil War, Acts of Public Enemies, Arrest or Re- 400
straint of Princes, Rulers or People, Insurrection, Riots or Civil Commotions 401
or Disturbances or other dangers of a similar nature then: 402

(i) If the Tug has not entered such area en route to the place of depar- 403
ture, or having entered has become trapped therein, the Hirer shall pay 404
a Delay Payment at the rate specified in Box 29 for every day of the re- 405
sulting delay. Provided that if the delay is for a period of more than 14 406
days either party hereto shall be entitled to terminate this Agreement by 407
telex, cable or other written notice in which event, save for liabilities al- 408
ready accrued, neither party shall be under any further liability to the 409
other but the Tugowner shall not be bound to repay to the Hirer any 410
payments already made and all amounts due shall remain payable. 411

(ii) If the Tug and Tow whilst en route to the place of destination have not 412
entered such area during the course of the towage or other service the 413
Hirer shall pay Delay Payment at the rate indicated in Box 29 for every 414
day by which the towage is prolonged by reason of waiting for such area 415
to become clear and/or safe and/or by reason of proceeding by a lon- 416
ger route to avoid or pass such area in safety. 417

(iii) If the Tug and Tow whilst en route to the place of destination have 418
become trapped in such area during the course of the towage or other 419
service, the Hirer shall pay a Delay Payment at the rate specified in Box 420
29 for every day of the resulting delay. Provided that if the delay is for a 421
period of more than 14 days either party hereto shall be entitled to ter- 422
minate this Agreement by telex, cable or other written notice in which 423
event, save for liabilities already accrued, neither party shall be under 424
any further liability to the other but the Tugowner shall not be bound to 425
repay to the Hirer any payment already made and all amounts due shall 426
remain payable. 427

21. Lien 428

Without prejudice to any other rights which he may have, whether in rem or 429
in personam, the Tugowner, by himself or his servants or agents or otherwi- 430
se shall be entitled to exercise a possessory lien upon the Tow in respect of 431

any sum howsoever or whatsoever due to the Tugowner under this Agree- 432
ment and shall for the purpose of exercising such possessory lien be entit- 433
led to take and/or keep possession of the Tow; provided always that the Hi- 434
rer shall pay to the Tugowner all reasonable costs and expenses howsoever 435
or whatsoever incurred by or on behalf of the Tugowner in exercising or at- 436
tempting or preparing to exercise such lien and the Tugowner shall be en- 437
titled to receive from the Hirer the Tug's Delay Payment at the rate specified 438
in Box 29 for any reasonable delay to the Tug resulting therefrom. 439

22. Warranty of Authority 440

If at the time of making this Agreement or providing any service under this 441
Agreement other than towing at the request, express or implied, of the Hirer, 442
the Hirer is not the Owner of the Tow referred to in Box 4, the Hirer expressly 443
represents that he is authorised to make and does make this Agreement for 444
and on behalf of the Owner of the said Tow subject to each and all of these 445
conditions and agrees that both the Hirer and the Owner of the Tow are 446
bound jointly and severally by these conditions. 447

23. General 448

(a) If any one or more of the terms, conditions or provisions in this Agree- 449
ment or any part thereof shall be held to be invalid, void or of no effect for 450
any reason whatsoever, the same shall not affect the validity of the remain- 451
ing terms, conditions or provisions which shall remain and subsist in full 452
force and effect. 453

(b) For the purpose of this Agreement unless the context otherwise requi- 454
res the singular shall include the plural and vice versa. 455

(c) Any extension of time granted by the Tugowner to the Hirer or any indul- 456
gence shown relating to the time limits set out in this Agreement shall not be 457
a waiver of the Tugowner's right under this Agreement to act upon the Hi- 458
rer's failure to comply with the time limits. 459

24. Time for Suit 460

Save for the indemnity provisions under Clause 18 of this Agreement, any 461
claim which may arise out of or in connection with this Agreement or of any 462
towage or other service to be performed hereunder shall be notified by te- 463
lex, cable or otherwise in writing within 6 months of delivery of the Tow or of 464
the termination of the towage or other service for any reason whatever, and 465
any suit shall be brought within one year of the time when the cause of ac- 466
tion first arose. If either of these conditions is not complied with the claim 467
and all rights whatsoever and howsoever shall be absolutely barred and ex- 468
tinguished. 469

25. Law and Jurisdiction 470

This Agreement shall be construed in accordance with and governed by 471
English law. Any dispute or difference which may arise out of or in connec- 472
tion with this Agreement or the services to be performed hereunder shall be 473
referred to the High Court of Justice in London. 474
No suit shall be brought in any other state or jurisdiction except that either 475
party shall have the option to bring proceedings in rem to obtain conservati- 476
ve seizure or other similar remedy against any vessel or property owned by 477
the other party in any state or jurisdiction where such vessel or property 478
may be found. 479

APPENDIX 3

TOWHIRE*

1. Date and place of Agreement	RECOMMENDED INTERNATIONAL OCEAN TOWAGE AGREEMENT (DAILY HIRE) CODE NAME: "TOWHIRE" PART I
2. Tugowner/place of business	3. Hirer/place of business
4. T o w (name and type)	5. Gross tonnage/displacement tonnage
6. Maximum length/maximum breadth & towing draught (fore and aft)	7. Flag and place of registry
8. Registered owners	9. Classification society
10. P. & I. liability insurers	11. General condition of tow
12. Particulars of cargo and/or ballast and/or other property on board the tow	
13. T u g (name and type)	14. Flag and place of registry
15. Gross tonnage	16. Classification Society
17. P. & I. liability insurers	
18. Certificated bollard pull (if any)	19. Indicated horse power
20. Estimated daily average bunker oil consumption in good weather and smooth water	
(a) at full towing power with tow	
(b) at full sea speed without tow	
21. Winches and main towing gear	

(continued)

Printed and sold by Fr. G. Knudtzons Bogtrykkeri A/S, 55 Toldbodgade, DK-1253 Copenhagen K
by authority of The Baltic and international Maritime Council (BIMCO), Copenhagen

* Reproduced by kind permission of BIMCO.

(continued)   **"TOWHIRE" INTERNATIONAL OCEAN TOWAGE AGREEMENT (DAILY HIRE)**   PART I

22. Nature of service(s) (Cl. 1)		

23. Place of departure (Cl. 7)	24. Date of departure	25. Place of destination (Cl. 8)

26. Contemplated route (Cl. 17)

27. Notices (state number of hours/days notice of arrival of tug at place of departure and to whom to be given)	28. Notices (state number of hours/days notice of arrival of tug and tow at place of destination and to whom to be given)

29. Riding crew to be provided by (also state number to be provided) (Cl. 9)	30. If riding crew provided by Tugowner state amount per man per day payable by Hirer (Cl. 9)

31. Mobilisation payment (optional, only to be filled in if expressly agreed) (Cl. 2(e))	32. Demobilisation payment (optional, only to be filled in if expressly agreed) (Cl. 2(f))

33. Daily rate of hire and advance payment period(s) (Cl. 2(a))	34. Payment of hire and for riding crew (if any) (state currency, mode of payment, place of payment and bank account) (Cl. 2(b))

35. Minimum period of hire, if any agreed	36. Commencement of period of hire (Cl. 2(a))

37. Termination of period of hire (Cl. 2(a))	38. Cancelling date, if any agreed (Cl. 16(e))

39. Interest rate (%) per annum to run from (state number of days) after any sum is due (Cl. 5)	40. Security (state sum, by whom to be provided and when) (optional, only to be filled in if expressly agreed) (Cl. 6)

41. Cost of bunker oil and lubricating oils (state whether included or excluded from daily rate of hire; if included state type of bunkers and cost per metric tonne (per litre for lubricating oils) (Cl. 2(d))

42. Cancellation fee (Cl. 16)	43. Numbers of additional clauses, covering special provisions, if agreed

It is mutually agreed between the party mentioned in Box 2 (hereinafter called "the Tugowner") and the party mentioned in Box 3 (hereinafter called "the Hirer") that the Tugowner shall, subject to the terms and conditions of this Agreement which consists of PART I including additional clauses, if any agreed and stated in Box 43, and PART II, use his best endeavours to perform the towage or other service(s) as set out herein. In the event of a conflict of terms and conditions, the provisions of PART I and any additional clauses, if agreed, shall prevail over those of PART II to the extent of such conflict but no further.

Signature (Tugowner)	Signature (Hirer)

PART II
"Towhire" International Ocean Towage Agreement (Daily Hire)

1. The Tow

"The Tow" shall include any vessel, craft or object of whatsoever nature including anything carried thereon as described in PART I to which the Tugowner agrees to render the service(s) as set out in Box 22.

2. Price and Conditions of Payment

(a) The Hirer shall pay the Tugowner the amount of hire set out in Box 33 per day or pro rata for part of a day (hereinafter called the "Tug's Daily Rate of Hire") from the time stated in Box 36 until the time stated in Box 37.

(b) (i) The Tug's Daily Rate of Hire shall be payable in advance as set out in Box 33; all hire or equivalent compensation hereunder shall be fully and irrevocably earned and non-returnable on a daily basis.

(ii) In the event of the Tug being lost, hire shall cease as of the date of the loss. If the date of the loss cannot be ascertained, then, in addition to any other sums which may be due, half the rate of hire shall be paid, calculated from the date the Tug was last reported until the calculated arrival of the Tug at her destination provided such period does not exceed 14 days.

(iii) In the event of the Tow being lost, hire shall continue until the Tug arrives at its destination or such nearer place, at the Tugowner's discretion, provided such period does not exceed 14 days.

(c) Within 14 days of the termination of the services hereunder by the Tugowner, the Tugowner will if necessary adjust in conformance with the terms of this Agreement hire paid in advance. Any hire paid by the Hirer but not earned under this Agreement and which is refundable thereunder shall be refunded to the Hirer within 14 days thereafter.

(d) (i) In the event that the Daily Rate of Hire includes the cost of bunkers and the average price per metric tonne of bunkers actually paid by the Tugowner differs from the amounts specified in Box 41 then the Hirer or the Tugowner, as the case may be, shall pay to the other the difference per metric tonne for every metric tonne consumed during the voyage. The average price specified above shall be the average of the prices per metric tonne actually paid by the Tugowner on the basis of quantities purchased at the last bunkering port prior to departure on the voyage, any bunkering port during the voyage, and the first bunkering port after completion of the voyage. The log book of the Tug shall be prima facie evidence of the quantity of bunkers consumed.

(ii) In the event that the Daily Rate of Hire excludes the cost of bunkers then the Hirer shall pay to the Tugowner the cost of the bunkers and lubricants consumed by the Tug in fulfilling the terms of this Agreement. The Tug shall be delivered with sufficient bunkers and lubricants on board for the tow to the first bunkering port (if any) or destination and be re-delivered with not less than sufficient bunkers to reach the next bunkering stage en route to the Tug's next port of call. The Hirer upon delivery and the Tugowner upon re-delivery shall pay for the bunkers and lubricants on board at the current contract price at the time at the port of delivery and re-delivery or at the nearest bunkering port.

*) (e) If agreed, the Hirer shall pay the sum set out in Box 31 by way of a mobilisation charge. This sum shall be paid on or before the commencement of the Tug's voyage to the place of departure, and shall be non-returnable, Tug and/or Tow lost or not lost.

*) (f) If agreed, the Hirer shall pay the sum set out in Box 32 by way of a demobilisation charge. This amount shall be paid tow lost or not lost, on or before the termination by the Tugowner of his services under this Agreement.

(g) The Hire and any other sums payable to the Tugowner under this Agreement (or any part thereof) shall be due, payable and paid without any discount, deduction, set-off, lien, claim or counterclaim.

*) Sub-clauses (e) and (f) are optional and shall only apply if agreed and stated in Boxes 31 and 32, respectively.

3. Additional Charges and Extra Costs

(a) The Hirer shall appoint his agents at the place of departure and place of destination and ports of call or refuge and shall provide such agents with adequate funds as required.

(b) The Hirer shall bear and pay as and when they fall due:-

(i) All port expenses, pilotage charges, harbour and canal dues and all other expenses of a similar nature levied upon or payable in respect of both the Tug and the Tow.

(ii) All taxes, (other than those normally payable by the Tugowner in the country where he has his principal place of business and in the country where the Tug is registered) stamp duties or other levies payable in respect of or in connection with this Agreement or the payments of hire or other sums payable under this Agreement or the services to be performed under or in pursuance of this Agreement, any Customs or Excise duties and any costs, dues or expenses payable in respect of any necessary permits or licences.

(iii) The cost of the services of any assisting tugs when deemed necessary by the Tugmaster or prescribed by Port or other Authorities.

(iv) All costs and expenses necessary for the preparation of the Tow for towing (including such costs or expenses as those of raising the anchor of the Tow or tending or casting off any moorings of the Tow).

(v) The cost of insurance of the Tow shall be the sole responsibility of the Hirer to provide.

(c) All taxes, charges, costs, and expenses payable by the Hirer shall be paid by the Hirer direct to those entitled to them. If, however, any such tax, charge, cost or expense is in fact paid by or on behalf of the Tugowner (notwithstanding that the Tugowner shall under no circumstances be under any obligation to make such payments on behalf of the Hirer) the Hirer shall reimburse the Tugowner on the basis of the actual cost to the Tugowner upon presentation of invoice.

4. War Risk Escalation Clause

The rate of hire is based and assessed on all war risk insurance costs applicable to the Tugowner in respect of the contemplated voyage in effect on the date of this Agreement.

In the event of any subsequent increase or decrease in the actual costs due to the Tugowner fulfilling his obligations under this Agreement, the Hirer or the Tugowner, as the case may be, shall reimburse to the other the amount of any increase or decrease in the war risk, confiscation, deprivation or trapping insurance costs.

5. Interest

If any amounts due under this Agreement are not paid when due, then interest shall accrue and shall be paid in accordance with the provisions of Box 39, on all such amounts until payment is received by the Tugowner.

6. Security

The Hirer undertakes to provide, if required by the Tugowner, security to the satisfaction of the Tugowner in the form and in the sum, at the place and at the time indicated in Box 40 as a guarantee for due performance of the Agreement. Such security shall be returned to the guarantor when the Hirer's financial obligations under this Agreement have been met in full.

(Optional, only applicable if Box 40 filled in).

7. Place of Departure

(a) The Tow shall be tendered to the Tugowner at the place of departure stated in Box 23.

(b) The precise place of departure shall always be safe and accessible for the Tug to enter, to operate in and for the Tug and Tow to leave and shall be a place where such Tug is permitted to commence the towage in accordance with any local or other rules, requirements or regulations and shall always be subject to the approval of the Tugowner which shall not be unreasonably withheld.

8. Place of Destination

(a) The Tow shall be accepted forthwith and taken over by the Hirer or his duly authorised representative at the place of destination stated in Box 25.

(b) The precise place of destination shall always be safe and accessible for the Tug and Tow to enter, to operate in, and for the Tug to leave and shall be a place where such Tug is permitted to redeliver the Tow in accordance with any local or other rules, requirements or regulations and shall always be subject to the approval of the Tugowner, which approval shall not be unreasonably withheld.

9. Riding Crew

(a) In the event that the Tugowner provides a Riding Crew for the Tow, such crew and their suitability for the work shall be in the discretion of the Tugowner. All expenses for such personnel shall be for the account of the Tugowner.

(b) In the event that any personnel are placed on board the Tow by the Hirer all expenses for such personnel will be for the account of the Hirer and such personnel shall be at all times under the orders of the Master of the Tug, but shall not be deemed to be the servants or agents of the Tugowner.

(c) The Riding Crew shall be provided at the Hirer's sole expense with suitable accomodation, food, fresh water, life saving appliances and all other requirements to comply as necessary with the law and regulations of the law of the Flag of the Tug and/or Tow and of the States through the territorial waters of which the Tug will pass or enter. It is a requirement that members of the Riding Crew provided by the Hirer shall be able to speak and understand the English language or any other mutual language.

10. Towing Gear and Use of Tow's Gear

(a) The Tugowner agrees to provide free of cost to the Hirer all towing hawsers, bridles and other towing gear normally carried on board the Tug, for the purpose of the towage or other services to be provided under this Agreement. The Tow shall be connected up in a manner within the discretion of the Tugowner.

(b) The Tugowner may make reasonable use at his discretion of the Tow's gear, power, anchors, anchor cables, radio, communication and navigational equipment and all other appurtenances free of cost during and for the purposes of the towage or other services to be provided under this Agreement.

11. Permits and Certification

(a) The Hirer shall arrange at his own cost and provide to the Tugowner all necessary licenses, authorisations and permits required by the Tug and Tow to undertake and complete the contractual voyage together with all necessary certification for the Tow to enter or leave all or any ports of call or refuge on the contemplated voyage.

(b) Any loss or expense incurred by the Tugowner by reason of the Hirer's failure to comply with this Clause shall be reimbursed by the Hirer to the Tugowner and during any delay caused thereby the Tug shall remain on hire.

12. Tow-worthiness of the Tow

(a) The Hirer shall exercise due diligence to ensure that the Tow shall, at the commencement of the towage, be in all respects fit to be towed from the place of departure to the place of destination.

(b) The Hirer undertakes that the Tow will be suitably trimmed and prepared and ready to be towed at the time when the Tug arrives at the place of departure and fitted and equipped with such shapes, signals, navigational and other lights of a type required for the towage.

(c) The Hirer shall supply to the Tugowner or the Tugmaster, on the arrival of the Tug at the place of departure an unconditional certificate of towworthiness for the Tow issued by a recognised firm of Marine Surveyors or Survey Organisation, provided always that the Tugowner shall not be under any obligation to perform the towage until in his discretion he is satisfied that the Tow is in all respects trimmed, prepared, fit and ready for towage but the Tugowner shall not unreasonably withhold his approval.

(d) No inspection of the Tow by the Tugowner shall constitute approval of the Tow's condition or be deemed a waiver of the foregoing undertakings given by the Hirer.

13. Seaworthiness of the Tug

The Tugowner will exercise due diligence to tender the Tug at the place of departure in a seaworthy condition and in all respects ready to perform the towage, but the Tugowner gives no other warranties, express or implied.

PART II
"Towhire" International Ocean Towage Agreement (Daily Hire)

14. Substitution of Tugs 186

The Tugowner shall at all times have the right to substitute any tug or tugs for 187 any other tug or tugs of adequate power (including two or more tugs for one, 188 or one tug for two or more) at any time whether before or after the com- 189 mencement of the towage or other services and shall be at liberty to employ 190 a tug or tugs belonging to other tugowners for the whole or part of the tow- 191 age or other service contemplated under this Agreement. Provided howev- 192 er, that the main particulars of the substituted tug or tugs shall be subject 193 to the Hirer's prior approval, but such approval shall not be unreasonably 194 withheld. 195

15. Salvage 196

(a) Should the Tow break away from the Tug during the course of the towa- 197 ge service, the Tug shall render all reasonable services to re-connect the 198 towline and fulfill this Agreement without making any claim for salvage. 199

(b) If at any time the Tugowner or the Tugmaster considers it necessary or 200 advisable to seek or accept salvage services from any vessel or person on 201 behalf of the Tug or Tow, or both, the Hirer hereby undertakes and warrants 202 that the Tugowner or his duly authorised servant or agent including the Tug- 203 master have the full actual authority of the Hirer to accept such services on 204 behalf of the Tow on any reasonable terms. 205

16. Cancellation and Withdrawal 206

(a) At any time prior to the departure of the Tow from the place of departure 207 the Hirer may cancel this Agreement upon payment of the cancellation fee 208 set out in Box 42. If cancellation takes place whilst the Tug is en route to the 209 place of departure or after the Tug has arrived at or off the place of depart- 210 ure then in addition to the said cancellation fee the Hirer shall pay any ad- 211 ditional amounts due under this Agreement. 212

(b) In the event that the towage operation is terminated after departure from 213 the place of departure, but before the Tow arrives at the place of destination 214 without fault on the part of the Tugowner, his servants or agents, the Tugow- 215 ner shall be entitled to be paid, and if already paid to retain all sums payable 216 according to Boxes 31/34 and any other amounts due under this Agree- 217 ment. The above amounts are in addition to any damages the Tugowner may 218 be entitled to claim for breach of this Agreement. 219

(c) The Tugowner may without prejudice to any other remedies he may ha- 220 ve leave the Tow in a place where the Hirer may take repossession of it and 221 be entitled to payment of cancellation fee or hire, whichever is the greater, 222 and all other payments due under this Agreement, upon any one or more of 223 the following grounds: 224

(i) If there is any delay or delays (other than delay caused by the Tug) at 225 the place of departure exceeding in aggregate 21 running days. 226

(ii) If there is any delay or delays (other than a delay caused by the Tug) 227 at any port or place of call or refuge exceeding in aggregate 21 running 228 days. 229

(iii) If the security as may be required according to Box 40 is not given 230 within 7 running days of the Tugowner's request to provide security. 231

(iv) If the Hirer has not accepted the Tow within 7 running days of arrival 232 at the place of destination. 233

(v) If any amount payable under this Agreement has not been paid with- 234 in 7 running days of the date such sums are due. 235

(d) Before exercising his option of withdrawing from this Agreement as 236 aforesaid, the Tugowner shall if practicable give the Hirer 48 hours notice 237 (Saturdays, Sundays and public Holidays excluded) of his intention so to 238 withdraw. 239

(e) Should the Tug not be ready to commence the towage at the latest at 240 midnight on the date, if any, indicated in Box 38, the Hirer shall have the op- 241 tion of cancelling this Agreement and shall be entitled to claim damages for 242 detention if due to the wilful default of the Tugowner. Should the Tugowner 243 anticipate that the Tug will not be ready, he shall notify the Hirer thereof by 244 telex, cable or otherwise in writing without delay stating the expected date 245 of the Tug's readiness and ask whether the Hirer will exercise his option to 246 cancel. Such option to cancel must be exercised within 48 hours after the 247 receipt of the Tugowner's notice, otherwise the third day after the date stat- 248 ed in the Tugowner's notice shall be deemed to be the new agreed date to 249 commence the towage in accordance with this Agreement. 250

17. Necessary Deviation 251

(a) If the Tug during the course of the towage or other service under this 252 Agreement puts into a port or place or seeks shelter or is detained or devia- 253 tes from the original route as set out in Box 26 because either the Tugowner 254 or Tugmaster reasonably consider 255

(i) that the Tow is not fit to be towed or 256

(ii) the Tow is incapable of being towed at the original speed contem- 257 plated by the Tugowner or 258

(iii) the towing connection requires rearrangement, or 259

(iv) repairs or alterations to or additional equipment for the Tow are re- 260 quired to safeguard the venture and enable the Tow to be towed to de- 261 stination, or 262

(v) it would not be prudent to do otherwise on account of weather con- 263 ditions actual or forecast, or 264

because of any other good and valid reason outside the control of the Tug- 265 owner or Tugmaster, or because of any delay caused by or at the request 266 of the Hirer, this Agreement shall remain in full force and effect. 267

(b) The Tug shall at all times be at liberty to go to the assistance of any ves- 268 sel in distress for the purpose of saving life or property or to call at any port 269 or place for bunkers, repairs, supplies, or any other necessaries or to land 270 disabled seamen, but if towing the Tug shall leave the Tow in a safe place 271 and during such period this Agreement shall remain in full force and effect 272 but any period so spent by the Tug in fulfilling or attempting to fulfil the pur- 273 poses permitted by this sub-paragraph other than for normal replenishment 274 of bunkers or fresh water or supplies shall not entitle the Tugowner to recov- 275 er from the Hirer the Daily Rate of Hire for the said period. 276

(c) The Tug shall have liberty to comply with any orders or directions as to 277 departure, arrival, routes, ports of call, stoppages, destination, delivery, re- 278 quisition or otherwise howsoever given by the Government of the Nation un- 279 der whose flag the Tug or Tow sails or any department thereof, or any per- 280 son acting or purporting to act with the authority for such Government or 281

any department thereof or by the committee or person having under the 282 terms of the War Risks Insurance on the Tug the right to give such orders or 283 directions and if by reason of and in compliance with any such orders or di- 284 rections anything is done or is not done the same shall not be deemed a de- 285 viation and delivery in accordance with such orders or directions shall be a 286 fulfilment of this Agreement and hire and/or all other sums shall be paid to 287 the Tugowner accordingly. 288

(d) Any deviation howsoever or whatsoever by the Tug or by the Tugowner 289 not expressly permitted by the terms and conditions of this Agreement shall 290 not amount to a repudiation of this Agreement and the Agreement shall re- 291 main in full force and effect notwithstanding such deviation, save that no hi- 292 re shall be paid for the period of such deviation, and shall be without preju- 293 dice to any other remedies which the Hirer may have against the Tugowner. 294

18. Liabilities 295

1. (a) The Tugowner will indemnify the Hirer in respect of any liability adjud- 296 ged due or claim reasonably compromised arising out of injury or death oc- 297 curring during the towage or other service hereunder to any of the following 298 persons: 299

(i) The Master and members of the crew of the Tug and any other serv- 300 ant or agent of the Tugowner; 301

(ii) The members of the Riding Crew provided by the Tugowner or any 302 other person whom the Tugowner provides on board the Tow; 303

(iii) Any other person on board the Tug who is not a servant or agent of 304 the Hirer or otherwise on board on behalf of or at the request of the 305 Hirer. 306

(b) The Hirer will indemnify the Tugowner in respect of any liability adjud- 307 ged due or claim reasonably compromised arising from injury or death oc- 308 curring during the towage or other service hereunder to any of the following 309 persons: 310

(i) The Master and members of the crew of the Tow and any other ser- 311 vant or agents of the Hirer; 312

(ii) Any other person on board the Tow for whatever purpose except the 313 members of the Riding Crew or any other persons whom the Tugowner 314 provides on board the Tow pursuant to their obligations under this 315 Agreement. 316

2. (a) The following shall be for the sole account of the Tugowner without any 317 recourse to the Hirer, his servants, or agents, whether or not the same is 318 due to breach of contract, negligence or any other fault on the part of the Hi- 319 rer, his servants or agents: 320

(i) Loss or damage of whatsoever nature, howsoever caused to or sus- 321 tained by the Tug or any property on board the Tug. 322

(ii) Loss or damage of whatsoever nature caused to or suffered by third 323 parties or their property by reason of contact with the Tug or obstruction 324 created by the presence of the Tug. 325

(iii) Loss or damage of whatsoever nature suffered by the Tugowner or 326 by third parties in consequence of the loss or damage referred to in (i) 327 and (ii) above. 328

(iv) Any liability in respect of wreck removal or in respect of the expense 329 of moving or lighting or buoying the Tug or in respect of preventing or 330 abating pollution originating from the Tug. 331

The Tugowner will indemnify the Hirer in respect of any liability adjudged 332 due to a third party or any claim by a third party reasonably compromised 333 arising out of any such loss or damage. The Tugowner shall not in any cir- 334 cumstances be liable for any loss or damage suffered by the Hirer or 335 caused to or sustained by the Tow in consequence of loss or damage how- 336 soever caused to or sustained by the Tug or any property on board the Tug. 337

(b) The following shall be for the sole account of the Hirer without any re- 338 course to the Tugowner, his servants or agents, whether or not the same is 339 due to breach of contract, negligence or any fault on the part of the Tugow- 340 ner, his servants or agents: 341

(i) Loss or damage of whatsoever nature, howsoever caused to or su- 342 stained by the Tow. 343

(ii) Loss or damage of whatsoever nature caused to or suffered by third 344 parties or their property by reason of contact with the Tow or obstruc- 345 tion created by the presence of the Tow. 346

(iii) Loss or damage of whatsoever nature suffered by the Hirer or by 347 third parties in consequence of the loss or damage referred to in (i) and 348 (ii) above. 349

(iv) Any liability in respect of wreck removal or in respect of the expense 350 of moving or lighting or buoying the Tow or in respect of preventing or 351 abating pollution originating from the Tow. 352

The Hirer will indemnify the Tugowner in respect of any liability adjudged 353 due to a third party or any claim by a third party reasonably compromised 354 arising out of any such loss or damage but the Hirer shall not in any circum- 355 stances be liable for any loss or damage suffered by the Tugowner or cau- 356 sed to or sustained by the Tug in consequence of loss or damage, how- 357 soever caused to or sustained by the Tow. 358

3. Save for the provisions of Clauses 11, 12, 13 and 16 neither the Tugow- 359 ner nor the Hirer shall be liable to the other party for loss of profit, loss of 360 use, loss of production or any other indirect or consequential damage for 361 any reason whatsoever. 362

4. Notwithstanding any provisions of this Agreement to the contrary, the 363 Tugowner shall have the benefit of all limitations of, and exemptions from, 364 liability accorded to the Owners or Chartered Owners of Vessels by any ap- 365 plicable statute or rule of law for the time being in force and the same bene- 366 fits are to apply regardless of the form of signatures given to this Agreement. 367

19. Himalaya Clause 368

All exceptions, exemptions, defences, immunities, limitations of liability, in- 369 demnities, privileges and conditions granted or provided by this Agreement 370 or by any applicable statute rule or regulation for the benefit of the Tugow- 371 ner or Hirer shall also apply to and be for the benefit of demise charterers, 372 sub-contractors, operators, master, officers and crew of the Tug or Tow and 373 to and be for the benefit of all bodies corporate parent of, subsidiary to, affi- 374 liated with or under the same management as either of them, as well as all 375 directors, officers, servants and agents of the same and to and be for the 376 benefit of all parties performing services within the scope of this Agreement 377 for or on behalf of the Tug or Tugowner or Hirer as servants, agents and 378 sub-contractors of such parties. The Tugowner or Hirer shall be deemed to 379

PART II
"Towhire" International Ocean Towage Agreement (Daily Hire)

be acting as agent or trustee of and for the benefit of all such persons, enti- 380
ties and vessels set forth above but only for the limited purpose of contract- 381
ing for the extension of such benefits to such persons, bodies and vessels. 382

20. War and Other Difficulties 383

(a) If owing to any Hostilities; War or Civil War; Acts of Terrorism; Acts of 384
Public Enemies; Arrest or Restraint of Princes, Rulers or People; Insurrec- 385
tions; Riots or Civil Commotions; Disturbances; Acts of God; Epidemics; 386
Quarantine; Ice; Labour Troubles; Labour Obstructions; Strikes; Lock-outs; 387
Embargoes; Seizure of the Tow under Legal Process or for any other cause 388
outside the control of the Tugowner it would be impossible or unsafe or 389
commercially impracticable for the Tug or Tow or both to leave or attempt to 390
leave the place of departure or any port or place of call or refuge or to reach 391
or enter or attempt to reach or enter the port or place of destination of the 392
Tow and there deliver the Tow and leave again, all of which safely and with- 393
out unreasonable delay, the Tug may leave the Tow or any part thereof at 394
the place of departure or any other port or place where the Hirer may take 395
repossession and this shall be deemed a due fulfilment by the Tugowner of 396
this Agreement and any outstanding sums and all extra costs of delivery at 397
such place and any storage costs incurred by the Tugowner shall there- 398
upon become due and payable by the Hirer. 399

(b) If the performance of this Agreement or the voyage to the place of de- 400
parture would in the ordinary course of events require the Tug and/or Tow 401
to pass through or near to an area where after this Agreement is made there 402
is or there appears to be danger of such area being blocked or passage 403
through being restricted or made hazardous by reason of War, Acts of Ter- 404
rorism, Trapping of Vessels, Civil War, Acts of Public Enemies, Arrest or Re- 405
straint of Princes, Rulers or People, Insurrection, Riots or Civil Commotions 406
or Disturbances or other dangers of a similar nature then: 407

(i) If the Tug has not entered such area en route to the place of departu- 408
re, or having entered has become trapped therein, for a period of more 409
than 14 days either party hereto shall be entitled to terminate this 410
Agreement by telex, cable or other written notice in which event, save 411
for liabilities already accrued neither party shall be under any further 412
liability to the other but the Tugowner shall not be bound to repay to the 413
Hirer any payments already made and all amounts due shall remain 414
payable. 415

(ii) If the Tug and Tow whilst en route to the place of destination have not 416
entered such area during the course of the towage or other service the 417
Hirer shall continue to pay the Daily Rate of Hire for every day by which 418
the towage is prolonged by reason of waiting for such area to become 419
clear and/or safe and/or by reason of proceeding by a longer route to 420
avoid or pass such area in safety. 421

(iii) If the Tug and Tow whilst en route to the place of destination have 422
become trapped in such area during the course of the towage or other 423
service either party shall, after a period of 14 days from the commence- 424
ment of such trapping, be entitled to terminate this Agreement by telex, 425
cable or other written notice, in which event, save for liabilities already 426
accrued, neither party shall be under any further liability to the other 427
but the Tugowner shall not be bound to repay to the Hirer any payment 428
already made and all amounts due remain payable. 429

21. Lien 430

Without prejudice to any other rights which he may have, whether in rem or 431
in personam, the Tugowner, by himself or his servants or agents or otherwi- 432

se shall be entitled to exercise a possessory lien upon the Tow in respect of 433
any sum howsoever or whatsoever due to the Tugowner under this Agree- 434
ment and shall for the purpose of exercising such possessory lien be entit- 435
led to take and/or keep possession of the Tow; provided always that the Hi- 436
rer shall pay to the Tugowner all reasonable costs and expenses howsoever 437
or whatsoever incurred by or on behalf of the Tugowner in exercising or at- 438
tempting or preparing to exercise such lien and the Tugowner shall be en- 439
titled to receive from the Hirer the Tug's Daily Rate of Hire throughout any 440
reasonable delay to the Tug resulting therefrom. 441

22. Warranty of Authority 442

If at the time of making this Agreement or providing any service under this 443
Agreement other than towing at the request, express or implied, of the Hirer, 444
the Hirer is not the Owner of the Tow referred to in Box 4, the Hirer expressly 445
represents that he is authorised to make and does make this Agreement for 446
and on behalf of the Owner of the said Tow subject to each and all of these 447
conditions and agrees that both the Hirer and the Owner of the Tow are 448
bound jointly and severally by these conditions. 449

23. General 450

(a) If any one or more of the terms, conditions or provisions in this Agree- 451
ment or any part thereof shall be held to be invalid, void or of no effect for 452
any reason whatsoever, the same shall not affect the validity of the remain- 453
ing terms, conditions or provisions which shall remain and subsist in full 454
force and effect. 455

(b) For the purpose of this Agreement unless the context otherwise requi- 456
res the singular shall include the plural and vice versa. 457

(c) Any extension of time granted by the Tugowner to the Hirer or any indul- 458
gence shown relating to the time limits set out in this Agreement shall not be 459
a waiver of the Tugowner's right under this Agreement to act upon the Hi- 460
rer's failure to comply with the time limits. 461

24. Time for Suit 462

Save for the indemnity provisions under Clause 18 of this Agreement, any 463
claim which may arise out of or in connection with this Agreement or of any 464
towage or other service to be performed hereunder shall be notified by te- 465
lex, cable or otherwise in writing within 6 months of delivery of the Tow or of 466
the termination of the towage or other service for any reason whatever, and 467
any suit shall be brought within one year of the time when the cause of ac- 468
tion first arose. If either of these conditions is not complied with the claim 469
and all rights whatsoever and howsoever shall be absolutely barred and ex- 470
tinguished. 471

25. Law and Jurisdiction 472

This Agreement shall be construed in accordance with and governed by 473
English law. Any dispute or difference which may arise out of or in connec- 474
tion with this Agreement or the services to be performed hereunder shall be 475
referred to the High Court of Justice in London. 476
No suit shall be brought in any other state or jurisdiction except that either 477
party shall have the option to bring proceedings in rem to obtain conservati- 478
ve seizure or other similar remedy against any vessel or property owned by 479
the other party in any state or jurisdiction where such vessel or property 480
may be found. 481

APPENDIX 4

SUPPLYTIME 89*

Issued by
The Documentary Committee of
The Baltic and International Maritime Council (BIMCO), Copenhagen
(First Edition published 1975)
REVISED 1989

Adopted by
International Support Vessel Owners'
Association (ISOA), London

Copyright, published by
The Baltic and International Maritime Council
(BIMCO), Copenhagen
September 1989

UNIFORM TIME CHARTER PARTY
FOR OFFSHORE SERVICE VESSELS
CODE NAME: "SUPPLYTIME 89"

PART I

1. Place and date	
2. Owners/Place of business (full style, address and telex/telefax no.) (Cl. 1(a))	3. Charterers/Place of business (full style, address and telex/telefax no.) (Cl. 1(a))
4. Vessel's name (Cl. 1(a))	5. Date of delivery (Cl. 2(a)) 6. Cancelling date (Cl. 2(a) and (c))
7. Port or place of delivery (Cl. 2(a))	8. Port or place of redelivery/notice of redelivery (Cl. 2(d)) (i) Port or place of redelivery (ii) Number of days' notice of redelivery
9. Period of hire (Cl. 1(a))	10. Extension of period of hire (optional) (Cl. 1(b)) (i) Period of extension (ii) Advance notice for declaration of option (days)
11. Automatic extension period to complete voyage or well (Cl. 1(c)) (i) Voyage or well (state which) (ii) Maximum extension period (state number of days)	12. Mobilisation charge (lump sum and when due) (Cl. 2(b)(i)) (i) Lump sum (ii) When due 13. Port or place of mobilisation (Cl. 2(b)(i))
14. Early termination of charter (state amount of hire payable) (Cl. 26(a))	15. Number of days' notice of early termination (Cl. 26(a)) 16. Demobilisation charge (lump sum) (Cl. 2(e) and Cl. 26(a))
17. Area of operation (Cl. 5(a))	18. Employment of vessel restricted to (state nature of service(s)) (Cl. 5(a))

(continued)

* Reproduced by kind permission of BIMCO.

19. Charter hire (state rate and currency) (Cl. 10(a) and (d))	20. Extension hire (if agreed, state rate) (Cl. 10(b))

21. Invoicing for hire and other payments (Cl. 10(d))	22. Payments (state mode and place of payment; also state beneficiary and bank account) (Cl. 10(e))
(i) state whether to be issued in advance or arrears	
(ii) state to whom to be issued if addressee other than stated in Box 2	
(iii) state to whom to be issued if addressee other than stated in Box 3	

23. Payment of hire, bunker invoices and disbursements for Charterers' account (state maximum number of days) (Cl. 10(e))	24. Interest rate payable (Cl. 10(e))	25. Maximum audit period (Cl. 10(f))

26. Meals (state rate agreed) (Cl. 5(c)(i))	27. Accommodation (state rate agreed) (Cl. 5(c)(i))	28. Mutual Waiver of Recourse (**optional**, state whether applicable) (Cl. 12(f))

29. Sublet (state amount of daily increment to charter hire) (Cl. 17(b))	30. War (state name of countries) (Cl. 19(e))

31. General average (place of settlement – only to be filled in if other than London) (Cl. 21)	32. Breakdown (state period) (Cl. 26(b)(v))

33. Law and arbitration (state Cl. 31(a) or 31(b) or 31(c), as agreed; if Cl. 31(c) agreed also state place of arbitration) (Cl. 31)	34. Numbers of additional clauses covering special provisions, if agreed

35. Names and addresses for notices and other communications required to be given by **the Owners** (Cl. 28)	36. Names and addresses for notices and other communications required to be given by **the Charterers** (Cl. 28)

It is mutually agreed that this Contract shall be performed subject to the conditions contained in the Charter consisting of PART I, including additional clauses if any agreed and stated in Box 34, and PART II as well as ANNEX "A" and ANNEX "B" as annexed to this Charter. In the event of a conflict of conditions, the provisions of PART I shall prevail over those of PART II and ANNEX "A" and ANNEX "B" to the extent of such conflict but no further. ANNEX "C" as annexed to this Charter is **optional** and shall only apply if expressly agreed and stated in Box 28.

Signature (Owners)	Signature (Charterers)

Printed and sold by Fr. G. Knudtzons Bogtrykkeri A/S, 55 Toldbodgade, DK-1253 Copenhagen K by authority of The Baltic and International Maritime Council (BIMCO), Copenhagen

PART II
"SUPPLYTIME 89" Uniform Time Charter Party for Offshore Service Vessels

1. Period

(a) The Owners stated in Box 2 let and the Charterers stated in Box 3 hire the Vessel named in Box 4, as specified in ANNEX "A" (hereinafter referred to as "the Vessel"), for the period as stated in Box 9 from the time the Vessel is delivered to the Charterers.

(b) Subject to Clause 10(b), the Charterers have the option to extend the Charter Period in direct continuation for the period stated in Box 10(i), but such an option must be declared in accordance with Box 10(ii).

(c) The Charter Period shall automatically be extended for the time required to complete the voyage or well (whichever is stated in Box 11(i)) in progress, such time not to exceed the period stated in Box 11(ii).

2. Delivery and Redelivery

(a) *Delivery.* – Subject to sub-clause (b) of this Clause the Vessel shall be delivered by the Owners free of cargo and with clean tanks at any time between the date stated in Box 5 and the date stated in Box 6 at the port or place stated in Box 7 where the Vessel can safely lie always afloat.

(b) *Mobilisation.* – (i) The Charterers shall pay a lump sum as stated in Box 12 without discount by way of mobilisation charge in consideration of the Owners giving delivery at the port or place stated in Box 7. The mobilisation charge shall not be affected by any cnange in the port or place of mobilisation from that stated in Box 13.

(ii) Should the Owners agree to the Vessel loading and transporting cargo and/or undertaking any other service for the Charterers en route to the port of delivery or from the port of redelivery, then all terms and conditions of this Charter Party shall apply to such loading and transporting and/or other service exactly as if performed during the Charter Period excepting only that any lump sum freight agreed in respect thereof shall be payable on shipment or commencement of the service as the case may be, the Vessel and/or goods lost or not lost.

(c) *Cancelling.* – If the Vessel is not delivered by midnight local time on the cancelling date stated in Box 6, the Charterers shall be entitled to cancel this Charter Party. However, if despite the exercise of due diligence by the Owners, the Owners will be unable to deliver the Vessel by the cancelling date, they may give notice in writing to the Charterers at any time prior to the delivery date as stated in Box 5, and shall state in such notice the date by which they will be able to deliver the Vessel. The Charterers may within 24 hours of receipt of such notice give notice in writing to the Owners cancelling this Charter Party. If the Charterers do not give such notice, then the later date specified in the Owners' notice shall be substituted for the cancelling date for all the purposes of this Charter Party. In the event the Charterers cancel the Charter Party, it shall terminate on terms that neither party shall be liable to the other for any losses incurred by reason of the non-delivery of the Vessel or the cancellation of the Charter Party.

(d) *Redelivery.* – The Vessel shall be redelivered on the expiration or earlier termination of this Charter Party free of cargo and with clean tanks at the port or place as stated in Box 8(i) or such other port or place as may be mutually agreed. The Charterers shall give not less than the number of days notice in writing of their intention to redeliver the Vessel, as stated in Box 8(ii).

(e) *Demobilisation.* – The Charterers shall pay a lump sum without discount in the amount as stated in Box 16 by way of demobilisation charge which amount shall be paid on the expiration or on earlier termination of this Charter Party.

3. Condition of Vessel

(a) The Owners undertake that at the date of delivery under this Charter Party the Vessel shall be of the description and classification as specified in ANNEX "A", attached hereto, and undertake to so maintain the Vessel during the period of service under this Charter Party.

(b) The Owners shall before and at the date of delivery of the Vessel and throughout the Charter Period exercise due diligence to make and maintain the Vessel tight, staunch, strong in good order and condition and, without prejudice to the generality of the foregoing, in every way fit to operate effectively at all times for the services as stated in Clause 5.

4. Survey

The Owners and the Charterers shall jointly appoint an independent surveyor for the purpose of determining and agreeing in writing the condition of the Vessel, any anchor handling and towing equipment specified in Section 5 of ANNEX "A", and the quality and quantity of fuel, lubricants and water at the time of delivery and redelivery hereunder. The Owners and the Charterers shall jointly share the time and expense of such surveys.

5. Employment and Area of Operation

(a) The Vessel shall be employed in offshore activities which are lawful in accordance with the law of the place of the Vessel's flag and/or registration and of the place of operation. Such activities shall be restricted to the service(s) as stated in Box 18, and to voyages between any good and safe port or place and any place or offshore unit where the Vessel can safely lie always afloat within the Area of Operation as stated in Box 17 which shall always be within Institute Warranty Limits and which shall in no circumstances be exceeded without prior agreement and adjustment of the Hire and in accordance with such other terms as appropriate to be agreed; provided always that the Charterers do not warrant the safety of any such port or place or offshore unit but shall exercise due diligence in issuing their orders to the Vessel as if the Vessel were their own property and having regard to her capabilities and the nature of her employment. Unless otherwise agreed, the Vessel shall not be employed as a diving platform.

(b) Relevant permission and licences from responsible authorities for the Vessel to enter, work in and leave the Area of Operation shall be obtained by the Charterers and the Owners shall assist, if necessary, in every way possible to secure such permission and licences.

(c) *The Vessel's Space.* – The whole reach and burden and decks of the Vessel shall throughout the Charter Period be at the Charterers' disposal reserving proper and sufficient space for the Vessel's Master, Officers, Crew, tackle, apparel, furniture, provisions and stores. The Charterers shall be entitled to carry, so far as space is available and for their purposes in connection with their operations:

(i) Persons other than crew members, other than fare paying, and for such purposes to make use of the Vessel's available accommodation not being used on the voyage by the Vessel's Crew. The Owners shall provide suitable provisions and requisites for such persons for which the Charterers shall pay at the rate as stated in Box 26 per meal and at the rate as stated in Box 27 per day for the provision of bedding and services for persons using berth accommodation.

(ii) Lawful cargo whether carried on or under deck.

(iii) Explosives and dangerous cargo, whether in bulk or packaged, provided proper notification has been given and such cargo is marked and packed in accordance with the national regulations of the Vessel and/or the International Maritime Dangerous Goods Code and/or other pertinent regulations. Failing such proper notification, marking or packing the Charterers shall indemnify the Owners in respect of any loss, damage or liability whatsoever and howsoever arising therefrom. The Charterers accept responsibility for any additional expenses (including reinstatement expenses) incurred by the Owners in relation to the carriage of explosives and dangerous cargo.

(iv) Hazardous and noxious substances, subject to Clause 12(g), proper notification and any pertinent regulations.

(d) *Laying-up of Vessel.* – The Charterers shall have the option of laying up the Vessel at an agreed safe port or place for all or any portion of the Charter Period in which case the Hire hereunder shall continue to be paid but, if the period of such lay-up exceeds 30 consecutive days there shall be credited against such Hire the amount which the Owners shall reasonably have saved by way of reduction in expenses and overheads as a result of the lay-up of the Vessel.

6. Master and Crew

(a) (i) The Master shall carry out his duties promptly and the Vessel shall render all reasonable services within her capabilities by day and by night and at such times and on such schedules as the Charterers may reasonably require without any obligations of the Charterers to pay to the Owners or the Master, Officers or the Crew of the Vessel any excess or overtime payments. The Charterers shall furnish the Master with all instructions and sailing directions and the Master and Engineer shall keep full and correct logs accessible to the Charterers or their agents.

(ii) The Master shall sign cargo documents as and in the form presented, the same, however, not to be Bills of Lading, but receipts which shall be non-negotiable documents and shall be marked as such. The Charterers shall indemnify the Owners against all consequences and liabilities arising from the Master, Officers or agents signing, under the direction of the Charterers, those cargo documents or other documents inconsistent with this Charter Party or from any irregularity in the papers supplied by the Charterers or their agents.

(b) The Vessel's Crew if required by Charterers will connect and disconnect electric cables, fuel, water and pneumatic hoses when placed on board the Vessel in port as well as alongside the offshore units; will operate the machinery on board the Vessel for loading and unloading cargoes; and will hook and unhook cargo on board the Vessel when loading or discharging alongside offshore units. If the port regulations or the seamen and/or labour unions do not permit the Crew of the Vessel to carry out any of this work, then the Charterers shall make, at their own expense, whatever other arrangements may be necessary, always under the direction of the Master.

(c) If the Charterers have reason to be dissatisfied with the conduct of the Master or any Officer or member of the Crew, the Owners on receiving particulars of the complaint shall promptly investigate the matter and if the complaint proves to be well founded, the Owners shall as soon as reasonably possible make appropriate changes in the appointment.

(d) The entire operation, navigation, and management of the Vessel shall be in the exclusive control and command of the Owners, their Master, Officers and Crew. The Vessel will be operated and the services hereunder will be rendered as requested by the Charterers, subject always to the exclusive right of the Owners or the Master of the Vessel to determine whether operation of the Vessel may be safely undertaken. In the performance of the Charter Party, the Owners are deemed to be an independent contractor, the Charterers being concerned only with the results of the services performed.

7. Owners to Provide

(a) The Owners shall provide and pay for all provisions, wages and all other expenses of the Master, Officers and Crew; all maintenance and repair of the Vessel's hull, machinery and equipment as specified in ANNEX "A"; also, except as otherwise provided in this Charter Party, for all insurance on the Vessel, all dues and charges directly related to the Vessel's flag and/or registration, all deck, cabin and engineroom stores, cordage required for ordinary ship's purposes mooring alongside in harbour, and all fumigation expenses and de-ratisation certificates. The Owners' obligations under this Clause extend to cover all liabilities for consular charges appertaining to the Master, Officers and Crew, customs or import duties arising at any time during the performance of this Charter Party in relation to the personal effects of the Master, Officers and Crew, and in relation to the stores, provisions and other matters as aforesaid which the Owners are to provide and/or pay for and the Owners shall refund to the Charterers any sums they or their agents may have paid or been compelled to pay in respect of such liability.

(b) On delivery the Vessel shall be equipped, if appropriate, at the Owners' expense with any towing and anchor handling equipment specified in Section 5(b) of ANNEX "A". If during the Charter Period any such equipment becomes lost, damaged or unserviceable, other than as a result of the Owners' negligence, the Charterers shall either provide, or direct the Owners to provide, an equivalent replacement at the Charterers' expense.

8. Charterers to Provide

(a) While the Vessel is on hire the Charterers shall provide and pay for all fuel, lubricants, water, dispersants, firefighting foam and transport thereof, port charges, pilotage and boatmen and canal steersmen (whether compulsory or not), launch hire (unless incurred in connection with the Owners' business), light dues, tug assistance, canal, dock, harbour, tonnage and other dues and charges, agencies and commissions incurred on the Charterers' business, costs for security or other watchmen, and of quarantine (if occasioned by the nature of the cargo carried or the ports visited whilst employed under this Charter Party but not otherwise).

(b) At all times the Charterers shall provide and pay for the loading and unloading of cargoes so far as not done by the Vessel's crew, cleaning of cargo tanks, all necessary dunnage, uprights and shoring equipment for securing deck cargo, all cordage except as to be provided by the Owners, all ropes, slings and special runners (including bulk cargo discharge hoses) actually used for loading and discharging, inert gas required for the protection of cargo, and electrodes used for offshore works, and shall reimburse the Owners for the actual cost of replacement of special mooring lines to offshore units, wires, nylon spring lines etc. used for offshore works, all hose connections and adaptors, and further, shall refill oxygen/acetylene bottles used for offshore works.

(c) The Charterers shall pay for customs duties, all permits, import duties

PART II
"SUPPLYTIME 89" Uniform Time Charter Party for Offshore Service Vessels

(including costs involved in establishing temporary or permanent importation 204
bonds), and clearance expenses, both for the Vessel and/or equipment, 205
required for or arising out of this Charter Party. 206

9. Bunkers 207

Unless otherwise agreed, the Vessel shall be delivered with bunkers and 208
lubricants as on board and redelivered with sufficient bunkers to reach the 209
next bunkering stage en route to her next port of call. The Charterers upon 210
delivery and the Owners upon redelivery shall take over and pay for the 211
bunkers and lubricants on board at the prices prevailing at the times and 212
ports of delivery and redelivery. 213

10. Hire and Payments 214

(a) *Hire*. – The Charterers shall pay Hire for the Vessel at the rate stated in Box 215
19 per day or pro rata for part thereof from the time that the Vessel is delivered 216
to the Charterers until the expiration or earlier termination of this Charter 217
Party. 218

(b) *Extension Hire*. – If the option to extend the Charter Period under Clause 219
1(b) is exercised, Hire for such extension shall, unless stated in Box 20, be 220
mutually agreed between the Owners and the Charterers. 221

(c) *Adjustment of Hire*. – The rate of hire shall be adjusted to reflect 222
documented changes, after the date of entering into the Charter Party or the 223
date of commencement of employment, whichever is earlier, in the Owners' 224
costs arising from changes in the Charterers' requirements or regulations 225
governing the Vessel and/or its Crew or this Charter Party. 226

(d) *Invoicing*. – All invoices shall be issued in the contract currency stated in 227
Box 19. In respect of reimbursable expenses incurred in currencies other 228
than the contract currency, the rate of exchange into the contract currency 229
shall be that quoted by the Central Bank of the country of such other currency 230
as at the date of the Owners' invoice. Invoices covering Hire and any other 231
payments due shall be issued monthly as stated in Box 21(i) or at the 232
expiration or earlier termination of this Charter Party. Notwithstanding the 233
foregoing, bunkers and lubricants on board at delivery shall be invoiced at 234
the time of delivery. 235

(e) *Payments*. – Payments of Hire, bunker invoices and disbursements for the 236
Charterers' account shall be received within the number of days stated in Box 237
23 from the date of receipt of the invoice. Payment shall be made in the 238
contract currency in full without discount to the account stated in Box 22. 239
However any advances for disbursements made on behalf of and approved by 240
the Owners may be deducted from Hire due. 241

If payment is not received by the Owners within 5 banking days following the 242
due date the Owners are entitled to charge interest at the rate stated in Box 24 243
on the amount outstanding from and including the due date until payment is 244
received. 245

Where an invoice is disputed, the Charterers shall in any event pay the 246
undisputed portion of the invoice but shall be entitled to withold payment of 247
the disputed portion provided that such portion is reasonably disputed and 248
the Charterers specify such reason. Interest will be chargeable at the rate 249
stated in Box 24 on such disputed amounts where resolved in favour of the 250
Owners. Should the Owners prove the validity of the disputed portion of the 251
invoice, balance payment shall be received by the Owners within 5 banking 252
days after the dispute is resolved. Should the Charterers' claim be valid, a 253
corrected invoice shall be issued by the Owners. 254

In default of payment as herein specified, the Owners may require the 255
Charterers to make payment of the amount due within 5 banking days of the 256
receipt of notification from the Owners; failing which the Owners shall have 257
the right to withdraw the Vessel without prejudice to any claim the Owners 258
may have against the Charterers under this Charter Party. 259

While payment remains due the Owners shall be entitled to suspend the 260
performance of any and all of their obligations hereunder and shall have no 261
responsibility whatsoever for any consequences thereof, in respect of which 262
the Charterers hereby indemnify the Owners, and their shall continue to 263
accrue and any extra expenses resulting from such suspension shall be for 264
the Charterers' account. 265

(f) *Audit*. – The Charterers shall have the right to appoint an independent 266
chartered accountant to audit the Owners' books directly related to work 267
performed under this Charter Party at any time after the conclusion of the 268
Charter Party, up to the expiry of the period stated in Box 25, to determine the 269
validity of the Owners' charges hereunder. The Owners undertake to make 270
their records available for such purposes at their principal place of business 271
during normal working hours. Any discrepancies discovered in payments 272
made shall be promptly resolved by invoice or credit as appropriate. 273

11. Suspension of Hire 274

(a) If as a result of any deficiency of Crew or of the Owners' stores, strike of 275
Master, Officers and Crew, breakdown of machinery, damage to hull or other 276
accidents to the Vessel, the Vessel is prevented from working, no Hire shall be 277
payable in respect of any time lost and any Hire paid in advance shall be 278
adjusted accordingly provided always however that Hire shall not cease in the 279
event of the Vessel being prevented from working as aforesaid as a result of: 280

(i) the carriage of cargo as noted in Clause 5(c)(iii) and (iv); 281

(ii) quarantine or risk of quarantine unless caused by the Master, Officers or 282
Crew having communication with the shore at any infected area not in 283
connection with the employment of the Vessel without the consent or the 284
instructions of the Charterers; 285

(iii) deviation from her Charter Party duties or exposure to abnormal risks at 286
the request of the Charterers; 287

(iv) detention in consequence of being driven into port or to anchorage 288
through stress of weather or trading to shallow harbours or to river or 289
ports with bars or suffering an accident to her cargo, when the expenses 290
resulting from such detention shall be for the Charterers' account 291
howsoever incurred; 292

(v) detention or damage by ice; 293

(vi) any act or omission of the Charterers, their servants or agents. 294

(b) *Liability for Vessel not Working*. – The Owners' liability for any loss, 295
damage or delay sustained by the Charterers as a result of the Vessel being 296
prevented from working by any cause whatsoever shall be limited to 297
suspension of Hire. 298

(c) *Maintenance and Drydocking*. – Notwithstanding sub-clause (a) hereof, the 299
Charterers shall grant the Owners a maximum of 24 hours on hire, which shall 300
be cumulative, per month or pro rata for part of a month from the 301
commencement of the Charter Period for maintenance and repairs including 302
drydocking (hereinafter referred to as "maintenance allowance"). 303

The Vessel shall be drydocked at regular intervals. The Charterers shall place 304

the Vessel at the Owners' disposal clean of cargo, at a port (to be nominated 305
by the Owners at a later date) having facilities suitable to the Owners for the 306
purpose of such drydocking. 307

During reasonable voyage time taken in transits between such port and Area 308
of Operation the Vessel shall be on hire and such time shall not be counted 309
against the accumulated maintenance allowance. 310

Hire shall be suspended during any time taken in maintenance repairs and 311
drydocking in excess of the accumulated maintenance allowance. 312

In the event of less time being taken by the Owners for repairs and drydocking 313
or, alternatively, the Charterers not making the Vessel available for all or part 314
of this time, the Charterers shall, upon expiration or earlier termination of the 315
Charter Party, pay the equivalent of the daily rate of Hire then prevailing in 316
addition to Hire otherwise due under this Charter Party in respect of all such 317
time not so taken or made available. 318

Upon commencement of the Charter Period, the Owners agree to furnish the 319
Charterers with the Owners' proposed drydocking schedule and the 320
Charterers agree to make every reasonable effort to assist the Owners in 321
adhering to such predetermined drydocking schedule for the Vessel. 322

12. Liabilities and Indemnities 323

(a) *Owners*. – Notwithstanding anything else contained in this Charter Party 324
excepting Clauses 5(c)(iii), 7(b), 8(b), 12(g), 15(c) and 21, the Charterers shall 325
not be responsible for loss of or damage to the property of the Owners or of 326
their contractors and sub-contractors, including the Vessel, or for personal 327
injury or death of the employees of the Owners or of their contractors and 328
sub-contractors, arising out of or in any way connected with the performance 329
of this Charter Party, even if such loss, damage, injury or death is caused 330
wholly or partially by the act, neglect, or default of the Charterers, their 331
employees, contractors or sub-contractors, and even if such loss, damage, 332
injury or death is caused wholly or partially by unseaworthiness of any vessel; 333
and the Owners shall indemnify, protect, defend and hold harmless the 334
Charterers from any and against all claims, costs, expenses, actions, 335
proceedings, suits, demands and liabilities whatsoever arising out of or in 336
connection with such loss, damage, personal injury or death. 337

(b) *Charterers*. – Notwithstanding anything else contained in this Charter 338
Party excepting Clause 21, the Owners shall not be responsible for loss of, 339
damage to, or any liability arising out of anything towed by the Vessel, any 340
cargo laden upon or carried by the Vessel or her tow, the property of the 341
Charterers or of their contractors and sub-contractors, including their 342
offshore units, or for personal injury or death of the employees of the 343
Charterers or of their contractors and sub-contractors (other than the Owners 344
and their contractors and sub-contractors) or of anyone on board anything 345
towed by the Vessel, arising out of or in any way connected with the 346
performance of this Charter Party, even if such loss, damage, liability, injury 347
or death is caused wholly or partially by the act, neglect or default of the 348
Owners, their employees, contractors or sub-contractors, and even if such 349
loss, damage, liability, injury or death is caused wholly or partially by the 350
unseaworthiness of any vessel; and the Charterers shall indemnify, protect, 351
defend and hold harmless the Owners from any and against all claims, costs, 352
expenses, actions, proceedings, suits, demands, and liabilities whatsoever 353
arising out of or in connection with such loss, damage, liability, personal 354
injury or death. 355

(c) *Consequential Damages*. – Neither party shall be liable to the other for, and 356
each party hereby agrees to protect, defend and indemnify the other against, 357
any consequential damages whatsoever arising out of or in connection with 358
the performance or non-performance of this Charter Party, including, but not 359
limited to, loss of use, loss of profits, shut-in or loss of production and cost of 360
insurance. 361

(d) *Limitations*. – Nothing contained in this Charter Party shall be construed or 362
held to deprive the Owners or the Charterers, as against any person or party, 363
including as against each other, of any right to claim limitation of liability 364
provided by any applicable law, statute or convention, save that nothing in 365
this Charter Party shall create any right to limit liability. Where the Owners or 366
the Charterers may seek an indemnity under the provisions of this Charter 367
Party or against each other in respect of a claim brought by a third party, the 368
Owners or the Charterers shall seek to limit their liability against such third 369
party. 370

(e) *Himalaya Clause*. – (i) All exceptions, exemptions, defences, immunities, 371
limitations of liability, indemnities, privileges and conditions granted or 372
provided by this Charter Party or by any applicable statute, rule or regulation 373
for the benefit of the Charterers shall also apply to and be for the benefit of the 374
Charterers' parent, affiliated, related and subsidiary companies; the 375
Charterers' contractors, sub-contractors, clients, joint venturers and joint 376
interest owners (always with respect to the job or project on which the Vessel 377
is employed); their respective employees and their respective underwriters. 378

(ii) All exceptions, exemptions, defences, immunities, limitations of liability, 379
indemnities, privileges and conditions granted or provided by this Charter 380
Party or by any applicable statute, rule or regulation for the benefit of the 381
Owners shall also apply to and be for the benefit of the Owners' parent, 382
affiliated, related and subsidiary companies, the Owners' sub-contractors, 383
the Vessel, its Master, Officers and Crew, its registered owner, its operator, its 384
demise charterer(s), their respective employees and their respective 385
underwriters. 386

(iii) The Owners or the Charterers shall be deemed to be acting as agent or 387
trustee of and for the benefit of all such persons and parties set forth above, 388
but only for the limited purpose of contracting for the extension of such 389
benefits to such persons and parties. 390

(f) *Mutual Waiver of Recourse (Optional, only applicable if stated in Box 28, but 391
regardless of whether this option is exercised the other provisions of Clause 12 392
shall apply and shall be paramount)* 393

In order to avoid disputes regarding liability for personal injury or death of 394
employees or for loss of or damage to property, the Owners and the 395
Charterers have entered into, or by this Charter Party agree to enter into, an 396
Agreement for Mutual Indemnity and Waiver of Recourse (in a form 397
substantially similar to that specified in ANNEX "C") between the Owners, the 398
Charterers and the various contractors and sub-contractors of the Charterers. 399

(g) *Hazardous and Noxious Substances*. – Notwithstanding any other 400
provision of this Charter Party to the contrary, the Charterers shall always be 401
responsible for any losses, damages or liabilities suffered by the Owners, 402
their employees, contractors or sub-contractors, by the Charterers, or by any 403
third parties, with respect to the Vessel or other property, personal injury or 404
death, pollution or otherwise, which losses, damages or liabilities are caused, 405
directly or indirectly, as a result of the Vessel's carriage of any hazardous and 406
noxious substances in whatever form as ordered by the Charterers, and the 407
Charterers shall defend, indemnify the Owners and hold the Owners harmless 408
for any expense, loss or liability whatsoever or howsoever arising with 409
respect to the carriage of hazardous or noxious substances. 410

PART II
"SUPPLYTIME 89" Uniform Time Charter Party for Offshore Service Vessels

13. Pollution 411

(a) Except as otherwise provided for in Clause 15(c)(iii), the Owners shall be 412 liable for, and agree to indemnify, defend and hold harmless the Charterers 413 against, all claims, costs, expenses, actions, proceedings, suits, demands 414 and liabilities whatsoever arising out of actual or potential pollution damage 415 and the cost of cleanup or control thereof arising from acts or omissions of 416 the Owners or their personnel which cause or allow discharge, spills or leaks 417 from the Vessel, except as may emanate from cargo thereon or therein. 418

(b) The Charterers shall be liable for and agree to indemnify, defend and hold 419 harmless the Owners from all claims, costs, expenses, actions, proceedings, 420 suits, demands, liabilities, loss or damage whatsoever arising out of or 421 resulting from any other actual or potential pollution damage, even where 422 caused wholly or partially by the act, neglect or default of the Owners, their 423 employees, contractors or sub-contractors or by the unseaworthiness of the 424 Vessel. 425

14. Insurance 426

(a)(i) The Owners shall procure and maintain in effect for the duration of this 427 Charter Party, with reputable insurers, the insurances set forth in ANNEX "B". 428 Policy limits shall not be less than those indicated. Reasonable deductibles 429 are acceptable and shall be for the account of the Owners. 430

(ii) The Charterers shall upon request be named as co-insured. The Owners 431 shall upon request cause insurers to waive subrogation rights against the 432 Charterers (as encompassed in Clause 12(e)(ii)). Co-insurance and/or 433 waivers of subrogation shall be given only insofar as these relate to liabilities 434 which are properly the responsibility of the Owners under the terms of this 435 Charter Party. 436

(b) The Owners shall upon request furnish the Charterers with certificates of 437 insurance which provide sufficient information to verify that the Owners have 438 complied with the insurance requirements of this Charter Party. 439

(c) If the Owners fail to comply with the aforesaid insurance requirements, the 440 Charterers may, without prejudice to any other rights or remedies under this 441 Charter Party, purchase similar coverage and deduct the cost thereof from 442 any payment due to the Owners under this Charter Party. 443

15. Saving of Life and Salvage 444

(a) The Vessel shall be permitted to deviate for the purpose of saving life at 445 sea without prior approval of or notice to the Charterers and without loss of 446 Hire provided however that notice of such deviation is given as soon as 447 possible. 448

(b) Subject to the Charterers' consent, which shall not be unreasonably 449 withheld, the Vessel shall be at liberty to undertake attempts at salvage, it 450 being understood that the Vessel shall be off hire from the time she leaves 451 port or commences to deviate and shall remain off-hire until she is again 452 in every way ready to resume the Charterers' service at a position which is not 453 less favourable to the Charterers than the position at the time of leaving port 454 or deviating for the salvage services. 455

All salvage monies earned by the Vessel shall be divided equally between the 456 Owners and the Charterers, after deducting the Master's, Officers' and Crew's 457 share, legal expenses, value of fuel and lubricants consumed, Hire of the 458 Vessel lost by the Owners during the salvage, repairs to damage sustained, if 459 any, and any other extraordinary loss or expense sustained as a result of the 460 salvage. 461

The Charterers shall be bound by all measures taken by the Owners in order 462 to secure payment of salvage and to fix its amount. 463

(c) The Owners shall waive their right to claim any award for salvage 464 performed on property owned by or contracted to the Charterers, always 465 provided such property was the object of the operation the Vessel was 466 chartered for, and the Vessel shall remain on hire when rendering salvage 467 services to such property. This waiver is without prejudice to any right the 468 Vessel's Master, Officers and Crew may have under any title. 469

If the Owners render assistance to such property in distress on the basis of 470 "no claim for salvage", then, notwithstanding any other provisions contained 471 in this Charter Party and even in the event of neglect or default of the Owners, 472 Master, Officers or Crew: 473

(i)   The Charterers shall be responsible for and shall indemnify the Owners 474 against payments made, under any legal rights, to the Master, Officers 475 and Crew in relation to such assistance. 476

(ii)   The Charterers shall be responsible for and shall reimburse the Owners 477 for any loss or damage sustained by the Vessel or her equipment by 478 reason of giving such assistance and shall also pay the Owners' 479 additional expenses thereby incurred. 480

(iii)   The Charterers shall be responsible for any actual or potential spill, 481 seepage and/or emission of any pollutant howsoever caused occurring 482 within the offshore site and any pollution resulting therefrom, 483 wheresoever it may occur and including but not limited to the cost of 484 such measures as are reasonably necessary to prevent or mitigate 485 pollution damage, and the Charterers shall indemnify the Owners 486 against any liability, cost or expense arising by reason of such actual or 487 potential spill, seepage and/or emission. 488

(iv)   The Vessel shall not be off-hire as a consequence of giving such 489 assistance, or effecting repairs under sub-paragraph (ii) of this sub- 490 clause, and time taken for such repairs shall not count against time 491 granted under Clause 11(c). 492

(v)   The Charterers shall indemnify the Owners against any liability, cost 493 and/or expense whatsoever in respect of any loss of life, injury, damage 494 or other loss to person or property howsoever arising from such 495 assistance. 496

16. Lien 497

The Owners shall have a lien upon all cargoes for all claims against the 498 Charterers under this Charter Party and the Charterers shall have a lien on the 499 Vessel for all monies paid in advance and not earned. The Charterers will not 500 suffer, nor permit to be continued, any lien or encumbrance incurred by them 501 or their agents, which might have priority over the title and interest of the 502 Owners in the Vessel. Except as provided in Clause 12, the Charterers shall 503 indemnify and hold the Owners harmless against any lien of whatsoever 504 nature arising upon the Vessel during the Charter Period while she is under 505 the control of the Charterers, and against any claims against the Owners 506 arising out of the operation of the Vessel by the Charterers or out of any 507 neglect of the Charterers in relation to the Vessel or the operation thereof. 508 Should the Vessel be arrested by reason of claims or liens arising out of her 509 operation hereunder, unless brought about by the act or neglect of the 510

Owners, the Charterers shall at their own expense take all reasonable steps to 511 secure that within a reasonable time the Vessel is released and at their own 512 expense put up bail to secure release of the Vessel. 513

17. Sublet and Assignment 514

(a) *Charterers.* – The Charterers shall have the option of subletting, assigning 515 or loaning the Vessel to any person or company not competing with the 516 Owners, subject to the Owners' prior approval which shall not be 517 unreasonably withheld, upon giving notice in writing to the Owners, but the 518 original Charterers shall always remain responsible to the Owners for due 519 performance of the Charter Party and contractors of the person or company 520 taking such subletting, assigning or loan shall be deemed contractors of the 521 Charterers for all the purposes of this Charter Party. The Owners make it a 522 condition of such consent that additional Hire shall be paid as agreed 523 between the Charterers and the Owners having regard to the nature and 524 period of any intended service of the Vessel. 525

(b) If the Vessel is sublet, assigned or loaned to undertake rig anchor 526 handling and/or towing operations connected with equipment, other than that 527 used by the Charterers, then a daily increment to the Hire in the amount as 528 stated in Box 29 or pro rata shall be paid for the period between departure for 529 such operations and return to her normal duties for the Charterers. 530

(c) *Owners.* – The Owners may not assign or transfer any part of this Charter 531 Party without the written approval of the Charterers, which approval shall not 532 be unreasonably withheld. 533

Approval by the Charterers of such subletting or assignment shall not relieve 534 the Owners of their responsibility for due performance of the part of the 535 services which is sublet or assigned. 536

18. Substitute Vessel 537

The Owners shall be entitled at any time, whether before delivery or at any 538 other time during the Charter Period, to provide a substitute vessel, subject to 539 the Charterers' prior approval which shall not be unreasonably withheld. 540

19. War 541

(a) Unless the consent of the Owners be first obtained, the Vessel shall not be 542 ordered nor continue to any port or place or on any voyage nor be used on 543 any service which will bring the Vessel within a zone which is dangerous as a 544 result of any actual or threatened act of war, war, hostilities, warlike 545 operations, acts of piracy or of hostility or malicious damage against this or 546 any other vessel or its cargo by any person, body or state whatsoever, 547 revolution, civil war, civil commotion or the operation of international law, nor 548 be exposed in any way to any risks or penalties whatsoever consequent upon 549 the imposition of sanctions, nor carry any goods that may in any way expose 550 her to any risks of seizure, capture, penalties or any other interference of any 551 kind whatsoever by the belligerent or fighting powers or parties or by any 552 government or rulers. 553

(b) Should the Vessel approach or be brought or ordered within such zone, or 554 be exposed in any way to the said risks, (i) the Owners shall be entitled from 555 time to time to insure their interest in the Vessel for such terms as they deem 556 fit up to its open market value and also in the Hire against any of the risks 557 likely to be involved thereby, and the Charterers shall make a refund on 558 demand of any additional premium thereby incurred, and (ii) notwithstanding 559 the terms of Clause 11 Hire shall be payable for all time lost including any loss 560 owing to loss of or injury to the Master, Officers, Crew or passengers or to 561 refusal by any of them to proceed to such zone or to be exposed to such risks. 562

(c) In the event of additional insurance premiums being incurred or the wages 563 of the Master and/or Officers and/or Crew and/or the cost of provisions and/ 564 or stores for deck and/or engine room being increased by reason of or during 565 the existence of any of the matters mentioned in sub-clause (a) the amount of 566 any additional premium and/or increase shall be added to the Hire, and paid 567 by the Charterers on production of the Owners' account therefor, such 568 account being rendered monthly. 569

(d) The Vessel shall have liberty to comply with any orders or directions as to 570 departure, arrival, routes, ports of call, stoppages, destination, delivery or in 571 any other way whatsoever given by the government of the nation under whose 572 flag the Vessel sails or any other government or any person (or body) acting 573 or purporting to act with the authority of such government or by any 574 committee or person having under the terms of the war risks insurance on the 575 Vessel the right to give any such orders or directions. 576

(e) In the event of the outbreak of war (whether there be a declaration of war or 577 not) between any of the countries stated in Box 30 or in the event of the nation 578 under whose flag the Vessel sails becoming involved in war (whether there be 579 a declaration of war or not) either the Owners or the Charterers may terminate 580 this Charter Party, whereupon the Charterers shall redeliver the Vessel to the 581 Owners in accordance with PART I if it has cargo on board after discharge 582 thereof at destination or, if debarred under this Clause from reaching or 583 entering it, at a near open and safe port or place as directed by the Owners, or 584 if the Vessel has no cargo on board, at the port or place at which it then is or if 585 at sea at a near, open and safe port or place as directed by the Owners. In all 586 cases Hire shall continue to be paid and, except as aforesaid, all other 587 provisions of this Charter Party shall apply until redelivery. 588

(f) If in compliance with the provisions of this Clause anything is done or is not 589 done, such shall not be deemed a deviation. 590

The Charterers shall procure that all Bills of Lading (if any) issued under this 591 Charter Party shall contain the stipulations contained in sub-clauses (a), (d) 592 and (f) of this Clause. 593

20. Excluded Ports 594

(a) The Vessel shall not be ordered to nor bound to enter without the Owners' 595 written permission (a) any place where fever or epidemics are prevalent or to 596 which the Master, Officers and Crew by law are not bound to follow the Vessel; 597 (b) any ice-bound place or any place where lights, lightships, marks and 598 buoys are or are likely to be withdrawn by reason of ice on the Vessel's arrival 599 or where there is risk that ordinarily the Vessel will not be able on account of 600 ice to reach the place or to get out after having completed her operations. The 601 Vessel shall not be obliged to force ice nor to follow an icebreaker. If, on 602 account of ice, the Master considers it dangerous to remain at the loading or 603 discharging place for fear of the Vessel being frozen in and/or damaged, he 604 has liberty to sail to a convenient open place and await the Charterers' fresh 605 instructions. 606

(b) Should the Vessel approach or be brought or ordered within such place, 607 or be exposed in any way to the said risks, the Owners shall be entitled from 608 time to time to insure their interests in the Vessel and/or Hire against any of 609 the risks likely to be involved thereby on such terms as they shall think fit, the 610 Charterers to make a refund to the Owners of the premium on demand. 611

PART II
"SUPPLYTIME 89" Uniform Time Charter Party for Offshore Service Vessels

Notwithstanding the terms of Clause 11 Hire shall be paid for all time lost 612
including any lost owing to loss of or sickness or injury to the Master, Officers, 613
Crew or passengers or to the action of the Crew in refusing to proceed to such 614
place or to be exposed to such risks. 615

21. General Average and New Jason Clause 616

General Average shall be adjusted and settled in London unless otherwise 617
stated in Box 31, according to York/Antwerp Rules, 1974, as may be amended. 618
Hire shall not contribute to General Average. Should adjustment be made in 619
accordance with the law and practice of the United States of America, the 620
following provision shall apply: 621
"In the event of accident, danger, damage or disaster before or after the 622
commencement of the voyage, resulting from any cause whatsoever, whether 623
due to negligence or not, for which, or for the consequence of which, the 624
Owners are not responsible, by statute, contract or otherwise, the cargo, 625
shippers, consignees or owners of the cargo shall contribute with the Owners 626
in General Average to the payment of any sacrifices, loss or expenses of a 627
General Average nature that may be made or incurred and shall pay salvage 628
and special charges incurred in respect of the cargo. 629
If a salving vessel is owned or operated by the Owners, salvage shall be paid 630
for as fully as if the said salving vessel or vessels belonged to strangers. Such 631
deposit as the Owners, or their agents, may deem sufficient to cover the 632
estimated contribution of the cargo and any salvage and special charges 633
thereon shall, if required, be made by the cargo, shippers, consignees or 634
owners of the cargo to the Owners before delivery". 635

22. Both-to-Blame Collision Clause 636

If the Vessel comes into collision with another ship as a result of the 637
negligence of the other ship and any act, neglect or default of the Master, 638
mariner, pilot or the servants of the Owners in the navigation or the 639
management of the Vessel, the Charterers will indemnify the Owners against 640
all loss or liability to the other or non-carrying ship or her owners insofar as 641
such loss or liability represent loss of or damage to, or any claim whatsoever 642
of the owners of any goods carried under this Charter Party paid or payable by 643
the other or non-carrying ship or her owners to the owners of the said goods 644
and set-off, recouped or recovered by the other or non-carrying ship or her 645
owners as part of their claim against the Vessel or the Owners. The foregoing 646
provisions shall also apply where the owners, operators or those in charge of 647
any ship or ships or objects other than or in addition to the colliding ships or 648
objects are at fault in respect of a collision or contact. 649

23. Structural Alterations and Additional Equipment 650

The Charterers shall have the option of, at their expense, making structural 651
alterations to the Vessel or installing additional equipment with the written 652
consent of the Owners which shall not be unreasonably withheld but unless 653
otherwise agreed the Vessel is to be redelivered reinstated, at the Charterers' 654
expense, to her original condition. The Vessel is to remain on hire during any 655
period of these alterations or reinstatement. The Charterers, unless otherwise 656
agreed, shall be responsible for repair and maintenance of any such 657
alteration or additional equipment. 658

24. Health and Safety 659

The Owners shall comply with and adhere to all applicable international, 660
national and local regulations pertaining to health and safety, and such 661
Charterers' instructions as may be appended hereto. 662

25. Taxes 663

Each party shall pay taxes due on its own profit, income and personnel. The 664
Charterers shall pay all other taxes and dues arising out of the operation or 665
use of the Vessel during the Charter Period. 666
In the event of change in the Area of Operation or change in local regulation 667
and/or interpretation thereof, resulting in an unavoidable and documented 668
change of the Owners' tax liability after the date of entering into the Charter 669
Party or the date of commencement of employment, whichever is the earlier, 670
Hire shall be adjusted accordingly. 671

26. Early Termination 672

(a) *For Charterers' Convenience.* – The Charterers may terminate this Charter 673
Party at any time by giving the Owners written notice as stated in Box 15 and 674
by paying the settlement stated in Box 14 and the demobilisation charge 675
stated in Box 16, as well as Hire and other payments due under the Charter 676
Party. 677
(b) *For Cause.* – If either party becomes informed of the occurrence of any 678
event described in this Clause that party shall so notify the other party 679
promptly in writing and in any case within 3 days after such information is 680
received. If the occurrence has not ceased within 3 days after such 681
notification has been given, this Charter Party may be terminated by either 682
party, without prejudice to any other rights which either party may have, under 683
any of the following circumstances: 684
(i)   *Requisition.* – If the government of the state of registry and/or the flag of 685
      the Vessel, or any agency thereof, requisitions for hire or title or 686
      otherwise takes possession of the Vessel during the Charter Period. 687
(ii) *Confiscation.* – If any government, individual or group, whether or not 688
      purporting to act as a government or on behalf of any government, 689
      confiscates, requisitions, expropriates, seizes or otherwise takes 690
      possession of the Vessel during the Charter Period. 691
(iii) *Bankruptcy.* – In the event of an order being made or resolution passed 692
      for the winding up, dissolution, liquidation or bankrupcy of either party 693
      (otherwise than for the purpose of reconstruction or amalgamation) or if 694
      a receiver is appointed or if it suspends payment or ceases to carry on 695
      business. 696
(iv) *Loss of Vessel.* – If the Vessel is lost, actually or constructively, or 697
      missing, unless the Owners provide a substitute vessel pursuant to 698
      Clause 18. In the case of termination, Hire shall cease from the date the 699
      Vessel was lost or, in the event of a constructive total loss, from the date 700
      of the event giving rise to such loss. If the date of loss cannot be 701
      ascertained or the Vessel is missing, payment of Hire shall cease from 702
      the date the Vessel was last reported. 703
(v)   *Breakdown.* – If, at any time during the term of this Charter Party, a 704
      breakdown of the Owners' equipment or Vessel results in the Owners' 705
      being unable to perform their obligations hereunder for a period 706
      exceeding that stated in Box 32, unless the Owners provide a substitute 707
      vessel pursuant to Clause 18. 708

(vi) *Force Majeure.* – If a force majeure condition as defined in Clause 27 709
      prevails for a period exceeding 15 consecutive days. 710
(vii) *Default.* – If either party is in repudiatory breach of its obligations 711
      hereunder. 712
Termination as a result of any of the above mentioned causes shall not relieve 713
the Charterers of any obligation for Hire and any other payments due. 714

27. Force Majeure 715

Neither the Owners nor the Charterers shall be liable for any loss, damages or 716
delay or failure in performance hereunder resulting from any force majeure 717
event, including but not limited to, acts of God, fire, action of the elements, 718
epidemics, war (declared or undeclared), warlike actions, insurrection, 719
revolution or civil strife, piracy, civil war or hostile action, strikes or 720
differences with workmen (except for disputes relating solely to the Owners' 721
or the Charterers' employees), acts of the public enemy, federal or state laws, 722
rules and regulations of any governmental authorities having or asserting 723
jurisdiction in the premises or of any other group, organisation or informal 724
association (whether or not formally recognised as a government), and any 725
other cause beyond the reasonable control of either party which makes 726
continuance of operations impossible. 727

28. Notices and Invoices 728

Notices and invoices required to be given under this Charter Party shall be 729
given in writing to the addresses stated in Boxes 21, 35 and 36 as appropriate. 730

29. Wreck Removal 731

If the Vessel sinks and becomes a wreck and an obstruction to navigation and 732
has to be removed upon request by any compulsory law or authority having 733
jurisdiction over the area where the wreck is placed, the Owners shall be 734
liable for any and all expenses in connection with the raising, removal, 735
destruction, lighting or marking of the wreck. 736

30. Confidentiality 737

All information or data obtained by the Owners in the performance of this 738
Charter Party is the property of the Charterers, is confidential and shall not be 739
disclosed without the prior written consent of the Charterers. The Owners 740
shall use their best efforts to ensure that the Owners, any of their 741
sub-contractors, and employees and agents thereof shall not disclose any 742
such information or data. 743

31. Law and Arbitration 744

*) (a) This Charter Party shall be governed by English law and any dispute 745
arising out of this Charter Party shall be referred to arbitration in London, one 746
arbitrator being appointed by each party, in accordance with the Arbitration 747
Acts 1950 and 1979 or any statutory modification or re-enactment thereof for 748
the time being in force. On the receipt by one party of the nomination in 749
writing of the other party's arbitrator, that party shall appoint their arbitrator 750
within 14 days, failing which the arbitrator already appointed shall act as sole 751
arbitrator. If two arbitrators properly appointed shall not agree they shall 752
appoint an umpire whose decision shall be final. 753
*) (b) Should any dispute arise out of this Charter Party, the matter in dispute 754
shall be referred to three persons at New York, one to be appointed by each of 755
the parties hereto, and the third by the two so chosen; their decision or that of 756
any two of them shall be final,and for purpose of enforcing any award, this 757
agreement may be made a rule of the Court. The arbitrators shall be members 758
of the Society of Maritime Arbitrators, Inc. of New York and the proceedings 759
shall be conducted in accordance with the rules of the Society. 760
*) (c) Any dispute arising out of this Charter Party shall be referred to arbitration 761
at the place stated in Box 33 subject to the law and procedures applicable 762
there. 763
(d) If Box 33 in PART I is not filled in, sub-clause (a) of this Clause shall apply. 764
*) (a), (b) and (c) are alternatives; state alternative agreed in Box 33 765

32. Entire Agreement 766

This is the entire agreement of the parties, which supersedes all previous 767
written or oral understandings and which may not be modified except by a 768
written amendment signed by both parties. 769

33. Severability Clause 770

If any portion of this Charter Party is held to be invalid or unenforceable for 771
any reason by a court or governmental authority of competent jurisdiction, 772
then such portion will be deemed to be stricken and the remainder of this 773
Charter Party shall continue in full force and effect. 774

34. Demise 775

Nothing herein contained shall be construed as creating a demise of the 776
Vessel to the Charterers. 777

35. Definitions 778

"Well" is defined for the purposes of this Charter Party as the time required to 779
drill, test, complete and/or abandon a single borehole including any side- 780
track thereof. 781
"Offshore unit" is defined for the purposes of this Charter Party as any vessel, 782
offshore installation, structure and/or mobile unit used in offshore 783
exploration, construction, pipelaying or repair, exploitation or production. 784
"Offshore site" is defined for the purposes of this Charter Party as the area 785
within three nautical miles of an "offshore unit" from or to which the Owners 786
are requested to take their Vessel by the Charterers. 787
"Employees" is defined for the purposes of this Charter Party as employees, 788
directors, officers, servants, agents or invitees. 789

36. Headings 790

The headings of this Charter Party are for identification only and shall not be 791
deemed to be part hereof or be taken into consideration in the interpretation 792
or construction of this Charter Party. 793

ANNEX "A" to Uniform Time Charter Party for Offshore Service Vessels
Code Name: "SUPPLYTIME 89" – dated

VESSEL SPECIFICATION

1. General

  (a) Owner: Name: _____

               Address: _____

                           _____

  (b) Operator: Name: _____

               Address: _____

  (c) Vessel's Name: _____ Builder: _____

  (d) Year Built: _____

  (e) Type: _____

  (f) Classification and Society: _____

  (g) Flag: _____

  (h) Date of next scheduled drydocking: _____

2. Performance

  (a) Certified Bollard Pull (Tonnes) _____

  (b) Speed/Consumption (Non-Towing)

      (Approx. Daily Fuel Consumption)
          (Fair Weather)

      Max Speed: _____ Kts (app.) _____ Tonnes

      Service Speed: _____ Kts (app.) _____ Tonnes

      Standby (main engines secured) _____ Tonnes

  (c) Approx. Towing/Working Fuel Consumption

      Engine Power   100% _____ Tonnes

  (d) Type(s) and Grade(s) of Fuel Used: _____

3. Dimensions and Capacities/Discharge Rates:

  (a) L.O.A. (m): _____ Breadth (m): _____ Depth (m): _____

      Max Draught (m): _____

  (b) Deadweight (metric tons): _____

                        Discharge Rate

  (c) ★ Cargo Fuel max (m³): _____ _____/hr at____head

  (d) ★ Drill Water max (m³): _____ _____/hr at____head

  (e) Potable Water (m³): _____ _____/hr at____head

  (f) Dry Bulk (m³/cu.ft):____ in Tanks _____/hr at____head

  (g) Liquid Mud (m³/barrels): _____ _____/hr at____head

      (max. SG) _____

      State type of recirculation system i.e.
      mechanical agitation, centrifugal pumps etc. _____

      _____

  (h) Cargo Deck Area (m²): _____ Capacity (m.t.): ___

      Length (m) x Breadth (m): _____

      Load Bearing Capacity _____

  (i) Heavy Weight Brine (m³/barrels): _____

      (max. SG) _____ _____/hr at____head

  ★ Multipurpose Tanks yes/no: _____

4. Machinery

  (a) BHP Main Engines: _____

  (b) Engine Builder: _____

  (c) Number of Engines and Type: _____

  (d) Generators: _____

      _____

  (e) Stabilisers: _____

  (f) Bow Thruster(s): _____

  (g) Stern Thruster(s): _____

  (h) Propellers/Rudders: _____

  (i) Number and Pressure Rating of Bulk Compressors:

      _____

  (j) Fuel Oil Metering System: _____

5. Towing and Anchor Handling Equipment

  (a)(i) Stern Roller (Dimensions): _____

    (ii) Anchor Handling/Towing Winch: _____

      _____

      _____

    (iii) Rig Chain Locker Capacity (Linear feet of

      3 in. Chain):_____

    (iv) Tugger Winches: _____

    (v) Chain Stopper Make and Type: _____

  (b)(i) Towing Wire: _____

    (ii) Spare Towing Wire: _____

    (iii) Work Wire: _____

    (iv) Spare Work Wire: _____

    (v) Other Anchor Handling Equipment
      (e.g. Pelican Hooks, Shackles, Stretchers etc.): ___

      _____

      _____

6. Radio and Navigation Equipment

  (a) Radios

      Single Side Band: _____

      VHF: _____

      Satcom: _____

  (b) Electronic Navigation Equipment: _____

      _____

  (c) Gyro: _____

  (d) Radar: _____

  (e) Autopilot: _____

  (f) Depth Sounder: _____

p.t.o.

APPENDIX 4

ANNEX "A"

VESSEL SPECIFICATION

7. **Fire Fighting Equipment**

    (a) Class (FF1, FF2, FF3, other): _____

    (b) Fixed: _____

    (c) Portable: _____

8. **Accommodation**

    (a) Crew: _____ (b) Passengers: _____

9. **Galley**

    (a) Freezer Space (m^3): _____

    (b) Cooler (m^3): _____

10. **Additional Equipment**

    (a) Mooring Equipment: _____
    _____

    (b) Joystick: _____

    (c) Other: _____
    _____

11. **Standby/Survivor Certificate**   Yes/No

    Nos: _____

**ANNEX "B" to Uniform Time Charter Party for Offshore Service Vessels
Code Name: "SUPPLYTIME 89" – dated**

INSURANCE

Insurance policies (as applicable) to be procured and maintained by the Owners under Clause 14:

(1) *Marine Hull Insurance.* – Hull and Machinery Insurance shall be provided with limits equal to those normally carried by the Owners for the Vessel.

(2) *Protection and Indemnity (Marine Liability) Insurance.* – Protection and Indemnity or Marine Liability insurance shall be provided for the Vessel with a limit equal to the value under paragraph 1 above or U.S. $5 million, whichever is greater, and shall include but not be limited to coverage for crew liability, third party bodily injury and property damage liability, including collision liability, towers liability (unless carried elsewhere).

(3) *General Third Party Liability Insurance.* – Coverage shall be for:

Bodily Injury .... per person

Property Damage .... per occurrence.

(4) *Workmen's Compensation and Employer's Liability Insurance for Employees.* – Covering non-employees for statutory benefits as set out and required by local law in area of operation or area in which the Owners may become legally obliged to pay benefits.

(5) *Comprehensive General Automobile Liability Insurance.* – Covering all owned, hired and non-owned vehicles, coverage shall be for:

Bodily Injury   According to the local law.

Property Damage   In an amount equivalent to _____ single limit per occurrence.

(6) Such other insurances as may be agreed.

ANNEX "C" to Uniform Time Charter Party for Offshore Service Vessels
Code Name: "SUPPLYTIME 89" – dated

AGREEMENT FOR MUTUAL INDEMNITY AND WAIVER OF RECOURSE

(Optional, only applicable if stated in Box 28 in PART I)

This Agreement is made between the Owners and the Charterers and is premised on the following:

(a) The Charterers and the Owners have entered into a contract or agreement dated as above regarding the performance of work or service in connection with the Charterers' operations offshore ("Operations");

(b) The Charterers and the Owners have entered into, or shall enter into, contracts or agreements with other contractors for the performance of work or service in connection with the Operations;

(c) Certain of such other contractors have signed, or may sign, counterparts of this Agreement or substantially similar agreements relating to the Operations ("Signatory" or collectively "Signatories"); and

(d) The Signatories wish to modify their relationship at common law and avoid entirely disputes as to their liabilities for damage or injuries to their respective property or employees;

In consideration of the premises and of execution of reciprocal covenants by the other Signatories, the Owners agree that:

1. The Owners shall hold harmless, defend, indemnify and waive all rights of recourse against the other Signatories and their respective subsidiary and affiliate companies, employees, directors, officers, servants, agents, invitees, vessel(s), and insurers, from and against any and all claims, demands, liabilities or causes of action of every kind and character, in favour of any person or party, for injury to, illness or death of any employee of or for damage to or loss of property owned by the Owners (or in possession of the Owners by virtue of an arrangement made with an entity which is not a Signatory) which injury, illness, death, damage or loss arises out of the Operations, and regardless of the cause of such injury, illness, death, damage or loss even though caused in whole or in part by a pre-existing defect, the negligence, strict liability or other legal fault of other Signatories.

2. The Owners (including the Vessel) shall have no liability whatsoever for injury, illness or death of any employee of another Signatory under the Owners' direction by virtue of an arrangement made with such other Signatory, or for damage to or loss of property of another Signatory in the Owners' possession by virtue of an arrangement made with such other Signatory. In no event shall the Owners (including the Vessel) be liable to another Signatory for any consequential damages whatsoever arising out of or in connection with the performance or non-performance of this Agreement, including, but not limited to, loss of use, loss of profits, shut-in or loss of production and cost of insurance.

3. The Owners undertake to obtain from their insurers a waiver of rights of subrogation against all other Signatories in accordance with the provisions of this Agreement governing the mutual liability of the Signatories with regard to the Operations.

4. The Owners shall attempt to have those of their subcontractors which are involved in the Operations become Signatories and shall promptly furnish the Charterers with an original counterpart of this Agreement or of a substantially similar agreement executed by its subcontractors.

5. Nothing contained in this Agreement shall be construed or held to deprive the Owners or the Charterers or any other Signatory as against any person or party, including as against each other, of any right to claim limitation of liability provided by any applicable law, statute or convention, save that nothing in this Agreement shall create any right to limit liability. Where the Owners or the Charterers or any other Signatory may seek an indemnity under the provisions of this Agreement as against each other in respect of a claim brought by a third party, the Owners or the Charterers or any other Signatory shall seek to limit their liability against such third party.

6. The Charterers shall provide the Owners with a copy of every counterpart of this Agreement or substantially similar agreement which is executed by another Signatory pertaining to the Operations, and shall, in signing this, and in every counterpart of this Agreement, be deemed to be acting as agent or trustee for the benefit of all Signatories.

7. This Agreement shall inure to the benefit of and become binding on the Owners as to any other Signatories on the later of the date of execution by the Owners and the date of execution of a counterpart of this Agreement or a substantially similar agreement by such other Signatory pertaining to the Operations.

8. Any contractor, consultant, sub-contractor, etc., performing work or service for the Charterers or another Signatory in connection with the Operations which has not entered into a formal contract for the performance of such work or service may nevertheless become a Signatory by signing a counterpart of this Agreement or a substantially similar agreement which shall govern, as to the subject of this Agreement, the relationship between such new Signatory and the other Signatories and also by extension its relations with the Charterers.

9. This Agreement may be executed in any number of counterparts or substantially similar agreements as necessary but all such counterparts shall together constitute one legal instrument.

APPENDIX 5

RULE 24 OF MERCHANT SHIPPING (DISTRESS SIGNALS AND PREVENTION OF COLLISIONS) REGULATIONS 1989 (S.I. 1989 No. 1798)

Rule 24. Towing and pushing

(a) A power-driven vessel when towing shall exhibit:

    (i) instead of the light prescribed in Rule 23(a)(i) or (a)(ii), two masthead lights in a vertical line. When the length of the tow, measuring from the stern of the towing vessel to the after end of the tow vessel exceeds 200 metres, three such lights in a vertical line;

    (ii) sidelights;

    (iii) a sternlight;

    (iv) a towing light in a vertical line above the sternlight;

    (v) when the length of the tow exceeds 200 metres, a diamond shape where it can best be seen.

(b) When a pushing vessel and a vessel being pushed ahead are rigidly connected in a composite unit they shall be regarded as a power-driven vessel and exhibit lights prescribed in Rule 23.

(c) A power-driven vessel when pushing ahead or towing alongside, except in the case of a composite unit, shall exhibit:

    (i) instead of the light prescribed in Rule 23(a)(i) or (a)(ii), two masthead lights in a vertical line;

    (ii) sidelights;

    (iii) a sternlight.

(d) A power-driven vessel to which paragraph (a) or (c) of this Rule apply shall also comply with Rule 23(a)(ii).

(e) A vessel or object being towed, other than those mentioned in paragraph (g) of this Rule, shall exhibit:

    (i) sidelights;

    (ii) a sternlight;

    (iii) when the length of the tow exceeds 200 metres, a diamond shape where it can be seen.

(f) Provided that any number of vessels being towed alongside or pushed in a group shall be lighted as one vessel:

    (i) a vessel being pushed ahead, not being part of a composite unit, shall exhibit at the forward end, sidelights;

    (ii) a vessel being towed alongside shall exhibit a sternlight and at the forward end, sidelights.

(g) An inconspicuous, partly submerged vessel or object, or combination of such vessels or objects being towed, shall exhibit:

    (i) if it is less than 25 metres in breadth, one all-round white light at or near the forward end and one at or near the after end except that dracones need not exhibit a light at or near the forward end;

    (ii) if it is 25 metres or more in breadth, two additional all-round white lights at or near the extremities of its breadth;

    (iii) if it exceeds 100 metres in length, additional all-round white lights between the lights prescribed in sub-paragraphs (i) and (ii) so that the distance between the lights shall not exceed 100 metres;

    (iv) a diamond shape at or near the aftermost extremity of the last vessel or object being towed and if the length of the tow exceeds 200 metres an additional diamond shape where it can best be seen and located as far forward as is practicable.

(h) Where from any sufficient cause it is impracticable for a vessel or object being towed to exhibit the lights or shapes prescribed in paragraph (e) or (g) of this Rule, all possible measures shall be taken to light the vessel or object towed or at least to indicate the presence of such vessel or object.

(i) Where from any sufficient cause it is impracticable for a vessel not normally engaged in towing operations to display the lights prescribed in paragraph (a) or (c) of this Rule, such vessel shall not be required to exhibit those lights when engaged in towing another vessel in distress or otherwise in need of assistance. All possible measures shall be taken to indicate the nature of the relationship between the towing vessel and the vessel being towed as authorised by Rule 36, in particular by illuminating the towline.

APPENDIX 6

Netherlands Tug Owners Conditions 1951

According to the law of the Netherlands, unless otherwise stipulated expressly and in writing, the towage within Dutch territorial waters carried out by a Dutch tugowner will be undertaken subject to the Conditions; outside the Netherlands the Conditions have to be expressly incorporated into the contract in order to bind the owner of the tow.

Article 1

The Tug Owners only make available their equipment and personnel on all waters and in all places in and outside the Netherlands on the following conditions:

Ship means in these conditions—unless the contrary is expressed—any vessel or floating object or unit which is towed, assisted, salved and/or moved under its own power in the Netherlands or Overseas, which is being assisted, supplied with steam and/or to which personnel is made available and to which or for which any other work is done.

Article 2

The Management decides for the execution of the work which tug and what personnel is to be employed for the required service.

Article 3

The work is carried out if possible in rotation of the orders received and until the place of destination or until such point as the tug and/or ship can reach safely on account of depth of water, bridges, sluices, locks or of any other reason whatsoever.

Distress signals will be attended to in priority.

If at the time agreed upon the ship is not ready or is not seaworthy or is not prepared for towage to the satisfaction of the management, then the Company is in default by the simple effluxion of time and liable to compensate the Tug Owner for all loss and/or damage.

The Tug Owner undertakes to make every effort in order to reach the place of destination without however giving any binding undertaking thereto.

267

Article 4

Unless otherwise agreed upon the contract price is due and payable before the commencement of the work.

Article 5

During the execution of the contract the ship may not cause any delay whatsoever.

Should such delay nevertheless occur the Company shall be in default by the mere occasion of the delay and responsible to the Tug Owners for any loss/or damage.

Article 6

The Company or the owner of the ship shall take for their account all damages also if sustained by third parties even if due to any fault or negligence on the part of the Tug Owners or of persons on board of the tug, including pilots, or of the personnel of the Tug Owners or any personnel supplied by the Tug Owners or to any defective equipment of the Tug Owners, or for which the Tug Owners might be held liable on any other ground.

Nevertheless, however, the Tug Owners will take for their account:
1. damage, which the tugs may have sustained by their own defects or through faults or negligence of their Masters and crews;
2. damage done to vessels or property of third parties through collision with the tugs and in so far as which the Company or the owner(s) of the ship can prove that this damage has not been contributed to or was caused by the ship.

Whenever pursuant to the provisions of this clause any damage is for account of the Company or the owner(s) of the ship neither the Tug Owners nor any other party who may have been instructed by the Tug Owners to carry out the work either entirely or in part shall be responsible for such damage, but the Company or the owner(s) shall be responsible to indemnify and keep indemnified the Tug Owners or any other party performing the work by order of the Tug Owners against all claims that third parties may have on account of this damage against the Tug Owners and/or other contractors whether jointly with the Company or owner(s) of the ship and to indemnify the other contractors against any damage to the boats of the other contractors in the same way as if this damage had been to the boats of the Tug Owners.

Article 7

In case of storm, drift ice, dense fog and darkness and in general in weather not favourable for navigation at the judgment of the Master of the tug, the tugs shall not be bound to tow.

If, however, the service of the tugs should be required in drift ice, the tariff shall no longer be in force and a special agreement shall have to be arranged.

If the hindrances as specified above should occur during the work, the Master of the Tug may cast off the ship or floating object towed, whenever in his judgment there will be danger for the tug.

He is bound, however, to take the ship and floating objects cast off in tow again when the circumstances necessitating the casting off have entirely disappeared; such again at his discretion.

Article 8

The Tug Owners and/or the Masters of the tugs are entitled without being liable for any loss and/or damage of whatever nature, to interrupt the work in order to go to the assistance of vessels in distress.

Article 9

The rates specified in the tariff of the Tug Owners shall not be applicable to ships which have struck a leak, which have lost their rudder, have sustained damage to the engines or have sustained other damage and in general also the ships which, without having sustained any damage, are in danger; but a special agreement will have to be arranged.

In case the Tug Owners have rendered any extraordinary services, which cannot be considered to be in performance of the towage contract, the Tug Owners shall be entitled to separate remuneration.

Article 10

The Tug Owners shall be entitled in case the contract has not been performed or, if it has already been partially performed by them, to cancel the contract entirely or for the unperformed part in the event of war or warlike operations in or outside Europe; prohibitions, restrictions and controls of shipping; requisitioning of ships; revolution, riots; civil commotions; blockade; strikes; lock-outs; abnormal increases in price and wages; scarcity of fuel and similar events, which in the judgment of the Tug Owners may prevent or impede the performance of the contract and the return voyage of the tugs to the Netherlands; by devaluation respectively depreciation of the currency in which the contract has been entered into, also at such change in circumstances that it must reasonably be assumed that the Tug Owners under those altered circumstances would not, or not on the same conditions, have entered into the contract.

Article 11

Those who make use of the Tug Owners' services accept conditions with which they are deemed to be fully conversant.

This agreement shall be subject to the Law of the Netherlands.

The settlement of all disputes arising from this agreement shall, to the exclusion of any other judge, be submitted to the District Court at Rotterdam subject to the right of appeal against the decision of the said Court, in accordance with the provisions of the Law of the Netherlands.

Article 12

These conditions which have been deposited with the Central Offices of the District Courts of Rotterdam and Amsterdam shall be referred to as the

"NETHERLANDS TUG OWNERS CONDITIONS 1951".

(Deposited with the Central Offices of the District Courts of Rotterdam and Amsterdam on the 15th of November, 1951.) [*Translation*].

Scandinavian Tugowners Standard Conditions of the Year 1959 Revised 1974 and 1985*

The tugboat enterprise (hereinafter called the Company) provides towage services on the following conditions.

(1) Definitions

The expression Hirer in these conditions means the body or person who has ordered the service or on whose behalf the service has been ordered.

The expression damage in these conditions means economical losses of all kinds including but not limited to total loss, damage, loss of income and expenses and also loss of and damage to cargo on board of the vessel in tow.

(2) The Company's liability towards the Hirer

The Company is not liable for damage caused to the Hirer in connection with the towage service unless the damage is a consequence of fault or neglect on the part of the Company's management. The Company is, however, not liable for fault or neglect committed by a person of the Company's management in such a person's capacity of master of a tug or member of its crew.

The Hirer is not in any case entitled to damages from a master of a tug, a member of its crew, a pilot, or anybody else in the service of the Company.

The liability of the Company shall in any case not exceed SEK 100.000.

(3) The Hirer's liability towards the Company

The Hirer shall indemnify the Company for all damage caused to the Company in connection with the towage service unless the Hirer shows that neither the Hirer nor somebody for whose acts the Hirer is liable totally or partly has caused the damage by fault or neglect.

Should the Company be held liable for damage caused to a third party in connection with the towage service, the Hirer shall indemnify the Company unless the Company

* Reproduced by kind permission of the Scandinavian Tugowners' Association.

would have been liable towards the Hirer in case the damage had been suffered by the Hirer.

In case of dispute, the Danish, respectively the Norwegian, respectively the Swedish text shall apply.

Index